Class War in America

Class War
in
America

How the Elites Divide the Nation by Asking:
ARE YOU A WORKER OR ARE YOU WHITE?

Jon Jeter

DRUM PUBLISHING

Printed in the United States of America

Published by DRUM Publishing
611 Pennsylvania Ave, #122
Washington DC 20003
www.drumpublishing.com

Hardcover ISBN: 978-1-965753-02-6
Paperback: ISBN: 978-1-965753-00-2
eBook ISBN: 978-1-965753-01-9

Library of Congress Control Number: 2024947297

Publisher's Cataloging-in-Publication
(Provided by Cassidy Cataloguing Services, Inc.)
Names: Jeter, Jon, author.
Title: Class war in America : how the elites divide the nation by asking: are you a worker or are you white? / Jon Jeter.
Description: Washington, DC : Drum Publishing, [2024] | Includes bibliographical references.
Identifiers: ISBN: 978-1-965753-02-6 (hardcover) | 978-1-965753-00-2 (paperback) | 978-1-965753-01-9 (eBook) | LCCN: 2024947297
Subjects: LCSH: Social conflict--United States--History. | Social classes--United States--History. | Elite (Social sciences)--United States--History. | Power (Social sciences)--United States. | Working class--United States--History. | Racism--United States--History. | Race discrimination-- Political aspects--United States. | Race discrimination--Economic aspects--United States. | United States--Race relations. | United States--Politics and government--History. | African Americans--Social conditions--History. | African Americans--Civil rights--United States--History. | BISAC: POLITICAL SCIENCE / General. | SOCIAL SCIENCE / General.
Classification: LCC: HM1121 .J48 2024 | DDC: 303.6--dc23

Cover and book design by: Málaga Smith

First Edition

Dedicated to

Mel Reeves, Mark Shannon, Forrest Palmer, Dave Heldman,

My father, Cecil Nathaniel Jeter,
who shone on me like the sun for 16,782 days

and finally,
for Palestine

Settle your quarrels, come together, understand the reality of our situation, understand that fascism is already here, that people are already dying who could be saved, that generations more will live poor butchered half-lives if you fail to act. Do what must be done, discover your humanity and your love in revolution.

–George Jackson

The universe is made of stories, not of atoms.

–Muriel Rukeyser

Contents

Prologue

In the spring of 2024, just as I was putting the finishing touches on this manuscript, college campuses across the United States erupted in anti-Israel protests.

That the livestreamed genocide of the Palestinian people would shock the conscience of a nation—even one as morally bankrupt as ours—is hardly surprising. What did shock me, however, were the images of a broad swath of Americans—whites and Blacks, Latinos, Arabs and Asians, Jews and Catholics and Muslims and Buddhists—shedding their tribal identities and laying it all on the line to do battle with the aristocrats who are financing the occupation, slaughter, and siege of Palestine.

If memory serves, the notion to write a book about America's class struggle occurred to me sometime in 2009 meaning that it has consumed the last 15 years, or more than a quarter of my 59 years on this earth. And were I to reduce my prodigious research and volumes of reading to a single declaratory sentence it would be this:

When the 99 percent comes together to fight for one another—rather than *against* each other—then the revolution is nigh.

I cannot predict with any certainty the quality of that revolution, or even its outcome, only that it is imminent, for the historical record clearly asserts that the nationwide uprisings on college campuses prophesy the resumption of hostilities between America's workers and their bosses.

In our ravening class war, past is prologue and empathy is the most powerful weapon on the battlefield.

Hardly anyone alive can recall the last time the country's working stiffs began to shake off the cobwebs to reorganize themselves into a fighting force capable of taking on Wall Street's fat cats. The year was 1931, in the depths of the Great Depression when police near Scottsboro, Alabama arrested nine African American teenage hoboes on charges of raping two white women. An all-white jury convicted them, sentencing all but the youngest to die in the electric chair, sparking international protests that were led in the U.S. by communists, many of whom were Jewish, and some of whom were Black.

It took 16 trials and 80 years but the movement would go on to win the release or pardon of all nine defendants but in the interim, the *cause célèbre* intersected with other grievances, including, most prominently, a dearth of democracy in the workplace, racial discrimination in the labor force, affordable housing, and police brutality.

In this fashion, the arrest of the Scottsboro Boys triggered 50 years of tumult in America's class relations, as a critical mass of whites forfeited their racial privileges to join with their Black co-workers and fight the wealthiest 1 percent who oppressed them all. Until roughly the moment that Ronald Reagan was sworn in as the nation's 40th president, employees went blow for blow with their employers, modernizing the state in the process.

Similarly, the students demanding that their university administrations divest from the munitions industry that fuels Israel's slaughter in Gaza are consciously committing class suicide by siding with a racialized group, the Palestinians, against the oppressors who are, in effect, their future employers.

This is especially true for those enrolled at elite Ivy League institutions and other prestigious schools such as the University of Southern California, New York University, Northwestern, Duke, the University of Michigan, Stanford, and the University of Chicago, where one graduate student identified as Christopher Iacovetti described to a local television reporter how police destroyed the protesters' encampment in a predawn raid that harkened back to the 1969 execution style slaying of the chairman of Illinois' Black Panther party, Fred Hampton, and the National Guard's massacre five months later of four, white student anti-war protesters at Kent State.

> Yeah, it was horrific. They waited like cowards until every single student was asleep in their tent basically and then they stormed in maybe 40 or 50 of them with riot gear screaming. They started throwing wood planks, throwing chairs, throwing absolutely everything in any direction to destroy the camp as fast as possible, to suppress this movement as fast as possible, and in fact, one of the chairs that they threw came within three inches of hitting my girlfriend in the head, and they had just woken us up. ...It was chaos. It was terrifying.

When the reporter asked Iacovetti about the disciplinary action faced by students, he said:

> They gave us some ridiculous notice out here saying that, like participants in the quad encampment, which no longer exists thanks to them, are facing like an interim leave of absence as well as a criminal trespass charge. I have no idea if that's just a scare tactic or if it's real but it doesn't matter because the difference between us and people like these cops is that there are limits to when we continue following orders. And when you're talking about a genocide visited upon a colonized population of 2 million people trapped in a ghetto that's as long as a marathon and six miles wide, when that ghetto is being systematically starved, slaughtered, every hospital bombed, every university bombed, 70 percent of homes destroyed, 40,000 people murdered, 15,000 children, the entire population on the brink of starvation . . . and if our government and our academic institutions are complicit in this, there comes a point where we say we're not following orders and it doesn't matter what you do to us because there are principles and there are human lives that matter more than our careers and our futures. And that's what separates us from people like Paul Alivisatos, the coward president of this university, and these coward cops

> that come in terrorizing an encampment where people are sleeping.
>
> I think that they thought that they could basically terrify us into inaction, into flight. But this is what this university has never understood, has never accepted, has never reckoned with this student movement. . . . And not just at UChicago but around the country is that the commitment to Gaza runs deeper than fears for our safety, fears for our careers, fears for our paychecks. It is a fundamental obligation we have as citizens of a country that is presiding over this genocide, arming this genocide, and as students at a university that is invested in those same weapons manufacturers and that is partnered with the same apartheid institutions that train that military and develop its technology.
>
> The next step is a simple one, whatever form it takes, which is to continue fighting with every breath we have, with everything we have for the people of Gaza because the blood of those kids is on our hands.

The reporter asks Iacovetti again if he is concerned about any disciplinary measures that the university might mete out. He responds:

> I don't care. It doesn't matter. There are things that matter more than my academic future and certainly every one of those children that is being murdered, starved, maimed, whose parents are having to choose, you know, do I let this kid starve first, or that one? This is such an ugly reality of such great magnitude that to even think, to really entertain questions about like, oh, what might happen if Paul puts me on a leave of absence, it's ridiculous, and it's insulting to the memory of every child that has been murdered in the course of this genocide, with the full complicity of the United States, of Joe Biden and people like Paul Alivisatos and his cops, that he sics on us in the middle of the night. They're hypocrites, they're cowards, and the blood of Gaza's kids is

> on their hands. The difference between them and us is that we know that and we reckon with it because we have a duty to them.

Iacovetti's impassioned pleas should concern the Western financiers who have profited from the Palestinians' violent dispossession because—if I may put too fine a point on it—he is white and it is the in-group's articulation of solidarity with a racialized out-group that has historically given workers in the U.S. the upper hand in the class struggle.

In the spring of 2024, there are myriad signs that an American Spring is taking shape.

For instance, Jews are in the vanguard of the student protests against Israel's siege of Gaza, as they were in the movement to free the Scottsboro Boys, and the ensuing struggles for labor and civil rights.

As another example, compare the apocryphal accusations of rape that triggered Jim Crow lynch mobs in Alabama to the Western media's unlikely accusations that Hamas systematically raped Israeli women in their October 7th assault. The white settler elite has historically deployed these false accusations to stir up murderous passions, creating a smokescreen for dispossession. The tactic dates back at least as far as the 1898 racial massacre in Wilmington, North Carolina when white supremacists overthrew the progressive, interracial government on the pretext of Black male predation despite a lack of any evidence.

And then there are the economic woes that undergird both the populist response to the Scottsboro scandal and today's class uprising, the DNA of which can be found in the deep financial downturn that began in 2008.

The key distinction is that the economic crisis that began in 1929 occurred within a mechanizing economy while the more recent slowdown occurred in a post-industrial context. Investors no longer make anything of value, and, like the mob, rely mostly on speculation, or loan sharking to turn a consistent profit.

Labor unions are another bellwether of change. Beginning to organize aggressively in the years after the Scottsboro arrests, labor leaders made racial integration a focus of their efforts. As a result, organized labor largely embraced a civil rights agenda in the period between the Scottsboro Boys' arrest and the postwar communist witch hunt, only to turn on students protesting the Vietnam War in the 1970s as American prosperity began to wane and competition for jobs began to intensify.

Similarly, organized labor in the U.S. is once again surging after years of decline.

According to Cornell University's Labor Action Tracker, 492,000 workers in the U.S. went on strike in 2023, and the 354 work stoppages that year represented a 70 percent increase from 201 strikes in 2021. Moreover, employees in 2024 are on a pace to nearly double the previous year's total, with more than 481,500 workers going on strike in the first four months of the year alone.

In the sixteen-month period between January of 2023 and May of 2024, 84,000 nurses, doctors and other medical professionals won 21 percent pay increases from Kaiser Permanente following a three-day walkout. The United Parcel Service agreed to wage increases for 34,000 Teamsters who went on strike, and 16,000 United Airlines pilots won pay increases of 34 to 40 percent. Simultaneously, writers and actors in Hollywood walked off their jobs in 2023; both won.

After a six-week strike, the United Auto Workers, or UAW, won a 68 percent increase in starting pay, and a 25 percent pay raise for current employees. In Los Angeles, hotel workers wearing shirts that read, "One Job Should Be Enough," staged more than 130 "rolling" or "pop-up" strikes in the summer of 2023 to demand higher wages and better working conditions. A year later, nearly half of the city's hotels had agreed to union contracts. In October of that same year, 3,700 casino workers walked off the job, closing all three hotels in downtown Detroit. Within 47 days, all three venues had settled with their striking employees, agreeing to the largest pay increases since the casinos opened in 1997, a reduced workload for housekeepers and Juneteenth as a paid holiday.

A month before the Detroit boycott began, tens of thousands of Las Vegas culinary workers authorized a citywide strike to begin nine days before the 2024 Super Bowl in the city. Casino owners caved to the workers' demands and quickly signed a new contract.

And even more telling than organized labor's impressive string of victories for its rank and file is its advocacy for the broader community, reminiscent of the trade union movement's influence in shaping social policy reforms in the New Deal era, and the generation that followed.

Today, autoworkers, Starbucks baristas and other labor unions endorse unambiguously the students protesting the mass murder of Palestinians. After police began to crack down on student encampments erected to protest the bloodshed in Gaza, the UAW local representing campus employees authorized a strike and Starbucks Workers United wrote on its social media platforms:

> SBWU stands with students around the country and condemns the brutal attempts to suppress their rights to free speech and political protest. Labor stands in solidarity with the students this May Day.

Had everything gone as planned, I would've published this book no more than 10 years ago, long before the proletarian uprising we are seeing across the U.S., and long before the publication of books such as Isabel Wilkerson's runaway bestseller, *Caste: The Origins of Our Discontents*, or Matthew Desmond's *Poverty, by America*. But man plans and God laughs, as the saying goes, and *Class War in America* arrived just in time to serve as my inadvertent rebuttal to Wilkerson's thesis, which lacks a foundational class analysis, and to Desmond's, which lacks a foundational racial analysis. Both are integral to understanding the precipice upon which the Republic stands nearly a quarter of the way through the 21st century.

This book, however, is not mine alone. I owe a great debt to far too many people that includes—but is not limited to—the many historians, scholars and public intellectuals such as Philip S. Foner, W.E.B. Du Bois, Walter Rodney, David Roediger, Howard Zinn, Glenda Gilmore, Malcolm X, Fred Hampton, James Baldwin, Antonio Gramsci, Frank Wilderson, Danielle L. McGuire, Achille Mbembe, Robert Rogers Korstad, Lorraine Hansberry, Joshua Freeman, and many others whose works and ideas I borrowed from in formulating my own; my friends Esther Iverem, Sunni Khalid, Nolu Crockett-Ntonga, Denise Young, Roger Chesley, Jose A. Monzon and Forrest Palmer who have either read portions of the manuscript or merely inspired me to—as Harriet Tubman may or may not have told slaves on the eve of their escape—keep going.

Moreover, it thrills me to no end that three generations of Smith women—Doris Smith, Málaga Smith, and Carla Appleberry—have read this manuscript and improved it, mightily, with their discerning eyes, and editing pens that are as sharp and red as blood-stained machetes. I am besotted with the three of them.

But no one person influenced my writing of this book more than my late father, Cecil Nathaniel Jeter, who died in 2011 at the age of 79. A case can be made that he is, in fact, my uncredited co-author, and that he planted the seeds for this tome on a summer afternoon in 1976 when I was 11.

What I remember vividly is my father pumping gasoline at a self-service station at 38th and Sherman Drive in northeast Indianapolis while I sat in the backseat of the family's Plymouth with my older brother. My mother sat in the passenger seat holding my little brother, the baby of the family. I watched as my father began to argue with the cashier, a middle-aged white woman, sitting in the glass booth.

My father accused the gas station attendant of cheating him out of the change he was owed; she insisted that he had handed her a $10 bill rather than the $20 that my father said he had given her. The old man ran hot normally so 90 seconds into the exchange he was irate, swearing at the cashier and pointing his finger at her while she stood nervously behind the glass.

"Sir, I am going to have to call the police," I remember her saying over the loudspeaker. "Go ahead," my father said defiantly. "I'll wait for him right here."

When the police officer arrived a few minutes later, the cashier told him her story, my father his. The white officer unsurprisingly chose the cashier's version of events and extended his hand to return the few coins the cashier said he was owed from the $10 bill.

"Motherfuck your change, peckerwood!" my father snarled, simultaneously slapping the coins from the officer's hand. I remember the hollow sound of metal pelting the pavement like tin rain and the officer placing his hand on his holstered gun. Suddenly, my mother's voice rang out from the passenger seat.

"Cecil," she said tersely, "c'mon, let's go."

While I did not fully comprehend what had transpired, I knew even then that my father did not blindly hate white people. He and my Jewish pediatrician, Bertram Roth, got along like a house afire, and he spoke approvingly of liberal Democrats in the U.S. Senate such as Hubert Humphrey, Ted Kennedy, and Indiana's Birch Bayh. It would take me years to grasp that my dad undoubtedly viewed the white gas station attendant and cop as traitors to their class, no better than marionettes on a string, manipulated into fighting a proxy war against their darker-skinned co-workers while the oligarchs laughed all the way to the bank.

"Daddy was my first lesson in the way the American system works," my older sister, Karen told me in one conversation. "He would always say that the white man and the Black man are like two rabbits chasing after a dollar bill and in the midst of chasing that dollar they start fighting each other.

That's why we never get anywhere."

Roughly six months after the incident at the gas station, in February of 1977, a white man of Greek ancestry, Anthony Kiritsis, walked into the office of his Indianapolis mortgage broker and used a clothes hanger to attach the muzzle of a shotgun to the back of the lender's head. The hostage standoff was broadcast live on local newscasts and while I don't recall my father exhorting Kiritsis to shoot the banker, his sympathies were clearly with the blue-collar borrower whose exploitation he identified with.

My old man always sided with the underdog. We were at that off-brand gas station in 1976 because he was boycotting Shell Oil which supported white minority rule in apartheid-era South Africa. Writing to my mother when he was a serviceman in the Korean War, he explained that his commanding officer had disciplined him for asking why the U.S. was always picking fights with people who'd done nothing to us. "So today," he wrote in his letter, "I'm cleaning the latrines."

If nothing else, I am my father's son, and I hope that this book does him proud.

And lastly, while the truth needs no vindication, African American authors who set out to write radical historiographies do. As the U.S. heads into the 2024 presidential election, there is every indication that the working class is regrouping for the dawn of America's third Reconstruction, as I suggest in the following pages. As such, I take great comfort in the Indian writer Arundhati Roy's words:

> Our strategy should be not only to confront empire, but to lay siege to it. To deprive it of oxygen. To shame it. To mock it. With our art, our music, our literature, our stubbornness, our joy, our brilliance, our sheer relentlessness—and our ability to tell our own stories. Stories that are different from the ones we're being brainwashed to believe.
>
> The corporate revolution will collapse if we refuse to buy

what they are selling—their ideas, their version of history, their wars, their weapons, their notion of inevitability.

Remember this: We be many and they be few. They need us more than we need them.

Another world is not only possible, she is on her way. On a quiet day, I can hear her breathing.

Jon Jeter
May 14, 2024

Introduction: Ground Zero

It's a class struggle, goddamit!

–Fred Hampton

At 4:44 a.m. on July 30th, 1864, Confederate sentries guarding a rebel stronghold east of Petersburg, Virginia, heard an awful, subterranean roar, followed in quick succession by a tremor underfoot that seemed to last, soldiers would say later, somewhere between a minute and a millennium. No sooner had the convulsions ceased than the ground below began to bulge as though it were a woman's belly, pregnant with peril, before erupting in a primeval, volcanic rage, and heaving flames as red and glowing as molten lava nearly 100 feet into the night sky.

The explosion ripped a yawning chasm through the meadow, littering the hillside with rock, metal, shards of tree bark and fugitive limbs, and dislodging clumps of dirt that returned to earth as misshapen graves, underneath which lay the dead and dying, their shrieks an aria of ineffable pain. From the ravine billowed plumes of thick white smoke, conspiring with the full moon to cast the encampment in a dreamy, shimmering half-light. Their ears still ringing from the blast, the able-bodied gray coats scrambled unsteadily to their feet, groping in the predawn darkness for their muskets, sabers, and each other, before wading into the scorching heat and suffocating gases to do a quick accounting. What they discovered astonished even the most hardened veterans: 278 soldiers, or a third of their South Carolina frontline regiment, lay fatally injured in the explosion's immediate aftermath.

The dead, however, could be buried later; of more immediate concern to the living was what fury would emerge from the abyss?

Curiously, it took a full 10 minutes following the explosion for federal troops to surface from the pit that was, by most accounts, 30-feet deep in some sections, and almost as wide as a football field. By that time, however, a phalanx of rebels had regrouped to meet the invaders head-on as they ascended from the slippery, clay-walled breach to mount an attack on the citadel, nicknamed, most appropriately, Fort Damnation.

Thus began what one Confederate officer would later describe as a "turkey shoot."

The final summer of the Civil War was a scorcher along the Atlantic seaboard and hotter still in Petersburg. Located at the nexus of four railway lines, the city was the supply hub for the Confederate capital of Richmond, 26 miles away, due north. A Union siege to overtake the rebel redoubt atop Cemetery Hill had failed, leaving Ulysses S. Grant's Army of the Potomac and Robert E. Lee's Army of Northern Virginia to settle in for a long stalemate featuring daily skirmishes but no real combat. As the month of June drew to a close, a lieutenant colonel who had worked as a Pennsylvania coal miner proposed a novel idea: What if federal troops carved a 510-foot-long mineshaft underneath the Confederate salient, packed it with 8,000 pounds of gunpowder and detonated it in the still of night?

The ensuing explosion was, at the time, the largest documented man-made blast ever, opening a gash so deep that the scar remains visible more than 150 years later. But the Northern command followed its spectacular technical achievement with a tactical blunder that was equally remarkable. Had things gone according to plan, the United States Colored Troops who had trained specifically for this maneuver would have led their Union comrades into battle by going *around* the treacherous tunnel rather than *through* it, which would've quickened their pace considerably and enabled them to engage the Southerners while they were still disoriented. But on the eve of battle, the commander of the Potomac Army, General George Meade, abruptly changed the plan; skeptical that the Colored Troops were combat-ready, he forbade[1] their deployment, according to the historian Richard Slotkin. His underling, Major General Ambrose Burnside, had the other division commanders draw straws to spearhead the mission, and as fate would have it, a drunkard named Brigadier General James H. Ledlie drew the shortest.

Failing to brief his men on the change in plans, Ledlie chose the most inopportune moment to go on a bender, leaving his war-weary unit to stumble into the fissure, half out of ignorance, half out of curiosity. Others followed, and a bottleneck formed in and around the crevice as federal troops slogged through the inky darkness only to be greeted by a barrage of rifle fire when they came up for air. A New Hampshire soldier who was blinded in the battle would later describe the logjam as a "mass of worms crawling over each other."[2]

Complicating matters for the Northerners was the quick thinking of General William A. Mahone, who led Virginia's 6th Infantry in a counterattack on the federal garrison—nicknamed Fort Hell—herding the bluecoats into the tunnel where only two viable outcomes—death or capture—awaited them on either side. Before lunging into battle, Mahone's soldiers stopped at a narrow, canopied pathway where the general slapped each of them on the shoulder and shouted "Give 'em hell, boys!"[3]

In a last-ditch attempt to elude disaster, Burnside finally ordered the United States Colored Troops to attack, which, by this juncture, bore all the signs of a suicide mission. To even reach the battlefield, the Negro infantrymen had to plow their way through a clot of demoralized whites huddled near the lip of the ravine, which was as raw and bloodied as a gunshot to the gut.

Surprisingly, the introduction of the Negro regiment turned out to be a gamechanger. Deploying a two-columned "pincer" attack, the Black soldiers fanned out, advancing from either side of the pit, fighting with such ferocity that they resurrected the white infantrymen who'd been cowering in fear only seconds earlier. With white and Black soldiers fighting valiantly side-by-side, Union troops captured 150 Southern prisoners and a clutch of battle flags, and it appeared, for a moment, that they just might pull off a comeback to rival Lazarus. Wrote one Confederate private of the Colored troops: "They fought like bulldogs and died like soldiers."[4]

But Meade's initial bungling ultimately proved insurmountable, and after nearly four hours of withering crossfire, combined with the occasional mortar shell tossed into the tunnel teeming with as many as a thousand men, the white flag materialized and the call went up: "The Yanks have surrendered." Confederate troops clambered into the hole, and the first men down, one soldier wrote, "plunged their bayonets into the colored wounded lying there." Colonel John Haskell of Virginia observed that "(o)ur men, who were always made wild by having negroes sent against them . . . were utterly frenzied with rage. Nothing in the war could have exceeded the horrors that followed. No quarter was given, and for what seemed a long time, fearful butchery was carried on."[5]

Confederate officers eventually stopped the massacre in and around the fissure, but there was a resumption of hostilities as the surviving Black prisoners passed, under guard, through the rebel reserves. Dorsey Binyon, a private in the 48th Georgia, regretted that "some few negroes went to the rear as we could not kill them as fast as they (passed) us." Capt. William Pegram of Virginia took satisfaction in the belief that fewer than half of the Blacks who surrendered on the field "ever reached the rear. . . . You could see them lying dead all along the route." He thought it "perfectly" proper that all captured Blacks be killed "as a matter of policy," because it confirmed the white race's innate superiority.

And then, in a horrific demonstration of racial solidarity, scores of white Union soldiers turned their bayonets, knives and sidearms on the Colored troops they had fought alongside just moments earlier. "The cry was raised that we would all be killed if we were captured among the negroes," one white soldier recalled later. When it was over, nearly 1,500 Confederates lay dead, compared to 4,000 federal soldiers, some resting atop pyramids piled with as many as eight corpses. The historian Slotkin wrote in a 2014 *New York Times* column that "it seems likely that more than 200 Blacks were killed after they had ceased fighting."

Viewed as a Biblical allegory, this forgotten firefight on a Godless swath of grassland at the nation's edge is a crucifixion, or an overwrought imagining of a Dantean underworld, Cain battling Abel to the death on the banks of the River Styx, between the fortresses of Damnation and Hell, with the sulfuric stench of burnt earth and rotting flesh wafting in the air. But the Battle of the Crater, as it's come to be known, is far more useful as a metaphor for the Republic's rise and fall. America's Big Bang cleaved from a Virginia knoll the epicenter of an enduring class war every bit as gaping and grotesque as a fistula, from which was shat a disfigured body politic in all its myriad contradictions.

Imagine a Zapruder film of the firefight in your mind's eye. What do you see? A white proletariat literally dug a hole for itself and managed to escape only with the help of the African Americans they had shunned and marginalized. But once the white settler has climbed from the chasm, they do not repay their Black rescuers with gratitude but a knife thrust in the back.

The worst racial massacre of the Civil War shines a spotlight on our maddening national metanarrative. From Abraham Lincoln to Joe Biden, the sons and daughters of Africa have proven their mettle as class warriors, responding to catastrophe by hurtling into the abyss alongside European emigres, and relying on little more than grit and guile and each other, *we, the people*, rise, like Spartans in crayon war paint, advancing on higher ground and glory.

And yet every victory is undone, every insurrection put down, with the 99 percent in full retreat, chased by the reactionaries' brutality, the managerial classes' muddle-headedness and the betrayal of a radical Black vanguard by their white allies who—like the Union soldiers at the Battle of the Crater—ineluctably choose "race" when the going gets tough.

The Petersburg inferno is the opening stanza of an American *Iliad*, or better still, the first caterwauling notes of an operatic odyssey depicting the plebeians coming together to assemble a new and resplendent land, only to inexplicably turn on each other with the suddenness and predictability of the tide, and cede their hard-won power to a gilded, gluttonous few. America's tribes are akin to dueling choruses, belting out a call and response as part of an unbroken pattern of ruinous dispossession, reconciliation and cathartic renewal, followed just as surely as night follows day by growing rancor between neighbors, and ultimately a deflating reversal of fortune.

Rinse-and-repeat.

You can, in fact, draw a geometrically straight line between the conflagration on the Atlantic seaboard and the moral panic that compelled a mostly white mob to descend on Capitol Hill 157 years later in an attempt to overturn a presidential election and restore order to the universe. And in both instances, the angry horde got it wrong, for the rebar of America's lost affluence is not sectarianism, but an atavistic class consciousness that reappears every 40 years or so, like a spectacular comet or an Old Testament epoch.

Consider that between roughly 1865 and 1900, every single state below the Mason-Dixon line experimented with some form of what academia has dubbed "racial democracy." These political movements did not have identical outcomes, but they all enjoyed some measure of success in redistributing wealth *downward*, from the haves to the have-nots as it were, and in the process laid the Keynesian cornerstone for a modern industrial state so prosperous that it would become the envy of nations as disparate as Botswana and Belarus. Jim Crow disbanded these post-Emancipation rainbow coalitions, but they began to regroup at the Great Depression's nadir, with African Americans, white liberals and Marxists forming a tripartite alliance to pressure their bosses, legislators and FDR to resuscitate a moribund economy by imbuing it with enough buying power to produce the singular achievement of the Industrial Age: the prosperous American middle class.

Embattled financiers re-branded "carpetbaggers" as "communists" and *poof!* like that, the interracial intifada at the heart of the New Deal began to disappear from our collective rearview mirror, and workers' share of national income along with it. In fact, when inflation is accounted for, wages for workers in America's private sector have not increased appreciably since Gerald Ford was in the White House.[6]

The term "racial democracy" is usually reserved for Brazil's highly-miscegenated population or post-apartheid South Africa. But the proletariat in the U.S. began forming rainbow coalitions years before Brazil even freed its slaves, and almost a century before South Africans of all races went to the polls for the first time. From Bacon's Rebellion in colonial Virginia in 1676 to the 1848 French Revolution, from the 1871 Paris Commune to the 1917 Russian Revolution, capitalists have loathed nothing so much as solidarity among their employees. So profound was their disdain for the interracial coalitions that emerged during the Reconstruction and Populist eras, the Great Depression and the turbulent 1960s, that investors in the U.S. could be said to suffer from a psychological disorder known as *iridophobia*, or fear of rainbows.

"I can hire one half of the working class," the railroad magnate Jay Gould is reported to have boasted in 1881, "to kill the other half."

Gould's macabre arithmetic is the raw stuff of racial democracy's arch-nemesis, racial *capitalism*, which eschews class solidarity for a market-based arrangement that is regulated by bigotry, patriarchy and narcissism. Imagine the American body politic as a hemophiliac, incapable of repairing the open wounds inflicted by class warfare without a transfusion of militant, dark T-cells which act as a coagulant, rallying the scattered troops to the battlefield, clotting the blood, healing the body.

Redolent of Kierkegaard's religious devotion, and the Mau Mau's feral aggression, African Americans' influence is as messianic as it is mathematical. With half of white voters historically pitted against the other, a Black electorate that is the nation's most progressive voting bloc casts the tie-breaking ballot in myriad statewide elections. Just as important, though, is the use of a political idiom that is grounded in African diasporic oral traditions, which adjudicates the despair and ennobles the unwashed with its prophetic vision of redemption, like a gospel choir's refrain, engineering language in a genuine effort to inquire—*Where are you? Can you meet me by the creek? Is your pain like mine? We can take them if we work together!*—and connect the African slave to the European indentured servant on their trek to the promised land. As irresistible and improvisational as the blues, this lyrical articulation of a profound fealty to God and each other has inspired everyone from Ho Chi Minh to Mark Twain, to the German cleric and Nazi-fighter Dietrich Bonhoeffer, the Beatles to Bruce Springsteen, to the white radical Bernardine Dohrn, who told me in 2015 that she spent her first year at the helm of Students for a Democratic Society touring college campuses nationwide, counseling student organizers to prioritize networking with their Black classmates or students at the nearest historically

Black college.

Losing a conflict in which they were vastly outnumbered, the oligarchs strategized long ago their only viable plan of attack:

Better, they surmised, to fight a race war than a class war.

As pro-Trump supporters stormed the U.S. Capitol in early 2021, another white mob of nearly two dozen demonstrators—several clad in "Make America Great Again" caps—pummeled a 25-year-old African American woman in downtown Los Angeles in full view of police officers. The woman, Berlinda Nibo, told the *Los Angeles Times:*[7]

> It seemed like these people were trying to kill me. To use me to make some kind of statement or something.

The problem, however, did not begin with the presidency of Donald Trump, who is a stock character in the denouement of a classic film that unspools from an antiquated movie projector, its images flickering hypnotically against a billowy tableau to depict the misfortunes of an extended American family over a span of seven generations, and counting. Much as Southern aristocrats deployed Jim Crow to put down a proletarian intifada, and Ronald Reagan schemed to undo the New Deal's rainbow mutiny nearly a century later with dog-whistle racial appeals, Trump is merely one of the latest—and loudest—in a long line of carnival barkers cast in the role of the Redeemer, climbing down from the mountaintop to sow the seeds of division and cleanse the land of heresy—by bloodshed if necessary—in an attempt to discredit the messengers of working-class solidarity. The news media's obsession with Trump, and increasingly Russian President Vladimir Putin, is part of the oligarchs' continuous effort to blame America's growing economic crisis on someone other than themselves.

Substantively speaking, U.S. politicians today are virtually indistinguishable from European viceroys in colonial Africa who exploited preferential treatment in hiring, education, and housing to pit one ethnic group against another, as evinced by the 1994 slaughter of an estimated one million civilians in the east African nation of Rwanda over a period of 100 days in violent clashes between the minority Tutsi tribe and the Hutu majority.

If classical macroeconomic theory interrogates a single question—Who gets ahead? —then America's interpretation of capitalism adds a codicil that demands a hard choice from its European settlers:

Are you a worker, or are you white?

Cui bono from this social fragmentation? The Marxist historian Philip Foner responds in his classic text, *Organized Labor and the Black Worker, 1619-1981:*

> When the president of the Fulton Bag and Cotton Mills in Atlanta, with 1,400 employees, hired 20 Negro women to work in the folding department of one of the mills in 1897, the entire white workforce (went on strike). The company agreed to fire the Black workers on one condition: the white workers would have to work overtime for free.

Contrast that with Argentina, a country that is 97 percent white, and for most of the 20th century, the wealthiest and most industrialized nation in South America, with gross domestic product typically divided evenly between employees and employers. It would be overblown to say that racism doesn't exist in Argentina—the *caudillos* or plantation owners sometimes referred to supporters of the populist president, Juan and his wife, Eva Peron, as *mierda de negro*, or nigger shit—but in 2003, a panhandler explained to me why the workers have historically been of one mind when it comes to tensions between rich and poor:

> We are all white and almost all Catholic so when something goes wrong for our neighbor we don't blame them because we know it could happen to us next. We know exactly who to blame: the upper class.

The slain Black political prisoner George Jackson once summed up the situation in a letter to another Black inmate at California's Soledad Correctional Facility:

> I'm always telling the brothers some of those whites are willing to work with us against the pigs. All they got to do is stop talking honky. When the races start fighting, all you have is one maniac group against another.[8]

It would be inaccurate to say that everything you thought you knew about American history is wrong, yet you almost certainly don't know the half of it.

The premise of this book is fairly straightforward, although born of a literary conceit on my part. By dint of good fortune, and a unique perspective as a journalist and foreign correspondent who was born at the zenith of American industrialism and the civil rights movement, the great-grandson of a slave, and the son of a millwright, I have traveled widely, listened intently, and managed, through nothing more than sheer dumb luck, to peek behind the curtain and see the U.S. for what it is: the westernmost front in the European settler's campaign to colonize the darker peoples of the world. At the risk of sounding immodest, I'd like to think of this book as an exhumation, or better yet a seance, to commune with our ancestors, reappraise our possibilities and remind a nation that has lost its way:

We once were warriors.

Emblematic of that fighting spirit is Viola Liuzzo, a white Detroit housewife and mother of five who watched televised accounts of law enforcement's savage attack on the more than 500 peaceful African American protesters marching across the Edmund Pettus Bridge in Selma, Alabama, on March 7th, 1965. Nine days later, the 39-year-old was moved to tears while watching Martin Luther King Jr.'s televised appeal for people of conscience to help register Black voters, and decided in that moment to heed King's call and make the trip to Selma in her '63 Oldsmobile.

Shuttling a Black volunteer from Montgomery to Selma on the night of March 25th, 1965, Liuzzo was accosted by a car carrying four Ku Klux Klan members, and fatally shot, her car veering into a ditch.

On the afternoon she left for Alabama, though, her husband, a business agent for the Teamsters, arrived home to find his wife packing a suitcase. He tried desperately to dissuade her from going, but she would have none of it. As she opened the front door to their home to leave, suitcase in hand, he made one final, desperate plea.

"Vi," he said, "this isn't your fight."[9]

"This," she said, "is everybody's fight." And with that she turned to walk out the door, headed south.

Part I

Shock and Awe

1.

Declarations of War

All warfare is based on deception.

–Sun Tzu, The Art of War

On the last day of the first leg of his final trip abroad as president, with Donald Trump waiting in the wings, a subdued Barack Obama waxed poetic on the essence of democracy as he toured the Acropolis in Greece.

"We've got the Parthenon behind us," he said as he surveyed the citadel's storied ruins in the soft light of an early winter sun. Dressed casually in a windbreaker, khakis, and sunglasses, Obama resembled a vacationing high school civics teacher from Poughkeepsie more than the outgoing leader of the world's sole superpower.

"It is here in Athens that so many of our ideas about democracy, our notions of citizenship, our notions of rule of law, began to develop," he said in his unhurried baritone. "And so when you visit a site like this not only are you getting a better understanding of Greece and Western culture, but you're also sending a signal of the continuity that exists between what happened here, the speeches of Pericles, and what happened with our Founding Fathers. And it's a very important role for the President of the United States to send a signal to the world that their culture, their traditions, their heritage, their monuments, are something of value, and are precious, and that we have learned from them. Because what that does then is send a strong signal around the world that we view ourselves as part of a broader humanity and a community of nations that can work together to solve problems and lift up what's best in humanity."

What was left unsaid in Obama's august soliloquy is that while Greece is typically acknowledged by Western scholars as the "cradle of democracy" the country could, in fact, learn a thing or two about governance from its *protégé* across the pond. As it turns out, the political and economic crisis that had by that time vexed Greece for nearly a decade following the 2008 global financial meltdown is virtually identical to the dilemma that confronted the state of Virginia some years earlier. With the state's coffers emptied by a deep recession, and legally forbidden from printing dollars—just as the European Union prohibits its member states from reproducing euros—Virginians couldn't merely manufacture legal tender to repay the lenders who loaned the state cash to pay its bills.

Tough choices had to be made.

Virginia, like Greece, could pay its creditors, or it could pay its citizenry, but it could not pay both.

And just as in Greece, Virginia's politicians largely underestimated the electorate's wrath, and rather than renegotiating the interest rates on their loans, both Democrats and Republicans opted to make full payment to the wealthy who advanced the state money by buying its bonds, while taking a fillet knife to the budget, gutting it like a thrashing, gasping trout that washed ashore in a rainstorm. Lawmakers closed nearly 100 public schools in a single calendar year, shuttered hospitals, sacked civil servants, shaved wages and pensions, and scaled back mail delivery. What's more, Virginia legislators' "let-them eat-cake" cuts to public spending—or what economists euphemistically call "austerity"—sapped consumers of what little buying power they had, worsening an already bad recession.

Virginians revolted, forming a third political party similar to the coalition of Greek progressives known as Syriza, meaning "from the roots" or "radically." After initially stumbling out the gate, Virginia's mavericks regained their footing, outpolling incumbents on both sides of the aisle, and seizing control of the state legislature, the Congressional delegation, both U.S. Senate seats, city halls in Richmond, Danville, Petersburg, and the governor's mansion, all within a single election cycle.

It was a bipartisan electoral bloodbath.

At this juncture though, the Old Dominion's narrative begins to diverge sharply from Greece's. For while Syriza blinked and ultimately agreed to a repayment plan that actually *deepened* government cost-cutting to satisfy the country's creditors, Virginia's Jacobins *stormed the Bastille.* Once ensconced in the state legislature, the upstart third party unilaterally reduced the interest rate paid on the state's outstanding bonds, infuriating Wall Street. The populist party was just getting started, however. With the cash saved from refinancing, lawmakers reopened shuttered schools and clinics and built scores of new ones in underserved areas, raised taxes on the rich and slashed them for everyone else. Moreover, because Black voters accounted for a sizable chunk of the party's rank and file, party leaders were responsive to their demands, reforming a criminal justice system that African Americans complained was discriminatory, and doling out patronage jobs to their Black constituents like so much surplus cheese. Three years into the political revolution, African Americans accounted for 54 percent of employees in the Secretary of State's office, 38 percent of the state's postal workers, 27 percent of employees in the Treasury Department, 28 percent at the state parks agency, and 11 percent of Virginia's pension board.

And in stark contrast to the modern nationwide trend of closing public schools and replacing seasoned teachers of color with the careerist, inexperienced college grads often hired by union-busting schemes like Teach for America, Virginia lawmakers *quadrupled* the number of Black teachers over a five-year span, effectively hiring scores of African American teachers to replace white teachers fired for low test scores on certification exams. So many African Americans were employed in Virginia's public sector, in fact, that at the movement's apogee, the manager of the Danville tax assessor's office wrote to a friend: "My office looks like Africa because there are so many [Black people] in it."

The year was 1881.

The Civil War would end a little more than eight months after the South's victory at Petersburg, which was insufficient to stave off the mounting rebel casualties and desertions. On the night before the Confederacy's surrender on April 9th, 1865, General Lee huddled inside his tent at Appomattox with his other generals, including William Mahone, the hero of the Battle of the Crater. "Well," Lee is reported to have said, "it is ended and forever. Slavery disappears never to be known again. The wise thing is to accommodate ourselves to the new order of things and go home and go to *work*."[10]

A few days after the general's wrap party, Mahone would gallop off to return to his Petersburg homestead determined, he would later write, to follow Lee's counsel with the same tenacity as he "would have . . . obeyed an order of his upon the battlefields."[11]

The Little General's tenacity would be needed. The federal government's postwar effort to regenerate the 11 Confederate states was arguably a larger undertaking than the war itself, in part because it required the restoration of bricks and mortar as well as arranging an unprecedented merger between 4 million freed slaves and 5.5 million white settlers, most of whom were firmly in favor of their enslavement. The preeminent question on the minds of the Southern aristocracy—that continues to preoccupy the capitalist class to this day as evidenced by the rush to reopen the economy at the height of the coronavirus pandemic—was how to maintain a steady and reliable supply of labor that is, if not free, then at least dirt-cheap?

White Southern workers were far less pragmatic than their bosses. Monopolizing their thoughts was the eviction of Yankee occupiers and the resurrection of a humiliated antebellum Dixie. Practicing a politics of aggrievement rather than reconciliation, Southern whites did their best in the early post-emancipation period to sabotage a rebuilding project they feared would introduce an era of "nigger government," denude them of their white-skin privileges and require them to compete unprotected against former slaves for jobs, resources, and status. The threat of a meritocratic order was wildly exaggerated, but the former slaves did enjoy some advantages in Southern labor markets.

One of the many ironies of slave labor is that it represented an investment in ways that free labor did not, and in their efforts to maximize returns, slave owners would occasionally increase the productivity of their slaves by upgrading their skills. For instance, when tobacco harvests began to exhaust the soil and produce dwindling crop yields, plantation owners in Maryland and Virginia began to lease their surplus labor to craftsmen in the District and Baltimore to learn carpentry and ironwork. By the time Lincoln signed the Emancipation Proclamation, there were more Negroes than whites in the skilled trades in Washington D.C., [12] helping foment a Faulknerian sense of loss among whites. Between 1865 and the mid-1870s, white vigilantes set fire to scores of Freedmen's schools, which were the precursor to universal public education. A crusading abolitionist before the war, the publisher of the *New-York Tribune*, Horace Greeley, wrote of the liberated slaves after the war:

> They are an easy, worthless race, taking no thought for the morrow.[13]

Greeley's reproach reflects the sophistry undergirding white supremacy. As noted by W.E.B. Du Bois and others, whites' worst fear is not that Blacks are inadequate but rather, like the Colored Troops at the Battle of the Crater, all too up to the task.

Compounding whites' insecurities was their dread of retribution. The historian John Hope Franklin wrote:

> Even before the war white Southerners had frequently entertained a wild nightmarish fear that the slaves would rise up, slay them, and overthrow the institution of slavery. It had happened in Haiti. Perhaps it would happen here. In 1865 Southern whites 'knew' that there was nothing to hold back the tide. Wild rumors flashed through the South that the freedmen would strike in vengeance. Some whites were even certain of the date. It would be New Year's Day 1866, they said. How could they keep their minds on rebuilding when their former slaves were poised to complete the destruction?[14]

The ambitious Mahone's myopia seemed to immunize him from such worriment, allowing him to focus on tasks with the laser-like intensity that General Lee had urged. Born in 1826 to slaveholding innkeepers in Southampton County—his father helped put down Nat Turner's 1831 slave revolt[15]—Mahone stood barely taller than five feet and weighed 100 pounds soaking wet, a result of the dyspepsia that plagued him his entire life and caused him to travel, even during wartime, with the cow and hens required for his ornery stomach. When told that her husband suffered a flesh wound in battle, Mrs. Mahone responded with alarm: "Flesh wound? It can't be a flesh wound; the General hasn't any flesh!"[16] He'd studied engineering at Virginia Military Institute, which he attended on a scholarship, and within two years of the war's conclusion, had parlayed his almost childlike fascination with trains—by all accounts, he delighted in riding the rails in a handcar to inspect roadbeds—into an appointment as president of the Atlantic, Mississippi and Ohio Railroad.

A slaveholder and ardent secessionist, Mahone was no John Brown, but like the freedpeople he did not sentimentalize the past, and unlike many whites of his day appeared to genuinely believe that Virginia's best days lay ahead of it, and not behind.

Similarly, if Negroes had surfaced from their enslavement with a taste for settling scores there is no historical record of it. It neither reduces nor romanticizes human bondage to suggest that the peculiar institution had the exact same effect on abducted Africans that a blast furnace has on iron ore, strengthening their resolve and cauterizing the wounds left by centuries of savage subjugation. The freedpeople yearned for nothing more than to build a Beloved Community, the pillars of which were land to farm, the reunification of families that had been scattered to the winds by chattel slavery and learning to read and write. Their motivations were, to be sure, practical—by most lights, any illiterate who signed a contract with the white man was a damn fool—but spiritual as well. Finding their strength through struggle and a stirring sense of purpose in serving a God whose love had delivered them from evil and redeemed their suffering, African Americans countered white Southerners' apostasy and brittleness of spirit with a steely faith and a profound understanding of class struggle.

In September 1868, for example, the Republican-dominated Georgia state legislature illegally expelled its duly elected Black lawmakers, many of whom had opposed the purge of former Confederates from the General Assembly.[17] Once reinstated by the federal government, the African American lawmakers immediately voted to compensate the white delegates who'd illegally deposed them, although it's possible that they saw the move as a bargaining chip to procure the mother lode of emancipation: universal public education.

Such was their enthusiasm for "book learnin" that one administrator for the Freedmen's Bureau—the federal agency responsible for managing the Reconstruction effort—compared it to a type of derangement, so "crazed" were they to learn. A newly liberated father in Mississippi proclaimed, "If I nebber does nothing more while I live, I shall give my children a chance to go to school, for I considers education [the] next best ting to liberty."

Consistent with their fears of Black tyranny, the white working class was, at best, ambivalent about public education: On the one hand, white Southerners recognized, much as the freed slaves, the doors it would unlock for posterity; on the other hand, they worried public education might finally put paid to the lie of white superiority by affording Blacks the same opportunities for advancement as whites. Whites were eventually persuaded to endorse universal, *segregated* free schools after the freedpeople helped convince the military government to relent in its insistence that ex-Confederates sign loyalty oaths. Within a few years of the opening of the state's first public schools in 1870, Virginians of all races simply couldn't imagine life without them.

The landowning elite could. They had for years paid for their own children's formal education and preferred a system mandating all parents do the same. They pounced on any opportunity to shirk their responsibility to the larger community, which arrived, conveniently enough, in the form of the first modern financial crisis.

The 2008 global economic downturn is most often compared to the Great Depression, but the better analogue is the six-year financial panic that began in 1873. Before and after the war, the wealthy invested heavily in real estate and the technological marvel of the day, the intercontinental railroad. Credit was easy, irrational exuberance high, and brokers in New York and

London created exotic new financial instruments to leverage their clientele's reckless speculation. As the historian James Ford Rhodes described it, the U.S. economy in the first half of 1873 bore a striking resemblance to its counterpart in the final months of 2007:

> Prosperity was written all over the face of things. Manufacturers were busy, workmen in demand. Streets and shops were crowded and everywhere new buildings going up. Prices of commodities were in high demand . . . Everybody seemed to be making money.

Until they weren't.

Beginning in Europe in late summer, the economic slowdown officially crossed the pond on Thursday, Sept. 18, 1873, when Northern Pacific Railroad's insolvency triggered a cash crunch at the investment house that had largely financed the Civil War, Jay Cooke & Company. Foreshadowing the collapse of Lehman Brothers 135 years later, the brokerage firm promptly announced it would suspend payments on the notes it had issued, which was tantamount to declaring bankruptcy. Twenty financial houses followed suit the next day.

Similar to the Federal Reserve's purchase of bank debt following the 2008 collapse of the subprime mortgage market, President Ulysses S. Grant's treasury secretary, William A. Richardson, announced a plan to relieve Wall Street of bad loans that would ultimately saddle the federal government's balance sheet with $13 million in bank debts representing more than one tenth of the nation's total economic output at the time. Brokers resumed trading the next day. But the hemorrhaging persisted, causing the New York Stock Exchange to suspend trading for the first time in its history. Banks across the U.S. continued to fail, however, among them the Freedman's Savings Bank. White savings and loan executives cynically hatched a plan to forestall a run on the bank by recruiting Frederick Douglass as a spokesman to urge calm. The plan took, for a while; in the six months following the crash, Black depositors in Richmond withdrew only $26,000 of their $166,000 in cumulative assets from the local branch of the savings and loan despite staggering unemployment.[18] That meant, however, that Black depositors were wiped out when the Freedman's Bank collapsed on June 29, 1874. African Americans wouldn't experience material dispossession on such a scale for another 135 years when the global real estate market imploded and financiers chose another African American, Barack Obama, to keep their graft going.

It wasn't just the money though. Formerly enslaved African Americans were under no illusions about their prospects of living harmoniously with white settlers. Their strategy was to carve out safe spaces for themselves using mutual aid societies, fraternal orders, education, the church, and of course, thrift, to improve their lot in life. Said one Black Virginian: "That little failure in 1874 did more to rob the Negro of hope . . . than any other occurrence."[19]

In the throes of recession, freedpeople living in the countryside earned between $6 and $10 a month on average (about $238 to $265 at 2023 prices) and life in the cities was hardly any better. In the *Journal of Southern History*, James T. Moore wrote:

> Jerry-built 'niggertowns' proliferated, gangs of ragged children roamed the streets; competition with laboring-class whites aggravated racial hatreds." So despairing were the times that some newspaper editorials openly questioned whether a generation of poverty, hunger and sickness might accomplish what 200 years of slavery had not, namely the extinction of an entire race.[20]

Aggravating matters was a coalition of deeply conservative politicians and planters who had seized on the 1870 withdrawal of federal troops from

Virginia to extend a wet blanket of political repression across the state that was every bit as suffocating as the police chokehold that would kill George Floyd a century-and-a-half later. Moore continues:

> This relentless machine hammered the blacks with poll taxes, gerrymanders and election fraud, reducing the number of Negroes in the state legislature from 30 in 1870 to only five in 1878. County officials excluded blacks from jury duty; local school boards employed white teachers for Black schools, rejecting the applications of qualified Negroes; Conservative judges ordered public whippings for Black criminals; hundreds of freedmen were disenfranchised for (petty) larceny and other minor offenses. Reflecting the rise of prejudice, moreover, patterns of segregation emerged in restaurants, hotels and other public places. Political impotence paved the way for public humiliation.
>
> Completing this cycle of despair, the Negroes' traditional allies—the white Republicans—seemed unwilling or unable to help them. The national Republican leadership set the pattern by virtually abandoning blacks after Reconstruction. President Rutherford Birchard Hayes adopted a "southern strategy" in 1877 which ignored racial issues altogether. Instead, he sought to build a respectable party in the region, one which could command the respect of the wealthier classes. His administration stressed reforms in the civil service, not civil rights.[21]

A Black newspaper, the *Petersburg Lancet*, dismissed the party of Lincoln in language that progressives might use to describe the Democrats today:

> The Republican party of the present is but a skeleton, a relic of the past.

White wage-earners weren't exactly living high off the hog though. Government statisticians hadn't yet begun calculating unemployment rates but so scarce were jobs that a new word entered the national lexicon to describe the thousands of men who'd taken to traipsing around the country on railcars looking for work: tramps. White laborers increasingly turned their ire on politicians' *laissez-faire* policies. By January 1876, some 18,783 white farmers, mostly in the Shenandoah Valley and the western portions of the state, chartered 685 local chapters of the Grange, or the Patrons of Husbandry, to champion the cause of agrarian reform.[22] Writing in the Southern Planter and Farmer, H.W. Crosby of Halifax wrote:

> We have long begged for our rights—let us now in solid column demand them! In Union there is strength. This is the colored man's secret. Let them agree on any measure and they are one for that measure. Let us take a lesson.[23]

At its height in the late 1870s, the Greenbackers accounted for 21 seats in the U.S. House of Representatives, but both they and the Grangers were simply outmatched by the wealthy planters and businessmen who'd already coalesced around the classical macroeconomic principles that tilted the playing field to favor the rich. Lawmakers working on behalf of the property owners ignored the Grangers' demands to lower railroad freight charges because they loathed regulations that ate into their profits. Concurrently, politicians rejected the Greenbackers' calls for stiffer trade tariffs because so-called "free trade" re-allocates money from the laborers who produce goods to the merchants who sell them. And proposals to increase consumer buying power by printing scrip such as that used by the federal government during the Civil War were also a non-starter because investors have historically believed that high wages trigger inflation, which they consider a type of fraud, reducing the value of their investments.

That was especially important to speculators who'd loaned Virginia's Board of Public Works $33 million between 1822 and 1861 to finance the construction of canals, toll roads, bridges, and most vitally, privately owned railroads. At an annual interest rate of 6 percent, the state was obliged to dole out $1.8million annually in interest payments, or more than half of the state's total revenue of $3.5 million for that year. [24]

On a per capita basis, Virginia's debt was the nation's largest, but with the money it borrowed, the state purchased a 40 percent stake in the railroad and canal companies, helped construct the James River and Kanawha Canal connecting Richmond to the breadbasket communities in the fertile Shenandoah Valley, and 2,483 miles of rail that crisscrossed the commonwealth. Moreover, the state's liabilities were offset by assets valued at $43 million at the end of 1860.[25] West Virginia's secession in 1861, however, left the state without a third of its territory, emancipation wiped its primary taxable asset off the books, and four years of war had pruned two million acres of productive farmland from the tax rolls, reduced the pounds of tobacco grown by two-thirds, corn and wheat crops by half, [26] and left the state's rail lines in a state of disrepair. Historian Jane Dailey wrote:

> Northern war correspondent Whitelaw Reid traveled at a snail's pace from Lynchburg to Bristol on straightened track whose gaps were plugged with stones. English journalist John Kennesaw spent most of his time on trains in Virginia peering out the window to see if the car had derailed. About all that remained intact of Virginia's extensive antebellum infrastructure was the debt the state incurred to finance its construction.

When Virginia was reinstated to the Union in 1870, the interest on the debt had ballooned the total outstanding debt to $45 million. Conservative Democrats cynically insisted on repaying the debt in full to preserve both the state's credit rating and its Southern honor. To meet the state's financial obligations, legislators began raising regressive taxes on everything from property to dogs to whiskey, while closing schools *en masse*. When Virginia's public schools opened its doors in 1871, there were 131,088 students enrolled in 3,047 schools. By the end of the 1878-1879 school year, the numbers had dropped precipitously to 108,074 students enrolled in 2,491 schools,[27] and the education deficit had soared to $526,000,[28] or approximately $12.5 million in 2020 dollars. As the political scientist Carl N. Degler wrote in 1971, it "was not for nothing that the Conservative Democrats were called Bourbons, after the royal house of France, which, at its restoration, was said to have learned nothing and forgotten nothing."

After vetoing an 1878 bill to reduce the interest rate on the debt, Virginia's Bourbon governor wrote with a smugness that would be echoed nearly a century later by President Gerald Ford in refusing to bail out a cash-strapped New York City:

> Our fathers did not need free schools to make them what they were . . . Free schools are not a necessity. The world, for hundreds of years, grew in wealth, culture, and refinement, without them. They are a luxury, adding, when skillfully conducted, it may be, to the beauty and power of the state, but to be paid for, like any other luxury, by the people who wish their benefits.[29]

Bankrupted by the 1873 Depression, Mahone fumed at the public spending cuts. "This twaddle about the honor of the state is sheer nonsense . . . "in light of the robbery of the school fund," he wrote to a friend.[30] Biographers and historians have alternately attributed to Mahone a Napoleonic complex, a soft spot for the underdog, and an understanding of the prosperity that would attend the shift from agriculture to industry. Whatever his motive, Mahone threw his name in the hat for governor in 1877; failing to win the Democratic nomination, however, only led him and other conservatives to abandon the party and organize an independent political party known as the Readjusters—as in readjust, or rewrite the debt—which was composed of Irish, German, and Jewish laborers concentrated in the regions west of the Blue Ridge Mountains and the Shenandoah Valley. Fearful of alienating whites, the Readjusters held "coloreds" at arm's length initially, while Republican President Rutherford

Hayes exploited the freedmen's loyalty to the party of Lincoln, urging "Negroes to spurn all forms of financial repudiation." [31]

The problem was that the Black electorate was suspicious of both camps. While they had no interest in ponying up their hard-earned cash to speculators—some of whom had owned them lock, stock and barrel only a few years earlier—neither were African Americans single-issue voters. Among their priorities were criminal justice reforms, including the repeal of the whipping post—which was used exclusively to sanction former slaves—anti-lynching legislation, a public accommodations law, and the right to integrate what had been, up to that point, all-white juries with a predilection for returning guilty verdicts against Negro defendants. The widely respected captain of a Richmond Black militia unit, Robert A. Paul, urged caution when it came to the Readjusters. "Those who had been the bitterest and most dangerous opponents to the Colored People were calling for our support. The one [Mahone] who had hurled hundreds of colored soldiers into the death-fraught crater of Petersburg had announced himself the leader and director of the new party." Black Virginians were immobilized between a rock and a hard place, much as their descendants would be forced to choose 141 years later between two conservative white presidential candidates with racial baggage, Donald Trump and Joe Biden.

The Readjusters' convening of February 25th and 26th, 1879, in Richmond broke the impasse, however. Of the smattering of African Americans in attendance, William T. Jefferson said that freedpeople had been waiting for an opportunity to resolve "the political leprosy which had fatally affected them."

> As for the debt, we don't want to pay a cent of it. We think we paid our share of it, if it ever was justly chargeable upon us, by long years of servitude. And then, as Virginia has been reconstructed in her territory and in her government we think her debt should be reconstructed too. We are humble

> citizens—the humblest in the Commonwealth—and we treat white people invariably with a great deal more courtesy than we receive because we are anxious not to offend you and to win your goodwill. We are for peace, and we accept the overture made to us as heartily as it is tendered for we feel that your interests and our interests are identical.[32]

Readjusters won 40 of 100 delegate seats in the 1879 poll but could command a legislative majority only if the 13 African American Republican delegates could be persuaded to vote with them. The party's chairman, Mahone, sprang into action, aggressively courting the Black legislators, and pledging the Readjuster's support for improved Negro schools, the abolition of the whipping post, repeal of the poll tax, the installation of Black jurors, and even a fair share of patronage jobs. The courtship succeeded. In one roll call vote after another, the Black delegates provided the margin of victory, appointing dozens of Readjusters to statewide offices and county judgeships, and passing legislation to slash the debt by 40 percent, although the measure could not withstand a veto by the Funder governor.

The 1880 presidential election threatened momentarily to derail the party's momentum. With no Readjuster on the national ticket, Mahone and the rest of the Readjuster leadership alienated their Black supporters by endorsing the Democrats' conservative nominee. African American voters bolted from the Readjuster coalition in droves. Not only did the Republican candidate, John A. Garfield, win the White House, but the Readjusters also finished a distant third in statewide elections. Mahone and the party's top echelon dismissed white Readjusters urging the party to weaken its ties to "uppity" Blacks and instead decided to double down on their biracial strategy to capture the governor's mansion in 1881. "We will know better next time," Mahone wrote in a letter to a white constituent. "We have been too sensitive, I suspect of combination."

Added a Readjuster lieutenant: "It is a case of neck or nothing."

The party moved decidedly left to win the Black vote, repealing the poll tax, integrating precinct chapters, committees and clubs, and doling out patronage jobs to African Americans in much the same way that Chicago's Democratic machine would to the Irish a century later. Mahone worked with Black Republicans to identify Black laborers to fill positions in the Construction Department, in the Norfolk Navy Yard, and in Washington, D.C. freedmen and women landed work as teamsters, firemen, engineers, riggers, iron platers, and day laborers, receiving wages as high as $1.50 per day. The number of African American teachers nearly doubled from 415 to 785 between 1879 and 1880, and while the schools remained segregated, the Readjusters went so far as to fire white teachers at Black schools and replace them with Black teachers who'd scored higher on statewide exams, in a scenario that is virtually the reverse of hiring practices at urban school districts in the 21st century. Following his election to the U.S. Senate in 1880, Mahone even voted typically with liberals in the GOP caucus.

Democrats exhorted white voters to reject the insurgents' race-mixing. "It is not the principal of the debt but the principle of pure white Saxon government that we stand for," read an editorial in one conservative Virginia newspaper.

Cheekily, the Readjusters taunted their adversaries.

"I don't propose to carry the war to Africa," said the party's 1881 gubernatorial candidate, William Cameron, "but to carry Africa into the war."[33]

Cameron and the Readjusters steamrolled the opposition in 1881, and as their first order of business, reduced the interest rate payments on the state's paper from 6 percent to 3 percent, saving taxpayers millions.

And then, like that, it was over. Owing obviously to African Americans' failure to accumulate much wealth in the 20 years since emancipation, whites in the city of Danville paid $38,000 of the $40,000 collected annually in property taxes, while Blacks occupied a majority of the city council seats, reflecting the jurisdiction's demographics. African Americans also accounted for all of Danville's justices of the peace, four of nine police officers, the lone health officer, the weighmaster, the clerk of the market and 20 of the 24 stalls rented there. A scuffle between a white man and a Black man over the right of way on a Danville sidewalk on the weekend before the 1884 election escalated into a riot, leaving three Blacks and a white fatally shot. The story quickly spread across the state. Exploiting tensions among Readjusters, Democrats claimed to restore law-and-order by assigning armed white mobs to patrol Black polling stations on horseback in Virginia's urban areas, turning Black voters away, ostensibly for security concerns. Readjusters did not intervene, and Blacks, sensing their party leaders' ambivalence, did not mount a robust effort to challenge voter suppression. In combination with record white turnout, the Democrats recaptured two-thirds of both state houses by a margin of 18,000 votes out of a total of 267,000 ballots cast.[34] Always sensitive to complaints that their policies were emboldening Negroes, Mahone and the party's leadership began to retreat from their more progressive policy positions to appease whites both within and outside their party. The pattern would be repeated a century later when Democrats began to increasingly ape Ronald Reagan's racist demagoguery, culminating in the party's nominations of Hillary Clinton and Joe Biden—both deeply unpopular with Blacks and progressives—in successive presidential elections.

The Readjusters remain the most powerful independent political movement in American history but the party was by no means an outlier. Between 1865 and 1900, every state below the Mason-Dixon line experimented with biracial coalitions that enjoyed varying degrees of success in expanding public education, building hospitals, extending transit lines, hiring Blacks for civil service positions, and reforming tax laws and the criminal justice system. The turning point was President Hayes' withdrawal of federal troops from the former Confederacy in 1877 to deliver on his promise to southern Democrats who supported him in a tight election the previous year. That effectively left Blacks unprotected from white lynch mobs such as the 500 gunmen, known as Red Shirts, who descended on the prosperous, all-Black South Carolina town of Hamburg in July 1876 just a few months before the presidential poll. Led by Ben "Pitchfork" Tillman, who would go on to a 24-year career in the U.S. Senate, the gang killed seven Blacks in a bid to intimidate African American voters and dismantle the biracial state government that, like the Readjusters, had created opportunities for Black and white workers alike. Stuffing the ballot box, the Democrats reclaimed control of the state, introducing the period of violent repression known as Jim Crow. Tillman and 93 other Red Shirts were charged but never prosecuted, and as a U.S. Senator, Tillman later boasted that "the leading white men" . . . had decided "to seize the first opportunity that the Negroes might offer them to provoke a riot and teach the Negroes a lesson."[35]

It was in this charged political atmosphere that my grandfather, James Jeter, was born in Union, South Carolina, in 1884.

The nomenclature has changed somewhat—carpetbaggers begat communists who begat liberals—but you can draw a straight, unbroken line that connects the Readjusters to modern American politics. Mahone's vacillating politics evoke comparisons to Vermont's U.S. Senator Bernie Sanders who has, in consecutive presidential campaigns, electrified people of color and young voters with his socialist platform only to betray his supporters by eventually urging them to endorse his rivals, modern-day Funders in the figures of Clinton and Biden. The Readjusters, in fact, even encountered an Obama-like character in the form of a moderate Black

Republican lawmaker who carried water for the bankers and landowning elite, often authoring bills challenging the Readjusters' progressive proposals.

Yet of all the features that the Readjusters etched into the face of American democracy, none is more enduring than the pillaging of public resources for private profits.

Austerity is a vicious circle: the deeper the spending cuts to public services, the more a city or state needs to borrow. And just as it was for Virginia's Bourbons, public education remains a high-value target. In 2013, Chicago Mayor Rahm Emanuel closed 50 public schools—the most by a single city at one time in the nation's history—with a combined enrollment that was 88 percent Black or Latino. Just days before he announced the school closures, Emanuel (or Mayor 1 Percent as he was widely known during his tenure in Chicago) announced the city's plans to invest $55 million to subsidize the construction of a new hotel and basketball arena for DePaul University, a private Jesuit university that charges each undergraduate roughly $30,000 annually in tuition and fees.[36] The best-of-times, worst-of-times tonality reflected the city's weaponization of a scheme that was initiated to jumpstart economic development in blighted neighborhoods.[37] In 2018, Chicago's tax increment financing districts, known as TIFs, siphoned off nearly $570 million, or roughly one-third of the city's annual operating budget, to spend on high-end development projects.

Chicago's tax increment financing districts freeze the property tax revenues for a defined neighborhood at, say, its 1990 level. For the life of the TIF district, the tax revenues collected above that fixed level, or the increment, is funneled into a slush fund that can be spent at the mayor's discretion, thereby evading democratic accountability. While Emanuel and his predecessor, Mayor Richard J. Daley, argued that student performance and declining enrollments were the primary determinants in school closures, a 2016 study by the Great Cities Institute at the University of Illinois at

Chicago found that race was the critical factor in deciding which schools closed between 2000 and 2013.[38]

The spate of school closings in Virginia and Chicago nearly 140 years apart bookend America's rise and fall yet almost no one in the public arena seems to make the connection.

"What," Saagar Enjeti, the co-host of the internet news program, *Rising*, bristled in a 2020 interview, "does white supremacy have to do with maximizing profits and sending a factory to China?"

Please come with me now on a journey through time to answer that question and assess what has been wrought by this ferocious, 150-year class war between the Americans who *built* the country, and those who *own* it.

Watch your step:

2.

A Call to Arms

The major obstacle to a united left in this country is white racism.

–George Jackson

History, it has been said, moves east to west. Yet there exists ample evidence that this transatlantic crossing represents the beginning of a dialogue that—if not quite as ancient as the sea—is at least as old as the first ship to cross it, resembling a flotilla of messages-in-bottles that transcend space and time and sometimes even language itself, affirming that in both our accords and our disunion, the course of human affairs is shaped by this unremitting chatter between the New World and the Old.

And so it came to pass that the shots fired on Fort Sumner occasioned a kind of tsunami that could be felt far beyond the bloodied battlefields of the Carolinas and Virginia extending east, across the pond, to the textile mills in Manchester and Liverpool, where dwindling cotton exports from the U.S. sliced into the bosses' profits and threw thousands of their employees out of work. While the robber barons lobbied the Queen to intercede militarily on behalf of the Confederacy, the British working class stood squarely in solidarity [39] with the Union, and their ensuing movement helped thwart the

Crown's plan to recognize the secessionists and revitalize the domestic textile industry. Speaking at a meeting in the spring of 1862, Karl Marx told 3,000 trade unionists:

> The English working class has won immortal historical honor for itself by thwarting the repeated attempts of the ruling classes to intervene on behalf of the American slaveholders by its enthusiastic mass meetings, even though the prolongation of the American Civil War subjects a million English workers to the most fearful suffering and privations.[40]

Owing to his experience as a war correspondent for the *New York Tribune* and Vienna's *Die Presse*, Marx's understanding of U.S. political economy was remarkably astute, and when the guns of war finally fell silent, he took a break from writing the first volume of *Das Kapital* to pen a letter to white American workers, urging them—out of basic self-interest if nothing else—to include the freedmen in their postbellum plans.

> An injustice to a section of your people has produced such direful results, let that cease. Let your citizens of today be declared free and equal, without reserve. If you fail to give them citizens' rights, while you demand citizens' duties, there will yet remain a struggle for the future which may again stain your country with your people's blood. The eyes of Europe and the world are fixed upon your efforts at reconstruction and enemies are ever ready to sound the knell of the downfall of republican institutions when the slightest chance is given. We warn you then, as brothers in the common cause, to remove every shackle from freedom's limb, and your victory will be complete.[41]

It's difficult to imagine Marx's exhortation falling on deafer ears. Most white laborers simply had no truck with the freedpeople—at least initially—choosing to regard the four million African Americans added to the ranks of the proletariat as competitors rather than comrades. This was a grave miscalculation; many of the former slaves had learned skilled trades as apprentices before the war, and thousands more had gained valuable experience in the Union army camps and relief associations. A traveling agent for the Freedmen's Bureau reported in 1868 that there were at least two Negro craftsmen for every white one in Mississippi and six Negro mechanics for every white mechanic in North Carolina. White workers, for the most part, flatly refused to integrate their unions, leaving Blacks no choice other than to work as scabs when the opportunity availed itself.

In their defense, one might argue (feebly) that white workers were just getting reacquainted with the tenets of labor organizing. The war's outbreak had decimated the unions that began to blossom in the 1850s, and workers had only begun to rebound in the summer of 1862. The war machine had quickened the development of the country's industrial sector and by the time the guns fell silent, American industrialists were making money hand-over-fist while wage-grunts were a tad slow to recognize the transition from farms to smokestacks. Employees steadily lost ground as prices soared but began to get their mojo back as the war wound down, tripling the number of union locals from 79 to 270 between December 1863 and December 1864, and increasing the number of national unions by 21 over the same period.[42] "Organize! Organize!" appealed Jonathan Fincher, editor of *Fincher's Trades' Review*, in December of 1863. "[O]rganize in every village and hamlet, and become tributary and auxiliary to district, county, state and national trade organizations."

In 1865, Black and white dockworkers on the New Orleans levee struck together for a pay hike. The country's first daily Negro newspaper, the *New Orleans Tribune*, endorsed the walkout as well as the eight-hour workday, but the Workingmen's Central Committee representing 11 segregated trade unions in the city, rather bizarrely petitioned the newspaper's editorial board to restrict their demands for a shorter workweek to white workers. The *Tribune* responded with a question: "How will you get justice if you yourself are unjust to your fellow laborers?" Shortly thereafter, when white bricklayers planning to strike discovered that the bosses intended to replace them permanently with scab workers, they called for an emergency meeting of all New Orleans bricklayers, regardless of color.

The *Tribune* hoped that white and colored bricklayers could work together but cautioned:

> . . . should the white bricklayers intend to use their colored comrades as tools, and simply to remove the stumbling block they now find in their way, without guaranty for the future, we would say to our colored brethren: Keep aloof, go back to your work, and insist upon being recognized as men and equals before you do anything.
>
> Labor equalizes all men; the handicraft of the worker has no color and belongs to no race. The best worker—not the whitest—is the honor and pride of his trade.[43]

As with Marx's admonition, the *Tribune's* plea went unheeded by white bricklayers, who refused to admit African Americans into their union, and lost the strike when Blacks were in fact hired as permanent replacements. Even this did not persuade white working men to recalibrate their strategy, however. When the Eight Hour League was formed in New Orleans the following year, Black membership was expressly forbidden, and when white laborers walked off the job in 1866 to win support for their cause, "Negroes did not hesitate to act as scabs and break the strike."[44] In contrast, Black and white workers in St. Louis joined forces in calling for a shorter workday; their demands were promptly met.[45]

Similarly, Northern whites often refused to work alongside Negroes, going so far as to demand their dismissal by walking off the job and picketing. One such "hate strike" occurred in October 1865 when Baltimore's white caulkers and ship carpenters successfully lobbied their bosses to fire 100 Black caulkers and longshoremen. And after surveying the city in 1869, *The New York Times* could not identify a single integrated labor union.

In May 1869, Frederick Douglass' youngest son, Charles Remond Douglass, landed a job at the Government Printing Office in Washington, D.C., and because it was a closed shop requiring membership in the union as a condition of employment, he simultaneously applied to join the Columbia Typographical Union. The union's financial secretary issued Douglass a temporary permit until a decision was made. At a meeting later that month, Douglass' application was hotly debated with some of the whites defending the "right of colored men to earn an honest livelihood on equal terms with whites"[46] and others voicing bitter opposition to Douglass' application because he was a scab. His application was ultimately withdrawn. Frederick Douglass noted that his son had been "denounced for not being a member of the Printers' Union by the very men who would not permit him to join such a union. . . . There is no disguising the fact—his crime was his color."

Other unions followed the lead of Washington's printers. In September 1869, the Carpenters and Joiners Union *whitesplained* their decision to rebuff overtures from Negro tradesmen:

> Resolved that we are ever willing to extend the hand of fellowship to every laboring man, more especially to those of our own craft; we believe the prejudices of our members against the colored people are of such a nature that it is not expedient at present to admit them as members or to organize them under the National Union.

This was no doubt music to the ears of the carpenters' bosses who, however genuine their actual disdain for Blacks, also understood bigotry, at least on some subliminal level, as a powerfully disruptive tool, and deployed it as a soldier would a grenade, hurling it into a crowd to distract and destroy, and keep a steady supply of strikebreakers at the ready. Occasionally, employers recruited hundreds or even thousands of Negro workers from the South to cross, sometimes unwittingly, picket lines in the North. Of the conundrum facing white labor, the famed historian C. Vann Woodward wrote that " . . . [t]wo possible but contradictory policies" are available: " . . . eliminate the Negro as a competitor by excluding him from the skilled trades either as an apprentice or a worker or take him in as an organized worker committed to the defense of a common standard of wages."[47]

While it is clear which approach carried the day, it's important to understand that there were exceptions to the policy of partition, notably the labor press, which began to proliferate in 1863. Within a decade some 130 new outlets had started to publish, with many of the more militant ones launched by printers who had been jettisoned for demanding a pay hike or trying to unionize their shop. The most arresting of these publications was the *Boston Daily Evening Voice.* Organized by locked-out printers, the *Daily Evening Voice* published its first edition on December 2, 1864, and went on to advocate for the rights of workers, without regard to "sex, complexion or birthplace." It championed education— "If we think so much of free schools, why do we not carry out the system and have our colleges free?"— and gender equality, appealing to men to open their unions and labor libraries to women, and to assist women in their efforts to procure voting rights, higher pay, and shorter hours.

> The laboring classes never will be elevated without the elevation of women—never. While woman is obligated to work like a slave to earn her daily bread, the country is as hopeless of any progress as Sahara of vegetation.

Similarly, a May 2, 1866 headline in the newspaper asked rhetorically:

> Can white workingmen ignore colored ones?

The reply from some quarters was a deafening "no." In his 1870 address to fellow Marxists at a convention of the New York Workingmen's

Assembly, William J. Jessup, a carpenter and the New York correspondent of the National Labor Union, urged integration:

> The negro will no longer submit to occupy positions of a degraded nature, but will seek an equality with the whites in the trades and professions. . . . If we discard this element of labor and refuse to recognize it, capital will recognize it and use it to our great disadvantage.[48]

In addition to white Marxists, the Irish immigrants who began to turn up in the U.S. fleeing poverty and British imperialism seemed of two minds about their racial affiliation, reflecting, at least in part, the broader society's uncertainty about how to classify "the niggers of Europe" who often toiled alongside Blacks, doing the most backbreaking work by day—digging canals, laying train tracks, loading and unloading cargo, and building dams—and routinely retired to slums teeming with Black neighbors by night. In antebellum Philadelphia, some considered the descriptor "Irishman" a slur on par with "nigger,"[49] and both were targeted by Boston "race" rioters in an 1829 pogrom.

Wrote the labor historian David Roediger:

> In cities like Worcester and Philadelphia, Blacks and Irish lived near each other without significant friction into the early 1830s. They often celebrated and socialized together, swapping musical traditions and dance steps. Even as late as the immediate post-Civil War years (the writer) Lafcadio Hearn described Black and Irish levee workers in Cincinnati as sharing a storehouse of jokes and tales, of jigs and reels and even of dialect words and phrases. Love and sex between Black men and Irish women were not uncommon.[50]

Irish attitudes on race would seem to reinforce the view of academics like Roediger, Noel Ignatiev, and the theologian Thandeka, that Europeans "learn" to be white in response to a barrage of cradle-to-grave social stimuli. "When the first Africans arrived in Virginia in 1619," begins the first volume of Theodore Allen's classic study, *The Invention of the White Race*, "there were no white people there; nor, according to colonial records, would there be for another 60 years."

Stemming from their marginalization by the British, Irish immigrants were slower than their European cousins to embrace a "white" identity. In 1842, for instance, 70,000 Irish signed an antislavery petition *in Ireland* appealing to their kith and kin across the pond to "*cling to the abolitionists*,"[51] in a bid to not only repeal slavery in the U.S. but to end racial discrimination in its entirety. It read: "Irishmen and Irishwomen! treat the colored people as your equals, as brethren." Likewise, in a letter dated April 1870, Marx tendered an opinion of the "Irish question" for two friends living in New York that could easily have doubled as a diagnosis of America's "Negro question," with Irish workers standing in for African Americans and English laborers as proxies for their Yankee counterparts. He wrote:

> And most important of all! All English industrial and commercial centres now possess a working-class split into two hostile camps: English proletarians and Irish proletarians. The ordinary English worker hates the Irish worker because he sees in him a competitor who lowers his standard of life. Compared with the Irish worker he feels himself a member of the ruling nation and for this very reason he makes himself into a tool of the aristocrats and capitalists against Ireland and thus strengthens their domination over himself. He cherishes religious, social and national prejudices against the Irish worker. His attitude is much the same as that of the 'poor whites' towards the 'niggers' in the former slave states of the American Union. The Irishman pays him back with interest in his own money. He sees in the English worker both the accomplice and the stupid tool of English rule in Ireland. This antagonism is artificially sustained and intensified by the press, the pulpit, the comic papers, in short, by all the means at the disposal

> of the ruling classes. This antagonism is the secret of the impotence of the English working class, despite its organisation. It is the secret which enables the capitalist class to maintain its power, as this class is perfectly aware.[52]

If the freedpeople had any hope of winning a war against both their bosses and their co-workers, they'd have to think outside the box. African Americans who were thrown out of work by the white caulkers and carpenters' 1865 strike in Baltimore held a brainstorming meeting a few days later. A Negro caulker named Isaac Myers made a bold proposal: What if Blacks pooled their resources to buy their own shipyard and managed it as a workers' cooperative?

The African American caulkers quickly raised $10,000 from a group of investors that included Frederick Douglass, borrowed another $30,000 from a white ship captain, took out a six-year mortgage, and purchased a shipyard and railway extension two days before Valentine's Day in 1866. Within six months the Chesapeake Marine Railway and Dry Dock Company employed 300 Blacks in Baltimore and other cities along the Atlantic seaboard at an average wage of $3 per day. Buoyed by several government contracts, the company repaid its mortgage and all outstanding debts within five years, and as the cooperative expanded, hired white laborers in addition to Blacks. At a meeting of the National Labor Union in Philadelphia in 1869, Myers pleaded with white delegates to integrate with Blacks:

> I speak today for the colored men of the whole country . . . when I tell you that all they ask for themselves is a fair chance; that you shall be no worse off by giving them that chance; that you and they will dwell in peace and harmony together . . . The white men of the country have nothing to fear from the colored laboring man. We desire to see labor elevated and made respectable; we desire to have the highest rate of wages that our labor is worth . . . And you, gentlemen, may rely on the support of the colored laborer of

> this country in bringing about this result . . . American citizenship with the Black man is a complete failure, if he is proscribed from the workshops of this country.[53]

Continuing, Myers invoked the Baltimore stevedores' cooperative efforts:

> We gave employment to a large number of the men of your race, without regard to their political creed, and to the very men who once sought to do us injury. So you see gentlemen, we have no prejudice.

Regardless, the NLU declined Myers' offer. Of the decision, W.E.B. Du Bois wrote:

> . . . the white worker did not want the Negro in his unions, did not believe in him as a man, dodged the question, and when he appeared at conventions, asked him to organize separately; that is outside the real labor movement, in spite of the fact that it was a contradiction of all sound labor policies.[54]

African Americans in Georgia staged the first postbellum labor stoppage on the Savannah docks, walking off the job in December 1866 after the city council voted to charge longshoremen $10 (about $182 in 2023 dollars) for a license to load and unload ships.[55] After a lengthy debate at their next meeting, city councilors agreed to lower the fee to $3 but that failed to satisfy the strikers, who formed a gauntlet to block scabs from reaching the harbor. The police arrested eight troublemaking Negroes for disorderly conduct and weapons possession, including Nero Thomas, who was shot in the melee but proclaimed as he was carted off that he would rather die for the cause than end his protest.[56]

The African American stevedores were unable to further reduce the license fee but their militancy inspired their ten white co-workers—eight of them Irish stevedores from Quebec City who spent their winters in

Georgia—to petition the court in January of 1869 to recognize their Workingmen's Benevolent Association of Savannah, or WBA. Although they organized much earlier, the Black maritime workers did not formally petition the court to recognize their labor union until 1885. Of the Workingmen's Union Association, or WUA, the historian John Blassingame wrote that it's "reasonable to speculate that some were former slaves, probably illiterate, and in many cases, new to the city," and "mixed freely with the city's poor Irish and used the same grocery stores and liquor saloons."[57] Collaboration between Blacks and whites did not eradicate racism on Savannah's docks; indeed, the vast majority of longshoremen not chosen for work by the pit boss in the daily "shape up" were African American. But those who were selected worked alongside white dockworkers in integrated "gangs" of six—typically three whites and three Blacks—and by 1888 received the same pay of $3.80 per day for stowing cotton, $3.40 for "roll-up," and $2.80 for "unhooking."

Also organizing across the evolving color line was the Noble Order of the Knights of Labor. Formed as a secret society in 1869 by nine, blacklisted white Philadelphia garment-cutters whose union had been dissolved, the Knights initially admitted only tailors but soon opened its membership to employees in other trades—known as "sojourners"—and eventually to any man 18 years of age or older who worked for a living, excepting lawyers, physicians, bankers, and liquor salesmen. By 1881, the Knights had begun to admit women as well, underscoring its slogan, "An injury to one is the concern of all."

When Scranton, Pennsylvania's former mayor, Terrence V. Powderly, was appointed Grand Master Workman in 1879, the Order was a collection of small, local assemblies with 20,151 members. By 1883, membership had ballooned to 51,914, and after winning two strikes in the spring and autumn of 1885 against the railroad magnate Jay Gould[58] (the Jeff Bezos of his day), membership peaked the following year at somewhere between 700,000 to a million, of which nearly ten percent was African American. While the Knights officially disapproved of strikes as a negotiating tactic in labor disputes, its leadership under Powderly "sought to organize the entire producing class into a single irresistible coalition that would work toward the abolition of the wage system and the establishment of a new society."[59] The Order campaigned for an eight-hour workday, an end to child labor, improved workplace safety, equal pay for women, unemployment insurance, compensation for on-the-job injuries, employee-managed cooperatives, and public ownership of utilities. Although the Knights did not formally disavow racism, the largest labor union of the 19th century was nothing if not pragmatic.

"Why," asked the Knights' official newspaper, *The Journal of United Labor*, in an 1880 editorial, "should workingmen keep out of our organization anyone who might be used as a tool to aid the employer in grinding down wages?"

Blacks poured into Knights locals in both the North and South, where the Order began organizing in 1878. Black women joined assemblies with Black men or formed their own locals composed of housekeepers, laundresses, and chambermaids. Bitter opposition from landlords, industrialists, and newspapers forced Knight organizers in the South to cloak their activities in names like "Franklin Lodge" or "Protective Lodge" and post sentinels outside meetings to defend against police raids.[60] Wrote a white organizer to Powderly from Raleigh, North Carolina in 1885:

> You have no idea of what I have to contend with [in] the way of prejudice down here. There is a continual cry of 'nigger,' 'nigger!' . . . I believe that our Order is intended to protect all people who work, the poor, ignorant, underpaid and overworked as well as the skilled mechanic, and have tried to act upon that principle. And for this alone I have incurred abuse and social ostracism.[61]

At its 1886 national convention in Richmond, the Knights not only insisted that the theaters and hotels accept African American delegates,[62] but that a Black delegate, Frank Ferrell, introduce Powderly to the assembly. Black membership in the Knights increased sharply from 60,000 to 90,000 by 1887[63] and that same year, a young, Black journalist, Ida B. Wells, wrote in the *Memphis Watchman*:

> I was fortunate enough to attend a meeting of the Knights of Labor . . . I noticed that everyone who came was welcomed and every woman from Black to white was seated with the courtesy usually extended to white ladies alone in this town. It was the first assembly of the sort in this town where color was not the criterion to recognition as ladies and gentlemen.

By the time Wells issued her endorsement, however, the Order had already begun to unravel. At a labor rally in Chicago's Haymarket Square on May 4, 1886, a bomb exploded and police opened fire on the crowd. Seven police officers and eight civilians were killed, and another 100 people were injured. Aided and abetted by newspaper publishers, Chicago's industrialists seized the opportunity to mount a counteroffensive against organized labor and the Knights in particular. With scant evidence, police arrested eight anarchists on conspiracy charges, painting them as terrorists, and ginning up anti-immigrant sentiment in a city that had only 15 years earlier accused an Irish saloon owner and her blameless cow for starting the Great Chicago Fire that killed 300 people, destroyed three square miles and left 100,000 homeless. Jurors convicted all eight defendants for the Haymarket bombing, sentencing seven to death, of which four were ultimately hanged and another committed suicide.

The Haymarket affair was the springboard for a nationwide campaign of intimidation intended to slow organized labor's momentum, partly by impressing upon whites the risks of organizing, especially in concert with

Blacks. Employers harassed, jailed, fired, locked out and beat troublemaking employees and when all else failed, they killed them. Rattled white workers began to abandon the Knights as quickly as they had joined. Official membership plummeted from 702,924 in 1886 to 221,618 in 1888.

One in every five Knights was Black by 1887[64] and by 1895, the Knights were a spent force, with no more than 20,000 mostly Black members nationwide.

A white Knights organizer in the Deep South, Hiram F. Hover, persisted, however, recruiting Negroes to join the Co-operative Workers of America.[65] While addressing an audience of more than 300 Negro workers at a Methodist church near the city of Warrenton, Georgia, in the early morning hours of May 20, 1887, a contingent of Klansmen fired a shotgun blast through the church window, ripping through the left side of Hover's face, and exiting on the other side, putting out his right eye.[66]

Hover miraculously survived but *the Augusta Chronicle* reported, apocryphally, that Hover had urged the "darkies" to "stick a torch to the white man's house" if their demands for higher wages were unmet, while a correspondent for *the Atlanta Constitution* referenced the violence at Haymarket a year earlier: "The Warrenton way of doing things is the very opposite of the Chicago method but will pan out better . . . Here is a pointer for Chicago that is worth considering."[67]

Local Knights in Georgia denounced the attack as a "case of capitalistic conspiracy against Labor," but Powderly and his top aides were conspicuously silent. In the aftermath of the Haymarket bombings, the Knights leadership was under pressure from white industrialists and landowners to rein in the more subversive elements within the Order just as Mahone was challenged by the Bourbons in Virginia to crack down on the most militant Readjusters. Rather than denounce Hover's shooting, Powderly railed against anarchists who had infiltrated the Order. Consonant with Mahone's leadership of the Readjusters, the Knights' tepid response to state violence against its constituents left Blacks isolated, allowing lawmakers to ratchet up further their campaign of terror, criminalizing Blacks who entered into collective bargaining agreements with employers and sending in state militias to massacre striking workers.

The truth of the matter is that the Knights were always of two minds on the issue of race. In a tacit nod to white supremacy, Powderly maintained that "it was the industrial, not the race question we endeavor to solve."[68] His ambivalence supports the hypothesis of the historian C. Vann Woodward that racial identities were not fully formed until the 1890s when the pattern of Jim Crow violence erected in the popular imagination an unscalable, impregnable wall between "us" and "them."

This parsing of working-class identities represents a reversal of Marx's theory that the class we are born into determines our social identity; rather, in the U.S., it is our social identity that prefigures our class relations.

Perhaps the best example of the meticulous construction of a social identity occurred on October 24, 1892, when nearly 3,000 New Orleans Teamsters, Scalesmen and Packers—known as the Triple Alliance or Triple A—walked off their jobs on the levees to demand overtime pay, a 10-hour-workday, and a closed shop. Representing merchants, railroad owners, and commodities exchanges, the Board of Trade announced that it would sign an agreement with the unions representing the white Scalesmen and Packers' unions but under no circumstance would it enter into an agreement with "niggers," as they referred to the Black Teamsters. *The New Orleans Times-Democrat* did its part to stoke racial anxiety by fabricating stories with headlines such as "Negroes Attack White Man" and "Assaulted by Negroes," but nothing took. Immunized by the sensibilities of the more recently settled German, Irish and Italian immigrants who had not yet grown accustomed to thinking of themselves as anything other than Germans, Irish, and Italians, the coalition held. The *Times-Democrat* retorted in an editorial:

> The very worst feature, indeed, in the whole case seems to be that the white elements of the labor organizations appear to be under the dominance of Senegambian influence, or that they are at least lending themselves as willing tools to carry out Senegambian schemes.[69]

Unmoved, nearly 50 union locals—including streetcar drivers and the typographers who had only recently signed new contracts—went on strike on November 8. One strike leader wrote to Samuel Gompers, head of the American Federation of Labor, which had succeeded the Knights as the nation's largest alliance of unions:

> There are fully 25,000 men idle. There is no newspaper to be printed, no gas or electric light in the city, no wagons, no carpenters, painters or in fact any business doing . . . I am sorry you are not down here to take a hand in it. It is a strike that will go down in history.[70]

With the exception of the closed shop, the Board eventually met all of their employees' demands, and the unity that was central to the Triple A's strength held fast for another generation before the financiers' relentless strategy of divide and conquer began to Balkanize the proletariat along racial lines.

In her superb book, *The End of Bias*, the author Jessica Nordell writes that a lie repeated often enough does not become the truth but invisible. The idea of whiteness as a thing apart is the principle around which modern American life is organized and yet few people either acknowledge or question it. The messaging communicated by the newspapers following the assault on Hover and during the New Orleans general strike is repeated almost daily in today's news and entertainment media in an effort to circumscribe a workers' movement.

Still, if we are conscious of it, we can catch the odd glimpse of workers who continue to practice the kind of class consciousness that animated the labor movement in the final years of the 19th century.

In 2009, two Black repairmen showed up at my Brooklyn apartment one Saturday afternoon to fix a problem I had with my Time Warner cable subscription. After 90 minutes, they had not yet resolved the issue, and mistakenly thinking their shop was nonunion, I suggested they leave it, and send someone back Monday. "I don't want the company to try and stiff you on overtime."

Not to worry, they assured me. They were represented by the International Brotherhood of Electrical Workers Local 3, and they described their shop steward as a middle-aged Italian from Bensonhurst, the tight-knit Brooklyn enclave that is notorious among New Yorkers for its racial hostility. The African American technicians liked to get a rise out of him by jokingly inquiring about his teenage daughter's availability.

Whether he was racist, my two guests couldn't say, but *this* they knew for certain:

> If the bosses try to fuck with us about overtime or anything,
> he will tear them a new asshole, guaranteed.

At roughly the same time, I met a young woman of Portuguese ancestry named Jennifer when I went to work in the Manhattan communications office of a liberal think tank, PolicyLink. I was excited to work for two African American women, Angela Glover Blackwell, the organization's founder, and my boss, the communications director, Milly Hawk Daniel.

None of my ideas ever seemed to find much traction with Milly, or Angela especially, who seemed to revel in her physical proximity to Obama at a White House summit far more than she valued systemic change. When I proposed ghostwriting an opinion piece about a series of Bay Area police killings of African American men, and pitching it to major newspapers, Angela dismissed it out of hand. When later I mentioned that African Americans did not share PolicyLink's enthusiasm for charter schools, Milly looked at me like I had a third eye in the middle of my forehead.

Far more disturbing, however, was Angela and Milly's mistreatment of the few African American staffers in the New York office, including Keith, who was my subordinate, and Twana, the receptionist.

If Milly's bullying of Keith and Twana was a dark and violent force that left them demoralized, then Jen's solidarity with Keith and Twana was a countervailing force of light. Once, when a white associate director loudly berated Keith, Jen ran to his defense, interrupting the tirade by pretending to ask Keith for a file that she urgently needed. The entire office closed ranks around the immensely popular Twana, but no one so much as Jen, who helped her brush up on her computer skills, adroitly defused questions from Milly about the hours Twana put in and provided Twana with any reconnaissance she gleaned from conversations with Milly, or other staffers in the Oakland office who Twana had little access to. Jen always went above and beyond her job description to help organize office birthday and holiday parties, was fiercely loyal to her ambitious African American supervisor, told the *Nuyorican* communications associate that she would handle her tasks while she took another sick day to recover from the flu, and although she was chronically overworked, was always the first to raise her hand when I needed some last-minute copy editing done. Once, Twana admitted to me that she viewed Jen as a sister, even though she was closer in age and complexion to Milly and Angela.

A few months into my time at PolicyLink, Jen pounced as I arrived for work one morning.

"Jon, can I have just a second?" she said, closing my office door behind her.

"Of course," I said, a little worried by her unusually sober mien.

"I know that you are going to be in on Keith's performance review later on today with Milly," she said. "And I just wanted to make a case for giving him a good review. He works really hard, but it's a hard job because you do so many different things for so many people that there's no one person who has a full view of everything you're doing. I know because I had that job before Keith and I can tell you that Keith is really doing an excellent job and. . . "

I held my hand up to interrupt. "Jen, you have no worries," I said. "I had already planned to give him an excellent review."

Jen exhaled, visibly relieved. "That's great, Jon. I thought you would but I was just worried that Milly might not have the whole picture."

A few months after my conversation with Jen, the U.S. Department of Agriculture fired an African American woman, Shirley Sherrod, from her job as Georgia's state director of rural development, after a conservative blogger had released excerpts from a speech she gave to the NAACP in 2010. The edited video made it appear that Sherrod was expressing racist views. Nothing could have been further from the truth.

In her address, Sherrod recalled the 1965 murder of her father and helping a white Georgia farmer stave off foreclosure decades later. The first time they met, she said, the farmer, Roger Spooner, "was trying to show me that he was superior to me. What he didn't know while he was taking all that time trying to show me he was superior to me was that I was trying to decide just how much help I was going to give him."

Continuing, she said: "I was struggling with the fact that so many Black people have lost their farmland and here I was faced with having to help a white person save their land."

Initially, she said, she palmed Spooner off on a white attorney who she thought would help Spooner file for bankruptcy protection. But the attorney dropped the ball, leaving Sherrod to scramble to find Spooner a competent attorney just a week before his property was to be sold.

After the NAACP released the unedited version of her speech, Obama's Agriculture Secretary, Tom Vilsack apologized to Sherrod and offered to rehire her—she declined—and Spooner and his wife, Eloise, defended Sherrod, who they credited with saving their farm.

In the full text of her speech, Sherrod recalled dedicating herself to a life of service after her father was murdered by a white man, but acknowledged to her audience that "when I made that commitment I was making that commitment to Black people and to Black people only, but you know God will show you things and he will put things in your path [so] that you realize that the struggle is really about poor people. . . . It's really about those who have and those who don't."

3.

Weapons of Mass Destruction

Those who can make you believe absurdities can make you commit atrocities.

–Voltaire

The party told you to reject the evidence of your eyes and ears. It was their final, most essential command.

–George Orwell, "1984"

'Twas a story of incomparable horror that gripped the nation in the autumn of 1994:

A young, white single mother is stopped at an intersection while driving with her two sons on a dark and desolate South Carolina road when suddenly she is accosted by a man who materializes, like an apparition, from the shadows. He is Black, armed, and in a hurry, hijacking the maroon Mazda compact and forcing the frantic 23-year-old Susan Smith to drive before finally kicking her out, and speeding off into the night with her two towheaded boys. When the car was dragged nine days later from the bottom of John D. Long Lake in Union, South Carolina, the bodies of the two toddlers were found still strapped in their car seats.

An hour's drive away across the state line in Charlotte, another white mother, Glenda Gilmore, was driving her own son to preschool when she first heard of the shocking affair on National Public Radio:

> I hugged my own little guy and stumbled out of the car. Some of the other mothers were crying. We said lingering goodbyes that morning and arrived early that afternoon to gather our children.[71]

That evening the television news broadcast the composite sketch of the gunman who had abducted Smith's sons, three-year-old Michael and 14-month-old Alex. On the screen appeared a scowling, dark-complexioned Black man, lithe as a bantamweight, with beady eyes that peered from underneath a knit cap. Suddenly, a wave of clarity washed over Gilmore like a riptide following a full moon.

"Susan Smith was lying, I realized in a rush,"[72] Gilmore would later write. "For I had 'seen' this man before in sources almost 100 years old. He was the incubus: in mythology, he is a winged demon that has sexual intercourse with women while they sleep; on the ground in 1898 he represented the Black beast rapist."

In her madness, Smith had subconsciously described for a police sketch artist the chimera conjured by three white supremacists-cum-warlocks who met in the spring of 1898 to plot the violent overthrow of North Carolina's liberal interracial government, known as the Fusionists. Holed up at the Chattawka Hotel in the coastal city of New Bern, the three men—Furnifold Simmons, chairman of the state Democratic Party, Josephus Daniels, the publisher of *the Raleigh News & Observer*, and a young attorney named Charles Brantley Aycock—conceded that their party could not win a fair ballot because the Democrats' record of accomplishment during their stint as North Carolina's governing party was abysmal. Humiliated by the rebels' surrender and the "despotism" of a state constitution that was rewritten to enfranchise the freedmen, North Carolina's race-baiting Democrats regained political control of the state when President Rutherford B. Hayes withdrew all remaining federal troops from the former Confederacy in 1877, and consolidated their power through gerrymandering, disenfranchising felons, and abolishing countywide elections. That was all well-and-good while the cotton was high, but enthusiasm for the do-nothing Democrats began to wane as cotton prices collapsed in the 1880s, forcing smallholder farmers to mortgage their crops as collateral for bank loans. With the onset of a depression in 1893, white farmers and industrial workers began to abandon the Democrats in droves, joining forces with Black voters to award control of both state legislative chambers to the Fusionists, so-named because the movement merged, or "fused" the Party of Lincoln—and its ardent Black following—with the Populists.

To repay farmers' onerous debts incurred as a result of the crop lien system, the Populists favored the monetization, or coinage, of silver as William Jennings Bryan famously championed in his "Cross of Gold" speech at the 1896 Democratic National Convention. Democrats, on the other hand, flatly rejected any monetary policies—such as the printing of Greenbacks, which functioned during the war much as bitcoin does today—that would weaken the dollar, accelerate inflation and slice into financiers' profits.[73]

The economist Doug Henwood explains:

> The Civil War was financed with easy money and a limitless supply of Greenbacks. Prices and production zoomed, and Yankee farmers prospered. After the war, however, Eastern bankers demanded a return to sobriety in the form of a valuation of gold that would enforce a return of pre-war

> prices. It succeeded all too well. Wheat that sold for $2.06 a bushel sold for less than 60 cents thirty years later. As prices fell, farmers borrowed to increase output and stay afloat, a strategy that only fed the deflation. Under the burden of falling prices and heavy debts, farms failed in droves, to be ceded to creditors, combined into larger operations and resold. Farmers expressed their displeasure in the populist rebellion, one of the greatest examples of spontaneous, radical revolt in our history.[74]

That revolt almost never happened in North Carolina. Redolent of the Readjusters, the Populists trafficked in white supremacist rhetoric early on, but hit the mute button in an attempt to woo Black support. The rebranding helped Fusionists capture a majority of seats in the state legislature in 1894, which paid immediate dividends for the working class. Championing local self-government, Fusion lawmakers mandated elections for all municipal and county boards and councils—ending the Democrats' policy of appointment—and eased restrictions on voter registration to increase Black participation at the polls in the 1896 election, when nearly nine of ten eligible African American voters cast ballots. The Fusionists ran the table, installing the first Republican governor since Reconstruction, Daniel Russell, who in a reenactment of the Readjusters' Cameron in Virginia 15 years earlier, went on to sign bills capping interest rates paid on bonds at 6 percent and used the savings to bolster funding for education, roads, and farm subsidies. Also mindful of the Readjusters was the Fusionists' doling out the spoils to its Black base, gerrymandering the electoral map to favor the election of African American candidates and appointing hundreds more as postmasters, police chiefs, constables, magistrates, coroners, and registers of deeds. By 1898, there were nearly 1,000 Negro officeholders in North Carolina.[75] "Once again," the historian Leon Prather noted, "the Black man constituted a formidable element within the Republican party and his voting power, which had been dormant since Reconstruction, reappeared as a force to be reckoned with."

That reckoning came early on November 10, 1898, when a mob of 2,000 heavily armed white men marched to the office of the only Black newspaper in Wilmington—the largest city in the state at that time—battered down the door, poured kerosene on the wooden floors, set it ablaze, and then joined scores of vigilantes on horseback in an attempt to "kill every damn nigger in sight."[76] When finally the guns fell silent and the flames ebbed, the mayor, board of aldermen, and police chief had been forced to resign, as many as 300 African Americans lay dead, and dozens more of their neighbors and "white nigger" allies chased from town to live the rest of their days in exile.

The *putsch* on the banks of the Cape Fear River is widely known as the first *coup d'etat* in U.S. history, and provides a textbook example of false consciousness, the term coined by Marx's partner, Friedrich Engels, to explain subordinate classes who assail their own material interests based on a misguided identification with their rulers. "Under thorough discipline and under command of officers," one witness to the Wilmington massacre wrote, "capitalists and laborers marched together. The lawyer and his client were side by side. Men of large business interests kept step with the clerks."[77]

Yet for all its inherent drama, the massacre itself was nowhere near as extraordinary as the public disservice campaign that preceded it, the objective of which was to speak something called a *nigger* into existence. For what was birthed by Simmons, Daniels and Aycock in that New Bern hotel room was as monstrous and farcical as any marketing strategy in the 19th century, surpassed in scale, horror and preposterousness only by the Belgian King Leopold's genocidal reconfiguration of the African Congo into the largest labor camp in history while grandstanding as the leader of a global campaign to abolish slavery.

The question puzzling Democratic operatives in 1898 was what issue could convince the white Everyman to abandon the political party that had demonstrably improved his family's standard of living in such a brief time span?

In his 1944 tome, *An American Dilemma,* the Swedish economist Gunnar Myrdal attributes racist attitudes in the U.S. to crude jealousies of both a sexual and material nature, and to be sure, whites in Wilmington were confronted daily with the quite real possibility that theirs was *not* the superior race. The city's Blacks had a higher literacy rate near the turn of the century, and according to a 2006 retrospective by *the Raleigh News & Observer*, African Americans*:*

> . . . owned 10 of the 11 eateries and 20 of 22 barbershops. Black entrepreneur Thomas Miller was one of Wilmington's three real estate agents. The city's business directory listed Black-owned Bell & Pickens as one of only four dealers and shippers of fish and oysters. Many of Wilmington's most sought-after craftsmen were also Black: jewelers and watchmakers, tailors, mechanics, furniture makers, blacksmiths, shoemakers, stonemasons, plasterers, plumbers, wheelwrights and brick masons. Frederick Sadgwar, an African American architect, financier and contractor, owned a stately home that still stands as a monument to his talents and industry.[78]

About the only thing Wilmington's Black community did not produce in abundance were sexual deviants, and so the three conspirators simply fabricated them out of whole cloth. With its broad circulation, Daniels' *News & Observer* was particularly useful in pathologizing the Black men who were key actors in the Fusion movement. Spearheading the daily newspaper's initiative was a young artist named Ethre Jennett, aka Sampson Huckleberry, who had left the state to enroll in what is today known as the Parsons School of Design in lower Manhattan. Daniels wrote to Jennett four months after the New Bern meeting to solicit his help and the artist complied, returning to North Carolina to produce nearly 75 single-panel cartoons between August and early November, supplying the white supremacists' public relations campaign with a potent visual element to help fill in the gaps—especially for barely literate whites—complementing headlines that shrieked of the deflowering of white womanhood, and furnishing posterity with archival material to reference whenever, like Susan Smith, the need arose for an alibi.

The criminologist Kathryn Russell-Brown has dubbed these attempts to exculpate white wrongdoing as "racial hoaxes," and prime examples include Boston's Charles Stuart, who murdered his pregnant wife in 1989 and fingered a fictitious Black carjacker as the culprit to throw the police off his own trail, or a white Milwaukee entrepreneur, Jesse Anderson, who stabbed his wife 21 times in a restaurant parking lot in 1992 and told police that the couple had been attacked by two African American men.

"The only way I can describe it," the white police officer Darren Wilson testified to a grand jury in 2014 after he gunned down an unarmed 18-year-old African American, Michael Brown, on a suburban St. Louis street, "it looks like a demon, that's how angry he looked."[79]

Accordingly, Jennett's illustrations more than a century ago would often pair the bearded, dignified "honest white man"—who bore an uncanny resemblance to Robert E. Lee—and the preening, big-lipped, blue-Black character known as Zip Coon. In one cartoon published just weeks before the 1898 slaughter, Zip Coon recoils from a smack to the nose by the honest white man wielding an oversized, rolled-up paper ballot.

There is a seamless historical continuity between Jennett's honest white man and the litany of heroic characters portrayed by Hollywood icons such as John Wayne, Gary Cooper, Clint Eastwood, and Tom Hanks, just as there is between Zip Coon's bug-eyed minstrelsy and the on-screen buffoonery of Mantan Moreland, Stepin Fetchit, Tyler Perry or Kevin Hart. These stock characters are tools of warfare, like propaganda leaflets stored alongside munitions in an armory, to be retrieved for rescuing the embattled reputations of the rich and the powerful. The Wilmington massacre debuted a genre of racial storytelling that casts white men as the cultural norms of virtue, intelligence, and even sex appeal, locked in mortal combat with aboriginal forces of barbarism and depravity.

This calumny has proven enormously effective at atomizing the class consciousness that has historically been the X factor in pluralist movements. And while it's impossible to say for sure, North Carolina's postbellum ghoul—with his sinewy, claw-like fingers, menacing gaze, spindly overbite, and bat-like wings emblazoned with the words "Negro Rule"—was likely inspired by a British novel published in 1897 that was all the rage at the time, Bram Stoker's *Dracula*.

Wilmington was hardly the first time the media deployed slander as a tactic, but it was among the first times that politicians and journalists coordinated a false flag operation to coerce Americans into going to war on a pretense. In this fashion, it was a forerunner to the media mouthing George W. Bush's warmongering insistence that Iraq's Saddam Hussein bore some responsibility for the 9/11 attacks.

Indeed, the mythological Black rapist was the original weapon of mass destruction.

Toppling the Fusion government remapped the modern political landscape, supplying the elites with a blueprint for how to stoke sectarian tensions and quarantine leftist cells. Just as importantly, Jim Crow's marriage of mass communications and mass murder impregnated a culture of make-believe, in which facts are rendered moot, critical thinking unnecessary, history inert, and antediluvian antagonisms inconsequential. As a party operative, Daniel Schenck, warned in the months leading up to the 1898 election: "It will be the meanest, vilest, dirtiest campaign since 1876. The slogan of the Democratic Party from the mountains to the sea will be but one word . . . Nigger."

The idealized nigger opened a Pandora's box. Two years after the Wilmington massacre, North Carolina stripped Black men of the vote and six years after that, Georgia newspaper publisher Hoke Smith consulted with Furnifold Simmons and North Carolina Democrats ahead of his bid for the governor's office. Pledging to "protect white womanhood," Smith won, and afterward white mobs took to the streets of Atlanta, murdering dozens of Blacks. Democrats in the state disenfranchised Blacks the following year, and by 1910 every state below the Mason-Dixon line had followed suit.[80]

Wilmington's framing of complex issues as Manichean battles remains a staple of political campaigns to this day. Barnstorming the country in 1976 in his unsuccessful bid to unseat President Gerald Ford in the GOP primary, former California Governor Ronald Reagan cynically invoked a woman in Chicago who "used eighty names, thirty addresses, fifteen telephone numbers to collect food stamps, Social Security, veterans' benefits for four non-existent deceased veteran husbands, as well as welfare."[81] New York City's billionaire Mayor Michael Bloomberg would double down on Reagan's dog-whistle politicking two decades later, defending the city's aggressive stop-and-frisk policy targeting New Yorkers of color as necessary to get handguns off the street. On the campaign trail in 2008, Barack Obama scolded African American men during a Fathers' Day sermon at an all-Black Chicago church:

> We need fathers to realize that responsibility does not end at conception. We need them to realize that what makes you a man is not the ability to have a child—it's the courage to raise one . . . don't just sit in the house and watch "Sports Center" all weekend long. That's why so many children are growing up in front of the television. As fathers and parents, we've got to spend more time with them, and help them with their homework, and replace the video game or the remote control with a book once in a while.

At a 2013 event to commemorate the 50th anniversary of the March on Washington, President Obama added more kindling to the fire:

> Legitimate grievances against police brutality tipped into excuse-making for criminal behavior. Racial politics could cut both ways as the transformative message of unity and brotherhood was drowned out by the language of recrimination. And what had once been a call for equality of opportunity, the chance for all Americans to work hard and get ahead was too often framed as a mere desire for government support, as if [they] had no agency in [their] own liberation, as if poverty was an excuse for not raising your child and the bigotry of others was reason to give up on yourself.

Reams of data refute these puerile storylines. In its 61 years of existence, the now-defunct Aid to Families with Dependent Children program generated a minuscule number of abuse complaints. Similarly, beneficiaries ripping off the federal government's nutrition assistance program, or SNAP, account for only one percent of all disbursements,[82] and fraud accounts for less than two percent of unemployment insurance payments.[83] Intelligence tests administered during World War I showed African American conscripts educated in the North outscoring their white peers from southern states,[84] and subsequent studies that adjust for prenatal care have consistently found no racial disparities in intelligence. (When gaps have been identified, they tend to be small and favor African Americans.) Data compiled by the FBI and Bureau of Crime Statistics indicate that the vast majority of rapes are *intra*-racial,[85] and that while there are profound disparities in arrests, white men and Black men *commit* felony crimes at similar rates.[86] An analysis of 2012 statistics by the New York Civil Liberties Union found that police confiscated 715 handguns in their 530,000 stop-and-frisk encounters that year, representing only a fraction of one percent. And a 2016 survey conducted by the National Institute of Health found that Black men reported significantly lower rates of drug dependency than did their white counterparts,[87] which is consistent with other studies. And a 2007 study by Boston College sociologist Rebekah Levine-Coley concluded that Black men are more likely to spend quality time with young children who live separately from them than are fathers of any other racial or ethnic group.[88]

Despite this wealth of evidence, the author Dennis Rome found that nearly half of all whites asked in a 2000 survey to rank Blacks' propensity for violence on a scale of one to seven chose the violent end of the spectrum, while only one in five chose the same rank for whites.[89]

Accounting for this non-sequitur is *Orientalism*, the term coined by the Occidental world to describe the exotic Arab lands to its east. In his eponymous 1978 book, the Palestinian American scholar Edward Said wrote that the West has historically qualified its imperialism by transferring blame from the colonizer to the colonized, dating the practice as far back as France's 1798 invasion of Egypt, when Napoleon encouraged artists, writers, and anthropologists to re-imagine the Nile's inhabitants, or to *Orientalize the Orient*. Of the famed French novelist Gustave Flaubert's depiction of a 19th-century dancer, Said wrote:

> Flaubert's encounter with an Egyptian courtesan produced a widely influential model of the Oriental woman; she never spoke of herself, she never represented her emotions, presence, or history. He spoke for and represented her. He was foreign, comparatively wealthy, male, and these were historical facts of domination that allowed him not only to possess [her] physically but to speak for her and tell his readers in what way she was 'typically Oriental.'

In his 1899 poem "The White Man's Burden," Rudyard Kipling both infantilizes and demonizes the typical Filipino as "half-devil, half-child" in exhorting the U.S. to annex the Philippines and nobly civilize the aboriginal menace. Likewise, the Hollywood director D.W. Griffith's landmark 1915 film, *The Birth of a Nation*, applies an *Orientalist* lens to his depiction of Black men as incorrigible rapists and drunkards whose loutish behavior doomed Reconstruction's ambitious experiment. Neither does it require particular exertion to recognize *Orientalism's* influence on the white savior complex at the center of banal films such as *Driving Miss Daisy*, *Ghost*, *The Blind Side*, *The Butler*, or *The Green Book*. Even when Hollywood gets it right, it gets it wrong: In the fabulous Academy Award-winning 1967 film, *In the Heat of the Night*, a meticulous, cerebral African American detective played by Sidney Poitier helps a loud, shoot-from-the-hip white sheriff, played by Rod Steiger, solve a murder in a Mississippi town. When the film was serialized for television 21 years later, the roles had been reversed, with Carroll O'Connor cast as the sage white sheriff whose probity and professorial demeanor calms the brash, Black, big-city detective, played by Howard Rollins Jr.

Left unchallenged, however, these racist flights of fancy turn to stone-tablet commandments in the popular white imagination, welding the events in Wilmington into a template for an authoritarian culture that shapes public opinion rather than reflects it, clearing the path for policy shifts that benefit the hegemons. A good example is the "super predator" narrative popularized by First Lady Hillary Clinton and the broken windows model of aggressive policing that emerged in the 1990s, asserting that serious crime could be abated by targeting low-level offenses such as vandalism, loitering, public nuisance, jaywalking and fare evasion. This crackdown merely increased interactions between law enforcement and communities of color, filling privatized prisons with inmates, supplying manufacturers with a pool of cheap labor, and fattening Wall Street's profits.

That the Wilmington mob's signal act was to destroy the city's sole Black newspaper was no accident: Ginning up white rage about imaginary Black rapists who resembled Dracula hinged, unsurprisingly, on drowning out appeals to common sense and decency. If, as the playwright Arthur Miller wrote, a great newspaper is a community in dialogue, Americans entered a red, white and blue Tower of Babel with the advent of Jim Crow and emerged on the other side, well, babbling, unable to either describe or address their discontent. As the Black activist and intellectual Kwame Ture was fond of saying, Americans don't think, they merely respond to stimuli.

So relentless is the barrage of disinformation that emanates from the media that it is easy to forget that the strategy's objective is regime change, similar to CIA Black Ops missions that led to the overthrow of populist democratic leaders such as Iran's Mohammad Mosaddegh or Chile's Salvador Allende. Fed a steady diet of racist tropes, the mob that attacked the U.S. Capitol on January 6th, 2021, fully intended to overturn the November election results—just as the Wilmington mob had 123 years earlier—and return to power an unrepentant bigot who vowed to honor the racial contract reserved for whites only.

An analysis of court records by the Chicago Project on Security and Threats, or CPOST,[90] found that 95 percent of the 377 protesters facing criminal charges for the January 6th attack are white, 85 percent are male and most live in counties that have experienced significant declines in the non-Hispanic white population. In *the Washington Post,* Robert Pape, a professor of political science at the University of Chicago and CPOST's director wrote:

> For example, Texas is the home of 36 of the 377 charged or arrested nationwide. The majority of the state's alleged insurrectionists—20 of 36—live in six quickly diversifying blue counties such as Dallas and Harris (Houston). In fact, all 36 of Texas's rioters come from just 17 counties, each of which lost White population over the past five years. Three of those arrested or charged hail from Collin County north of Dallas, which has lost White population at the very brisk rate of 4.3 percent since 2015.

> When compared with almost 2,900 other counties in the United States, our analysis of the 250 counties where those charged or arrested live reveals that the counties that had the greatest decline in White population had an 18 percent chance of sending an insurrectionist to D.C., while the counties that saw the least decline in the White population had only a 3 percent chance. This finding holds even when controlling for population size, distance to D.C., unemployment rate and urban/rural location. It also would occur by chance less than once in 1,000 times.
>
> Put another way, the people alleged by authorities to have taken the law into their hands on Jan. 6 typically hail from places where non-White populations are growing fastest.

Dubbed the "Great Replacement" by white nationalists, the anxiety that led to a failed coup in January 2021 is entirely consistent with fears of a "nigger government" that produced a successful one in Wilmington in 1898. In both cases, however, the white working class was inspired by faith—the evidence of things unseen—rather than any serious interrogation of history or material facts. This helps explain why the political discourse in the U.S. typically spurns intellectual inquiry and why white supremacist violence is often attended by an energy akin to a religious fervor.

Of this irrational, spellbound element, Gilmore wrote:

> Looking back on the racial massacre in 1936, a Wilmington resident recalled the compelling power of the incubus. Colonel John D. Taylor, a one-armed Confederate hero, and his son, J. Alan Taylor, allegedly talked in the weeks just prior to the 1898 election. 'Alan,' the old veteran warned, 'we are a conquered people. . . . The day is coming, however, when Northerners will regard our cause "State's rights" as just. . . . Meanwhile we must continue to grin and bear it.' To which his son, a rising young man, was said to have replied, 'But my little daughter, Mary, and young son, Douglas, now in their teens, are representative of a new

> generation; and I am going to do my utmost to make sure that Wilmington is a clean, happy and safe place. . . . I do not want them, and their little friends, growing up [among] rapists!' Together with eight other white men, J. Alan Taylor organized an armed militia to patrol each of the city's five wards, block by block. This group, known among themselves as the "Secret Nine," refashioned their identities. From the clay of upstanding businessmen, they remolded themselves into "revolutionaries."

Yet the question remains: Why did Simmons, Daniels and Aycock seize upon a narrative depicting Black men as rapists? Perhaps my experience at PolicyLink offers some clues. Labor law in the U.S. does not require employers to provide a reason for firing a non-union or "at-will" employee. Consequently, Angela Glover Blackwell did not identify her reasons for firing me in April 2010. Before my termination, however, she had informed me that there were vague complaints made by senior staffers that I had addressed them using profanity and in a threatening tone of voice, effectively creating a hostile work environment. I responded, calmly, that I had never conducted myself in such a manner in a workplace setting in a career that had, at that point, spanned nearly a quarter-century. When I pressed her for specifics about the complaints made against me, she demurred.

While there exists no evidence of the misbehavior of which I was accused, there were dozens of complaints about a white male co-worker at PolicyLink, mostly lodged by women of color within the organization. Despite these grievances from multiple sources, he was promoted, reminiscent of George Bernard Shaw's reproach:

> All criticism is a form of autobiography.

According to Edward Baptist, author of *The Half Has Never Been Told: Slavery and the Making of American Capitalism*, early European patriarchs envisioned the New World as their "sexual playground" in which the exalted status of head of household was conferred through access to land and cheap labor to farm it. And of her splendid book, *At the Dark End of the Street: Black Women, Rape and Resistance—a New History of the Civil Rights Movement from Rosa Parks to the Black Power Movement*, Danielle McGuire told me in a 2018 interview:

> Patriarchy does not recognize women as full human beings or even citizens. They were the property of their fathers first and then their husbands. It's similar—though not identical—to the treatment of African Americans as chattel, or livestock.

The rape of slave women was especially heinous because it enabled slave owners to replenish their stable of slaves on the cheap. Wrote a diarist, Mary Chestnut, of life on a South Carolina slave plantation:

> God, forgive us but ours is a monstrous system, a wrong and an inequity!
>
> Like the patriarchs of old, our men live all in one house with their wives and their concubines; and the mulattos one sees in every family partly resemble the white children. Any lady is ready to tell you who is the father of all mulatto children in everybody's household but her own. Those, she seems to think, drop from the clouds.

The popular understanding of the patriarch as the honest white man whose virtue and hard work entitles him to Native Americans' land, African Americans' labor and women's loins help explain Harvey Weinstein's reign of terror in Hollywood; the media's gaslighting of Tara Reade, the former congressional aide who alleged that Joe Biden assaulted her in 1993; Christine Blasey Ford, who accused Supreme Court Justice Brett Kavanaugh of sexual assault; or the slap on the wrist administered to Brock Turner, a 20-year-old white Stanford University swimmer who was sentenced to six months in jail for the rape of a young woman near a garbage bin outside a campus fraternity house.

"What these men all have in common is that they're powerful, and they're male and they're almost all white," Melissa Minds VandeBurgt, the head of archives, special collections and digital initiatives at Florida Gulf Coast University told me in 2018. "Americans are convinced that we're better than that, and so we've put the blinders on. The culture that enables rape is everywhere."

The reassignment of the role of rapist to Black men, however, raises yet another question, which is why are so many white women complicit in the scheme to recast their oppressors as their protectors? In the weeks leading up to the Wilmington massacre, for example, the feminist white writer, Rebecca Felton, urged white men to "lynch a thousand negroes a week" to avenge the phantom rapes.

A white journalist named Anne Braden would write of this perverse social construct in a 1972 brochure for the Southern Conference Educational Fund:

> For me the awareness began in 1946 in a courtroom in Birmingham, Alabama. I was 22, a young newspaper reporter, covering the courthouse. That day, a young Black man was being tried—not for rape but for something called 'assault with intent to ravish.' A young white woman testified that he passed her on the opposite side of a country road and looked at her in an 'insulting' way. He was sentenced to 20 years.
>
> I was appalled by the case. Torn by what was happening to the Black man. But torn too, as I watched the white woman. She appeared to be very poor but she had obviously dressed in her best—and for that day she was queen in the courtroom. The judge, the prosecutor, her father who told of her fright when she came in from that walk—all rallied round to defend her honor. . . . I realized the horror of what she was doing to herself. Tomorrow, after her day as queen, she would go back to a life of poverty and boredom; waiting

> on her father, on her brothers, and someday on a husband—paying with a lifetime of drudgery for those magic moments when she could achieve the status of a wronged white woman.[91]

Wrote Gilmore of the Black rapist throughout history:

> White politicians created him to seize political power and to extend white male 'protection' to white women of the lower classes. This figure gave the Wilmington racial massacre its force; it haunted white women's dreams and pushed white men to reach deep inside themselves to fan a rage that became murderous. A century later, when all else failed Susan Smith—parents, marriage, career, love—she used the one morsel of status left to her as a poor white Southern woman with a past. If threatened by a Black man, she could become loved again, cleansed in the blood of her lambs. She could even use the power of the Black male rapist myth to get away with murder. Or so she thought.[92]

Ironically, the mythology of the Black rapist is intended as a kind of social prophylactic, for while the patriarchs might find miscegenation unseemly, their worst fear was never really that white women and Black men might *fuck,* but that they would *talk* and possibly join forces against their common enemy.

The daughter of a Jewish Los Angeles criminal defense attorney, Leila Steinberg is often credited with discovering Tupac Shakur, the slain son of a Black Panther, who is widely regarded as the greatest rapper of all time. In a 2020 radio interview, however, she took great pains to disabuse listeners of that misperception. Listen:

> Pac really found me . . . we discovered each other, he was 18 when we really got started working, I was 27 with three kids and more on my plate than I could handle and he really thought I'd be a great business person and he taught me and trained me and we came up together and so like the myth of

some white savior shit that has to go. . . . In this country where there's Black success there's always a white person claiming it, and I really want it to be clear that we both helped each other . . . but I want people to know that he helped me find my voice and my purpose. . . . I have had a career in the music business for years now because he felt like I could do business when I didn't even have self-esteem and I did not think I could sit at the table with mostly white men doing business . . . and so you have to imagine I had a young coach saying 'you got this!' and literally read every book and helped train me. The real story is so much more powerful than the Michelle Pfeiffer Dangerous Minds white woman comes to the hood and saves Black kids. . . . We were a perfect combination for this storm that was created.[93]

4.

The Surge

The purpose of racism is to control the behavior of white people, not black people. For blacks, guns and tanks are sufficient.

–Otis Madison

The paradox of the murderous flame is that it turns even the blackest skin ash white.

Perhaps this is what ultimately drove the disillusioned Black poet mad in Jean Toomer's haunting 1923 novel *Cane.* Ralph Kabnis has already begun to lose his bearings when he visits the home of a friend, Layman, who recalls a recent lynching. It's a Sunday afternoon in the fictional Georgia town of Sempter and with the "high-pitched and hysterical sounds" from a nearby church providing a soundtrack, Layman recounts in *sotto voce* the white mob that alighted upon a Negro woman who tried to defend her fugitive husband:

> She was in the family-way, Mame Lamkins was. They killed her in th street, an some white man seein th risin in her stomach as she lay there soppy in her blood like any cow, took an ripped her belly open, an th kid fell out. It was living; but a nigger baby aint supposed t live. So he jabbed

> his knife in it an stuck it t a tree. And then they all went away.

Layman's climactic finish is echoed by the sound of a woman in the nearby church choir testifying euphorically "Jesus, Jesus, I've found Jesus. Oh Lord, glory t God, one mo sinner is acomin home," which is in turn accompanied by Kabnis shrieking at the unspeakable horror visited on Lamkins and her fetus: "Christ no!" Precisely then, the parlor window is smashed with a rock warning the "northern nigger" to go home.

Toomer's modernist classic was an attempt to untangle the Gordian knot of identity, language, and racial terror, and make some sense of the author's 1921 trek to Georgia where Lamkins' proxy, 21-year-old Mary Turner, had been mutilated in a small town near the Florida border after vowing to avenge her husband, who was one of 11 Black men lynched in retaliation for the killing of a white farmer. Perhaps it is a testament to the unbearable gravity of being Black in white America that Toomer's dramatization of her ordeal downplays the monstrousness of the assault.

Mary Hattie Graham bore Hazel "Hayes" Turner two children before marrying him in Colquitt County. The young couple moved to Brooks County, Georgia, where they took jobs with white plantation owner Hampton Smith, who was known for beating his Black workers, often after bailing them out of jail and having them work off their debt on his plantation. One beating left Mary Turner in such bad shape that her husband threatened to return the favor, resulting in criminal charges and a stint on the chain gang.

On the evening of May 16, 1918, a worker fatally shot Smith, and the ensuing dragnet rounded up several of Smith's employees and even a few African Americans who were incarcerated in the county jail. Mary Turner, who was eight months pregnant at the time, denied that her husband had anything to do with Smith's murder and threatened to file criminal charges against the mob's ringleaders. One local newspaper would later write that "the people in their indignant mood took exceptions to her remarks as well as her attitude."[94]

Turner fled after getting wind of rumors that she was in imminent danger, but the mob caught up with her on May 19, dragged her to the Folsom Bridge overlooking the Little River, tied her ankles together, strung her upside down, doused her in gasoline and set her on fire. While she was still alive, a man split open her stomach with a long knife used to butcher hogs, causing her fetus to plunge to the ground. On impact, the infant cried out before the quick, forceful stomp of a man's boot ended its cries and its life in one fell swoop. Mary Turner's corpse was riddled with bullets and later that night, her remains and that of her baby were buried a few feet away from where they were slain.

Smith's killer was cornered and killed three days later in a shootout with police, culminating a weeklong rampage that compelled more than 500 African Americans to flee from the area near the Brooks and Lowndes County border, abandoning scores of parcels of arable farmland that were quickly snatched up by whites.

No one was ever prosecuted for Turner's killing although another newspaper would hang Turner in effigy a few years later in an editorial mocking her as a "she bear" who deserved her fate because she "flew into such a rage and uttered such vile curses upon the women of Brooks County."[95]

The mixed-race grandson of a Louisiana governor who had disowned him, the Harlem Renaissance writer Toomer was himself struggling with questions of identity, closure, and healing, assigning his literary avatar Kabnis to lead *Cane's* Ulyssean search for truth. The lyrical novel concludes on a note that is at once inchoate and redemptive, reimagining the grisly sacrifice of Mame Lankins and her expunged fetus as a kind of alternative Nativity scene, or a prayer for a new and troubled land, west of Eden, and far from grace.

> Outside, the sun arises from its cradle in the tree-tops of the forest. . . . Gold-glowing child, it steps into the sky and sends a birth-song slanting down gray dust streets and sleepy windows of the southern town.

But like Kurtz in Joseph Conrad's *Heart of Darkness*, Kabnis' descent into madness is morally ambiguous and anything but sanguine. When we are first introduced to the failed writer who has journeyed south to teach school, he agonizes over the pulchritude of a still Georgia night.

> God Almighty, dear God, dear Jesus, do not torture me with beauty. Take it away. Give me an ugly world. Ha, ugly. Stinking like unwashed niggers. Dear Jesus, do not chain me to myself and set these hills and valleys, heaving with folk-songs, so close to me that I cannot reach them. There is a radiant beauty in the night that touches and . . . tortures me. Ugh. Hell. Get up, you damn fool. Look around. What's beautiful there? Hog pens and chicken yards. Dirty red mud. Stinking outhouse. What's beauty anyway but ugliness if it hurts you?

The trance that afflicts Kabnis when we first meet him accrues from his inability to summon the language that fully conveys the trauma of Black life and Mame Lamkins only worsens his ennui.

> Th form thats burned int my soul is some twisted awful thing that crept in from a dream, a godam nightmare, and it wont stay unless I feed it. An it lives on words. Not beautiful words. God Almighty no. Misshapen, splitgut, tortured, twisted words.

By the end, it is all over but the shouting for Kabnis, who seems throttled by paranoia that he will meet the same end as Lamkins. When last we see him he "is stumbling over a bucket of dead coals that he jerks from the floor, Sisyphus-like, and carries up the stairs . . ."[96]

Literary critics struggle to reconcile Toomer's pairing of Kabnis' spiritual death with that of a bastard nation spilling from Mary Turner's mangled womb. Was Kabnis' impotence intended to impart an act so debauched that it is not, as Toni Morrison wrote in her chilling novel of infanticide, *Beloved*, a story to pass on? Yet in its unspokenness, in our forgetting of a Madonna and child left slaughtered and blasphemed by the side of a dirt road, are we condemned to 100 years of soul-rotting solitude, brought on by a horror that we can perjure but never *unsee*?

One hundred and two years later and roughly 120 miles east of where Mary Turner was gutted like a wild boar, African blood would again stigmatize Georgia's red soil when a white father and son hunted down and summarily executed an unarmed 25-year-old Black jogger named Ahmaud Arbery while their friend videotaped the snuff film to be enjoyed later, I can only assume, like porn. "Fucking nigger," Travis McMichael reportedly said as Arbery writhed on the ground, mortally wounded.

Three weeks later, on March 13, Mary Turner's ghost hovered in Louisville's midnight skies when police burst into the apartment of 26-year-old Breonna Taylor, and opened fire, hitting the African American emergency medical technician at least five times. The officers who fatally shot her were executing a no-knock arrest warrant for a suspected drug dealer who was already in custody. And 10 weeks after that, the killing of 46-year-old George Floyd by a white Minneapolis police officer, Derek Chauvin—who knelt on the neck of the handcuffed, compliant and prostrate African American for eight minutes and forty-six seconds, ignoring his final, gasping pleas of "I can't breathe"—sparked the largest protests in U.S. history.

The technology used to record the white lynch mob's handiwork has evolved dramatically—from snapshots photographed on cardboard box cameras to cell phone videos—just as the size, shape, and organization of the bloodthirsty hordes have metastasized from vigilantes to the local *gendarme*. What remains disturbingly constant, however, is the white settlers' ritualized desecration of the Black body.

To fully understand this peculiar sacrament of white settler colonialism, it helps to scrutinize the murderous rabble as we might imagine a criminal profiler would investigate a time-traveling serial killer in, say, the pilot episode of *CSI: American Lynch Mob*.

Poring over the evidence reveals an unmistakable pattern: Our killer's appetite for bloodshed is whet by some combination of disorienting change in his economic circumstances and African Americans' loudening demands for equal treatment under the law, which, in tandem, threaten whites' privileged position in society. According to a compilation of data begun by the Tuskegee Institute in 1882, the lynchings of whites outnumbered Blacks until 1885, but that trend reversed abruptly in 1886 as employers stepped up their efforts to bully a labor movement that was finding some success in organizing across racial lines. As the economy contracted with the concomitant rise of Jim Crow and the Gilded Age, the numbers of African Americans lynched nationwide soared to 113 in 1891, 161 the following year, 118 the year after that and 134 in 1894 in the throes of a steep financial downturn.

Conversely, as the country began to dig itself out of the rubble of the Great Depression, the number of Blacks lynched plummeted to three in 1943, two in 1944 and one in 1945. By 1952, there wasn't a single lynching reported anywhere in the U.S., according to Tuskegee's registry.

Therein lies the nigger in the woodpile, if you'll pardon my pun: That same year, wages for American workers climbed to what was, at the time, their historic high, accounting for roughly 51 percent of the country's gross domestic product, or GDP.[97] Nine of every 10 working-age men were gainfully employed.

It's worth mentioning that the most robust economic expansion in history coincided with the civil rights movement and a decline in the number of lynchings so precipitous that Tuskegee discontinued its registry in 1968 with a final tally of 4,742 victims of extralegal homicides, of whom

3,445 were Black and 1,297 white.[98] The term "lynching" today is typically used metaphorically yet the threat of violence against Blacks continues unabated in legal, rather than extralegal, form. In its motivation (an assertion of power), result (death), and penalties (none), mob justice today is virtually indistinguishable from its previous iteration, as evinced by the videotaped murders that have become regular segments on evening news broadcasts and podcasts. Authorities reported a sharp spike in hate crimes following Trump's 2016 election, and a 2013 study by the Malcolm X Grassroots Movement titled "Operation Ghetto Storm" found that police or security personnel kill an unarmed African American every 28 hours in the U.S. An analysis of FBI statistics shows that African Americans are three times more likely to be killed by police than are whites.[99]

Why?

The short answer is the rejoinder popularized by Bill Clinton's campaign manager, James Carville: "It's the economy, stupid." Compared to 1952 when 51 cents of every dollar in national income went into workers' pockets, employees' share of GDP had plummeted to 43 cents of every dollar produced by 2023, according to the U.S. Bureau of Economic Analysis.

So wobbly are the pillars of racial capitalism, the late intellectual Cedric Robinson was fond of saying, that they must constantly be reinforced. Consider that white Georgians exploited Turner's 1918 lynching to pilfer the farms left behind by Black flight much as the U.S. ultimately occupied the oilfields abandoned by Iraqis fleeing the military's 2007 assassination program, euphemistically called the "Surge." Frustrated at losing ground, unable to envision the myriad possibilities of coalescing with a Black proletariat, and anxious that the well of white privilege may have finally run dry, a fragile American *herrenvolk*, or master race, lashes out instead, doubling down on an extortion scheme predicated on *killing the competition* through a combination of gratuitous violence and social alienation. Wrote the sociologist Oliver Cromwell Cox of lynching:

> It was the most powerful and convincing force of racial repression operating in the interest of maintaining the status quo.

A Memphis mob in 1892 lynched three African American men for defending a Black-owned grocery store from goons sent by an envious white competitor. Their slayings launched Ida B. Wells' career as an anti-lynching crusader. Foreshadowing Myrdal's conclusions about white jealousy in *An American Dilemma*, Wells' reportage led her to similarly conclude that lynching was seldom used to sanction rape but rather to condemn *consensual* sex between Black men and white women, or, alternately as "an excuse to get rid of Negroes who were acquiring wealth and property and thus keep the race terrorized and 'keep the niggers down.'"[100] Conversely, during the 1906 Atlanta riots, a 13-year-old Walter White, who would go on to serve as president of the National Association for the Advancement of Colored People, or NAACP, recalled a white mob attacking the home of a neighbor "that was too nice for a nigger to live in."[101]

The killing season of 1919 goes to Wells' point. Five months after Mary Turner's immolation, a lanky, dark-skinned Black man named Aaron Gaskins boarded a commuter train in Alexandria, Virginia, and took a seat in the rear. He had recently purchased a war bond to support the troops in World War I. Why, he wondered, couldn't he sit anywhere he damn well pleased just like white passengers who paid the same fare as he did?[102]

Finally, like Turner, he decided to speak his mind. He rose from his seat, ambled to the front of the train car, and announced to the startled passengers: "I am as good as white people riding in this car," he declared. "After this war is over we are going to get our rights; we will have a race war if we don't."

The train's engineer reported the incident to authorities who declined to pursue the matter, but the end of the Great War two months later was followed by what the historian John Hope Franklin described as the "worst outbreak of racial violence in the nation's history."

"Some years ask questions," wrote Toomer's Harlem Renaissance peer, Zora Neale Hurston, "others answer."

The year 1919 *testified.*

Between April and November 1919, there were roughly 25 race riots nationwide, including 97 lynchings and a three-day siege in Elaine, Arkansas, where 200 African American men, women and children were slain after Black sharecroppers threatened to organize a union.[103] According to the writer Abigail Huggins:

> At the same time, cities across the north were being reshaped by the Great Migration. By the end of 1919, about 1 million African Americans had fled segregation and a total lack of economic opportunities in the south for northern cities. Between 1910 and 1920, the black population in Chicago grew by 148 percent and in Philadelphia by 500 percent, creating massive anxiety among white people in northern cities that black people were taking jobs, housing, and security from them.[104]

Blacks doubtless shared whites' disquietude yet mined their fears for artistic inspiration rather than homicidal schemes. Centered in New York, the Harlem Renaissance, or New Negro movement as it was known at the time, would eventually migrate to every corner of the African diaspora in the interwar years, and in its production of *avant garde* music, fashion, poetry, dance and literature, provided the canon for an American Enlightenment.

Describing the bloodshed in 1919, the Harlem Renaissance writer, James Weldon Johnson, coined the term "Red Summer," and yet another, Claude McKay, steadied his mind and hand long enough to write a defiant poem, "If We Must Die," as Blacks and whites clashed in Washington D.C.

If we must die, let it not be like hogs
Hunted and penned in an inglorious spot,
While round us bark the mad and hungry dogs,
Making their mock at our accursèd lot.
If we must die, O let us nobly die,
So that our precious blood may not be shed
In vain; then even the monsters we defy
Shall be constrained to honor us though dead!
O kinsmen! we must meet the common foe!
Though far outnumbered let us show us brave,
And for their thousand blows deal one death-blow!
What though before us lies the open grave?
Like men we'll face the murderous, cowardly pack,
Pressed to the wall, dying, but fighting back!

It is no coincidence that Red Summer followed the 1917 Russian Revolution or coincided with the greatest strike wave in U.S history that began in 1919, influenced by the 13 million immigrants from southern, eastern and central Europe who poured into the country between 1886 and 1925, bringing with them all manner of anarchist and Marxist ideals. Attorney General A. Mitchell Palmer began to round up dissidents for arrest and deportation, culminating in the execution of the Italian anarchists, Nicola Sacco and Bartolomeo Vanzetti, for a fatal armed robbery in 1920, despite scant proof of their guilt. The combination of the Palmer Raids and Red Summer's season of racial terror was a reminder of the campaign of repression and intimidation tactics that followed the Haymarket bombing

33 years earlier. Much as they had managed to dismantle the Knights of Labor, employers hoped to again reverse the proletariat's momentum by isolating the most radical actors. Moreover, the combination of government raids and vigilante violence impressed upon immigrants the importance of choosing race over class. "You soon know something about this country," said one Serbian worker in the era, "Negroes never get a fair chance."[105]

Prior to World War I, the labor force had been largely fragmented, with Blacks employed mainly in the agricultural and service sector as domestics, gardeners, or chauffeurs, while immigrant laborers who turned up at Ellis Island provided the industrial sector with a steady supply of cheap labor. The first wave of the Great Migration (which included my grandfather James Jeter, who fled South Carolina for New Jersey before landing in Indianapolis) coincided with labor organizing by unskilled white workers, causing Theodore Roosevelt to warn Congress that "every farsighted patriot should protest, first of all against the growth in this country of that evil thing which is called 'class consciousness.'"[106] Nine months after the 1911 fire at the Triangle Shirtwaist Factory in Greenwich Village left 146 employees dead, the thundering Everett Mill in Lawrence, Massachusetts, fell suddenly silent after the mostly Polish employees opened their pay envelopes on the afternoon of January 12, 1912, to discover 32 cents—enough to buy three loaves of bread—missing. A newly enacted state law had reduced the workweek for women and children from 56 to 54 hours, but mill owners broke with custom in cutting workers' wages proportionally.

Thirty miles north of Boston, Lawrence was the nation's capital of worsted goods in 1912. Feeding the spinning machines were the Italians, Lithuanians, Armenians, and Poles—more than 50 nationalities in all—who flocked to this New England hamlet of only seven square miles on the banks of the Merrimack River to find work. Between 1890 and 1910, Lawrence's population doubled, earning it the moniker "Immigrant City."

As word of the Everett strike spread through Lawrence's tenements, workers began to seethe. By the end of the next workday, January 13, more than 10,000 textile workers—mostly teenage girls who had been in the country for less than five years—had walked off the job, pouring into the streets as the snow fell, shouting "Short pay! All out!" overwhelming security guards, slashing machine belts, threads and cloth, and shattering windows.

New England's immigrant workforce endured grueling conditions on the shopfloor, including respiratory illnesses such as tuberculosis and pneumonia. What the workers lacked in terms of a common culture or language to unite them was more than offset, however, by their common grievances against their bosses. Within two weeks, their numbers swelled to as many as 25,000, squaring off in the snow and bitter cold against state militiamen, ladling soup, picketing and demanding both living wages and dignity—"We want bread, and roses, too"—in paraphrasing a 1911 poem that gave the work stoppage its name. The first two stanzas go:

As we go marching, marching, in the beauty of the day,
A million darkened kitchens, a thousand mill lofts gray,
Are touched with all the radiance that a sudden sun discloses,
For the people hear us singing: Bread and Roses! Bread and Roses!
As we go marching, marching, we battle too for men,
For they are women's children, and we mother them again.
Our lives shall not be sweated from birth until life closes;
Hearts starve as well as bodies; give us bread, but give us roses.

Mill owners hired saboteurs to plant dynamite in a botched attempt to discredit their employees. Finally, on January 29, Lawrence erupted when strikers attacked a streetcar carrying scabs and an errant gunshot from police killed one protester, while a bayonet killed another. The slayings only strengthened public support for the strike. Writing a century later, the historian Christopher Klein described the aftermath of the violent clashes on January 29:

> With the city on a hair trigger, striking families sent 119 of their children out of harm's way to Manhattan on February 10 to live with relatives or, in some cases, complete strangers who could provide food and a safe shelter. A cheering crowd of 5,000 greeted the children at Grand Central Terminal, and after a second trainload arrived from Lawrence the following week, the children paraded down Fifth Avenue. The "children's exodus" proved to be a publicity coup for the strikers, and Lawrence authorities intended to halt it. When families brought another 46 children bound for Philadelphia to the city's train station on February 24, the city marshal ordered them to disperse. When defiant mothers still tried to get their children aboard the train and resisted the authorities, police dragged them by the hair, beat them with clubs and arrested them as their horrified children looked on in tears.[107]

Public outrage sparked calls for a congressional inquiry, where 14-year-old Carmela Teoli recounted for lawmakers how she had been scalped when her hair got caught in a mill machine, hospitalizing her for seven months. Nonetheless, she was forced to return to work two years later because her family needed the money.[108] Exposed, the mill owners agreed to a 15-percent wage hike, an increase in overtime pay and a promise not to retaliate against strikers, ending the nine-week strike on March 14. Before the month was over, 275,000 New England textile workers received similar pay packages.

One New England mill town that failed to capitalize on Lawrence's success, however, was Middletown, Connecticut, and class attitudes help explain why. When one of the town's largest employers, Russell Manufacturing, refused to negotiate with a bargaining unit, 400 of the company's employees walked off the job on June 4, 1912. Middletown was also home to a large immigrant community; about a quarter of the city's population, 13,000, was Italian, mostly from the Sicilian town of Melilli. As in Lawrence, the Industrial Workers of the World, or Wobblies, sent their representatives to organize the Middletown strikers who were met by state violence and intimidation coordinated by a local elite that was unified in its disdain for their employees. Yet, Russell broke the strike without meeting a single demand made by their employees. Why? The Irish who had settled in Middletown a generation before the Sicilians began to arrive had, by 1912, already become "white." Or, as one scholar wrote:

> On top of it all, there were xenophobia and ethnic tensions among the workers themselves, with few Irish and U.S.-born workers participating, *if any did at all.*[109]

Despite the Wobblies' failure in Middletown, by 1919, one in five workers belonged to a labor union—including half of all textile workers—and nearly four million employees walked off the job in roughly 300 labor disputes that year. Industrialists countered by hiring African Americans as scabs, increasing competition for jobs and housing, compounding the tensions that undermined Middletown's Italian workers. Tin Pan Alley songwriters attempted to console anxious whites with lyrics intended to disabuse African Americans of any fanciful notions they may have had. Ditties such as "That's Why Darkies Were Born" were par for the course, exhorting Blacks to stay in their lane, and continue to work the fields and entertain without complaint.

Of particular concern to whites were the Black soldiers returning from World War I with a renewed sense of pride. Wrote one postal agent:

> As far back as the first movement of the American troops to France the negro publicists began to avail themselves of the argument that since the negro was fit to wear the uniform he was, therefore, fit for everything else.

One Black veteran, 21-year-old Harry Haywood was working as a waiter in the dining car on the Michigan Central railroad line between Chicago and New York, when he stepped off the train on July 28, 1919, and into a streetscape that reminded him of the European battlefields he had left only three months earlier.

> Southside Chicago, the Black ghetto, was like a besieged city. Whole sections of it were in ruins. Buildings burned and the air was heavy with smoke, reminiscent of the holocaust from which I had recently returned. . . .
>
> The battle at home was just as real as the battle in France had been. As I recall, there was full-scale street fighting between Black and white. Blacks were snatched from streetcars and beaten or killed; pitched battles were fought in ghetto streets; hoodlums roamed the neighborhood, shooting at random. Blacks fought back.[110]

Continuing, he wrote:

> The whole country seemed gripped in a frenzy of racist hate. Anti-Black propaganda was carried in the press, in magazine articles, in literature, and in the theater. D.W. Griffith's obscene movie *The Birth of a Nation*, which glorified the Ku Klux Klan and pictured Blacks as depraved animals, was shown to millions.[111]

Haywood's vivid description comports nicely with the tenets of a philosophical school known as *Afropessimism* which compares America's liturgy of Black sacrifice and its faintly erotic overtones to a sacrament, similar to Toomer's portrayal of Mame Lamkins' crucifixion with the cries of church evangelists in the background, or the Eucharist's symbolic cannibalization of the body of Christ to authenticate followers of Christianity. Frank Wilderson, a best-selling author and professor of African American studies at the University of California at Irvine who is widely regarded as the founder of *Afropessimis*m, told me in a 2018 interview that whites generally are both unwilling and unable to identify themselves as a part of the working class. Consequently, the vast majority seek to strengthen their racial identity in times of crisis by reproducing the idea of master and slave through everything from microaggressions to racial terror.

> What we're seeing is that the world secures its rights and privileges through this ritualistic violence against Black people. It is through our reproduction of the idea of a slave that we come to understand freedom. Violence against Black people is absolutely necessary to build a sense of community and assure the psychic health of everybody else.[112]

As evidence, Wilderson points to multiple studies that reveal whites typically grow more confident after seeing news reports of police killings of Blacks and Latinos because it reassures them that regardless of what societal changes are underfoot, they remain at the top of the pecking order. Said Wilderson:

> Marx assumes the essential oppressed unit in any society is the worker, and radical feminism posits that women suffer because they are, in fact, women. But Marxism and theories of feminist subjugation have an inadequate analysis of violence and are concerned chiefly with exploitation and alienation. Neither addresses the essential nature of Black subjugation, which is murder.[113]

The sadistic countenance evident on Chauvin's face as he choked George Floyd to death, or the leaked audiotape of then-Los Angeles City Council President Nury Martinez threatening a colleague's adopted toddler with violence, and the remorselessness of the mob that murdered Mary Turner all support Wilderson's theory that violence against African Americans is a unifying force for non-Black Americans. The Black-owned newspaper, the *Richmond Planet*, tallied 123 nationwide lynchings in 1897 for offenses that included rape, murder, asking for a drink of water and sassing a white woman. An eight-year-old boy identified only as "Parks" was lynched for "nothing."[114] Wrote no less an expert than Thomas Jefferson:

> Blacks being unable to forget the terrible wrongs done to

> them would nurse murderous wishes . . . while whites would live in a state of anticipatory fear that urged preemptive violence.

Mindful of the white Union soldiers at the Battle of the Crater, *Afropessimism* posits that the slave must die so that his owner may live. But it's important to understand that in terms of political economy, death can take on myriad forms; ownership alone has historically not defined the relationship between master and slave. In his Pulitzer Prize-winning book, *Inhuman Bondage: The Rise and Fall of Slavery In The New World*, the historian David Brion Davis describes enslavement, in its most irreducible form, as the vassal's "perpetual condition of dishonor," which provides the "master class with a resource for parasitic and psychological exploitation." This, Davis argues, imposes on the slave a type of "social death" leaving him "wholly excommunicated from civic life," not unlike livestock (the etymology for the word "chattel" is derived from the Latin word for both "capital" and "cattle"). Davis quotes the Greek 6th-century B.C. reformer Solon who explained his decision to abolish slavery:

> All the common people are in debt to the rich.

Whether the principal commodity is cotton, cars or credit, the white settler state reduces African Americans to a sprawling network of ATMs from which white wealth is extracted. Lynchings are meant to intimidate African Americans who don't pony up, or challenge the Ponzi scheme that assigns them the permanent role of laborers, debtors, and deadbeats. Black tenant farmers who were fleeced by white plantation owners were evicted if they protested (social death) and lynched if they did so too loudly (physical death).

Set in a small, Georgia town during the Eisenhower administration, Pete Dexter's 1988 novel, *Paris Trout*, pivots on the fatal shooting of a 14-year-old Black girl by the eponymous white merchant trying to collect a debt. Newly hired by the state to clean "crazy people's shit" off the walls of a local asylum for $30 each week, Henry Ray Boxer buys an $800 lemon of a car from Trout, who tacks on another $227 for insurance. After agreeing to pay weekly installments of $17.50, the young African American drives off beaming like a lottery winner, only to be promptly rear-ended.

When he is reminded that he just purchased "insurest," he returns the car, demanding that his creditor either repair it or cancel his debt. Trout bellows:

> It ain't that kinda insurance. You just ask your people about . . . what happens if you don't pay Paris Trout.

Convinced that no white jury would ever convict him, Trout visits the shack Boxer shares with his mother and the girl to extract his pound of flesh.

Winner of the 1988 National Book Award, *Paris Trout* is an absorbing work of literature, yet shines an even brighter light on America's class war.

It's no coincidence that unarmed Blacks are three times more likely to be killed by police today than are unarmed whites[115]—6.5 times more in Chicago—and up to their ears in debt. According to a 2021 study, more than half of all African Americans, 54 percent, have bad credit, compared to 37 percent of whites.[116] In fact, whites earning $25,000 annually are likely to have better credit than Blacks earning between $65,000 and $75,000.[117]

Nine of every ten Black college students enrolled in four-year public universities rely on federally-subsidized student loans compared to six in ten whites, and African Americans who earned their bachelor's degree from a four-year public university in 2012 owed an average of $3,500 more in school loans than white graduates that year. Regulators have fined lenders such as Toyota, Fifth Third Bank, and Ally Bank for overcharging Blacks and Latinos for car loans, and African Americans, on average, pay between $300 and $500 more for an auto loan than do white borrowers, despite incomes that are, on average, slightly more than half that of whites. One in three Blacks between the ages of 18 and 64 have overdue medical bills compared to one in four whites in the same age cohort. African Americans are twice as likely to be in arrears on bills including water or utility and more likely to have their service disconnected or even lose their home as a result of a lien.

Wells Fargo bankers testified that they peddled "ghetto loans" targeting "mud people," which is consistent with an Economic Policy Institute analysis that found that 53 percent of all Black borrowers were issued subprime loans, compared to 47 percent of Latinos and a quarter of white borrowers. In New York City, African American home buyers in 2006 were four times more likely than whites to be saddled with a subprime mortgage,[118] and another study found that between 2004 and 2008, only 6.2 percent of white borrowers with a credit score of 660 or higher received a subprime loan while the rate for Black borrowers with similar credit scores was 21.4 percent. In fact, lending disparities actually widened when households with *higher* incomes were compared, meaning that an African American family earning $200,000 annually was more likely to be saddled with a subprime loan than a white family making less than $30,000, leaving New York University Sociology Professor Jacob Faber to conclude that borrowers of color were targeted not because they were credit risks, but because they *weren't*.

Hence, racial terror is a kind of promissory note, or guarantee to the lender that all debts will be repaid in full, or in blood. Lynching is a form of collateral, meant to hearten white capital that its privileged position in society is safe, and to warn Blacks who challenge the system that they are decidedly *not*.

In the early morning hours of December 8, 1969, 17-year-old Bernard Arafat awoke to the sound of footsteps on the roof of Panthers' headquarters at 41st and Central Avenue in South Central Los Angeles, followed by gunfire. Arafat had never fired a gun before but he instinctively " . . . found an automatic shotgun and defended myself."

Arafat and 12 of his Panther comrades—of whom three were women and five were teenagers—fended off 350 police officers who detonated explosives on the roof and even called in a tank for backup. When the militants finally surrendered, 5,000 rounds of ammunition had been exchanged, and six Panthers and four officers had been injured, none fatally. Similar to the Philadelphia police department's 1985 bombing of a Black separatist sect known as MOVE—to serve a misdemeanor summons for noise violations—the LAPD defended the raid as necessary to execute arrest warrants on armed combatants.

More importantly, the dramatic standoff represented the nationwide debut of the Special Weapons and Tactics, or SWAT, team, which was an experiment in reorganizing the lynch mob. Created putatively to handle sniper and hostage incidents such as those encountered during the 1965 Watts Rebellion, SWAT has "become a mainstay of modern policing," according to the *Los Angeles Times*.[119] "Between 2000 and 2008, more than 9,000 of the nation's roughly 15,000 law enforcement agencies employed a SWAT unit," and between 1980 and 2000, "SWAT deployments increased by more than 1,500% nationwide."

A 2019 analysis[120] of militarized arrests in Maryland by Jonathan Mummolo, an assistant professor of politics and public affairs at Princeton, found that less than 5 percent of SWAT raids involved terrorism, hostage situations or active shooters, and that 90 percent of deployments were to execute rather mundane activities such as search or arrest warrants.

"SWAT uses Navy SEAL techniques to go on fishing expeditions," Peter Kraska, a professor of police studies at Eastern Kentucky University, told the *Los Angeles Times*. "They bust down the door, throw flash grenades, handcuff everyone inside, ransack the place and leave. And these techniques are predominantly used on communities made up of racial minorities."

The numbers are all the more interesting when you consider that the Los Angeles Panthers deployed no snipers, held no hostages and were *pinned down* by gunfire rather than barricaded inside their headquarters. Much like Mary Turner and Aaron Gaskins aboard the D.C.-bound commuter train in 1919, their sin was a belligerent insistence on civil rights. Said Arafat to the *Times* in 2019:

> SWAT evolved as a way to control people, places and things. It started with us. Now it's everywhere.

Still, the lynch mob is forever a work in progress. Consider that 33 states have conveniently passed Stand Your Ground laws since the height of the subprime market in 2006, by which time economists had been warning of a housing bubble for at least four years. Well before the downturn, it had become abundantly clear that the real estate market was propped up by fraudulent loans—targeting African Americans and Latinos—that far outstripped borrowers' ability to repay. What if millions of Blacks had begun to get ideas like the one espoused by the defiant Henry Ray Boxer?

Florida was the first of 33 states in the U.S. to extend, rather preposterously, the Castle Doctrine—the legal principle that states that a man's home is his castle—dating back to a 17th-century British common law exempting a homeowner from assuming a defensive posture against a burglar or intruder. As a result of Florida's Stand Your Ground legislation authorizing the use of lethal force outside the home, the legal consequence for killing an unarmed African American in the state is less than that for killing a beaver in Maine.

In fact, a 2010 study [121] by Texas A&M University economics professor Mark Hoekstra and research assistant C. Cheng found that Stand Your Ground laws actually *increased* the homicide rate by an average of 8 percent.

The authors wrote:

> It is clear that the primary impact of these laws, beyond

> giving potential victims additional scope to protect themselves, is to increase the loss of human life.

A statistical analysis of 204 Stand Your Ground cases between 2005 and 2013 by a St. Louis University researcher found "disturbing" proof that "there indeed is a quantifiable racial component in the impact of the law in Florida; namely, a suspect is twice as likely to be convicted of a crime if the victim is white, compared to when that victim is not white." The article compares its findings to a civil rights-era study that similarly found "strict enforcement for crimes when the victim is white and less rigorous enforcement when the victim is non-white."

In her 2017 book *Stand Your Ground: A History of America's Love Affair With Lethal Defense*, author Caroline Light wrote:

> (A)s the Black Lives Matter and #SayHerName movements are teaching us now, our current insecurities will not be mitigated by endowing more citizens with the right to shoot first and ask questions later. Indeed, eliminating gun restrictions and the duty to retreat has only intensified the violence against our nation's most vulnerable citizens. It should not surprise us that SYG laws and more liberal gun-carry laws—in spite of their ostensibly race-neutral framing—continue to place people of color outside of our nation's protective boundaries. The deliberate misidentification of criminality and vulnerability is embedded in our very ideals of citizenship.

The correlation between the proliferation of Stand Your Ground legislation and the simultaneous dispossession of Black wealth through fraudulent home loans is clear. By 2019, the median white family owned almost eight times more in net assets than the median Black household, according to Ann F. Thomas, a law professor at New York University.

And much as whites responded violently to Mary Turner's appeals for justice in 1918, the summer of protests that followed the police murder of

George Floyd was met with the same hysteria that attended her lynching. In 2021 state legislative sessions, Republican lawmakers in 34 states introduced 81 bills that toughen penalties on protesters who block roads, more than twice as many proposals as in any other year, Elly Page, a senior legal adviser at the International Center for Not-for-Profit Law, told *The New York Times*. These include, incredibly, bills passed by lawmakers in Oklahoma and Iowa immunizing motorists whose vehicles plow into protesters. Other proposals include an Indiana bill to bar anyone convicted of unlawful assembly from holding state employment, including elected office, and a bill in Minnesota to prohibit anyone convicted of unlawful protesting from receiving student loans, unemployment benefits, or housing assistance.

I am getting a bit ahead of myself, but Mary Turner's grisly murder set in motion a pattern of racial terror and larceny that continues to thwart worker unity by assigning a material value to a white identity. In the spring of 2015, Darren Seals, an African American activist in St. Louis lamented the ineffectiveness of the public response to Michael Brown's slaying, concluding in a social media post:

BLACK DEATH IS BIG BUSINESS.

Sixteen months later, the 29-year-old Seals was fatally shot and the car he was sitting in set on fire. His murder remains unsolved.

Part II

The Fire Last Time

5.

Prisoners of War

If we know, then we must fight for your life as though it were our own— which it is—and render impassable with our bodies the corridors to the gas chamber. For if they come for you in the morning, they will be coming for us that night.

–James Baldwin

The first time the white boy stepped on his hand, 18-year-old Haywood Patterson said nothing. He and his three friends from Chattanooga had stowed away on the Southern Railroad freight car looking for work, not trouble. He assumed that the gaggle of white teenage boys sharing the top of the railcar with his crew were doing the same. It was the first week of spring in 1931, and the country was two years into the Great Depression. Hobos sprouted like cherry blossoms after a spring rain, traipsing the country in search of shorter breadlines, an empty bed, or Lord willing, a paying gig.

But as the train sped west through northern Alabama headed for Memphis, the same white boy stepped on young Haywood's hand again, provoking a response. "The next time you want by, just tell me you want by and I let you by."

"Nigger," the white teen snarled, "I don't ask you when I want by. What you doing on this train anyway?"

Patterson kept his cool: "Look, I just tell you, the next time you want by you just tell me you want by and I let you by."

The white youth exploded: "Nigger bastard, this is a white man's train. You better get off. All you Black bastards better get off!"

"That," Patterson would say later of what would become the most important criminal trial of the 20th century, "is how the Scottsboro case began—with a white foot on my Black hand."[122]

Had his adversary been in a position of authority, such as an engineer, fireman, or "railroad dick," Patterson said, he might well have shied away from confrontation. But the bully in his face obviously didn't have two nickels to rub together or else he wouldn't be here hitching a ride on a freight car, same as him. So Patterson barked back. "You white sons-of-bitches, we got as much right here as you."

As James Goodman describes the encounter in his masterful account, *Stories of Scottsboro*, the train at that moment began to slow as it climbed a steep hill and the band of white boys jumped off to hurl rocks at the Black youths, who took cover inside another car. When the train stopped in the town of Stevenson, Patterson and his friends met up with six other Black teenage stowaways riding in another section of the train who agreed to help if their white rivals reappeared.

No sooner had the train left the station than the bombardment resumed, not from the ground but from an adjoining railcar. The ensuing brawl was brief with the Black teens heaving all but one of their counterparts, Orville Gilley, from the slow-moving train. Gilley would have met the same fate as his friends, but by the time the Black youths got to him, the train had picked up considerable speed, and he was hanging perilously from the gondola. Fearing Gilley might fall underneath one of the railcars, two Black teenagers pulled him back to safety and stood down.

Forty miles down the tracks, near Paint Rock, the train began to slow again. Having vanquished the threat, the Black youths had returned to their original cliques, unaware that one of the white teens tossed from the train had reported the melee to the Stevenson station master who had in turn wired ahead to law enforcement. When a couple of the Black youths peeked outside as the train rolled to a stop, they were shocked to see two Jackson County sheriff's deputies and a phalanx of white men armed with rifles, pistols, and shotguns rushing towards them. The posse grabbed Patterson and his three friends, and the other group of Black youths, peppered them with questions, and unsatisfied with their answers, arrested them on charges of vagrancy and assault, tied them to one another with a plow line, herded them onto the back of a flatbed truck, and drove them to the jail in the county seat of Scottsboro, 21 miles east of Paint Rock.

As they were led away, sheriff's deputies stood on the depot platform interrogating two young white women dressed in overalls. Twenty-three-year-old Victoria Price and 18-year-old Ruby Bates were from the city of Huntsville in northern Alabama on the banks of the Tennessee River. With a population of 32,000, Huntsville was, at the time, the state's third-largest city behind only Birmingham and Mobile, and home to no fewer than seven cotton mills. Price and Bates worked in the oldest, most antiquated and least prosperous of the city's mills, the Margaret, owned by a consortium of local businessmen who couldn't compete with the deep pockets of the financiers from up North who'd invested in the newer mills in town. The Margaret's owners compensated by paying workers next to nothing, and they even cut into that pittance when times got truly tough.

By 1931, Price was earning only $1.20 daily, or roughly half of what she'd been making in 1929 before the onset of the Great Depression. Making matters worse was that the mill was only operational two or three days a week by the spring of 1931, and shutting down entirely every other week, leaving Price and Bates with no more than six days' pay in a good month.

Uneducated, unmarried and practically unemployed, Price and Bates could've been the inspiration for Boo Radley's sisters in *To Kill a Mockingbird* if indeed Harper Lee had bequeathed her ghoulish character with siblings. Both women lived with their mothers in unpainted wooden shacks in Huntsville's worst slum and had few options for making ends meet, none of them good. Price's family was, in fact, the lone white household in a Black neighborhood. She had first gone to work in the mills when she was ten and became the family's sole breadwinner after her mother suffered a debilitating back injury on the job. Bates had worked at Margaret for only two years. Her mother, Emma, was a sharecropper who'd ended up in Huntsville after fleeing an abusive marriage to her second husband, Ruby's father, who spent most days tending to his still. Wrote Goodman:

> Once, on a binge, he sold their house, four rooms in the middle of eighty decent acres thirty miles south of Decatur, without telling her, then disappeared and didn't come back until he was sober and broke. Emma saved and bought another house and he did it again.

Destitute and desperate, Price and Bates turned to prostitution, cementing their place among a marginalized subset of the proletariat who are stigmatized for their exaggerated backwardness, drunkenness, criminality, and Calvinist failings to produce offspring capable of pulling themselves up by their bootstraps, according to Nancy Isenberg, author of the best-selling book, *White Trash: The 400-Year Untold History of Class in America.* Price and Bates, according to Goodman, "lived among Black people, played with them as children, roamed the streets with them as teenagers, bootlegged liquor and got drunk with them as young adults." They also "dated them, slept with them and fell in-and-out of love with them," with Huntsville police once ticketing Bates for hugging a colored man in public. One exasperated Huntsville social worker went so far as to complain that the city's white mill workers were "as bad as the niggers."

When asked initially by sheriff's deputies if the Negroes had "bothered them," both Price and Bates denied flatly that the contingent of Black hobos had made any contact with them. Already on probation for prostitution at the time, Price explained that she and Bates had merely hitched a ride aboard the train to look for work at the Chattanooga mills, and finding none, were returning home. By most accounts, it was only under pressure from the solicitor who prodded the two women ("Go ahead and say they did it, that boy attacked you didn't he?") that Price recalibrated the hand she'd been dealt and recognized, we can safely assume—just as surely as Susan Smith would recognize 63 years later in blaming her infanticide on a phantom Black carjacker—an opportunity to be reborn, at long last, as *white,* a damsel-in-distress, baptized in the virginal blood of respectability, her slate wiped clean of poverty's mortal sins and her womanhood redeemed and entrusted for safekeeping to the heroic patriarchs who had rejected her heretofore.

Yes, Price, the older and more confident of the pair acknowledged, they had been raped, savagely so, by the Negroes who beat them, ripped off their clothes, and threatened them with guns and knives. In an almost laughable story, Price repeatedly told police, reporters, and jurors that as many as six of the Black teenagers had attacked her. Nineteen-year-old Olen Montgomery was the first, she said, penetrating her while 13-year-old Eugene Williams held a knife to her throat, 15-year-old Willie Roberson pried her legs apart and the others cheered fanatically: "Pour it to her, pour it to her." What's more, Price said, the dastardly Negroes' plans extended far beyond one-time sexual gratification, forewarning the fair maidens of their plans to kidnap them, or failing that, to kill them. In Price's version of events, 19-year-old Andy Wright seemed to have an almost theatrical penchant for exposition similar to the comedian Mike Myers' camp parody of cinematic villains in his *Austin Powers* franchise. "When I put this in you and pull it out you will have a Negro baby," she recalled him saying.

"When I saw them nab those Negroes," Price would tell reporters the day following the arrests, "I sure was happy. Mister, I never had a break in my life. Those Negroes have ruined me and Ruby forever. The only thing I ask is that they give them all the law allows."

Sixty miles away in Chattanooga, the editors of the *Southern Worker* heard of the arrests on the radio that evening. Born Solomon Auerbach in 1906 and raised in a Jewish immigrant neighborhood of Philadelphia, James Allen had joined the Communist Party USA in 1928 and was teaching philosophy at the University of Pennsylvania when his handlers asked him two years later to launch the party's first newspaper in the South. He initially tried Birmingham but soured quickly after discovering that the town was so hot that Party organizers were forced to move as often as three times in a single month to keep ahead of the Klan and the sheriff's Red Squad. He settled instead on the slightly more progressive Chattanooga just across the Tennessee state line and home to the publishing empire of the Adolph Ochs family that owned *the New York Times* and *the Chattanooga Times*. His wife, Ida Kleinman, joined him as Isabelle Allen a few weeks later, and the couple rented a small apartment for both home and office, traveling light with only their personal effects, a small, portable typewriter, some boxes and books, so they could pack up and move at a moment's notice if need be. They found a printer six miles away across the Georgia state line in Rossville who agreed to print 3,000 copies a week for $60 cash. (The printer's partner, ironically enough, was a Klansman but unable to turn away business in the depths of the Depression; with disclosure assuring mutual destruction, the odd bedfellows kept their deal a secret from everyone but each other.) Using a Birmingham dateline to throw police off his trail, the inaugural issue of the *Southern Worker* was published on August 16, 1930, calling for "full social, economic and political equality for Negro workers and farmers," in an editorial entitled "What Do We Stand For?" The Birmingham police reportedly raided every known communist hangout in the city searching for "Jim Allen."

As an extension of the *Daily Worker* newspaper published in New York City, the *Southern Worker* "gathered the kind of news that the regional and national papers often ignored,"[123] expanding the party's footprints in the region with coverage of lynchings, the relationship between management and employees in the coal, steel and textile industries, police brutality, and sharecropper uprisings in Arkansas and Alabama. Allen's editorials encouraged interracial collaboration, supported federal anti-lynching legislation, and had gained quite a following among Black Southerners who circulated the paper widely, often reading it aloud to illiterate co-workers.

When the Allens learned that law enforcement had barely thwarted a lynch mob of nearly 100 whites who had swarmed the Scottsboro jail, the couple wired the New York office of the International Labor Defense. Founded in the aftermath of the Palmer raids, the ILD, as it was known, sent their southern representative, Lowell Wakefield, and a top Black organizer, Doug McKenzie to Scottsboro, where they met up with Isabelle Allen. McKenzie was the first to report that Price and Bates were sex workers, and Allen, writing under the pseudonym Helen Marcy, humanized the defendants through interviews with their parents. Characterizing the case as a "crude frame-up,"[124] the articles in the *Southern Worker* called for mass protests almost from the start, contrasting sharply with the opprobrium heaped upon the youths by the national press corps.

Among those reading the dispatches from Alabama was Walter White, the 37-year-old secretary of the National Association for the Advancement of Colored People, founded in 1909 by white liberals and Black intellectuals. While he privately expressed doubts about the youths' guilt, the ambitious White was new to his job and reticent to antagonize either his biracial executive board or the bourgeois donors of all races who he was relying on to keep the reformist civil rights organization afloat in the Depression. His statement read in part:

> The N.A.A.C.P. is not an organization to defend Black criminals. We are not in the field to condone rape, murder and theft because it is done by Black men. . . . When we hear that eight colored men have raped two white girls in Alabama, we are not first in the field to defend them. If they are guilty and have a fair trial the case is none of our business.[125]

With the NAACP keeping a low profile, the Chattanooga Negro Ministers' Alliance did the best they could on short order, hiring a local defense attorney, Stephen Roddy, who was reputed to be a former Klansman. After the judge denied Roddy's request for a change of venue, the first of the four trials began less than two weeks after the arrests, with throngs of whites assembled outside the courthouse and a band playing "There'll Be a Hot Time in the Old Town Tonight."[126] Offering scant resistance, Roddy did little to challenge the prosecution's lack of physical evidence or impeach conflicting testimony from witnesses, nor did he even attempt a closing argument, his dispirited defense amounting to barely more than pleading with the 12 white jurors to spare his clients' lives. Full of vim and vigor but not so much as a dollop of mercy or an ounce of common sense, the white Scottsboro jurors convicted Clarence Norris, Charles Weems, Haywood Patterson, Olen Montgomery, Ozie Powell, Willie Roberson, Eugene Williams, and Andy Wright of murder and sentenced all eight to die in the electric chair—nicknamed "Yellow Mama" —at Kilby State Prison. The trial of 13-year-old Roy Wright, the youngest of the Scottsboro Boys, ended in a mistrial when jurors held out for the death penalty even though the prosecution asked only for life imprisonment.

The four trials took all of four days and barely three weeks for the state to arrest, indict, prosecute, convict, and sentence the defendants.

Before blitzkrieg justice had been meted out, however, the communists began strategizing their next steps. "What's the party going to do?" an African American organizer named Sol Harper challenged his comrades at the CPUSA's Harlem office. Harry Haywood, the Black waiter who had waded through Chicago's riots 12 years earlier, had just returned stateside after three years of language training and political education courses in Moscow. In his autobiography, he recalled Harper accusing the NAACP of selling the nine teenagers out. "We have to step in now," Harper said. "We must take over the legal defense. Send our lawyers down and get them to line up the boys and their parents."

After meeting with the International Labor Defense, a plan came together. The ILD's Wakefield wired Alabama's governor to request a stay of execution, which was granted immediately. The ILD's chief lawyer, Joseph Brodsky, and an associate traveled to Birmingham and Chattanooga to meet with the parents while a local ILD attorney, Allen Taub, traveled to Kilby State Prison outside Montgomery to meet with their sons. By April 10, the day of sentencing, virtually all the defendants had agreed to allow the communists to represent them on appeal. That same day, the Central Committee published a statement in the *Daily Worker* referring to the case as a "courthouse lynching" carried out by the "Southern white ruling class." The statement called upon "all working-class and Negro organizations to adopt strong resolutions of protest and to wire these to the Governor of Alabama." Those resolutions alone, however, "will do no good; you must organize such at greatest possible speed mass meetings and militant mass demonstrations against this crime." In conclusion, the communique blared, "Death penalty for lynchers!" and "Stop the legal lynching at Scottsboro!" Two days later, nearly 1,300 workers demonstrated in Cleveland to protest the verdicts, 20,000 attended a rally the next day in New York City, followed by massive demonstrations in Philadelphia, Milwaukee, Omaha, Sioux City, Kansas City, Boston, Buffalo, Niagara Falls, New Haven, and Elizabeth, New Jersey.

And just like that, the liberation of the American working class had begun.

That one of the first battles of the Cold War was fought in a Dixie county named for Stonewall Jackson may come as a shock and yet the communists would descend on the northeastern corner of Alabama in the months to come much as the Western allies would storm the beach at Normandy 13 years later.

Often left unsaid in any discussion of the 1917 October Revolution are the similarities between the oppression of Russian workers under the czars and the subjugation of the American precariat under the thumb of monopoly capital. Among Vladimir Lenin's first official acts as the head of the newly formed Union of Soviet Socialist Republics was the nationalization of all foreign assets in the country and, in a move that put both Virginia's Readjusters and Greece's Syriza to shame, he didn't merely renegotiate the interest rate, he repudiated the USSR's sovereign debt entirely. Between 1769 when Catherine the Great took out the country's first loan from Amsterdam, and the outbreak of the Great War, Russia's indebtedness had ballooned to the largest of any nation's in the world, totaling 8.8 billion roubles, of which railroad construction accounted for more than a third, similar to Virginia's postbellum financial woes.[127] To repay their creditors, the czars resorted to the Bourbons' policy of dipping into government funds earmarked for social spending and slashing interest rates paid to bank depositors.

Vladimir Ilyich Lenin was also of the opinion that the Bolsheviks could not govern without ridding the proletariat of the ancient ethnic rivalries that were stoked by the czars in a cynical attempt to divide and conquer the more than 100 nationalities—a "prison-house of nations," as pre-revolutionary Russia was often referred to—inhabiting a land mass accounting for nearly a sixth of the Earth's surface. To cite one illustrative example, a Ku Klux

Klan-like outfit known as the "Black Hundreds" was infamous for nighttime massacres targeting Jewish communities. (The Yiddish word "pogrom" was invented by Russian Jews to specifically describe these assaults.) Alexander III's ascension to the throne in 1881 escalated anti-Semitic violence, causing Russian Jews to flee in droves for enclaves such as New York City. Tribalism re-emerged years later under Stalin but in the revolution's formative years, bigotry was expressly forbidden, culture exalted, and self-determination in the form of republicanism encouraged. In 1934, Harry Haywood said to a mostly Black crowd in Detroit:

> Here we have the same sort of race-inciting propaganda which was carried out by the Czarist regime in old Russia against the Jewish people.
>
> The Jews are also branded by the Czarist reactionaries as killers of Christian children, the blood of whom was used in the ceremonies. This slander against Jews was calculated to inflame the minds of the Russian toilers and to justify mass murder of the Jewish people. In this way, the Czarist reactionaries attempted to divert the attention of the toilers from the struggle against their common oppressors.[128]

Also in his autobiography, Haywood recalled a drunk staggering aboard a half empty Moscow streetcar one late afternoon in the late 1920s. Seeing Haywood with a group of his Black classmates, the inebriate mumbled loud enough for everyone to hear "Black devils in our country." Here is what happened next, according to Haywood:

> A group of outraged Russian passengers thereupon seized him and ordered the motorman to stop the car. It was a citizen's arrest, the first I had ever witnessed. 'How dare you, you scum, insult people who are the guests of our country!'
>
> What then occurred was an impromptu, on-the-spot meeting, where they debated what to do with the man. I was to see many of this kind of "meeting" during my stay in

> Russia. It was decided to take the culprit to the police station, which, the conductor informed them, was a few blocks ahead. Upon arrival there, they hustled the drunk out of the car and insisted that we Blacks, as the injured parties, come along to make the charges. At first, we demurred, saying that the man was obviously drunk and not responsible for his remarks. 'No, citizens,' said a young man . . . 'drunk or not, we don't allow this sort of thing in our country. You must come with us to the militia (police) station and prefer charges against this man.'
>
> The car stopped in front of the station. The poor drunk was hustled off and all the passengers came along. The defendant had sobered up somewhat by this time and began apologizing before we had even entered the building. We got to the commandant of the station.
>
> The drunk swore that he didn't mean what he'd said. 'I was drunk and angry about something else. I swear to you citizens that I have no race prejudice against those Black gospoda [gentlemen].'

It was not lost on Haywood and other Black servicemen that they were treated better by their Russian hosts than by their own military commanders who secretly sent a memo during the war encouraging their French counterparts to favor white soldiers. The CPUSA was born the year after the war ended, 1919, as Red Summer raged and Palmer raided, when the Socialist Party expelled militants who proposed to import bolshevism.[129] That proved serendipitous for Blacks such as Haywood, Paul Robeson, Du Bois, and the journalist Cyril Briggs who founded the secretive, self-defense order known as the African Blood Brotherhood, which became a seedbed for Black Reds. Searching for solutions led many African Americans to reject the narrow nationalism of Marcus Garvey—who encouraged African Americans to cross picket lines manned by whites—and the reductionism of white socialists such as Eugene Debs, who wrote in a 1903 article that appeared in the *International Socialist Review*:[130]

> The history of the Negro in the United States is a history of crime without a parallel. [And yet,] [t]here is no Negro question outside of the labor question. . . . The class struggle is colorless. The capitalists, white, black and other shades are on one side and the workers, white, black, and all other colors, on the other side.

The socialist writer, Kate Richards O'Hare, put it far more crudely when she wrote in 1912:

> SOCIALISTS WANT TO PUT THE NEGRO WHERE HE CAN'T COMPETE WITH THE WHITE MAN.[131]

Said Du Bois, who was briefly a Socialist:

> No recent convention of Socialists has dared to face the Negro question fairly.[132]

Worse still was the Black respectability politics increasingly promoted by an African American bourgeoisie that, however well-meaning, operated from a misguided understanding of Black laborers as a defeated people whose best chance was to obey white folks and hope for the best. In that context, the Black elite appointed themselves race interlocutors tasked with managing the assimilation of their brethren. Similar to Marx's description of the Irish attitude towards the English, the African American working class regarded Black aristocrats as stooges, who were, as James Baldwin would say years later, complicit in their own murder.

When marauding white lynch mobs attacked African Americans in Atlanta in 1906, Black militias dutifully patrolled segregated neighborhoods, including those populated by the academics and administrators who worked at the city's historically Black colleges, Morehouse, Spelman, and Clark

University. Once the smoke had cleared, Atlanta's Urban League organized neighborhood clubs to teach "better housekeeping" practices to Black maids and washerwomen, Karen Ferguson wrote in her resplendent book, *Black Politics in New Deal Atlanta.* The domestics attended, listening intently to lectures on cleanliness and punctuality, but when, they began to wonder, would the forum address the subject of pay raises for making an extra effort? Told that no pay raises would be forthcoming, the Black domestics bolted, presumably giving their Urban League sisters the side-eye on the way out the door. In a letter written to a white friend just days after the 1906 riots, a prominent African American educator named William Crogman wrote:

> Here we have worked and prayed and tried to make good men and women of our colored population, and at our very doorstep the whites kill these good men. But the lawless element in our population, the element we have condemned fights back, and it is to these people that we owe our lives.[133]

Similarly, Black mercantilists opposed efforts to organize Black workers at the North Carolina cigarette maker R.J. Reynolds in 1919. According to Robert Rodgers Korstad, author of *Civil Rights Unionism: Tobacco Workers and the Struggle for Democracy in the Mid-Twentieth Century South*, one Black banker, J.H. Hill, implored 'my people' not to be tempted by 'strangers. . . . There is no need for a poor laboring class of people to try to make demands on any rich corporations. We are dependent upon these corporations for employment.' Underwhelmed, Black tobacco workers boycotted stores that did not support the union and threatened to withdraw their money from Hill's bank. Similarly, when another Black merchant tried to dissuade the tobacco workers from unionizing, he was met with 'hoots and jeers.'[134]

Dissatisfied with the game plans such as those put forth by Debs and the Talented Tenth (as Du Bois famously dubbed the Black community's best educated), scores of African Americans enrolled in the Communist

University of the Toilers of the East—known by its Russian acronym KUTVA—to pore over texts by Marx and Lenin and study topics that included Russian language, economics, labor organizing, and revolutionary theory. The Bolsheviks opened the university in 1921 to train the scores of nationalities within the Soviet Union's borders and revolutionaries from around the world. The university would close in the late 1930s as World War II dawned, but its graduates include such historical figures as Ho Chi Minh, Jomo Kenyatta, and Deng Xiaoping.

At the 6th Congress of the Communist International, or COMINTERN, the assembly proclaimed in 1928:

> It is essential for the Communist Party to make an energetic beginning now—at the present moment—with the organization of joint mass struggles of white and black workers against Negro oppression. This alone will enable us to get rid of the bourgeois white chauvinism which is polluting the ranks of the white workers in America, to overcome the distrust of the Negro masses caused by the inhuman barbarous Negro slave traffic still carried on by the American bourgeoisie—in as much as it is directed even against all white workers—and to win over to our side these millions of Negroes as active fellow-fighters in the struggle for the overthrow of bourgeois power throughout America.

The aristocratic war on terror that began in earnest in 1919 had taken its toll on the workforce, reducing the percentage of organized employees from 19.4 percent in 1920 to 10.2 percent in 1930, according to Kim Phillips-Fein in her book *Invisible Hands: The Businessmen's Crusade Against the New Deal.* Yet, when the stock market crashed in 1929 the Communist Party could claim no more than 7,000 members in the U.S., of whom an estimated 6,000 were foreign-born; half of them had trouble conversing with their co-workers in English.[135]

When the Scottsboro case fell into their laps, the party was actively scouring the country for a good narrative that improved upon their didactic pamphlets and glib sloganeering to activate the proletariat stateside.

Inundated with speaking requests, the African American director of the International Labor Defense, William Patterson, made a decision that changed the course of history: Rather than attorneys or party organizers speaking on behalf of the Scottsboro youths, they would send the mothers of the boys across the nation and around the world to tell their own stories and raise funds for their sons' legal defense.

In an editorial published in the *New York Daily Worker* in January of 1932, Ada Wright joined Bernice Morris, Viola Montgomery, Janie Patterson and Josephine Powell to write:

> We are the mothers of the nine Scottsboro Negro boys who have been sentenced to death in the electric chair. The world knows our poor boys are innocent. We appeal to all working-class mothers to help us save our boys from being killed.[136]

Known as "Mother Wright," Ada Wright was a domestic worker and widow who turned 41 the year that her sons Roy and Andy were arrested. She was not well-traveled, had no public speaking experience, and couldn't discern an "elephant from a Communist" as one activist wrote of her. Yet she was an irresistible force, writing in a communist newspaper in September 1931 that she learned of the arrests from her sister, who read about the incident in a Chattanooga newspaper.

> Well, I quit work and started to collect money for a lawyer. Then this lawyer, Stephen Roddy, he's no good, and a drunkard, he says he wants ninety dollars. So we collected it for him and what did he do? Why, he just told the judge that he wasn't there to defend the boys and he did not want to defend them in court. He just plain railroaded them to the chair. He told them all to plead guilty and to get life. But the boys refused to plead guilty. They weren't guilty and

> they did not plead guilty. But what could I do, just a poor widow?
>
> And then the International Labor Defense came to see us. They told us they were a defense organization for the working class and they said they wanted to defend our boys and do everything possible to get them free. Well, you can just imagine how we felt then. Here we thought we were alone in the world without friends and suddenly we found people wantin' to defend our boys.[137]

Accompanied by thc secretary of the International Labor Defense, J. Louis Engdahl, she embarked on a six-month tour of 16 European countries in the spring of 1932, addressing enthusiastic, working-class crowds, and comparing her sons' plight to "class war prisoners all over the world." In a 2001 paper, George Washington University English Professor James A. Miller, and historians Susan Dabney Pennybacker and Eve Rosenhaft wrote:

> She spoke in London, Manchester, Dundee, Kirkaldy, Glasgow, and Bristol, along with ILD organizers. Prime Minister Eamon De Valera prohibited Wright from entering Ireland. She traveled instead to Scandinavia, where 10,000 people reportedly demonstrated in Copenhagen alone. Wright and Engdahl again crossed the Belgian border illegally to visit thc coal district of Wallonia in late August 1932. She addressed audiences of women in Charleroi and in Gilly, the heart of the "moving and often murderous arena" of the Borinage. When she was arrested in Charleroi, a crowd of mothers with babes in arms accompanied her to the police station. She was again arrested in Kladno, Czechoslovakia, on suspicion of spreading Communist propaganda with the intent to interfere in local politics: 'I answered that I don't know anything about local conditions in Kladno, that I'm not trained enough to give a political speech and I don't know enough about Communism yet to be a good Communist.'[138]

When the 48-year-old Engdahl died of pneumonia in Moscow, Wright returned to the U.S. with his ashes. A flier promoting a Harlem speaking engagement beamed:

> We ask you workers of Harlem, Negro and White, to join the SCOTTSBORO VICTORY PARADE and greet MRS ADA WRIGHT, THE AMBASSADRESS OF THE NEGRO PEOPLE TO THE WORKERS OF THE WORLD.

Wright's star power helped turn the Scottsboro case into an international *cause celebre*. President Roosevelt began asking his staff for regular updates on where she was speaking, to whom, and what was said. Letters of support poured into the ILD offices from the Ukrainian Labor Temple, the Frederick Douglass Interracial Forum; Russian, Finnish, Scandinavian, Croatian, Hungarian and Jewish toilers; the Lithuanian Working Women's Alliance; "we white and Black workers" in Birmingham, Kansas City and Milwaukee; from Albert Einstein, Bill "Bojangles" Robinson, H.G. Wells, Theodore Dreiser, Fiorello La Guardia, Thomas Mann and John Dos Passos. Protests erupted in Johannesburg and Beirut, where the U.S. consulate was attacked, its windows shattered and a note attached "to the door [that] protested the execution of the Negroes involved in the Scottsboro affair."[139]

Wrote the defendant Patterson of the mail and cigarettes sent to the Scottsboro defendants by supporters:

> Mail from white people was confusing to me. All my life I was untrusting of them. Now their kind words and presents was more light than we got through the bars of the window.[140]

The communists used the Scottsboro case to reunite Black and white workers who had begun to drift apart following the end of radical Reconstruction a half century earlier. "There is no group in America," the iconic Harlem Congressman Adam Clayton Powell Jr. wrote in 1945, "which practices racial brotherhood one-tenth as much as the Communist Party."

Such tributes earned the Reds the enmity of African American liberal reformers like the NAACP's White, who viewed the Communists both as a threat to his organization's prestige and a band of merry lunatics who were perfectly willing to sacrifice Black folks on their utopian red altar. While privately disparaging the Scottsboro mothers as hayseeds, the NAACP continued to solicit the defendants and their families to take over their defense. None did. In 1932, Claude Patterson wrote to his son in prison: "You will burn sure if you don't let those preachers alone and trust in the International Labor Defense [to] handle the case."[141] That same year, the defendants were heard singing in their cells:

I looked over yonder and what did I see
Comin' for to carry me home?
Mr. William Patterson and the ILD
Comin' for to carry me home.

Also in 1932, Ada Wright wrote:

> The Defense Committee sent lawyers down to Scottsboro and invited some of us mothers up north to help with the defense. We told Roddy that we never wanted to have anything to do with him again. But the N.A.A.C.P. has been pesterin' us ever since to let them take the case and to keep Roddy on the job. But we told them plain we know our friends when we see them and we're a goin' to stick to the League of Struggle for Negro Rights and the International Labor Defense Committee. I've been speaking at meetings all over New York, Chicago and other places, and I never knew we had so many friends. Why, it seems there are thousands of working people in this country, white and

> black, that just wants to do all they can to get the boys out. It just gives me so much courage and makes me feel so good. I want my boys out but I want all the other boys free just as well. I can see where we all got to stick together. And I think if we get all our boys free that there are a lot of Negro mothers in the South who will be happy for once in all their lives, because they know that there is a real fight goin' on against lynchin' our people in the South.
>
> So I am sticking by the International Labor Defense and they are stickin' by us, and if we all pull together some good got to come from it.[142]

Born as a kind of supplicant organization charged with pleading for the lives of Blacks victimized by Jim Crow courts, the NAACP could never quite make the revolutionary leap when the Black proletariat went on the offensive against its class enemies. That divide within the Black community has only widened in the intervening years, producing a roster of African American "misleadership"—to use a phrase popularized by *Black Agenda Report's* late Executive Editor Glen Ford—that includes Obama, Kamala Harris, and practically the whole of the Congressional Black Caucus.

Conversely, though it took nearly 40 years, and seven retrials, the Scottsboro mothers, the International Labor Defense and public indignation eventually won either freedom or a pardon for all nine defendants. The communists in those days came to think of African Americans as the "most class conscious" of Americans, and while Blacks would eventually grow critical of the CPUSA for its waning commitment to their liberation struggle, African Americans would account for 950 of the party's 1,000 members in Alabama in 1934.[143] Reminiscent of the Black workers who flocked to the Knights of Labor as white workers fled in the violent period following the Haymarket bombing, Alabama's communists were commonly referred to as the "nigger party" according to the historian Robin D.G. Kelley, and for a period of time in the mid-to-late 1930s, the party had more members in Birmingham than did the local chapter of the NAACP. For her part, Ada Wright expressed her gratitude to the party until the day she died.

Harry Haywood wrote of the ordeal:

> The courtroom farce at Scottsboro was a part of a wave of racist terror sweeping the South that had resulted in ten known lynchings in the previous three months. Clearly its purpose was to 'keep the nigger in his place,' to prevent unity of Blacks and poor whites—in other words, to divert the unrest of Black and white workers into channels of interracial strife.

Victoria Price stuck to her story for the remainder of her life, but Ruby Bates experienced a Damascene conversion at the second trial, recanted her testimony and went on to write to the defendants in prison, appearing at rallies with four of them upon their release in 1937 and writing newspaper editorials with Ada Wright. Appearing at St. Nicholas Arena in Manhattan, she told an audience of more than 5,000 people that she initially lied in the case because she had been "excited and frightened by the ruling class of white people," leading her hometown newspaper, the *Huntsville Times*, to describe her as "Harlem's darling" in an editorial petitioning prosecutors to charge her with perjury. Bates' epiphany recalled the slave trader, John Newton, who composed the Christian hymn, *Amazing Grace*, amid a lashing sea storm to atone for his sins, augured Viola Liuzzo's spiritual awakening, and heralded a new phase in America's class war, characterized by mass desertions of conscripts from the "white" army. In 1933, Bates told a Baltimore crowd:

> I want to tell you that the Scottsboro boys were framed by the bosses of the south and two girls. I was one of the girls and I want you to know that I am sorry I said what I did at the first trial, but I was forced to say it.
>
> Those boys did not attack me and I want to tell you all right here now that I am sorry that I caused them all this

> trouble for two years, and now I am willing to join hands with black and white to get them free.[144]

6.

The Battle on the Bay

I was taking care of myself and to take care of myself I had to line up with other people and help take care of them.

–Harry Bridges

In 1927, a 47-year-old ironworker named John Norris emptied his savings account to make the down payment on a Chicago two-flat that set him back a cool $17,500, worth about $293,443 in 2023 dollars.[145] The idea was to pay off the mortgage in ten years with his wages and the rent collected from tenants living in the second apartment, providing Norris and his wife with a tidy nest egg upon retirement. But the Great Depression was to dreams as Grendel was to flesh, tearing into Norris' best-laid plans by subjecting him to one layoff after another until he lost his job entirely. And the tenants he'd depended on for rental income were of no help either, vacating the apartment owing Norris $300 and leaving him unable to pay his mortgage. When the bank foreclosed in October 1930, he lost all of the $8,100 he'd acquired in equity—about $150,517 in 2024 dollars—and when the couple was evicted 18 months later, they traipsed the city wearily pleading with friends for a place to sleep for a night or two.

Deserted by her husband in 1925, Rose Majewski managed to raise the couple's five children on her own for a while by scrubbing floors at the First Trust and Savings Bank in Chicago for $21.50 a week.[146] When the stock market crashed in October 1929, however, she was laid off. She cobbled together enough work over the next year to keep her family afloat, cleaning the Merchandise Mart Building for $18 a week and cleaning chickens at a packinghouse for weekly wages between $10 and $12. But by June 1930, Mrs. Majewski's luck had run out; unable to find another job after she was laid off yet again, her 16-year-old daughter became the household's primary breadwinner, catching on as a domestic for $4 a week and food. The family quickly ran through their $50 in savings, fell behind on their rent, insurance policies, a radio they were buying on installment, and their account with the grocer, who cut them off. When they were eventually evicted, the Majewski clan found four rooms on the top floor of a converted barn for $14 a month. Finally, Mrs. Majewski, who was born in Poland, spoke little English and had never applied for citizenship, went on the dole, supporting her brood with $5 a week from a charity, and a monthly box of food staples from the Cook County Bureau of Public Welfare.

"The depression," the Harlem Renaissance writer Langston Hughes wrote, "brought everybody down a peg or two. And the Negro had but few pegs to fall."

Indeed, by the time the stock market lost $2 billion—12 percent of its value—in a single day of trading on October 21, 1929, Blacks had been experiencing widespread unemployment for nearly three years, according to the Bureau of Labor Statistics' monthly bulletins. In the early months of 1929, with the economy supposedly at full throttle, 300,000 African American industrial workers, about 20 percent of all Blacks employed in smokestack industries, had already been thrown out of work.[147] Moreover, a quarter of all urban Black workers were employed as household domestics on the eve of the Great Depression, and the remainder concentrated in entry-level construction jobs and bituminous coal mining, which were among the sectors hit first and hardest by the slowdown.

Travis Dempsey lost his job selling the city's Black newspaper, *the Chicago Defender*, on the day after Black Thursday, when the stock market nosedived, triggering the downturn.[148] He was ten. Two months later, his favorite uncle, Otis, known as a spendthrift, was laid off from his job at the packinghouse three days before Christmas in 1929. And in a replay of the closing of the Freedman's Bank in 1874, Uncle Otis lost every penny to his name when government regulators that summer closed the Binga State Bank. Otis Dempsey would be dead within two years' time, a broken man in a barren, broken land.

African Americans tried to steer clear of whites' worsening moods that often found expression in what we might refer to as microaggressions today, to include spitting and harassment such as that exhibited by the white hobos riding the rails outside Scottsboro. There were also reports of encounters that fell short of lynching yet were nonetheless deadly.

On a gorgeous late summer Saturday in 1935, a then-27-year-old-Theodore Goodloe was the driver of a truck shuttling 33 young, festive hay riders from Indianapolis' historically Black neighborhood of Haughville when it was sideswiped by a truck driven by a white man. Seven people were seriously injured and two were killed: 22-year-old Arthur Kelley and a 14-year-old boy who were both apparently dangling their legs from the left side of the truck when the collision occurred. The teenage boy died instantly; both his legs were severed at the knee.

His name was John Jeter, and 30 years later my parents would pay homage to the older brother my father never knew by naming their second son, and third child—me—after him. In a front-page article, the city's Black newspaper, the *Indianapolis Recorder*, described the driver of the second truck, Earl Bramlet, as white and 24. He was not charged, but I am familiar with that westside street where the accident occurred and it is plainly too narrow to accommodate two trucks driving side-by-side (the *Recorder* describes the road width at 18 feet, which is exactly the width of the two nine-foot-wide trucks). Had Bramlet been Black and my uncle white, prosecutors would've almost certainly filed charges equivalent to manslaughter or vehicular homicide. The *Recorder* suggests that Blacks gathered at the hospital were in a near-riotous state. My father was just months shy of his fourth birthday and my family speculates that he was never told the full story of what happened to his brother. Earlier that year he had lost his mother to tuberculosis, and his father and siblings likely wanted to spare him the trauma. Approximately 40 years later, when I was nine or ten, I accompanied my father to the Indianapolis farmers' market on an Indian summer weekend. We had likely devoured a few German sausages and cheese, and with our work done, were preparing to return home when I spotted an older Black man shuffling towards us. As I remember the incident now nearly a half-century later, the man was north of 70 with a frame so slight that his chest appeared caved-in, or sunken, like a toppled bird's nest. But he was, as we used to say, cleaner than the board of health, dressed to the nines in a worn brown suit, necktie, and fedora. I remember the man approaching us slowly, and the closer he got, the more I could discern a look of unmistakable anguish on his face, that left me wondering, in the seconds before his arrival, if he wasn't planning to attack my old man.

Instead, he clasped my father's right hand tightly in his, and in a raspy voice repeated these words, like a mantra, for what seemed an eternity:

> I'm sorry, son. I'm so sorry. I'm so very sorry.

It was the driver of the truck that my uncle was riding in when he was killed, Theodore Goodloe.

Clearly embarrassed, my father withheld absolution because none was warranted, and instead tried to console the man while simultaneously attempting to regain control of his annexed hand. "It's okay, Mr. Goodloe.

It wasn't your fault. No one ever blamed you."

During the Depression, Blacks were shortchanged by the relief rolls just as they were on the payrolls. In Miami, for example, jobless Blacks were paid $1.25 per diem, or about half of the $2.45 paid to unemployed whites. Nationwide, African American households in 1932 averaged only $1.25 per week in government food subsidies.[149]

Even this meager amount was only achieved due to massive mobilizations of both Black and white workers through the Unemployment Councils organized by the Communist Party. Historian Roy Rosenzweig estimated that "easily two million jobless workers engaged in some form of activism at some time in the thirties,"[150] although the consensus is that this figure is a dramatic undercount and may have been as high as 10 percent of the population of about 125 million.

Again, Blacks were front and center. In nationwide protests on National Unemployment Day in March 1930, 2,000 of the 3,000 demonstrators in Birmingham, Alabama, were Black, many of them children, who sang:

Empty is the cupboard, no pillow for the head
We are the hunger children who fight for milk and bread
We are the workers' children, who must, who must be fed.[151]

In April 1931, *The New York Times* reported that 50 hunger marchers—of whom 40 were African American—burst into an assembly of the Maryland House of Delegates in Annapolis demanding that lawmakers reroute funds earmarked for a new penitentiary to finance a fund for unemployment insurance. That same month, just weeks after the Scottsboro defendants were arraigned, the price of cotton dropped to six cents per pound—roughly a third of its price from two years earlier—causing planters in Alabama's Tallapoosa County to suspend credit at their commissaries for tenant farmers. Black sharecroppers were encouraged to look for work at a nearby mill, but they had other ideas.

At a sharecropper meeting later that month in Camp Hill, a 21-year-old African American school teacher from Birmingham, Estelle Milner, a CPUSA member and the daughter of a county sharecropper, read aloud from an article published in the *Southern Worker* on efforts to organize farm relief councils in a neighboring county. Ralph Gray and his brother Tommy agreed to reach out to communist organizers on the farmworkers' behalf. The grandson of a Reconstruction-era state senator, Ralph Gray was a World War I veteran with a reputation as a troublemaker, once refusing to chop Sheriff Kyle Young's cotton for the going daily rate of 50 cents. Young warned Gray that "white folks aren't going to stand for Negroes setting the price of labor in Tallapoosa."[152]

The two CPUSA organizers—one Black, one white—led strategy sessions in which the croppers developed their list of demands, which included the repeal of planters' protectionist trade restrictions prohibiting croppers from selling their wares to buyers outside Tallapoosa County; this measure, often associated with socialist governments, lowered the price that tenant farmers could demand for their product. Additionally, the croppers wanted written contracts, and day laborers wanted cash payments.

In May, the fledgling Croppers and Farmworkers Union sent four delegates to the All-Southern Scottsboro Defense Conference in Chattanooga where they were arrested for loitering. One white woman who tried to attend was badly beaten by her husband; their daughter had him arrested, but the judge congratulated the defendant and urged him to use a shotgun on the agitators the next time.

By Independence Day, the union counted 800 members, and on July 15th, acting on an informant's tip, Sheriff Young and several deputies raided an abandoned building just south of Dadeville where eight croppers and a communist organizer were drafting a letter to the governor demanding the release of the Scottsboro teens. The locals managed to hustle the CPUSA organizer out the back door, but Young was outraged by Blacks meddling in white folks' business.

The next day Young and a posse burst in on 150 union members meeting in Dadeville's St. Mary's Catholic Church, and seeing his nemesis, Ralph Gray, shot him, though Gray managed to return fire before fleeing, hitting the sheriff in the stomach. The posse pursued the wounded Gray to his cabin where they finished him off, fractured his widow's skull, and roughed up several of his friends, before rushing off to find Milner, the uppity schoolteacher who'd dared to read the *Southern Worker* aloud at the sharecroppers' meeting, beating her so badly that several of her vertebrae ruptured. In total, the mob arrested 33 sharecroppers and murdered five others whose bodies were never found. Gray's corpse was deposited on the Tallapoosa County Courthouse steps in Dadeville and used for target practice.

Notwithstanding Hughes' poignantly poetic assessment of the Depression years, the downturn didn't quite knock *everyone* back. Some West Coast investors weathered the storm quite nicely, thank you, owing in large part to the Jones-White Act of 1928, which paid massive taxpayer subsidies in the form of lucrative mail contracts to shipowners operating in overseas ports, putatively to stimulate job creation for civilian maritime employees, and create a naval auxiliary in the case of war. Foreshadowing the Obama administration's auction of foreclosed homes to speculators in 2012 as a means of reviving a moribund real estate market, Jones-White bore the strong whiff of collusion between the plutocrats and their cronies in elected office. Under the law, the federal government agreed to sell aging naval vessels to private steamship companies at a steep discount of less than ten cents on the dollar, with liberal terms and plenty of time to pay. Secondly, Congress created a $250 million fund to lend shipowners as much as 75 percent of the construction costs to build new vessels at interest rates as low as one percent. And third, the shipping magnates were awarded 44 different contracts to deliver the mail internationally for the ungodly sum of $30 million annually.

One of the biggest beneficiaries of the Jones-White boondoggle was Robert Stanley Dollar's eponymous Dollar Lines, which employed cheap Chinese labor on its ships and retrofitted their fleets in Chinese shipyards using unskilled workers, known pejoratively as "coolies." On October 2, 1922, Dollar launched the Admiral Oriental line with an initial cash outlay of $500, issuing notes for capital stock in the amount of $499,500. A month later, the Dollar Lines began operating a service to the Asian-Pacific rim using vessels leased from the U.S. government. In a span of four years, the Dollar Lines reported a profit of $533,714, having already retired the notes they had issued for capital stock. Owing to the largesse of lawmakers on Capitol Hill, Dollar went on to purchase a fleet of ships from the U.S. Navy, enabling the company to rack up profits of $6,767,958 between 1922 and 1934; for negotiating the purchase of these ships, R. Stanley Dollar—named, ironically enough, for the British explorer Stanley Livingstone, whose expeditions opened up the African Congo to the Belgian King Leopold's colonial predations[153]—collected the princely sum of $698,750 in commissions, equivalent to nearly $16 million in 2024 dollars. In total, the San Francisco-based Dollar Line and its subsidiary, the Admiral Oriental Line, entered into mail contracts with the U.S. government worth more than $48 million over a ten-year period beginning at almost the precise moment as the Great Depression. On the East Coast, the Export Steamship Corporation did at least as well as its West Coast counterparts, buying a fleet of 18 ships that cost taxpayers $42 million to build, for less than $1.1 million. Between August 1928 and June 1929, company vessels transported all of three pounds of mail, for which the government paid them $234,980. In 1931, as the Depression cranked up, Export Steamship transported eight pounds of mail, for which taxpayers paid the company just shy of $26,000 per pound. In *The Big Strike*, the journalist Mike Quinn wrote of the Jones-

White Act:

> When Mr. Heberman, president of the Export Lines, returned from Washington where he had negotiated this deal, he turned in an expense account of $300,000.

United States Senator Homer Truett Bone said that the unseemly transaction "constitutes a bold challenge thrown in the teeth of the hungry people of the nation. We made multimillionaires overnight under the Jones-White Act . . . "[154] Buoyed by the taxpayer-funded windfall, the Pacific Coast's "Big Three"—the Dollar Lines, the Matson Navigation Company, and American Hawaiian—pocketed profits totaling $29 million between 1920 and 1935 (when Roosevelt ended the program), paid cash dividends to shareholders of $16 million, stock dividends valued at $27 million, retired $5 million in debt, and nearly quadrupled their net worth from $10 million to $39 million.

Unsurprisingly, the millionaire shippers did not share their good fortune with their employees.

The postwar upheaval that began with Red Summer and the Palmer raids had virtually reorganized the workforce by 1929, reducing union membership nationwide from a peak of 5,047,800 in 1919 to 3,442,600 on the eve of the Great Depression,[155] out of a workforce of nearly 30 million employees at that time,[156] representing a rate of unionization that is remarkably similar to 2020 before the pandemic's onset. The American Federation of Labor, which had succeeded the Knights of Labor as the country's largest union, was a spent force after the first World War, having devoted virtually all its energies to organizing craft—a synonym for "white" —workers rather than the unskilled, which included most African Americans. Despite appeals from such distinguished figures as A. Philip Randolph, Du Bois, and the Urban League, AFL President William Green refused to integrate affiliates. At the onset of the Great Depression, mining was the only core industry represented by the AFL, while rubber, steel, and car manufacturing remained unorganized.

San Francisco's Riggers and Stevedores Unions went on strike for higher wages in 1919; shipowners responded by hiring African American strikebreakers for even less money. Few, if any, Black workers preferred segregated locals, but the Pacific Coast International Longshoremen's Association, or ILA, had barred "coloreds" since its inception in the mid-19th century. Weary of pleading with white workers for an opportunity to unite and fight the bosses together, Black workers didn't hesitate to pounce on any opportunity to earn a paycheck. One African American explained his motivation for crossing the 1919 picket line:

> I was living in Oakland and I had a wife and ten kids, out of work, and the news came out that they had a strike on the waterfront, which the Negroes weren't allowed to work.[157]

Shipowners fired the strikers on the San Francisco docks in 1919 and required new workers to join the closed, and toothless, company shop—known colloquially as "yellow dog unions" —which replaced the ILA. Membership in the yellow dog union was indicated by possession of a "Blue Book" that a longshoreman was required to produce to participate in the daily "shape-up," whereby the company's pit boss randomly chose the crew, or gang, to load or unload ships that day, similar to the modern practice of casual labor. The writer Cal Winslow described the practice:

> The San Francisco longshoremen called the Embarcadero 'the slave market'—there, each morning at 8 am, workers would gather, as often as not desperate for any opportunity to work. Many more would gather than were needed, some would be skilled, 'regular men,' others transients, then all grades in between. The hiring boss, the petty dictator on the dock, would stand before them; he could take any man he wanted, reject anyone he pleased.[158]

With Black strikebreakers prohibited from joining the Blue Book union, the number of employed longshoremen fell from a peak of 86,000 in 1920 to 74,000 a decade later. In a bid to do more with less, shipowners squeezed the workforce that remained through the use of dangerous speed-ups that would continue to haunt, cripple and kill industrial workers with astonishing regularity for the next half-century. Speaking of the machine that hoists cargo, a longshoreman in the 1930s described working conditions in menacing terms:

> Now the winch driver is not supposed to hang a load over the men working in the square of the hatch, well, just listen to that man, (the boss) holler 'come in with it' while there are two loads landed in one section and the men are flooring off. Safety rules don't mean anything if he can cheat the men out of a half-hour's pay. I wonder how he would like to work and have a load (very seldom less than two ton [sic]) hanging over his head. [He] hollers and shouts and makes the men very uneasy.[159]

With a clear electoral mandate, Franklin Delano Roosevelt hit the ground running after he was inaugurated in March 1933, signing into law the National Industrial Recovery Act, or NIRA, just three months later. The NIRA asserted workers' rights to collectively negotiate terms of employment with their employer through the representative of their choice and specified minimum wages for each geographic region. Boycotts reappeared almost overnight; the next year, 1.47 million workers took part in 1,856 work stoppages. But the NIRA actually worsened working conditions for Blacks; rather than pay Negroes the higher wage, employers merely fired them and replaced them with whites. Within two months of the law's passage, Blacks were referring to the federal agency that managed the NIRA, the National Recovery Administration, as the "Negro Removal Act."

Six months before the passage of the NIRA, the CPUSA published its first edition of the *Waterfront Worker*, and much like the *Southern Worker* did for Alabama's laborers, it helped maritime workers begin to construct a class identity that was separate and apart from their tribal clan. Written anonymously by "Rank and File Stevedores," the newsletter turned hidebound media narratives on their head, valorizing the besieged longshoremen, or "the boys," and portraying the bosses and the union leaders as lazy, corrupt, "slave drivers" who "feathered their nests" through the sweat and blood of others.[160] In stark contrast to Jennett's race-baiting cartoons in North Carolina in 1898, the *Waterfront Worker* published cartoons of Black and white unionists standing together underneath the banner "Solidarity."

Circulated by hand, the *Waterfront Worker* excoriated the corrupt leadership of the American Federation of Labor—which most employees agreed was in bed with management—and ginned up support to form an ILA local, albeit one controlled by the rank and file rather than the AFL's leadership.

Three factions competed for control of the local that was beginning to take shape: a moderate, Catholic bloc led by Lee Holman; a slightly more progressive faction; and the most radical grouping, led by a cadre of communists that included an Australian longshoreman and former Wobbly by the name of Harry Bridges.

Named for their meeting place in San Francisco's Mission District, the Albion Hall bloc distinguished itself through its *Waterfront Worker* editorials championing a vision for workplace democracy, a call for elections for rank-and-file union leadership, and perhaps most importantly, direct action on the docks including work slowdowns and stoppages. When four longshoremen were effectively fired for their union activities, the Albion Hall camp organized a strike of nearly 150 dockworkers. The blacklisted workers were eventually reinstated, and Albion Hall grew both in stature and membership.

Under pressure, the employers raised hourly wages by a dime to 85 cents plus $1.25 for each overtime hour in December 1933, but that fell well short of the demands agreed upon three months later by 14,000 longshoremen who attended a San Francisco convention. While the Holman faction won most of the seats on the new union's executive committee, it was the Albion Hall bloc that captured the delegates' imagination with proposals calling for a $1-an-hour wage, 30-hour workweeks, coastwide contracts, unemployment insurance, a resolution against working ships flying the Nazi flag, and most importantly, a union hiring hall.[161] Calling the dockworkers a "bunch of communists,"[162] the shipowners flatly rejected their proposals. Officials from the ILA's New York office hijacked the ensuing talks, unsuccessfully pressuring the rank-and-file to agree to a plan in which the waterfront bosses recognized the longshoremen's union, but not their unquestioned authority over the hiring hall. Said Bridges:

> Settlement for mere recognition may mean a lot to national heads of the International Longshoremen's Association who get fat salaries. But the workers are going to hold out for nothing less than a closed shop.[163]

By April 29, it had become clear to the longshoremen that the shipowners were dragging their feet, and they gave the ILA bigwigs until May 9 to hammer out a deal or else they planned to strike.

To prevent employers from resorting to their old tactics of recruiting Blacks as strikebreakers, Albion Hall went on the offensive, quickly dispatching the timid Holman (who was later found to have mob ties) and his team from the Executive Board, rounding up support for a strike, and addressing the 800-pound elephant in the room, which was that the only way for the ILA to win a labor stoppage was to admit Blacks into their shop and prevent them from crossing the picket line.

The relationship, historically, between white and Black workers in the U.S. approximates a mating ritual or teenage courtship of a kind depicted in a 1940s Mickey Rooney film. In the role of the smitten bobbysoxer are African Americans who have futilely pursued whites to join them on the picket lines until a crisis spurs a moment of clarity, and the white working class comes-a-courting those they had spurned earlier. The Great Depression marked just such an epiphany for the white worker who began to woo the Black cohort like his life depended on it. With his similar slight frame, Bridges reprised Mahone's role as a coalition-builder in Virginia 50 years earlier. According to the African American journalist, Thomas Fleming, co-founder of the Bay Area's Black weekly newspaper, the *Sun-Reporter*:

> Bridges went to black churches on both sides of San Francisco Bay and asked the ministers: could he say a few words during the Sunday services? He begged the congregation to join the strikers on the picket line, and promised that when the strike ended, blacks would work on every dock on the West Coast.

Two Blacks were appointed to the strike committee headed by Bridges, and whites and Blacks collaborated in outreach efforts on the docks as well as in the broader African American community. Their most high-profile convert was the union organizer C.L. Dellums—uncle of the future Congressman and Oakland Mayor Ron Dellums—of the Sleeping Car Porters Union who helped discourage Blacks from crossing the picket line. Recounting the initial awkwardness of the nascent rainbow coalition, Dellums recalled one meeting:

> There was a white man and a Negro running the meeting. . . . They whispered and told me to sit down, that I couldn't take the floor, I couldn't speak. So I turned to the crowd and said 'Most of you fellows know me by sight. I am C.L. Dellums. I want to speak to you. . . . If you want to hear what I have to say, make this guy shut up and let me talk.' And so they did. . . . So I gave them a good rabble-rousing. I gave them first a good educational talk on labor and civil

> rights where we had so much in common. Then I asked them to give me their word, and I told them, 'I know you'll keep your word with me, I always keep mine with you. Give me your word you will not break the strike, all who will stand.' And they stood almost to the man. So I said 'Ok, since we're not going to break the strike, the meeting is over. Let's get the hell out of here.'[164]

With that, the battle lines were sharply drawn: On one side was the community, which included a women's auxiliary comprised mostly of the longshoremen's wives, the unemployed councils, small farmers from the area who donated food, and the San Francisco branch of the International Labor Defense, whose primary representative, Elaine Black Yoneda, was known as the Red Angel for the aid she provided the burgeoning unionists. On the other side was the Chamber of Commerce, the AFL bureaucrats with the Teamsters and New York-based International Longshoremen's Association, local politicians such as San Francisco Mayor Angelo Rossi, and the newspapers, including two owned by William Randolph Hearst in which the shippers were major investors.

On May 9th at 8 p.m., longshoremen walked off the job at all Pacific Coast ports between Seattle and San Diego and within two days, the strike clogged up nearly 2,000 miles of coastline.

In addition to "help wanted" ads calling for scabs, the shipowners published an advertisement in the newspapers. Addressed to the longshoremen, it read:

> We want to pay you as good wages as the industry can afford. We always have paid top wages—and hope to keep it up. Recovery is not yet here—it is only on the way. You are hurting, not helping, to bring it back for yourselves, for us, and for San Francisco. It is an ill-advised strike. Be reasonable!

As the strike went on, rank-and-file Teamsters and seamen joined longshoremen on the picket line in a gesture of solidarity, and the Boilermakers and Machinists Union boycotted all ships worked by scabs. San Francisco's Embarcadero began to resemble a war zone as skirmishes between police and pickets broke out sporadically. With the strike's third month approaching, shipowners were beginning to feel the pinch. Nearly 100 ships were tied up in San Francisco's ports, leaving tons of perishables to rot in the summer sun. In Alaska, salmon season was beginning and the work stoppage left canneries without the supply they needed to fill orders. A few Blacks seized on the opportunity to earn a paycheck, but the strike held. The bosses' attempt to forcibly reopen the port on July 2nd was turned back by 8,000 combative strikers.

The port was closed for Independence Day, but hostilities resumed when shippers again tried to reopen the ports on July 5th. The police shot three strikers, two fatally: Nick Coundeorakis, who went by the alias Nick Bordoise, was an active CPUSA member, and had been shot in the back; Howard Sperry was a longshoreman and World War I veteran.

Mayor Rossi ignored Bridges' plea to call off the police and the fighting continued throughout the day, while a fleet of ten ramshackle trucks continued to haul freight from the docks to a makeshift warehouse. Governor Frank Merriam declared a state of emergency and summoned the National Guard to the Embarcadero. Strikers named the clash "Bloody Thursday."

That weekend, the bodies of the dead lay in wake at the ILA headquarters, where thousands gathered to pay their respects. Thousands more marched alongside the trucks in a solemn funeral procession the following week with yet thousands more lining the streets. With the dead buried, Bridges lobbied the Bay Area's workforce for a general strike.

By a margin of 1,220 to 271, the city's largest union local, the Teamsters, voted for a general strike if maritime workers had not approved a contract by July 12.[165] Twenty other unions followed suit, some unanimously.

On the morning of July 16th, 1934, the general strike officially began with thousands walking off the job. Mom-and-pop stores closed as did bars, nightclubs and liquor stores; the big department stores remained open, as did a handful of restaurants to serve the emergency personnel who remained on the job.

Hastily scribbled signs and placards in the windows of most small shops and restaurants read:

"CLOSED TILL THE BOYS WIN";
or
WE'RE WITH YOU FELLOWS.
STICK IT OUT;
or
CLOSED TILL THE LONGSHOREMEN GET THEIR HIRING HALL;
or
"CLOSED. ILA SYMPATHIZER."[166]

The desertion of the bustling city by its workforce sparked employers and civic officials to claim, absurdly, that the shutdown was a Soviet attempt to annex San Francisco. Shipowners and California politicians continued to inundate the public with anti-labor messages, and even appealed to President Roosevelt to intervene. With Roosevelt vacationing, the decision was left to Labor Secretary Frances Perkins, who counseled the cabinet that "shooting it out with working people" would not be a good look for the administration.[167]

Self-proclaimed "rank-and-file" journalist Mike Quinn's masterful account, *The Big Strike*, provides a textbook example of reportage and storytelling and illustrates, with startling clarity, the failures of a modern news media that centers on the authority of pundits like Rachel Maddow, Tucker Carlson, and Glenn Greenwald rather than the agency of the people who literally make history. Listen:

> An uncanny quiet settled over the acres of buildings. For all practical purposes not a wheel moved nor a lever budged. The din of commercial activity gave way to a murmur of voices in the streets.
>
> Along the Embarcadero and in front of the National Guard Armory self-conscious-looking schoolboys wearing steel helmets and ill-fitting khaki uniforms paced up and down fingering heavy automatic rifles.
>
> Highways leading out of the city bore a continuous stream of expensive cars carrying well-to-do refugees to distant sanctuaries. They were fleeing from bombs and rioting mobs.
>
> There were no bombs.
>
> There were no rioting mobs.
>
> These existed only in the pages of the daily press which characterized the event as a Bolshevik revolution, and conjured up visions of tempestuous throngs sweeping, torch in hand, through the city streets.
>
> Telephone and telegraph wires burned like an inflamed nervous system.
>
> Unconvinced pedestrians bought copies of newspapers whose headlines exceeded the signing of the Armistice. These papers declared that the city was in control of communists who were threatening bloodshed and ruin. In residential sections some uninformed citizens were frightened out of their wits; they barricaded their doors and trembled in expectation of chaos.
>
> But the people, in general, were unimpressed by headlines that screamed of communist violence. They knew better. They could look around and see for themselves that the General Strike was disciplined and orderly. Mobs and

bombs had no part in it.

The 83-day strike ended with the longshoremen reluctantly agreeing to arbitration, resulting in a coastwide contract, wage increases, a reduction in work shift hours, and a hiring hall that was jointly controlled by the employers and the union but with a dispatcher chosen by the union who effectively tipped the balance of power in favor of the employees. The arrangement meant that the companies could not discriminate against workers who were blacklisted because of their union work, or Black longshoremen.

As part of the deal, African Americans insisted on a "last-shall-be-first" hiring process in which longshoremen who had gone jobless the longest moved automatically to the front of the line the next shift. The historian Philip S. Foner quoted a dockworker saying:

> Negro-white unity has proved to be the most effective weapon against the shipowners, against the raiders and all our enemies.[168]

Spurred by strikes in Minneapolis and Toledo the same year as the West Coast boycott, Congress passed the Wagner Act in 1935, strengthening workers' rights to organize. But it was the dockworkers' strike that formed the template for the Congress of Industrial Organizations, or CIO, which denounced racial discrimination at its founding convention the following year.

Bridges was hounded by immigration agents who tried to deport him almost until his death at the age of 88 in 1990. In his monthly newsletter to the rank and file, he once wrote:

> Discrimination against Negroes is anti-labor, anti-American, and anti-white.

On another occasion, he wrote:

> Obstacles standing out like mountains—this defines the

> racial prejudices, which have been so carefully guarded by the capitalist groups down through the ages. White trash will never agree to work with colored folks and the Negro must not attempt to introduce his presence into a group of white worker[s.] Just how carefully the employers have guarded these untrue statements has been revealed in the recent Pacific Coast strike . . . There is just one fence—the minority group of capitalists on the one side; the workers including all casts and creeds on the other, with the power of the majority group.[169]

A Black longshoreman named Cleophas Williams recalled a union meeting near the end of World War II:

> One of the old-timers asked Harry when the war is over what are you gonna do about these black guys who have come here to take our jobs away from us? Harry said he wished we had a system where we could have full employment for everybody but if things reached the point where only two workers were left on the waterfront, if he could make the decision, one would be a black man. I had never heard this kind of talk before.[170]

Testifying before Congress after the 1934 strike, Bridges offered a transcendent vision of industrial unionism:

> It's also a union that recognizes that from time to time it's got to stand up and fight for certain things that might not necessarily be just wages, hours and conditions: civil liberties, racial equality and things like that.[171]

As one example, African Americans looking for work in the shipyards during the war often found housing in San Francisco's Fillmore neighborhood. Invoking eminent domain, the city's redevelopment agency began razing thousands of "blighted" homes in the neighborhood shortly after the war ended, eventually forcing nearly 10,000, mostly Black households to relocate, and transforming Geary Street into an eight-lane monstrosity that sealed off the Fillmore from the whiter and wealthier Pacific Heights. Bridges' second-in-command at the rebranded International Longshore and Warehouse Union (ILWU), Lou Goldblatt, had a thought:

> There was no reason why the pension funds should just be laying around being invested in high-grade securities. I thought there was no reason why that money shouldn't be used to build some low-cost housing.[172]

The ILWU created the Longshore Redevelopment Corporation to pounce on the three city blocks—out of a total of 60—that the city had set aside for affordable housing construction. In her 1964 letter to the *San Francisco Chronicle,* Josephine Solomon described her new digs:

> I've just moved into my new home in St. Francis Square . . . and living here is quite clearly going to be exhilarating and, more important, the best possible place in which I can raise my children. About 100 families have already moved in . . . and we have representatives of all races and colors living together as neighbors. There is no more beautiful sight in this town than our marvelous, mixed-up collection of white, brown, and yellow children playing together in the sunny community square every afternoon.

7.
Giant Killers

The sun did not divide off a portion of its rays for one class and a portion for the other, a part for the white and a part for the blacks, but shone equally for everybody. All that grew on the earth and live in the seas were equally the property of all mankind as all were provided with the same organs, had the same necessities and required the same nourishment and sustenance.[173]

–Ramon Pagas
New Orleans Cigar Maker, 1893

East of the mountains, and west of the sea, Winston-Salem is less than an hour's drive from North Carolina's border with Virginia, and less than that from Mount Airy, the bucolic town that inspired *the Andy Griffith Show's* fictitious Mayberry. The city sits in a low-slung corridor of the Piedmont Plateau that stretches from central Alabama to upstate New York, intersected along the way by a network of streams and rivers, its soft, sandy soil vomiting up bountiful harvests in segments: cotton in the South, fruit orchards in the North, and tobacco from its midsection.

Winston-Salem is the belt buckle affixed to that midsection. The city and its environs sizzle in summer, freeze in winter and radiate in autumn with seemingly every color in the natural world, resembling the palette of a metaphysical painter, its colorful streetscapes of church steeples, lofts, and mills doused in a soft amber light. On the morning of June 17, 1943, a Thursday, the midsummer sun was beginning to heat up just as the employees of the R.J. Reynolds Tobacco Company reported to work for their 7:30 a.m. shift, Blacks spilling like raindrops from the buses, whites tumbling in clots from their cars, everyone filing through the factory gates marked "White Only" or "Colored."

By the time the Japanese attacked Pearl Harbor, R.J. Reynolds—the maker of the iconic Camel cigarette brand—operated the world's largest tobacco manufacturing plant, and along with the global leader in diamond production, South Africa's De Beers Group, the company would go on to pioneer the practice of product placement, encouraging—and by some accounts even paying—Hollywood producers to include their merchandise in film scenes, perhaps as a background prop or small plot device. Ironically, the business model for both companies was based on the exploitation of overworked, low-wage Black workers, De Beers in fetid underground African mines and R.J. Reynolds in its sweltering North Carolina leaf houses, which employed approximately 12,000 employees year-round, two-thirds of whom were African American and half women. In the slowest of times, the Reynolds plant resembled a slave plantation with whites manning practically all of the supervisory jobs and operating the heavy equipment. In May 1943, with laborers in short supply and wartime demand for tobacco products soaring—the Pentagon purchased 20 percent of the company's products for its soldiers—Reynolds' management sped up production and increased quotas across the shop floor.

Ranging in age from 16 to 60, African American women were the linchpins of the cigarette manufacturing process, responsible for virtually all "stemming" at the plant, which is the critical step in reconfiguring aged tobacco leaves into cigarettes, smoking and chewing tobacco. Until the mid-1930s, stemming was done entirely by hand; by 1943 however, most stemmers worked on a machine that, like the cotton gin, separated the leaf from the stem. According to the historian Robert Korstad's definitive account, *Civil Rights Unionism: Tobacco Workers and the Struggle for Democracy in the Mid-Twentieth-Century South*:

> Three women worked at each of the fifth floor's sixty-six stemming machines. Black women from the nearby casing room brought the tobacco to the machines in large boxes. One woman removed a 'hand' of tobacco from the box, untied it, and passed it on to a coworker who spread the leaves out on top of the machine. A third woman fed the tobacco onto a moving chain that carried it between two circular knives that cut the stem. Each job required dexterity and intense concentration. The room was hot, the work numbingly repetitive, and the dust from the leaf covered everyone from head to foot by the end of the day. The tobacco moved continuously, with the speed of the work in the stemmery geared to the needs of the manufacturing division it supplied.

In exchange for this back-breaking work, most women at the plant took home between $16 and $20 weekly, representing about half of what the federal government categorized as "subsistence" level in a city the size of Winston-Salem, with a population of 80,000.

Said one Reynolds employee, Geneva McClendon:

> We was catching so much hell in Reynolds that we had to do something. In the first place they gave you a great big workload, more than you could do. Instead of cutting down on the boxes of work, if the foreman discovered a box not tightly packed, he would roll it back to the casing room to be repacked. If you'd tell them they put too much work on you, they'd fire you. And then they stood over you and cussed you out about doing it: 'If you can't get this work out, get your clothes and get out.' . . . Everybody would almost cry every day the way they would work you and talk to you.

> Working conditions was so bad that you needed God and a union.[174]

Finally, she said:

> It got so we wasn't going to take it any more; we had had it.

Recalling the straw that broke the camel's back (pun very much intended) on that June morning in 1943, an African American stemmer in Reynolds' Plant Number 65, Theodosia Simpson, said:

> The lady who worked on the machine next to me, she was a widow with five kids, and she was sick that day. Oh, you could get sick up there in a minute, the way you had to work. She couldn't keep up with her work. . . . The foreman came up and told her that if she didn't catch up, 'there was the door that the carpenter left.' She started crying because she had these children to rear and nobody working but her. And that sort of got next to me. I called a couple of people I thought I could trust 'down house,' down to the lavatory. I said, 'When we come in here tomorrow, let's not work until we get some understanding on how these people are going to be treated.[175]

Somehow, a white foreman got wind of the women's plans. "He came around telling everybody, 'We hear there's going to be a work stoppage. You better not do that. You'll lose your job,'" said Geneva McClendon. "And that frightened a few people. So at lunchtime we got together, and decided instead of doing it tomorrow morning, let's do it after lunch."

A Black man who worked in the adjoining casing room, Leon Edwards, said the women told co-workers beforehand about the plan they'd hatched. "They said, 'We want you all to stick with us,' and when they returned from their lunch break, they executed their plan like an elite squadron of commandos." The company, Edwards said, "had a little whistle they'd blow (when it was time to start work) and when that whistle went 'whwhwh,' them women about-faced just the same as if they were in the army. Everyone turned their back to the machine. You [never saw] anybody turn so quick."

Said McClendon:

> The foreman looked at us as if we were crazy. He pulled the whistle again and nobody moved. He asked what was wrong. Several of us told him that we weren't going to work until our working conditions improved, our workload cut to where we could get our work out, and we wanted our wages equalized. The foreman said he couldn't do nothing and if we didn't want to work to get out. We told him we wanted to work but not under these conditions and if he couldn't do nothing we would like to talk to the person that did have the authority to remedy the situation.

It was at this point that a 38-year-old African American man, James McCardell, who had worked for 15 years in the casing room, spoke up. "If these women'll stand up for their rights, I'm with them."

And with that he crashed to the floor, dead, from a cerebral hemorrhage, doctors would later determine. He'd been sick that entire week, his co-workers said, but each time he went to the on-site nurse, she would say she could find nothing wrong and send him back to work.

McCardell's death was tantamount to throwing dry kindling on a bonfire. Refusing to return to their stations, the stemmers shouted down the head foreman, laying the responsibility for McCardell's death squarely at the feet of abusive managers. The supply of stemmed tobacco that typically dropped from fifth-floor tables to the fourth came to a halt, idling 198 employees on the fourth floor and 25 on the third. As the women waited, the strike leaders passed instructions:

> 'Sit right there, don't move.' And: 'Just stay there until time to go home. If you've got to go to the bathroom, go to the bathroom, come right back on your job.'

Within minutes the overwhelmed foreman had summoned the bigwigs, chief among them John C. Whitaker, vice president in charge of manufacturing. "We told him that we were tired of the workload," said McClendon, "tired of the bosses standing over us with a whip in his hand. We wanted better working conditions, and we wanted more money."

Whitaker then took the floor, playing good cop to the bullying foreman's bad cop. In a commanding yet non-combative voice, he addressed the strikers:

> Let me first remind you of the very important responsibility we all have to maintain production during this very crucial period of the war. Neither you nor I want to have our boys overseas think badly of our effort here in Winston-Salem. I know you have some grievances, and I want you to tell me about them so that the company can study them and make some changes where they are necessary. I want you to remember, however, that this is a very large company, and many different people make demands on our time and resources. Your demands are part of that, but so are the workers over in Number 12, or the stockholders who furnish us with the capital to operate.[176]

Nonplussed, the women elliptically reiterated their grievances:

> 'We can't work this hard.'
>
> 'I don't make enough money to give my family a decent meal.'
>
> 'We're tired of those foremen treating us like dirt.'

Whitaker took the floor again, reassuring the women that the company would look into their complaints but reminded them that wartime price controls were in effect; a pay raise would require approval from the federal government.

And with that Whitaker had broken the first rule of warfare, class or otherwise: He underestimated the enemy.

"Mr. Whitaker," Theodosia Simpson interjected, "according to the Little Steel formula you can give us a wage increase."

"Who told you about the Little Steel formula?" Whitaker snapped.

"Whether you know it or not, I can read and I can think. It's been in all the newspapers."

"I don't know anything about the Little Steel formula, but I'll have the company attorneys look into it."

"Well, you start talking to them about that wage increase," Simpson said, and continued to light into Whitaker about the foreman's abuse of the ailing widow. The other women chimed in and the exchange resembled an African ritual in which women villagers gather in a circle around the tribal chief and articulate a laundry list of complaints to be addressed if the chief has any plans to retain his position. It was at this point that Whitaker made his second mistake, telling the employees to form a select committee to meet with him the next morning. No sooner had Whitaker left the room than the men who moved the tobacco and cleaned floors joined with the women stemmers to appoint a committee with Simpson as its chairperson.

Almost a year had passed since the United Cannery, Agricultural, Packing, and Affiliated Workers of America, or Cannery Workers Union, had created an exploratory group, the Tobacco Workers Organizing Committee, to lay the groundwork for unionizing Reynolds. In the intervening months, the TWOC had steadily been signing up disgruntled Reynolds employees who were emboldened by frequent newspaper accounts of miners, rubber and autoworkers walking off the job to demand—and often winning—higher wages and better working conditions. Most of those unions in the news belonged to the same Congress of Industrial Organizations that had spearheaded the triumphant 1934 general strike in San Francisco.

So, too, did the Cannery Workers Union, which had organized the Reynolds' working group.

Said Geneva McClendon:

> Every worker should be in a union. In the union you take

> the whip out of the boss's hand. I knew about unions from reading newspapers and the pamphlets. I read about the benefits the unions had gotten. I figured the CIO was a good union.[177]

News of the afternoon's uprising in Plant 65 spread quickly to other buildings. Simpson and McClendon left work and made a beeline for the Cannery Workers Union offices to confer with organizers William DeBerry and Frank Hargrove. Wrote Korstad:

> DeBerry and Hargrove were excited. Months of meetings, discussions, and training had paid off. The union had neither planned nor foreseen the protest in Number 65, but solid preparation had carried the sit-down in its direction. TWOC members had been in the forefront of the action, and they were among the most articulate workers and quick-witted leaders. Their tactical maneuvering and articulation of workers' grievances had transformed the protest into a sit-down strike.
>
> Still, organizers for the Cannery Workers Union found themselves in a quandary. The union supported the 'no strike pledge' taken by the CIO for the duration of the war. It was important, therefore, to try to arrange a settlement so that production of tobacco, which was considered a vital war commodity, could be resumed. At the same time, the sit-down presented a great opportunity to bring more people into the union.

Dozens of Reynolds' employees attended a Tobacco Workers Organizing Committee meeting held at Winston-Salem's Union Mission Holy Church that evening to strategize next steps. DeBerry and Hargrove stressed the importance of solidarity.

> If you go to them one at a time you might get fired, but if you stick together, they're not going to fire you.

A sense of foreboding washed over the city as Reynolds' employees filed into work the following morning. Referring to Theodosia as "[t]he Simpson woman," a story in the *Winston-Salem Journal* reported on the sit-down strike in Number 65 and the scheduled meeting between management and employees demanding pay raises and a reduced workload. But something was clearly amiss when the employees reached the entrance of the largest stemmeries. Wrote Korstad:

> Instead of entering one by one, they stopped. They whispered among themselves, passing the word. Then they made their way to the dressing rooms, changed clothes, and streamed out onto the plant floor. Sixteen hundred women took up their positions. The whistle blew, but all but a few stood stiffly still. Quickly the few machines that had started screeched to a halt. An eerie silence fell. When the superintendent came out, a TWOC spokeswoman stepped forward to say that the company's problems were not limited to Number 65. Workers in Number 60 also had grievances; they too wanted a face-to-face meeting with the executives over in the Reynolds building. And they demanded that the company allow Robert "Chick" Black to help them present their demands.[178]

Known for his fearlessness, honesty, and charisma, Black was one of the Tobacco Workers Organizing Committee's earliest recruits. He worked in a "secret" department that cut tobacco leaf stems into fine pieces for use in cigarettes and smoking tobacco, a bit like a slaughterhouse using meat scraps to make sausage. His wife, Minnie, worked as a stemmer in Plant Number 60. Black refused Whitaker's entreaties to coax the women to return to work.

> Now, Mr. Whitaker, you want me to go over there and speak for the company. I'm not going to do that. I've got a wife working over there. Just to let you know how I feel about it, we're going to close down this plant. I think it's wrong for me working in Number 64, with my wife over in Number 60 trying to better her condition with all those

> other people. I'm going to send word up and down this five-floor factory and in thirty minutes we'll have everyone of those machines at a standstill.

And just to show he meant business, Black walked over to a co-worker and instructed him to have the men cut off the machines. Within 20 minutes, there wasn't a single machine running in the entire building.

Reprising his remarks to the women in Number 65 a day earlier, Whitaker appealed to Black's sense of patriotism, reminding him of the soldiers, far from home, relying on the plant's workforce to produce their smokes. He mentioned Black's unblemished work record and questioned whether he wanted to squander the goodwill he'd accumulated over the years on such a quixotic gesture. Black refused to budge, agreeing only to instruct the men on his floor to finish processing the stems before walking out because there was a risk of fire if they were allowed to sit for a full weekend.

Meanwhile, Theodosia Simpson's committee from Number 65 waited for Whitaker with their list of demands. Preoccupied with the factory-wide boycott, he never came, leaving the women in Number 65 with no good reason to return to work; and their co-workers followed suit. By early afternoon, thousands of Black workers were on the streets outside the factory gates, milling around, chatting. "The thing that really hurt Reynolds," Black would say later, "was these workers, none of them went home. They were just out in the streets. Out on the company's premises. That was really embarrassing for the company. Everybody knew."

As the employees began to leave, TWOC members waited outside the gates with union cards. Hundreds signed up on the spot. Black addressed one group of women from Number 60:

> If you want to pin a contract on the company, I can't promise you anything, but if you stick together and don't let

> the company intimidate you, we'll build a union in Reynolds.

In July 1935, President Roosevelt signed into law the National Labor Relations Act, recognizing employees' right to bargain collectively with their employers. Named for the U.S. senator from New York—first name Robert—who sponsored the bill, the Wagner Act required employers to bargain in good faith with any local supported by a majority of their employees and established the rules governing union certification. The fledgling CIO wasted no time, launching the biggest organizing campaign in U.S. history in the hopes of unseating the AFL as the labor movement's powerhouse institution.

This was ambitious but hardly impossible. The CIO had, to some extent, demonstrated its organizing chops with the successful 1934 West Coast longshoremen's strike that opened the doors of the house of labor to all workers, regardless of race. This was consistent with the big-tent approach of the Knights of Labor and the Wobblies but in stark contrast to the American Federation of Labor's exclusionary policies. Formed in 1886—the same year the Knights were scandalized at Chicago's Haymarket Square—the AFL was a loose grouping of craft unions, led for its first 38 years by a New York cigar-maker named Samuel Gompers, whose narrow view of trade unionism defied both common sense and math in limiting membership to white craft workers and steering clear of larger political concerns to focus strictly on paycheck issues. Gompers' conservative ideology survived his death in 1924, and even amid the Great Depression, the federation continued to organize only skilled tradesmen, leaving unorganized huge swaths of unskilled employees in critical industries such as steel, auto, rubber, and meatpacking.

Symbolic of the AFL's antagonistic relationship with African American workers, several of the militant Black longshoremen who had participated in the 1934 San Francisco general strike joined local Negro leaders in picketing the trade union's 1935 national convention in Atlantic City with signs reading: "Labor Cannot Be Free While Black Labor Is Enslaved" and "White Unions Make Black Scabs." Despite their stated commitment to organize workers regardless of color, however, the AFL rebuffed even modest proposals for reform made by delegates as eminent as A. Philip Randolph. That was the last straw for African Americans who simply could not afford to wait any longer.

Two years in, the New Deal had begun to lift millions of whites out of poverty, but Blacks continued to suffer horribly. The winter and spring of 1935 were especially bleak; in Pittsburgh, for example, nearly three of every five Negroes remained on the relief rolls, and in Harlem, more than 43 percent of the 56,157 Negro households were on the dole.[179] Said James W. Ford, secretary of the Communist Party's Harlem section:

> The masses live on the brink of starvation. Disease and pestilence stalk the community. Police brutality drives the people to the point of desperation.[180]

On March 19th, 1935, Harlem exploded, resulting in the deaths of three Blacks at the hands of the police and $2 million in property damage. The news media unimaginatively dubbed the disturbance the "Black Ides of March," attributing the violence to "Communist agitation." The pastor at Harlem's Abyssinian Baptist Church, Adam Clayton Powell Jr., disagreed:

> It was not a riot, it was an open, unorganized protest against empty stomachs, overcrowded tenements, filthy sanitation, rotten foodstuffs, chiseling landlords and merchants, discrimination in relief, disfranchisement, and against a disinterested administration.[181]

Led by a bushy-eyebrowed ex-miner, John Lewis, the CIO's leadership saw unskilled labor as its sweet spot and the African American worker as the centerpiece of a new workers' movement that would be able to stand up for itself on shop floors across the country. Lewis himself made no bones about this, hiring known communists as organizers because of the party's strong relationship with the Black working class, as demonstrated by their handling of the Scottsboro case, and the San Francisco dockworkers' strike. The CIO's strategy was a tacit acknowledgment that the white working class could not prosper absent Black participation. African Americans at the time accounted for 8.5 percent of all iron and steel workers, 17 percent of the workforce in the nation's abattoirs and packinghouses, 9 percent of all coal miners, and a whopping 68 percent of tobacco workers in North Carolina, Virginia, and Kentucky.

Because of their checkered experience with the AFL, however, African American workers initially expressed ambivalence towards the newly formed CIO. Community leaders in the NAACP, Urban League, and many Black churches were slow to embrace the new industrial union, in no small part because of their relationships with employers and donors who were fiercely opposed to organized labor. At the NAACP's 1936 convention in Detroit, several local African American ministers who received financial support from Henry Ford opposed a motion to invite CIO representatives to address conferees, instead adopting a resolution urging Blacks to "go into no labor organization blindly but . . . instead appraise critically the motives and practices of all labor unions and . . . bear their full share of activity and responsibility in building a more just and more intelligent labor union."[182]

Such equivocations provoked a scorching reproach from the African American journalist George S. Schuyler, who accused "educated Negroes" of abandoning "the struggling Negro workers," singling out African American preachers for openly "siding with the employers," and even recruiting strike-breakers "to take the jobs of Black unionists."[183]

Serendipitously, more than 250 Black leaders—chief among them Randolph, Dr. Alaine Locke and Dr. Ralph Bunche of Howard University, and the poet Langston Hughes—called for a "united front of all Negro organizations," at the opening session of the National Negro Congress on Valentine's Day, 1936 in Chicago. Chosen the organization's first president, Randolph stressed to the more than 800 delegates the obsolescence of craft unionism, and counseled members to "seek to broaden and intensify the movement to draw Negro workers into labor organizations and break down the color bar in the trade unions that now have it."

Combined with other Black militants working under the auspices of groups such as the Southern Youth Congress and the Workers' Alliance, the National Negro Congress played a key role in helping the CIO win support from African Americans, especially in the South. In June 1936, the CIO replaced the ineffective Amalgamated Association of Iron, Steel and Tin Workers with the Steel Workers Organizing Committee, or SWOC, and named the United Mine Workers Vice President Philip Murray as chairman, and his colleague at the UMW, William Mitch, to head the Southern region. This was not, to put it mildly, Mitch's first rodeo; he had led the expansion of Alabama's two UMW locals from 225 members in 1933 to 23,000, two years later. African Americans accounted for 60 percent of the rank-and-file membership.

In doing so, Mitch had to overcome the Alabama press that labeled him a "carpetbagger," the Klan's outsized influence on white miners, and the Alabama State Federation of Labor, which described as communist a United Mine Workers' tradition requiring locals to be headed by a white president, secretary, and treasurer and a Black vice president. Mitch was one of 400 CIO organizers deployed in steel towns in Pennsylvania, Ohio, Illinois, and Alabama to organize more than 500,000 steel workers.

Industry bosses flooded newspapers with full-page red-baiting ads insisting that no "Godfearing, patriotic American worker" would sign up with "the emissaries from Moscow," and denouncing their opposition to "any attempt to compel its employees to join a union or to pay tribute for the right to work."[184]

Accounting for 20 percent of steelworkers nationwide, African Americans were typically hired for the worst and most dangerous jobs, for which they were paid between $16 and $22 a week. With support from the Black middle class, employers had turned back efforts to unionize the workforce during the tumultuous period after World War I, but the National Negro Congress was determined to offset the corrupting influences of an African American comprador class this time around. Congress co-founder John P. Davis wrote early in 1936: "There is no effort in which the National Negro Congress could possibly engage at this time more helpful to large numbers of Negro workers . . . than the organization of Negro steel workers. . . . 85,000 Negro steel workers with union cards will signal the beginning of the organization of all Negro workers."

Davis recommended to the CIO the names of a dozen Black organizers, some of whom were dues-paying communists. A United Mine Worker organizer for 35 years, James Hart, was instrumental in convincing Negro steel workers in Gary, Indiana, that the CIO "is not going to discriminate against Blacks."[185] A Black communist who led hunger marches for public relief on behalf of jobless workers, Benjamin Careathers, persuaded nearly 2,000, mostly African American steel workers in and around Pittsburgh to join the union. The Congress sent militias of volunteer organizers into the Black community to address local churches and clubs, and pressure African Americans to join, distributing, during the drive, more than a quarter of a million pro-union leaflets nationwide. Read a typical leaflet:

> We colored workers must join hands with our white brothers. . . to establish an organization . . . which shall deliver us from the clutches of the steel barons. We appeal to all colored workers in the steel mills to join the union.

Addressing a convention of the National Negro Congress in 1937, Philip Murray said:

> There is no other labor organization in this country that affords the Negro the same opportunity as do the great international and national unions affiliated with the CIO. I can conceive your situation—90 to 95 percent of our entire colored population poor. Thousands of them are undernourished and underprivileged. They have the same ideals and aspirations and the same hopes beating within their breasts that beat within the breast of a white man. Their wives and children have the same feelings and emotions and they are entitled by all the laws of nature itself to the same opportunity in the game of life as any white man. We tell you your economic and political salvation lies in assisting the CIO in the course of its activities . . . and I beseech your support and the support of your officers . . . in this great undertaking which the CIO has now begun.[186]

Ultimately, the combination of the Steel Workers Organizing Committee, the National Negro Congress, women's auxiliaries, and Black newspapers like *the Pittsburgh Courier* and *Chicago Defender* made a more compelling case *for* joining the CIO than industry executives made *against* it. Indeed, in some areas of Pittsburgh and Chicago, Black workers signed up in larger percentages than did white steel workers. One Black minister in Gary, Indiana, is reported to have told his parishioners after listening to a pitch from a Congress organizer working for the SWOC:

> I have always been against the AF of L and organized labor, but I am convinced that this CIO move is the only thing for my people. I want every steelworker of my church to sign up for this union. And . . . I want you . . . to sign up every steelworker you come into contact with in Chicago Heights. If anybody asks you what you are doing, tell them Rev. Pinkett told you to sign them up and he has God and the people with him.

On March 2nd, 1937, the U.S. Steel Corporation reached an agreement with the SWOC without the need for a strike. Within two weeks, the company raised wages by 10 percent and agreed to pay time and a half for overtime. Several smaller steel companies followed suit, and by the end of 1937, the SWOC had signed with about 450 employers. Bethlehem, Republic, Youngstown Sheet and Tube, and Inland—the "Little Steel" formula that Theodosia Simpson referenced in her confrontation with Whitaker—held out until 1941, by which time the SWOC was the sole bargaining agent for 550,000 steel workers, raising industry wages by a third, reducing working hours, and abolishing Jim Crow discriminatory practices where they were found.

For starters, Blacks accounted for only 4 percent of all autoworkers in 1940, 11,000 of whom were employed by Ford's mammoth River Rouge plant. Nearly half of the Blacks at River Rouge toiled in the backbreaking foundry rather than on the assembly lines or in the skilled trades, and yet, the relationship between Henry Ford and Detroit's Black community was complicated. What Ford didn't pay his employees he invested in goodwill, donating frequently to the city's Black churches and the NAACP, hosting high-profile Negro friends such as the scientist George Washington Carver at Ford's suburban laboratories, and hiring two Black personnel managers, unheard of at the time. It was not uncommon for eligible African American bachelors in the 1930s and 1940s to wear their Ford plant badges on their lapel while attending Sunday church service.

Conversely, Black autoworkers in the city typically had no relationship with their white co-workers, many of whom were born and bred in the South, and did not readily shed their hostilities towards Negroes, nor their memberships in organizations such as the Ku Klux Klan and the Black Legion. Chrysler tapped into racial divisions in 1939, hiring Black scabs to replace striking white employees, and it surfaced again in 1940, during the CIO organizing drive, when African American employees were reticent to join the union, continuing to work throughout a strike at the Ford plant in April 1941. The United Auto Workers redoubled their efforts to re-educate white workers and provide Black workers with viable alternatives to Ford's patronage. Foner describes a small Detroit plant organized by the UAW in 1936:

> Although blacks made up about 25 per cent of the working force, the local had refused to allow them to become members, defying international union representatives who pointed out that they were in violation of the UAW constitution. Eventually it became clear that the only way the local could win its demands from management was through a strike. It dawned on the white members that no strike could succeed with one-fourth of the workers in the shop barred from union membership. A committee of black workers was invited to discuss the recruitment of Negroes into the local. A spokesman for the blacks put it on the line: 'We represent most or all of the Negro workers in the plant. If we recommend that they join the union or participate in the strike, they will do so. We think we should be in the union and support the strike if one is necessary. We cannot recommend that unless we are guaranteed full membership privileges and equal consideration under the contract.' The response of the chairman of the meeting was immediate: 'Anything you want, brothers, just get in there and help us win the strike.' All the white auto workers present applauded the statement. Black workers came into the union and, a few weeks later, joined with the white members in the first of the auto workers' famous sitdown strikes. 'Negro and white workers sat down together in the plant,' an on-the-spot observer wrote, 'marched the picket line outside the plant, shared the food from the strike kitchen, and when the strike was won they had a victory dance.'

Cigarettes were introduced in the U.S. at roughly the same time that Henry Ford was born in 1863. Before the Civil War, tobacco in North

America was consumed almost entirely via cigars, or pipes, or as snuff. Skilled hand rollers could produce as many as 2,500 cigarettes in a day, but machines invented closer to the turn of the 20th century spit out up to 120,000 daily. In the four decades since reactionaries had begun their revolution against postwar workers' movements, factories that processed and manufactured tobacco had proven particularly impervious to unionization of a type that improved employees' working conditions and living standards. To consolidate racial capitalism, corporate monopolies combined with the AFL's timidity, the federal government's indifference and white workers' biases to create a separate low-wage labor market in the South that treated African Americans as guest workers rather than citizens. This financial arrangement so circumscribed consumer buying power that by 1938 President Franklin D. Roosevelt declared the Dirty South "the Nation's No. 1 economic problem."

Reynolds cut wages and sped up production schedules in 1927, prompting the AFL affiliate, the Tobacco Workers' International Union, or TWIU, to meekly send organizers to gauge the appetite for a union, causing a groundswell of Black and white employees to talk openly of unionizing. Reynolds dispatched with the effort rather easily, however, firing employees identified by spies in planning meetings. By some accounts, Reynolds fired 1,799 of its employees on a single day in 1928 and pressured local landlords to evict jobless workers if they fell behind on their rent. A boycott of Reynolds products organized by the toothless TWIU fell flat, as did their warnings to company management that it would be far better for them to deal with the devil it knew, the union, rather than the devil it didn't, the communists, who were lurking in the shadows.

While intended as a bluff to force Reynolds to the bargaining table, there was some truth to the TWIU's admonition. A year later, the Communist Party helped lead a protracted walkout at a textile mill in nearby Gastonia, N.C. The owners of the Loray Mill accused the organizers of "race mixing" and called in the National Guard to crush the strike. Gastonia's police chief and Ella May Wiggins—the striking workers' balladeer—were killed in the violent clashes.

The main difference between Gastonia's textile workers in 1929 and Winston-Salem's tobacco workers in 1943 was that in the latter the federal government leveled the playing field by asserting the legal rights of labor to organize and made explicit precisely what employers could and could not do to abridge those rights. And other New Deal initiatives—most notably the Fair Employment Practices Committee, or FEPC—had little direct authority, but provided Black workers with a platform from which they could tell their stories.

Following the June 17th standoff, the Cannery Workers Union quickly signed up 8,000 Reynolds employees—virtually all Black—organized a committee to negotiate with the management, and formally requested an election under the National Labor Relations Board.

For their part, management used lower-level supervisors to intimidate the rank and file and discourage white workers from joining. As the election approached, a company controlled—or yellow dog—union, the R. J. Reynolds Employees Association, appealed to the NLRB for a place on the ballot. Simultaneously, the Chamber of Commerce organized an Emergency Citizens Committee to fend off the union, warning that attempts to alter longstanding race relations would "likely lead to riots and bloodshed."

These defensive measures almost certainly would've won the day in the past, but with the National Labor Relations Board as a referee, the company's attempts to stall or divide the workers into bargaining units were denied. When local judges sought to delay the election, government attorneys remanded the case to federal court.

After months of delay, Reynolds' employees finally cast their ballots on December 16th and 17th, six months to the day after Plant 65 had sat down on the job. A few hours after the polls closed, an NLRB representative announced the tally: the CIO had won by a margin of more than two-to-one, 6,833 to 3,175.

Local 22 of the Food, Tobacco, Agricultural and Allied Workers union would go on to sign its first contract with Reynolds a year later. While fairly standard for CIO contracts, the pact was radical in the context of Winston-Salem's race relations, shifting power to the employees on the basis of seniority, formalized grievance procedures, and wage schedules. The contract did not attack segregation on the shop floor, per se—white workers continued to monopolize the better-paying jobs—but it empowered the 100 elected shop stewards who were, in the words of one union activist, the "most important people in the plant." Armed with an understanding of both their rights and responsibilities as spelled out in the contract, the shop stewards used the collective bargaining agreement to transform Reynolds' paternalistic traditions into "a bill of rights."

Perhaps just as importantly, the reconfiguration of relations on the Reynolds shop floor helped Winston-Salem's Black community reimagine itself as a political actor. Within months of signing a contract with Reynolds' management, the union hall, located only a few blocks from the Reynolds plant, hosted meetings, plays, musical performances, classes on labor history, Black history, and national and international news events. Local 22 sponsored softball leagues, checkers tournaments, sewing circles, and swimming clubs, and stocked a library that opened the world up to many Black workers, and a few whites as well.

Said one Local 22 activist, Viola Brown:

> You know, at that little library they [the city of Winston-Salem] had for us, you couldn't find any books on Negro history. They didn't have books by Aptheker, Dubois, or Frederick Douglass. But we had them at our library.

In stark contrast to the AFL's focus on paycheck issues, the CIO's vision of social transformation informed the 20th century's most radical and progressive movements. Local 22 registered thousands of voters, revitalized the NAACP's Winston-Salem chapter, and spearheaded the election of a Black minister to the city council, representing the first time that a Black candidate had outpolled a white opponent in the South since Reconstruction.

Led by African American women like Simpson and Local 22's President Moranda Smith, union activists called for low-income housing, price controls, unemployment compensation, and expanded educational opportunities. During the CIO's postwar organizing drive, dubbed "Operation Dixie," Local 22 helped organize an additional 10,000 leaf house workers in the Piedmont region.

As Robert Black would later recall:

> After we built our union, we told the people that just to build a union is not going to solve all of our problems. We have got to get control of the election system and get people in public office. . . . If you are going to defeat these people, not only do you do it across the negotiating table in the R.J. Reynolds Building, but you go to the city hall, you elect people down there that's going to be favorable and sympathetic and represent the best interest of the working class.[187]

8.
‘Cats is Cats’

Rise, like lions after slumber
In unvanquishable number!
Shake your chains to earth, like dew
Which in sleep had fallen on you:
Ye are many—they are few!

–Percy Bysshe Shelley

Filmed on the Salton Sea in southern California’s Mojave desert, the World War II thriller *Sahara* raked in more cash at the box office than any other movie released by Columbia Pictures in 1943. Feted by audiences and critics alike for its striking photography, strong performances, and pithy dialogue, *Sahara* starred Humphrey Bogart as a tough-as-nails tank commander named Joe Gunn who, in one suspenseful scene, sardonically reassures a Nazi prisoner that he needn’t worry about the African scout who is guarding him. “This man’s ancestors were men of culture and learning while yours were still crawling in the jungle on all fours.”

To the film critic, Joseph Foster, this was a revelation. He wrote:

> This Sudanese Scout, who is meant to represent all Negroes

> in the United Nations, assumes qualities of leadership never before accorded to a Negro in the films. Not only is he endowed with a knowing ability upon which the expedition depends for its safety, but he demonstrates the discipline of only the most responsible of leaders.

Of *Sahara's* screenwriter, John Howard Lawson, Foster wrote:

> His purpose was "to have the Negro serve as the symbol of democracy in the fight with captured Nazis. When the Nazi has to be disarmed, the Negro does it. . . . Again, when the Nazi escapes, the Sudanese goes after him, chokes him with his bare hands, and gives up his life in the effort.

Sahara was sandwiched between two films that showcased another Golden Age A-list actor, Myrna Loy, who had a penchant for lobbying studio executives to cast African Americans against type. In the 1940 romantic comedy, *Third Finger, Left Hand,* a Black train porter who is studying law by correspondence saves the day for the newlywed couple played by Loy and her co-star, Melvyn Douglas. In another Loy vehicle released in 1948, *Mr. Blandings Builds His Dream House*, it's the African American maid, Gussie, played by Louise Beavers, who comes up with the advertising slogan that has eluded her distracted boss, an agency account executive played by Cary Grant. Known primarily for her role as Nora Charles opposite William Powell in the *Thin Man* franchise, Loy had once asked her bosses at the MGM studio:

> Why does every black person in the movies have to play a servant? How about a black person walking up the steps of a courthouse carrying a briefcase?[188]

In tandem with the CIO's frenetic energy, the country's ingress into war abroad sparked a reconsideration of the class struggle by its discontents at home. Eager to avoid a recurrence of the repression that followed the First World War, millions of Blacks exuberantly embraced the "Double V" public relations campaign launched by what was at the time the nation's largest Black newspaper, *the Pittsburgh Courier*, urging victories over fascist enemies both foreign (the Axis powers) and domestic (Jim Crow). This odd blend of jingoism and justice seemed to augur the coming of an American Spring, and the changing of the season infected an ample number of whites with a class consciousness resembling that displayed by the Bolsheviks who were outraged by their drunken countryman's racist mistreatment of Harry Haywood aboard a Moscow streetcar.

When a 1942 tax default transferred ownership of the massive Shriners Temple to New York City, the mostly Jewish Clothing, Garment and Musicians union and a Jewish workers' fraternal organization, the Workmen's Circle, loaned Mayor Fiorello LaGuardia the money to convert the shuttered Midtown rotunda into the City Center for Music and Drama, which would go on to house the New York City Opera Company. With a top ticket price of only two bucks—less than a third of what the Metropolitan Opera charged for an orchestra seat at the time—the City Opera Company was an innovator, hiring young American singers who had not yet achieved international reputations. One such artist was Todd Duncan, whose debut in September 1945 was the first time a major opera company in the U.S. featured a Black performer in a leading role. Four years later, the Harlem Renaissance composer, William Grant Still, premiered his composition about the Haitian revolutionary Jean-Jacques Dessalines, *Troubled Island*, representing the first time a grand opera written by an African American was produced by a major theater company.

Likewise, when fans in Cincinnati heckled Major League Baseball's first African American player, Jackie Robinson, during a 1947 game, his white Brooklyn Dodgers teammate, shortstop Pee Wee Reese, a Southerner, walked calmly over to the second baseman, put his arm around him, and offered words of encouragement, in a gesture that was at once simple and seismic.[189] A few years later, Jack Kerouac, Allen Ginsberg, William S.

Burroughs, Neal Cassady and Lawrence Ferlinghetti were struggling, young writers who spent their days pumping out poems and novels that they couldn't get published, and their nights commiserating in Greenwich Village, listening to jazz, drinking, smoking weed and popping pills. Finally, one night, after a particularly rousing set by Charlie "Bird" Parker, someone in the group—some say it was Kerouac, others Cassady—had an epiphany, and posed the question to his chums: "What if we try to write the way that Bird sounds?" The young writers found their voice that night, and of course, went on to become the Beat Poets, who were as acclaimed as any writers in 20th century American literature. The jazz trumpeter Clark Terry seemed to sum up the ethos of the day. When criticized by Black jazz musicians for employing so many whites, Terry shrugged, saying simply:

> Cats is cats.

In his booklet published in 1976, *The Fate of Empires*, the retired British commander of Jordan's Arab Legion, General John Glubb, theorized that all empires in history experienced six cycles, usually occurring over a period of roughly 250 years: the Age of Pioneers; the Age of Conquests; the Age of Commerce; the Age of Affluence; the Age of Intellect; and the Age of Decadence and Decline. Traumatized by the violent interwar years and the Japanese assault on Pearl Harbor, Americans were searching their souls and discovering, at long last, their blues, their voice, and their love of revolution.

Wrote a white Flint housewife in the aftermath of the triumphant 1936-7 General Motors sit-down strike:

> I found a common understanding and unselfishness that I'd never known in my life. I'm living for the first time with a definite goal. Just being a woman isn't enough anymore. I want to be a woman with the right to think for myself.[190]

Such epiphanies were the capstone of an American Enlightenment that began to liberate the production of knowledge and art from political mandates. A nation's evolving truths increasingly found expression in song, poetry, literature, murals, theaters and perhaps most profoundly on the silver screen, hailed by no less an authority than Vladimir Lenin as the most revolutionary of art forms. In his book, *Bright Boulevards, Bold Dreams: The Story of Black Hollywood*, the historian Donald Bogle wrote:

> Heading a special wartime filmmaking division, director Frank Capra worked with the young black scriptwriter Carlton Moss to create *The Negro Soldier*, a tribute to the contributions of black military personnel throughout the nation's history. Another tribute, *The Negro Sailor*, was also filmed.
>
> The NAACP's executive secretary, Walter White, became more vocal about the inequities on-screen. On two occasions, White traveled to Hollywood with Wendell Willkie, the NAACP's counsel and a one-time Republican presidential candidate as well as a board member of Twentieth Century Fox. Both men attended an Academy Awards dinner, went to studio commissaries, and sought meetings with studio executives to discuss movie roles for African Americans. At a Hollywood luncheon, Willkie delivered a speech that strongly criticized racial stereotypes. Throughout his visits, he 'pointed out the incalculable harm that continued picturization of Negroes, Asians, Africans, and Latin Americans as either savages, criminals, or mental incompetents was doing both abroad and in the United States.' White also made his case, urging 'the film industry to use more courage and imagination in the handling of roles of dark-skinned minorities.' White wanted to see Negro extras in scenes depicting everyday American life—blacks on city streets or in restaurants or at train stations. In this way, the diverse fabric of American life would be revealed.
>
> White also grew increasingly critical of the roles played by Hattie McDaniel. Some studio executives chose not to meet with White. But Darryl F. Zanuck and Walter Wanger were

> among those who did. David O. Selznick and Zanuck agreed to new guidelines for using extras and also agreed to bring more blacks into the studios in technical and craft positions.

A pivotal figure in Hollywood's redemptive efforts was John Howard Lawson, the scriptwriter for Bogart's film, *Sahara*. Born to a wealthy Jewish family in 1894, Lawson was the dean of the Hollywood Ten, a group of leftist screenwriters who made a conscious effort to imbue their scripts with progressive political messages. Lawson, in particular, had been radicalized by his participation in rallies for Sacco and Vanzetti, the two Italian anarchists convicted in Massachusetts in 1921 on dubious charges of killing two men in the course of a payroll robbery. And in the 1930s, he traveled to Alabama to write newspaper articles condemning the state for railroading the Scottsboro defendants and exposing the role played in the sordid affair by a vigilante organization known as the White Legion. In both Massachusetts and Alabama, Lawson was arrested for his activism.

That seemed only to encourage him. If Brantley, Aycock, Simmons and Jennett could conspire to speak something called a nigger *into* existence in the lead-up to the Wilmington massacre, Lawson and his cohort seemed intent on speaking the nigger *out* of existence.

Contrast, for instance, Griffith's cartoonishly drawn Black characters in *The Birth of a Nation* with the 1960 Hollywood classic, *Spartacus*, written by the most fabled of the Hollywood 10 screenwriters, Dalton Trumbo. Were it not, perhaps, for Stanley Kubrick's deft direction, the fight scene between the African gladiator, Draba, and Kirk Douglas's Spartacus, might well have been laughable. At 6-feet-4 inches tall, Woody Strode's Draba towered over the diminutive Douglas yet the two actors, both in their mid-30s at the time of filming, gave credible performances. Ironically, when the moment came to deliver the cinematic *coup de grace*, Draba spared Spartacus' life, turning his instrument instead on his enslavers, leaping into the coliseum's stands before he is murdered by a guard's spear and a quick knife thrust from the smirking villain, played by Sir Laurence Olivier. Later, Draba's corpse is seen hanging from the rafters of the slaves' quarters as a warning to anyone who would dare follow his example

Of course, some of Hollywood's change of heart wasn't motivated entirely by altruism; it was also good PR, as the scrutiny of the Nazis invited unflattering comparisons to America's brutalization of an ethnic minority. Still, some unknowable but significant portion of the industry's response to the country's racial fragmentation seemed genuine and motivated by good faith. In 1951, a young Nebraskan named Marlon Brando revolutionized cinema with his sensitive portrayal of Stanley Kowalski in *A Streetcar Named Desire*. Around the same time, Brando befriended a struggling Black writer named James Baldwin, and he would go on to be associated for the remainder of his life with radical organizations such as the Black Panthers, the American Indian Movement, and the Student Nonviolent Coordinating Committee. When asked his favorite of his more than four dozen films, Brando chose his role as an agent provocateur in the 1969 movie *Burn*, depicting a fictional 19th-century slave revolt.

In 1957, a young New York actor named John Cassavetes started production on his first feature film, entitled *Shadows*, which depicts two weeks in the lives of three African American siblings during the Beat Generation years in New York City. With a largely improvised dialogue, the film's plot turns on the revulsion written on the face of a white jazz musician when he discovers that his lover is, in fact, a Black woman whose complexion is light enough to allow her to pass for white. Financed with money raised mostly from friends and Cassavetes' agent, the film shocked audiences upon its release by turning the "concept of race upside down."[191] In 1994, the film critic Leonard Maltin wrote that the film was considered a "watershed in the birth of American independent cinema."

Another example of Hollywood's role in demystifying the racial superstitions that brake working-class movements can be found in one Tallulah Bankhead. Google the actor's name and you will be regaled (or mortified if your mores tend to the Victorian) by tales of her libertine appetites, her breakout performance in the Hitchcock classic *Lifeboat*, or her half-camp, half-vamp villainess in the 1960s Batman television series. Wikipedia references her patrician mien—*dahling* not darling—her crusade to get to know Gary Cooper (biblically if not especially well) and her elegantly debauched riposte to Chico Marx's prurient proclamation over the punch bowl at a dinner party.

"Hello Ms. Bankhead," he said.

"Nice to meet you, Mr. Marx," Bankhead replied. There was a pregnant pause and then:

"You know I really want to fuck you," Marx blurted out.

"And so you shall my good ol' fashioned boy," was Bankhead's unhesitating retort.[192]

The rebellious daughter of an aristocratic Southern family, Bankhead made a point of appearing on stage and screen with African Americans such as Canada Lee, helped raise cash for exploited sharecroppers and championed anti-lynching legislation. It was her advocacy for liberal causes that led organizers to recruit her for a 1947 rally in support of a Black Chicago steelworker, James Hickman, who was on trial for fatally shooting the slumlord who set fire to his apartment, killing his four youngest children. Concluding the remarks that were prepared for her that autumn afternoon, she said:

> So long, however, as there exists anywhere on Earth one minority that is treated with contempt, that is herded into black slum areas, that is abused and insulted, so long will we have violence, hate, brutality, savagery. So long as there exists a Jewish problem, or a Mexican problem—or a problem of any minority—so long will one form of violence

> beget another. I am proud to be one of the humble gladiators in this struggle against narrow prejudice and stupidity. I am glad to lend my efforts so that there shall be no more James Hickman tragedies.[193]

In his terrific retelling of the case, *People Wasn't Made to Burn: A True Story of Race, Housing and Murder in Chicago,* the author Joe Allen wrote that the mostly Black audience of 1,200 people responded to Bankhead's remarks with tears and raucous applause, causing her to ad-lib for an encore:

> I love the Negro race.

This brought the house down and the rainbow coalition of African Americans, Trotskyites, and trade unionists went on to win Hickman's release and a crackdown on abusive landlords, adding another trophy to the mantle of a multicultural workers' movement.

Ironically, World War II dealt the laboring class a much better hand to play. The jobless rate bottomed out at 24.9 percent in the spring of 1934, and despite the best efforts of the New Dealers and the CIO, had dropped only six percentage points by 1939, leaving it at a woeful 19 percent. By comparison, the war machine had, by 1944, produced the tightest labor market in U.S. history with the unemployment rate plummeting to 1.2 percent.

Additionally, the establishment of the National War Labor Board promoted organized labor to full partnership in the tripartite alliance between big business, government and employees. The Board settled all wartime labor disputes and worked in tandem with the Economic Stabilization Act—which froze wages and prices at the level of September 15, 1942—to broker a rapprochement between industrial combatants and keep war production humming along without hiccups. In return, AFL President William Green and CIO President Philip Murray agreed to a no-strike pledge for the duration of the war, and other than the United Mine Workers' successful 1943 strike, there were no labor stoppages sanctioned by the leadership between the attack on Pearl Harbor and V-J Day, although wildcat strikes began to surge as the war in Europe wound down, partly as a rebuke to union leadership who'd grown complacent and palmed off much of their collective bargaining responsibilities to the federal government.

Included in these unauthorized work stoppages were an outbreak of "hate strikes" protesting the promotions of Black employees to job classifications traditionally reserved for whites, recalling their forefathers who forced employers to fire freedmen after the Civil War. The difference was that the wartime hate strikes were just as likely to be met with indifference from the broader community—if not outright hostility—than were the racial boycotts 75 years earlier. The CIO locals representing steel, electrical, and shipbuilding employees in Baltimore managed to put down just such a racist insurgency at the Sparrows Point Bethlehem shipyards in July, 1943 but had no such luck five months later when white employees at the Western Electric Company's Point Breeze plant in Baltimore demanded separate toilet facilities for their 1,750 Black co-workers. Unable to convince the striking workers to return to work, the CIO asserted that they were exploiting the race issue "in the interests of the nation's enemies" and asked Roosevelt to intervene. He complied, ordering the army to take over the plant; the strikers returned to work. Eight months later on August 3, 1944, the worst "'hate strike" of the war era began when white streetcar workers in Philadelphia walked off the job to protest the hiring of eight Blacks to the job of motorman—rather than in the traditional menial positions of porters or sweepers—leaving the city without public transportation for six days. Read one flier exhorting white transit workers to take action:

> Your buddies are in the Army fighting and dying to protect the life of you and your family and you are too yellow to protect their jobs until they return. Call a strike and refuse to teach the Negroes. The public is with you.
>
> The CIO sold you out.[194]

When the bus and trolley transit workers called in sick on the day the Black trainees were scheduled for their first run, the striking white laborers were surprised by the backlash they received from the Transport Workers Union (TWU), the Philadelphia CIO Industrial Union Council, the newspapers, and perhaps most shockingly, Black and white Philadelphians from all walks of life. Unable to persuade the strikers to return to work, the Transport Workers Union, the CIO Committee to Abolish Discrimination, and the Philadelphia Industrial Union Council joined with the African Methodist Episcopal Church, the American Jewish Congress, the Catholic Interracial Council, the NAACP, the Baptist Ministers Conference of Philadelphia, and the Society of Friends Committee on Race Relations to place a full-page advertisement in the local papers denouncing the strike as "treason against the American war effort," and "traitorous to the fundamental principles of American liberty and the right of all men to live and earn their living without discrimination."[195] The signatories urged denizens to reject outright the "unreasonable demands of the inciters of this strike." The Roosevelt administration sent 5,000 soldiers to Philadelphia to guard the cars on August 7th, and the strike was broken in little more than a week. While not a single AFL union condemned the racist strike, the CIO's local held an election for officers the following month, with the rank-and-file transit workers choosing an African American as one of their union's four vice-presidents.

In all, the country lost nearly 2.5 million man-hours to hate strikes between March 1 and May 31, 1943, according to the Bureau of Labor Statistics. White workers' dueling responses to the twin terrors of war and poverty, or reminders of death—*memento mori* in Latin—evoke the image of the pensive white Everyman with the angelic CIO whispering into his ear on one shoulder while the devilish AFL proselytizes in the other. No clear winner ever emerged, but white laborers' re-evaluation of their class identity provided a glimpse of what an American proletariat united across racial (and gender) lines might achieve

The scales couldn't have fallen from the eyes of the converted at a more opportune moment. On the morning of April 13th, 1945, the headline of a one-page special edition of *The Worker's Voice* proclaimed solemnly that "President Roosevelt is Dead," and channeling the energy from both the Double V campaign and Reconstruction, challenged its readership to finish the job it had started. "We must resolve to carry through to victorious conclusion the war—the complete defeat of the fascist forces in the world—and build a permanent and lasting peace that the Brotherhood of Man may be realized in this world." Continuing, the labor periodical asserted: "History must not be allowed to repeat itself. We cannot allow the traitors to triumph as they did in the tragic period following the death of another great leader—Abraham Lincoln."[196]

When the atomic bombs dropped on Japan brought the Second World War to a close in September 1945, the national economy was confronted with the loss of $74 billion in military production and charged with absorbing 12 million GIs into the workforce. The unemployment rate tripled from 1.2 percent in 1944 to 3.9 percent by 1946, and price controls expired in June of that same year, causing food prices to skyrocket by 28 percent over the next six months, erasing most of the gains made by the proletariat during the war years. Workers nationwide began to carpet-bomb Congress and newsrooms with telegrams, postcards, and letters to the editor demanding that the federal government continue its wartime regulation of consumer prices which, like the printing of scrip during the Civil War, had subsidized wages. In November 1945, Christine Gardner, a seasonal employee at Piedmont Leaf in North Carolina and a Local 22 member, testified before a Senate Education and Labor subcommittee that was weighing a hike in the minimum wage to sixty-five cents an hour.

"My husband and I have been married ten years," the mother of three told the senators, "during which time he has never had a suit of clothes. His greatest ambition is to buy for me a Christmas present, and for himself a complete set of clothes."[197]

With the federal ban on strikes lifted, employees in the petroleum, coal and textile industries walked off the job in October, followed by 200,000 United Auto Workers in November, demanding a 30 percent pay increase from their employer, General Motors. Yet, in a nod to the country's blossoming class consciousness, the UAW demanded that the company raise employees' pay without passing it on to consumers—or fellow workers—in the form of an increase in prices. An analysis by the Office of War Mobilization and Reconversion found that auto manufacturers could, in fact, raise their employees' wages by 25 percent without adjusting prices and still pocket more cash than they had before the war. Similar disputes that paired product pricing with wage increases informed strikes by electrical, meat-packing, and agricultural equipment workers.

The strike wave continued the following year with nearly 750,000 steelworkers walking off the job in January 1946, followed by coal miners in the spring, inducing a nationwide brown-out. A railroad strike threatened to bring commerce to a standstill and before the year was over, schoolteachers, municipal employees, utility and communications workers walked off their jobs. For the year, the Bureau of Labor Statistics recorded 4,985 strikes, a figure rivaled only by the labor upheaval of 1919.

In San Francisco's East Bay, a campaign by Retail Clerks Local 1265 to organize two downtown Oakland department stores—the men's clothiers, Hastings and Kahns—was met with staunch resistance from a trade group, the Retail Merchants Association, representing the employers.

"I was working in the shoe department and I was making, I believe, $28 a week at that time," said Al Kidder, a returning war veteran. "The only problem was that when I found after talking to other workers in specialty stores . . . they were making $10 or more per week than I was so I went to the union and asked why they didn't organize the store."[198]

Negotiations began in the summer of 1946 but quickly stalled. Store clerks—including many women who had found work in retail after losing their jobs in the local munitions plants when their husbands, sons, and nephews returned from the war—began picketing for union recognition at Hastings in late October and at Kahn's in early November.

Initially, the advantage went to the bosses who were flush with windfall profits they'd pocketed during the war and could afford to play hardball. But as the holidays approached, the Teamsters refused to cross picket lines to deliver merchandise to the department stores, tipping the balance of power ever so slightly to the store clerks.

Mindful of the 1934 waterfront strike across the bridge in San Francisco, the Retail Merchants Association decided to break the strike by renting trucks and hiring non-union drivers from Los Angeles to transport merchandise valued at $500,000 from Southern California to a Berkeley warehouse where it would be stored until Sunday, December 1st, when it was scheduled to be delivered. Kahn's Vice President, John Sullivan, notified Oakland Police Chief Robert Tracy of the store's plans and on Saturday, November 30th, the city government warned the clerks' union that the delivery would take place at 2 a.m. Sunday morning. Intending to disrupt the deliveries, nearly 70 unarmed pickets arrived hours before daybreak at the heart of the downtown shopping district on 15th and Broadway where Hastings and Kahn's occupied opposite ends of the block. Beginning at 5 a.m., police squadrons in riot gear and gas masks began to overwhelm the pickets, forcing them to scatter. Simultaneously, police tow trucks began hauling cars parked legally on the streets. The historian Philip J. Wolman describes what happened next:

> The first streetcar began its run down Broadway before 7 a.m. It was stopped at the police cordon, but when the authorities tried to move the streetcar through the crowd the pickets balked. Al Brown, a business agent for the Carmens

and Bus Drivers Union, happened to be driving the first streetcar to reach 17th and Broadway. When the police ordered him to continue down Broadway, he refused to cross the picket line. He pulled the controls out of the streetcar, just left it sitting in the middle of the intersection, and walked away from it! He stopped the following streetcars and urged the drivers to do (the same). They responded as did the bus drivers whose routes crossed the downtown district. Most joined the angry ranks of the pickets. All north-south traffic in the heart of Oakland was soon tied up. Shortly after 7 a.m., with the pickets watching helplessly behind police lines, the first deliveries were made to the struck stores. Six trucks from the so-called Veterans Truck Lines, Inc., covered with tarpaulins and with their license plates bent under, arrived with a police escort of fifteen or sixteen motorcycles and twelve squad cars. The merchandise was delivered to both stores (five truckloads to Kahn's and one truckload to Hastings) without incident although both the police who had herded the pickets away from the stores and the strikebreakers were subject to vehement verbal abuse from pickets and a sizeable crowd of spectators. After unloading, the six trucks started back for the police patrolled Berkeley warehouse as the 200-300 policemen guarding the stores held their ground waiting for the second delivery. Traffic built up throughout the morning, and crowds continued to gather. The trucks arrived back in the downtown area before 11 o'clock with six more truckloads of merchandise for Kahn's. Again, there was no mass violence.

Throughout the morning the situation in the streets was peaceful but tense. Picket captains and union officials circulated among the crowds admonishing them to remain calm. One incident marred the non-violence of the day. A police three-wheeler, whether intentionally or accidentally, ran down Newton Selvidge, a motorman who had joined

> the pickets and had tried to stand in the way of the police caravan. Selvidge's injuries, serious enough to demand an ambulance to rush him to the hospital, angered the crowds.[199]

When the deliveries were completed sometime around midday, seething workers from across Alameda County flocked downtown to survey the aftermath of the battle, joining their co-workers who had witnessed the incident and continued to mill angrily in the streets.

As the afternoon went on, rank-and-file unionists, both white and Black, met with their representatives from locals across the Bay Area. What they could not abide, they quickly agreed, was the police and elected officials meddling in a fight that was none of their business. The consensus was to give the municipal leadership an opportunity to apologize; by the end of the workday Monday, December 2nd, no such gesture of contrition emanated from City Hall. Carpenters, steamfitters, bakers, and laborers representing most of the locals in the county met to discuss their options and in short order they decided to shut the city down. That evening, the attorney for the Central Labor Council, James F. Galliano, announced that a work holiday had been called beginning at 5 a.m. the next day and union members were notified by telephone. Beginning at daybreak on Tuesday, December 3rd, 1946, and ending 54 hours later, more than 100,000 workers from 142 AFL locals failed to show up for their shift.

Shipyards and factories were closed, building construction suspended, bus, trolley, and streetcar services shuttered, which caused schools to close as well. Taxis were not running, and bars, hotels, and retailers were mostly closed; those that weren't operated with skeleton crews composed of management. A few corner grocery stores and gas stations remained open, as did the bank branches, but they did very little business. Managers at the four biggest newspapers in the county, the *Berkeley Daily-Gazette*, the *Alameda Times-Star*, William Randolph Hearst's *Oakland Post-Enquirer*, and Joseph

Knowland's rabidly anti-union *Oakland Tribune*, arrived at work that morning to find their employees on strike and picketing rather than putting out the next day's newspaper. Organized labor had hardly forgotten the cynical role that the press played in the San Francisco general strike 12 years earlier, and for all intents and purposes, made it impossible for the Big Four to disseminate propaganda during the strike. San Francisco's Teamsters refused to deliver that city's dailies across the bridge to Alameda County, leaving the *People's Daily World* as the only newspaper in mass circulation in Oakland during the general strike, although radio stations KRON and KRE were allowed to function as usual.

By 9 a.m. a crowd estimated at nearly 5,000 had gathered in the streets between the department stores. One of the picketers, a woman, began singing:

I'm a picket, I'm a picket, I'll be a picket 'till I die.
But I'd rather be a picket than a goddamn company spy.

By 10 a.m. thousands had joined her in song. During the strike's peak activity, the crowd swelled to more than 20,000 people squeezed into a four-block area of downtown Oakland. The defiant display of workers' solidarity transformed the city's streetscape into a triptych of rotating frescoes, scenes from a class war unfurling like swatches of textured, colorful fabric against the Bay Area's skyline: a church revival teeming with parishioners belting out spirituals; a battleground upon which combatants skirmished intermittently; and perhaps most peculiarly, a biracial, blue-collar bacchanal that seemed an odd mixture of New Orleans' Mardi Gras and the 1871 Paris Commune.

A gaggle of nearly 150 strikers tussled with officers to retrieve a lone picketer who had crossed into enemy territory behind a police barricade. Picketers blocking the entrances to the two department stores angrily repelled a couple who tried to force their way through the crowd to enter

Kahn's, and later a San Francisco newspaperman who attempted to do the same. A house painter working in a residential neighborhood near the city center was confronted by strikers who asked him accusingly "don't you know there's a strike on?"

Local organizers were keenly aware that the general, or "accidental" strike was unauthorized by the international leadership, and they tried to avoid antagonizing union executives such as Teamsters' National Vice President Dave Beck, who called the general strike "a lot of foolishness" and "more like a revolution than an industrial dispute." Despite a few scuffles, there was never any sense of danger and most observers noted that the patrol officers seemed to sympathize with the strikers, some of whom were friends or even relatives. That lack of real tension added to what strikers and observers consistently referred to as a "carnival" atmosphere, especially in the work stoppage's first 24 hours. By nightfall Monday, the strikers had instructed all stores except pharmacies and food markets to close. Bars were allowed to stay open, but they could serve only beer and had to put their jukeboxes out on the sidewalk to play at full volume and at no charge. "Pistol Packin' Mama, Lay That Pistol Down," the number one hit of the day, echoed off all the buildings. Said one striker, Joe Chaudet:

> Everybody was having a good time . . . it was a holiday mood, it was a feeling of comradeship, it was the feeling that, well, we're all together in this thing, you know and it was a good, warm, healthy feeling, it was more like what this country should be.[200]

Come Tuesday morning the picketers had cordoned off downtown. Another striker, Stan Weir said:

> Anyone could leave, but only those with passports (union cards) could get in. The comment made by a prominent national network newscaster, that 'Oakland is a ghost town tonight,' was a contribution to ignorance. Never before or

> since had Oakland been so alive and happy for the majority of the population. It was a town of law and order. In that city of over a quarter million, strangers passed each other on the street and did not have fear, but the opposite.

The 1946 strike ended on Thursday, December 5 at 11 a.m., when the AFL international called it off because they were worried that the more radical CIO unions would join and reorganize the Bay Area's industrial relations in a fashion that would exclude the older and more conservative union leaders. As a result of their leadership's timidity, the department store clerks did not win recognition from the retailers.

Still, the general strike sparked a revolution at Oakland's City Hall with the labor unions running their own slate of candidates for alderman and winning four of the nine council seats in the next election.

Sixty-five years later, on the other side of the country, a young African American activist, Omar Wilks, rediscovered the workers' secret sauce when the New York City Police Department arrested hundreds of dissidents participating in a 2011 Occupy Wall Street protest on the Brooklyn Bridge. In an interview he told me:

> You know when they were handcuffing us and loading us into the wagons we were singing, all of us, and we kept singing even as they put us into the cells. And there was a point there, man, I don't know how to explain it but there was just this feeling, and you know everybody felt it, where it just didn't matter how old you were, or what color, or what religion, it was just the people, fighting for each other.

Marx wrote that capitalism alienates workers from nature, from each other, and even from our true selves. The psychoanalyst and anti-colonial resistance leader from the French colony of Martinique, Frantz Fanon, wrote that the antidote to capitalism's isolation is the formation of a revolutionary consciousness, expanding communities beyond your household, or church, or enclave or tribe to include a wider swath of humanity. In finding common cause with each other, Fanon wrote, we create the New (Wo)Man.

And the comedian Dave Chappelle would put it even more succinctly many years later:

> You need to know how to solve your problems. You need to know where your power lies; you are Americans so your power lies in each other.

And that is precisely why the 1946 Oakland general strike remains the last general strike in U.S. history.

Part III

Everybody's Fight

9.

The Patriot Act

The laws which enforce segregation do not presume the inferiority of a people; they assume an inherent equalness. It is the logic of the lawmakers that if a society does not erect artificial barriers between the people at every point of contact, the people might fraternize and give their attention to the genuine, shared problems of the community.

–Lorraine Hansberry

On the final day of February in 1952, a leap year, a 34-year-old newspaperman named Elliott Maraniss received a subpoena to testify before the House Committee on Un-American Activities, which was in town investigating "Communism in the Detroit Area."

That wasn't entirely accurate, of course. Communism was merely the Rosetta stone that helped workers of different backgrounds crack the code and translate their discontent into a political *lingua franca.* Far more problematic for the wealthy was communism's role in bridging the gap between Black and white laborers, and the ensuing transformation of warring tribes into a cohesive, fighting unit. In the context of America's bitter and protracted class war, the Red Scare's sole objective was to identify the country's most radical and outspoken actors—inordinately African

Americans and Jews—and discredit them.

Widely known by the acronym, HUAC, the panel rode shotgun for this operation that was, for all intents and purposes, the Palmer Raids 2.0, with FBI Director J. Edgar Hoover reprising the role of Woodrow Wilson's attorney general this time around, and providing Congress with a network of informants who dropped a dime on the leaders of an uprising that was beginning to draw blood. Buoyed by their postwar list of demands, employees pocketed nearly half of the nation's annual income in 1951, the year before the Detroit hearings, and would go on to take home more than 50 percent of GDP for each of the next seven years.[201] Still smarting from the punch to the nose delivered by organized labor in battlefields as far-flung as California's docks to Carolina's tobacco farms, the oligarchs had discovered, much to their chagrin, the meaning of the aphorism, "it ain't no fun when the rabbit has the gun." To reclaim their unquestioned authority in the nation's decision-making, industrialists at the 20th century's midpoint would have to answer the exact same question that perplexed Charles Brantley Aycock, Josephus Daniels, and Furnifold Simmons in North Carolina in 1898: How could they persuade white workers to jump from a ship that had not only rescued them when they were lost at sea, but now had them halfway to shore?

What the oligarchs needed was an intervention of the sort that slowed the momentum of the Readjusters, the Fusionists, and the Knights of Labor. The Scottsboro imbroglio demonstrated that the material conditions were such that merely invoking the folkloric Black rapist was no longer sufficient. Their mission this time around would require a new boogeyman—bigger, better, badder—who could exploit whites' sense of themselves as a model for other races to emulate and weaken their growing identification with more radical workers. Rather unimaginatively, postwar financiers merely repackaged their grandparents' slander of the African American's intellect, morality and libido, adding to their bill of indictment a charge of sedition for gullibly aiding and abetting the Soviets' rumored plan to raise the hammer and sickle on U.S. soil.

Born in Boston to a Jewish family, Maraniss was raised on Coney Island in the same neighborhood that produced the playwright Arthur Miller. According to his son, David Maraniss, a Pulitzer Prize-winning *Washington Post* reporter and editor and a best-selling author, his father moved east to enroll at the University of Michigan, where he did indeed fall in with the Reds. His was one of scores of names handed over to the committee by an FBI informant. By the time he walked into the Federal Building in downtown Detroit and took a seat at the witness table in Room 740, he'd already been summarily fired by the *Detroit Times*, which was owned by the stridently anti-communist Hearst newspaper group.

With the committee's counsel playing the role of prosecutor, the hearings resembled a trial, but witnesses had almost none of the rights typically afforded to defendants in the judicial system. Citing his Fifth Amendment protections against self-incrimination, Maraniss refused to say whether he was a party member, but did bring a prepared statement that he was not allowed to read at the hearing.

Maraniss would pay a heavy price; the witch hunt left him unemployable for five years, and he was forced to move his young family from one marginal job opportunity to another before finally landing a stable gig at a Wisconsin newspaper that coincidentally took a dim view of the red-baiting hometown senator, Joseph McCarthy. But Maraniss was only collateral damage; the primary target of HUAC's Detroit hearings was the militant cell of African Americans attached to the world's largest union affiliate, Local 600 of the United Auto Workers, representing 60,000 workers at the Ford Motor Company's River Rouge complex.

Allusive of the Colored Troops rushing to the aid of their white comrades at the Battle of the Crater, the Great Migration's second wave saw more than two million African Americans in the South trek north, and another million relocate from the rural areas in the South to big southern cities like Atlanta, Birmingham, Memphis, Charlotte, and Winston-Salem. The number of Black voters in the North doubled between 1940 and 1948, and African American voter registration in the eleven states of the Old South quadrupled, reaching more than one million by 1952. This acutely politicized proletariat was hardly dazzled by the big city's bright lights and, in the tradition of their activist freedpeople forefathers, hit the ground running, aggressively advocating for civil and labor rights simultaneously. In 1940, the NAACP counted 50,000 members in 355 branches nationwide; six years later, those figures had ballooned to 450,000 members in 1,073 branches.[202]

Despite its expanding membership rolls and the organization's public relations disaster in Scottsboro, the NAACP's politics continued to mimic the bourgeois values of its liberal donors and board members, and its leadership was growing increasingly virulent in its denunciation of communism as the Cold War got underway. Of much more concern to the ruling class than the NAACP were the half-million African Americans who had joined CIO locals over roughly that same span, most notably the aforementioned UAW. Only four percent of autoworkers were Black in 1940; by 1960 that figure had quintupled to 20 percent, although, much like their grandchildren and great-grandchildren nearly 70 years later who were at greater risk of being exposed to the coronavirus, Blacks were the essential workers of their day, consigned to the physically taxing but absolutely critical job classifications in the foundry, paint shop, and wet-sanding operations.

By 1950, there were almost 100,000 organized African American employees in metropolitan Detroit, nearly 12,000 of whom worked at the vast River Rouge complex, which was famously depicted by the iconoclastic Mexican painter Diego Rivera, a devout Marxist, in his 1933 series of frescoes known as the Detroit Industry Murals. Consisting of 16 buildings—

each staffed by full-time union officials—the River Rouge shopfloor was the sun around which the city's radicals orbited. With Black committeemen leading the way, workers stood up to foremen, challenged top managers, and broke Ford's spy system. Lamented one supervisor: "We noticed a very definite change in attitude of the working man. It was terrible for a while . . . the bosses were just people to look down on after the union came in."[203]

At its height, the Rouge foundry sent more than 20 Black delegates to every national UAW convention, accounted for half of all Black staffers hired by the head office and, by custom, supplied Local 600 with at least one top officer, wrote the labor historian Nelson Lichtenstein. An African American foundryman, Shelton Tappes, who would later serve as the union's recording secretary, helped negotiate an unprecedented antidiscrimination clause into the UAW's first contract with Ford in 1941. In the March 1951 union election, candidates affiliated with the progressive caucus won three of the local's four highest offices, the presidencies of several buildings, and nearly half the seats on the executive board and general council. With progressives leading the way, Local 600 staked out a wide range of leftist positions, including calls for a ceasefire in the Korean War, which began in June 1950 and ended 37 months later.

Also interrogated by HUAC at the Detroit hearings were two Local 600 spinoffs. The Civil Rights Congress, or CRC, was founded in 1946, merging the International Labor Defense—which had played such an instrumental role in defending the Scottsboro Boys—and the National Federation of Constitutional Rights. In 1951, Paul Robeson and his close friend and hero of the Scottsboro case, ILD Director William Patterson, presented to the United Nations the Civil Rights Congress' human rights petition, *We Charge Genocide*, embarrassing the U.S. government in its propaganda war with the Soviet Union. The director of the Detroit chapter of the CRC, Anne Shore, said the organization "depended on a coalition of labor, white, Black, middle class, and intellectuals and it had been a very effective organization over the years."

The other organization that had caught HUAC's eye was the National Negro Labor Council. Founded in 1951 by an African American foundry worker at a New Jersey radiator plant, the NNLC was intended to recapture the militant energy of the CIO's early years, which had begun to wane in the postwar period as the political class ratcheted up the Red Scare. Elected to national leadership positions at the NNLC's inaugural convention were William Hood, the top-ranking African American official at Local 600, and Coleman Young of the Amalgamated Clothing Workers, who would go on to be elected Detroit's first Black mayor in 1973.

Born in Alabama in 1918, Young had moved to Detroit with his family in 1923 and was initiated into politics at a barbershop in the city's Black Bottom neighborhood. Landing a job at Ford, Young joined the union in the underground days but was fired after, as Young recalled it, he wielded a pipe to knock cold a company "thug." He was also fired from a post office job because he was a union organizer. Later, as a CIO organizer, he worked on housing issues, and he wrote for African American newspapers under the pseudonym "Captain Midnight." He led unionization drives and protests against police brutality.

The representatives serving on the HUAC panel were staunch supporters of the poll tax and ardent anti-communists. The committee's first chairman, Martin Dies Jr. of Texas, endorsed the Klan; Mississippi Congressman John Rankin routinely referred to Blacks and Jews as "niggers" and "kikes;" and the panel's chairman at the time of the Detroit hearings, Georgia's Democratic Congressman John Stephens Wood, was likely part of the white Atlanta mob that lynched a Jewish factory owner, Leo Frank, in 1915.

Accordingly, picketers marched up and down the sidewalk outside Detroit's federal courthouse, hoisting placards that read:

NEGRO-WHITE UNITY IS NOT SUBVERSIVE

EVERYONE IN LOCAL 600 CAN VOTE:
HOW ABOUT IN GEORGIA?

WOOD VOTED FOR POLL TAX

WHY DON'T YOU SPEND OUR MONEY INVESTIGATING LYNCHINGS IN FLORIDA?

Appearing before the committee on February 28th, 1952, Young immediately made it clear that he was a hostile witness who held the court in contempt. When the panel's chief counsel, Frank Tavenner, asked Young if he was a communist, the combative future mayor shot back:

> I refuse to answer that question, relying upon my rights under the Fifth Amendment, and, in light of the fact that an answer to such a question, before such a committee, would be in my opinion a violation of my rights under the First Amendment, which provides for freedom of speech, sanctity and privacy of political beliefs and associates. And further, since I have no purpose of being here as a stool pigeon, I'm not prepared to give any information on any of my associates or political thoughts.

From Virginia's Shenandoah Valley, Tavenner, who spoke with a pronounced southern drawl, had a reputation for directness and imperturbability. He persisted but it quickly became clear that he'd met his match.

> Mr. Tavenner: You told us you were the executive secretary of the National Negro Congress . . .
>
> Mr. Young: The word is Negro, not Nigra.
>
> Tavenner: I said Negro. I think you are mistaken.

Young: I hope I am. Speak more clearly.

The chairman, Wood, chimed in.

Mr. Wood: I will appreciate it if you will not argue with counsel.

Young: It isn't my purpose to argue. As a Negro, I resent the slurring of the name of my race.

Wood: You are here for the purpose of answering questions.

Young: In some sections of the country, they slur . . .

Tavenner: I am sorry. I did not mean to slur it.

With the committee now clearly on its heels, Young went on the offensive, like Ali coming off the ropes to pummel Foreman. He reminded the panel that its former chairman, John Rankin, had once declared the NAACP a subversive group and that it was his opinion that HUAC was un-American. When the committee continued to press him to identify communists, Young mocked them.

Young: You have me mixed up with a stool pigeon.

Representative Charles Potter, Michigan Republican: I have never heard of anybody stooling in the Boy Scouts.

Young: I was a member of the organization.

Potter: I don't think they are proud of it today.

Young: I will let the Scouts decide that.

Later, Representative Wood asked Young to differentiate between the National Negro Labor Council and the National Negro Congress.

Young: I would inform you also, the word is Negro.

Wood: I am sorry. If I made a different pronouncement of it, it is due to my inability to use the language any better than I do. I am trying to use it properly.

Young: It may be due to your southern background.

Wood: I am not ashamed of my southern background. For your information, out of the 112 Negro votes cast in the last election in the little village from which I come, I got 112 of them. That ought to be a complete answer of that. Now, will you answer the question?

Young: I happen to know, in Georgia, Negro people are prevented from voting by virtue of terror, intimidation, and lynchings. It is my contention you would not be in Congress today if it were not for the legal restrictions on voting on the part of my people.

The conversation turned to Young's wartime experience.

Potter: I believe in your statement that you said that you were in the service fighting fascism during the last war.

Young: That is right.

Potter: Then it is proper to assume that you are opposed to totalitarianism in any form, as I am.

Young: I fought and I was in the last war, Congressman that is correct, as a Negro officer in the Air Corps. I was arrested and placed under house arrest and held in the quarters for three days in your country because I sought to get a cup of coffee in a United States Officers Club that was restricted for white officers only. That is my experience in the United States Army.

Potter: Let me say this, I have the highest admiration, yes, the highest admiration for the service that was performed by Negro soldiers during the last war. They performed brilliantly.

Young: I am sure the Negro soldiers appreciate your admiration, Mr. Potter.

Potter: At the same time, while I am just as much opposed to Nazism and fascism as you are, I am opposed to totalitarianism in any form. As you well know the

> Communist International as dictated from Soviet Russia is probably the most stringent form of totalitarian government in the world today. In case, and God forbid that it ever happens, but in case the Soviet Union should attack the United States, would you serve as readily to defend our country in case of such eventuality as you did during the last war?
>
> Young: As I told you, Congressman, nobody has had to question the patriotism, the military valor, of the Negro people. We have fought in every war.
>
> Potter: I am not talking about the Negro people. I am talking about you.
>
> Young: I am coming to me. I am part of the Negro people. I fought in the last war and I would unhesitatingly take up arms against anybody that attacks this country. In the same manner, I am now in the process of fighting against what I consider to be attacks and discrimination against my people. I am fighting against un-American activities such as lynchings and denial of the vote. I am dedicated to that fight and I don't think I must apologize or explain it to anybody . . ."

His testimony complete, Young rose from the witness table and strode toward the rear of the chamber, surrounded by supporters and other witnesses who reached out to shake his hand and offer words of praise. He had bucked the committee in a way no one else had, and the effect was electric. Conversely, reporters were stunned. How, they quizzed Tavenner and his peers, had Young received such wide latitude to spar with his inquisitors. "It just happened," a reporter for the *Detroit Free Press* was told. The headline the following day read "Committee Loosens Reins, Defiant Witness Runs Wild," with the subhead "Fight over Terminology Bitterest of Hearing."

For days thereafter, as Coleman Young moved through the streets of

Black Bottom and the city's other Black neighborhoods, he was hailed as a hero. "I felt like Joe Louis home from a fight," he later told the oral historian Studs Terkel.[204] "People called out my name as I walked down the street and small crowds gathered when I stopped. . . . That single incident endeared me to the hearts of Black people. Fighting back, saying what they wanted to say all their lives to a southern white."

After a decade in the White House, the Democratic Party had a quandary on its hands. How could it continue to oblige its most steadfast supporters, African Americans, while also accommodating the party's white supremacist southern wing? By the 1944 presidential election, the answer was clear:

It couldn't.

This didn't bode well for Roosevelt's vice president, Henry Agard Wallace, whose championing of the common man and reproach of imperialism and racism clashed with the aristocrats' investment portfolios. Of a 1943 race riot in Detroit, Wallace proclaimed "that we cannot continue to crush Nazi brutality abroad and condone race riots at home." Fearing (correctly as it turned out) that the ailing Roosevelt might not survive his fourth term, party apparatchiks drummed the immensely popular Wallace out of the vice president's chair and replaced him with the conservative Kansas City haberdasher, Harry Truman.

Wallace left Truman's cabinet in 1946, emerging as a leading critic of the Cold War. He was named editor of the staunchly liberal *New Republic* magazine and in 1948 announced his candidacy for the presidency on the Progressive Party ticket, openly defying Jim Crow laws and refusing to address segregated audiences while campaigning in the South. Despite Wallace's spirited support from African Americans—including Local 22—voters returned Truman to the White House by a slim margin.

In the 1946 midterm elections, Republicans won huge majorities over Democrats—246 to 188 in the House and 51 to 45 in the Senate—for the first time since 1931. Rejuvenated by new blood that included a freshman GOP congressman from California named Richard Nixon, yet bloodied by nearly 5,000 work stoppages, the "Class of 1946" was eager to begin repealing as much of the New Deal as it could. The first order of business was to amend the Wagner Act.

Sponsored by Republican Senators Robert Taft of Ohio, the son of a former U.S. president, and Fred Hartley of New Jersey, the Republican-controlled Congress overrode President Truman's veto to pass the Labor-Management Relations Act of 1947 in June of that year, a little more than six months after Oakland's general strike. Labor leaders and the Democratic leadership, including Truman, referred to the Taft-Hartley Act as a "slave labor" bill.

In essence, Republicans argued, ridiculously, that the Wagner Act disadvantaged employers and that the Taft-Hartley Act would restore some equilibrium to industrial relations by prohibiting secondary boycotts—when employees strike to persuade their employer to stop doing business with another employer—sympathy or general strikes such as the 1946 Alameda County boycott or the 1934 citywide San Francisco walkout, and jurisdictional boycotts intended to coerce an employer to choose one union's employees over another. Also criminalized was the closed shop in states that forbade them leading to the passage of union-busting "Right to Work" laws in a number of states, mostly in the South.

The prohibition against general strikes removed from labor's quiver its sharpest arrow. General strikes remain the nuclear option for workers across the world; in November 2020, more than 250 million workers took part in a nationwide boycott in India bringing commerce in the world's most populous democracy to a standstill. Like sit-down strikes, general strikes are especially nettlesome for business owners because they raise uncomfortable questions about what value bosses add to the product and who should own the means of production.

Taft-Hartley's primary target, however, was no particular arrow but the quiver itself, represented by the sparse daylight between Blacks like Coleman Young and whites like Elliot Maraniss. Said one white woman organizer during the CIO's steel campaign:

> The Communists think a Negro is just the same as they are. They are very strong for that sort of stuff.[205]

From a tactical standpoint, Taft-Hartley was tantamount to shutting down an adversary's ability to communicate on the battlefield by scrambling its signals, as underscored by the legislation's requirement that union officers sign government affidavits affirming that they were not communists. This provision, in turn, led to the creation of loyalty boards, charged with investigating workers suspected of having links to organizations identified as subversive. Unsurprisingly, these efforts impacted Blacks disproportionately. A newsletter for the longshoremen's union, the *ILWU Dispatcher*, found that "sixty-five percent of the longshoremen screened off the waterfront are Negroes" who are "among the most militant ILWU members because they have found in our organization the sort of democracy and freedom from discrimination they seldom find elsewhere."[206]

A reporter for a Black weekly, the San Francisco *Sun-Reporter*, wrote of the witch hunts:

> Screening is an attempt to drive Negroes from the waterfront and to undermine the unions that have fought for racial equality. I have found that Negroes with key jobs have been the first to be screened.[207]

Similarly, a survey concluded that "approximately 70 percent of the screened members of the National Union of Marine Cooks and Stewards have been Negroes."[208]

The loyalty boards established for the purpose of screening union members showed the government's hand. Among the questions put to African Americans were:

> Have you ever had dinner with a mixed group?

And:

> Have you ever danced with a white girl?

White employees were asked whether they had ever entertained Blacks as guests and white witnesses were asked:

> Have you had any conversations that would lead you to believe [the accused] is rather advanced in his thinking on racial matters?

Similar to the picketers protesting HUAC outside the federal courthouse in Detroit, labor leaders also called out the divide-and-conquer strategy. Warned UAW President Walter Reuther:

> So let's all be careful that we don't play the bosses' game by falling for the Red Scare. Let's stand by our union and fellow unionists. No union man, worthy of the name, will play the bosses' game. Some may do so through ignorance. But those who peddle the Red Scare and know what they are doing are dangerous enemies of the union.

The irony is that no one played the bosses' game better, or with more relish, than National Maritime Union President Joseph Curran, or Walter Reuther who, as the head of his local union, led the sit-down strikes at Flint's General Motors plant that made the UAW a household name nationally. The two headed a purge of 11 unions, representing nearly a million workers, from the CIO over a two-year period beginning in 1949.

Among progressives, the scouting report on Reuther was that he always feinted left and drove right. As evidenced by his exhortation urging workers to reject the bosses' Red Scare tactics, Reuther talked a good game, helping to quell hate strikes and championing civil rights during the war. The UAW was, in fact, the only predominantly white institution to defend the Black community and denounce police brutality following the 1943 Detroit race riot, when police and marauding white mobs murdered 25 African Americans. Yet, from the moment he defeated African Americans' preferred candidate, George Addes, for the UAW's presidency in 1946, he seemed as obsessed with ridding the union of Marxists as he was with negotiating contracts for rank-and-file autoworkers. His antagonism of African Americans and their strongest allies within the UAW fulfilled Reuther's short-term objectives of consolidating his support among second-generation Polish and Hungarian skilled tradesmen and assembly line workers who had no investment in colorblind shop floor policies that would eat away at their racial privileges.

At the 1943 UAW convention, Reuther and his supporters managed to defeat a resolution introduced by Addes' supporters calling for a special Negro representative. Reuther's response was that this was tantamount to "racism in reverse," an argument he deployed again in defeating a 1949 proposal calling for a Black vice president to advocate for African American workers with as much energy as Reuther and his lieutenants advocated for white workers.

As head of the UAW, Reuther's hand-picked choice to head Local 600 was Carl Stellato, who was elected to the top post in 1950. His first order of business was a mandate requiring that all 550 elected and appointed representatives of Local 600 sign loyalty oaths consistent with Taft-Hartley. Stellato's efforts to remove five unit officers from their positions on the grounds that they were communists failed, however, and the blowback nearly cost him his re-election in 1951.

If Reuther couldn't purge a CIO union that was, in his estimation, too Red, he would challenge the local in a certification election, known in organizing circles as a "raid." That was the case with the United Farm Equipment and Metal Workers Union.

With more than 70,000 members spread among 22 union locals at its zenith in 1948, the FE, as it was widely known, was the dominant union in the farm equipment industry, but there was some overlap with the UAW.

While both unions belonged to the CIO, they had vastly different visions for industrial unionism. Similar to the dockworkers' Bridges, the radical leadership of the United Farm Equipment and Metal Workers Union believed that capital and labor had nothing in common and as such, any agreement reached with management represented only a truce in the class struggle, not its end. Under Reuther, on the other hand, the UAW subscribed to a more conciliatory model of organized labor. "We make collective bargaining agreements," Reuther was fond of boasting, "not revolutions." The differing viewpoints were reflected in the number of work stoppages undertaken by the rival unions. Between October 1, 1945, and October 31, 1952, the UAW held 185 strikes compared to 971 by the FE.[209]

The United Farm Equipment and Metal Workers Union and UAW first clashed in 1946 at the International Harvester plant in the Chicago suburb of Melrose Park. Constructed in 1941, the shop manufactured the Pratt Whitney radial aircraft engines used in the B-24 bomber. International Harvester purchased the site from General Motors after the war and in 1946, the FE challenged UAW Local 6 in a certification election. The UAW won handily but the margin was split largely along racial lines, with whites—many of them returning servicemen—preferring the UAW, and African Americans—representing only a fraction of the workforce and mostly relegated to janitorial positions—casting ballots for the more progressive FE, which had a reputation of coaxing employers to hire and promote Blacks to the assembly line or machinist positions.

In the spring of 1949, an acrimonious jurisdictional dispute erupted between the UAW and the FE at International Harvester's McCormick Works factory in Chicago. Leading up to the vote, UAW organizers distributed leaflets accusing the FE of being "Communist-dominated" and the FE countered with charges of the UAW's red-baiting. A full-page FE ad in the Midwest edition of the *Pittsburgh Courier* asked:

> Why hasn't the UAW ever elected a Negro to national office, to its international executive board or as a district director? At the recent national convention of the FE-CIO, William Smith of Chicago, a worker in the McCormick Works plant, was elected vice-president of the union. . . . WALTER REUTHER'S MACHINE IN THE UAW DOESN'T WANT NEGROES IN ITS LEADERSHIP. This union is currently trying to raid the FE-CIO at McCormick.

With the Black vote playing a decisive role, the FE won the election.

Back in Detroit, Young, following his explosive testimony to HUAC, found himself blacklisted in the job market by employers and by the UAW. So complete was Reuther's control that he saw to it that no UAW affiliates would endorse for elected office any candidate who had shown a propensity to work with communists, including Young.

In his 1973 book, *The Company and the Union*, William Serrin, the Pulitzer Prize-winning reporter of the *Detroit Free Press*, excoriated the UAW's deal with General Motors that "transformed a natural antagonism into a socially destructive partnership." Serrin was particularly critical of Reuther, referring to him as a "gasbag" in an interview with Studs Terkel,[210] and noting the deep reservoir of mistrust in the UAW expressed by Black autoworkers especially. While the celebrated Reuther was the only non-Black person invited to speak at the 1963 March on Washington, it was later revealed that his union was at that time "negotiating discriminatory union contracts that locked Black workers in *de facto* segregated job classifications in violation of Title VII of the Civil Rights Act." By 1960, according to data compiled by the U.S. Commission on Civil Rights, Black workers accounted for seven-tenths of 1 percent of the skilled labor force in Detroit auto plants, yet 42.3 percent of the entire workforce.[211]

Reuther, who would go on to head the CIO, would lead the successful effort at the 1949 convention to expel the FE and several other left-leaning unions, including the United Electrical Workers, which had endorsed Henry Wallace's 1948 presidential bid for the Progressive Party.

When I arrived in Detroit in 1991 as a City Hall reporter for the *Free Press*, I quickly discovered how proud Black Detroiters were of Young, who was by that time in his fifth term as the city's mayor. Once, a Black county commissioner warned me to steer clear of parroting my co-workers' hypercritical reportage of Young. "You have to understand, Mayor Young is Black Detroit's Martin Luther King," I recall him saying.

Conversely, many whites, believing they were out of earshot, would mockingly, sophomorically, refer to him as *Coal-man*, and brag about how long it had been since they stepped foot in the city, a boast I would recall nearly a decade later when I would overhear white South Africans saying the exact same thing about visiting that country's all-Black townships. Once, at lunch, I told an aide to Mayor Young that I was considering writing a book on Reuther, who died in a 1970 plane crash.

"Whatever you do," the aide said, "don't mention that to the mayor . . . don't even say Reuther's name around the mayor. He hates him to this day."

It's natural to draw comparisons between the CIO and the Readjusters, who built a promising movement and just as quickly dismantled it, in a gesture of solidarity with other whites, or even the Union troops who turned on the colored soldiers at the Battle of the Crater. In recent decades, many academics—most notably the African American historian Herbert Hill—have spearheaded a re-evaluation of the CIO, recasting its reorganization of the workforce in the 1940s as nothing more than a cynical ploy by white workers to get ahead; once they attained a beachhead on the shop floor, most reverted to their white supremacist ideology.

Here again, my own experience as an African American worker is instructive. In rejecting the grassroots approach exemplified by the longshoremen's Harry Bridges, Reuther's management was a throwback to the sclerotic leadership of the AFL's Samuel Gompers and anticipated modern labor leaders such as the American Federation of Teachers President Randi Weingarten, or RoseAnn DeMoro, executive director of National Nurses United, or NNU.

I went to work in the Oakland headquarters of the nurses' union in January 2015. My first assignment on the job was to attend a public hearing on the sale of a nonprofit hospital, O'Connor. Opened in 1889, O'Connor Hospital was the first in the city of San Jose, and the second in California to be chartered and managed by the Daughters of Charity, a 400-year-old Catholic mission founded by St. Vincent de Paul. The 2008 recession left millions of Californians unable to pay their hospital tab, and the Daughters of Charity Health System was awash in unpaid medical bills.

Dubbed by the *Nation* magazine as the country's most progressive trade union, NNU and its better-known affiliate, California Nurses Association, endorsed a proposal by hospital executives to sell the chain to Prime, a southern California-based healthcare provider with a reputation for ripping off Medicaid, its patients, and its workforce. A 2014 federal audit of Prime hospitals, for instance, found 217 cases of improperly diagnosed kwashiorkor, a form of malnutrition that is seldom seen in the U.S., and typically found only in the Global South. Unsurprisingly, Medicaid's reimbursement rate for the disease is quite high when compared with other maladies.

The Service Employees International Union, or SEIU, on the other hand, favored a sale to Blue Wolf, a Wall Street hedge fund with no management experience in the healthcare industry but a demonstrated proficiency for dismantling businesses, auctioning their parts off to the highest bidders.

More startling still was that San Jose's working-class communities—a rainbow coalition of Latinos, South Asians, Blacks and whites—wanted *neither*, Prime least of all.

"We never trusted Blue Wolf, but the community was much more worried about Prime," Bob Brownstein, the executive director of the civic organization, Working Partners USA, told me in 2016. Had they bothered to show up for any of the dozen or so community stakeholder meetings held in 2014, the nurses' union might have known this, but Brownstein didn't recall seeing a California Nurses Association labor representative at more than one of the meetings.

Brownstein was part of a coalition of 15 civic groups that wrote a joint letter to California's then-Secretary of State, Kamala Harris, urging her to veto the sale to Prime. The group's clear preference was Santa Clara County, which had bid on O'Connor and whose health care network had a regional reputation for providing quality care to the uninsured that was second only to O'Connor's.

But Daughters of Charity executives preferred selling all six hospitals to a single bidder.

"I don't know why the California Nurses Association didn't help us push the county's bid," said Grace-Sonia E. Melanio, communications director for Community Health Partnership, which was one of the authors of the letter to the attorney general's office.

By January 2015, Brownstein, Melanio, and others knew that shifting the conversation from the two labor-backed bidders to the county's bid was a longshot, at best. Still, Melanio recalls her astonishment at seeing the tsunami of nurses clad in robin's breast red (CNA's colors) and Egyptian blue (SEIU's colors) as she pulled into the O'Connor parking lot ahead of that January public hearing.

"I was shocked," she said, "to see that the unions had the community outnumbered by roughly 100 to 1."

Shortly after Harris nixed the Prime deal, DeMoro called an emergency meeting in March 2015, attended by roughly 65 staffers.

"If we don't do something different now, we're going to die," she said.

A young Latina labor organizer raised her hand and said: "Why don't we start to build partnerships with the immigrant-rights community that's politically active and organizing across California?" I recall her saying. "We could really strengthen our own organizing capacity and deepen our roots in a community that is looking to join forces with institutional allies."

You could've heard the proverbial gnat piss on cotton in Georgia.

Later, the young organizer would tell me privately that had she been a white, male labor organizer, and replaced the immigrant rights community with some off-brand faction of Silicon Valley white liberals like Facebook founder Mark Zuckerberg, DeMoro would've been over the moon.

"Everybody knows that RoseAnn loves her white boys," she said.

Rifts such as this loom large in a nation facing the possibility of a financial meltdown that many economists predict could rival the Great Depression, if not surpass it. Few Americans of any race can recall with any specificity the history of organized labor in the U.S., but practically every adult has an opinion of whether labor unions have delivered anything of value to them, their co-workers, their family or their community. After 75 years of estrangement and treachery, the question is whether white labor leaders like DeMoro will reach out to non-white workers, and will African Americans and Latinos trust them if they do?

The Congress of Industrial Organization's bait-and-switch tactics also shine a light on the Democratic Party's use of identity politics today to control the political narrative. Angered by Local 22's robust endorsement of

Henry Wallace and his Progressive Party slate in the 1948 election, the CIO's Executive Council sent the African American president of the United Transport Service Employees union, Willard Townsend, to raid Local 22 in an NLRB election the following year. Townsend was the first Black member of the CIO's executive board, and more importantly, as virulently anti-communist as the NAACP's Walter White. His arrival coincided with a public relations campaign financed by R.J. Reynolds that was intended to persuade white members of Local 22 that it was their patriotic duty to quit a union dominated by communists.

Winston-Salem's mayor went on the radio to read excerpts from an anti-communist screed authored by the first chairman of the House Un-American Activities Committee, Martin Dies, the Texas congressman. As an unknown in Winston-Salem, Townsend had a snowball's chance in hell of winning the election but that was hardly the point; when the votes were tallied, Townsend managed to pull just enough African American votes from Local 22 to weaken its support at the plant, paving the way for the CIO to expel the tobacco workers' union for its communist leadership the next year.

Most prominent among Local 22's Reds was Moranda Smith, who in 1949 was named Southern Regional Director of the Food and Tobacco Workers union—representing more than 100,000 workers—and as a member of the union's national executive board, she occupied the highest position held by an African American woman in the labor movement up to that point. In that position, "Sister Smith," as she was known, traveled widely across the South in an attempt to defend the Food and Tobacco Workers' affiliates from raids by the CIO's conservative leadership.

On a hot and dusty Indian summer day in September 1949, the then-34-year-old Smith ambled defiantly down Main Street in Apopka, Florida. The night before, a group of Klansmen had kidnapped a Black man and tortured him to compel him to reveal where Smith was staying in town. The man would not talk, and the Klan left him, bloodied and battered, on the street as a warning.

Hearing of this, Sister Smith marched alone through the city the next day to show the Klan that neither she nor her union were afraid.

But the life span of a Black, communist, chain-smoking, lesbian labor organizer is not long, and she would drop dead of a stroke in April 1950. Five thousand mourners turned out for her funeral in Winston-Salem, and Paul Robeson sang to celebrate the life of one of the greatest, unknown soldiers in America's enduring class war.

10.

Days of Rage, Days of Grace

All power to all people.
We say white power to white people.
Brown power to brown people.
Yellow power to yellow people.
Black power to black people.
X power to those we left out.

–Fred Hampton

First, her eyes:

In one photograph after another taken between the time of her arrest in 1950 on espionage charges and her execution three years later, Ethel Rosenberg—née Greenglass—stared knowingly into the camera, unsmiling, undefeated and seemingly unafraid, with eyes the color of a moonless night, her lips pursed together in polite contempt for anyone who dared judge her, resembling the defiant wife of some indicted mob kingpin rather than a doting Jewish mother who'd not traveled west of New Jersey and never lived farther than five miles away from the Lower East side tenement where she'd been born.

Was she a communist? Certainly in spirit if not in name. And what of it? All she'd ever wanted was a career in theater, but fat chance of that when your dad makes his living repairing the overworked sewing machines used by overworked seamstresses in the garment district's sweltering sweatshops. At Seward Park High she was a fixture in school plays, leaving quite the impression on classmates who wrote under her yearbook photo, "Can she act? And how!" A friend would later recall Ethel belting out impromptu songs to describe the quotidian sights and smells they encountered as they walked to and from school each day. When a 15-year-old Ethel graduated from high school at the deflationary nadir of the Great Depression in 1931, there was barely enough money for three square meals a day, let alone college, so she enrolled in a six-month course to brush up on the secretarial skills she'd neglected while focusing on college preparatory courses.

While her mother thought it unbecoming for a proper Jewish girl, Ethel joined an amateur theater group, the Clark Players, that met in the neighborhood settlement house and managed to earn some nice coin singing in amateur talent programs, bringing home prizes of between $2 and $10, which helped put food on the Greenglass family's table. In 1934 she started work as a clerk at the National New York Packing and Shipping Company on West 36th Street where she would eventually earn wages of $7 per week. When clerks, porters, and other unorganized workers in the textile industries went on strike in the autumn of 1935, 19-year-old Ethel was the only woman on the plant's four-member strike committee, helping organize pickets and collaborating with her female co-workers in one particularly gutsy move to persuade truck drivers to respect their work stoppage. Wrote *the New York Times* in August 1935:

> [A]bout 150 young women pickets moved in squads through the garment district. . . . They lay on the pavement in front of trucks and dared the drivers to move.

After the strike, Ethel was fired. Formed earlier that same year, the National Labor Relations Board wrote that the move was retaliatory:

> There is no allegation or evidence that she was not an efficient employee. The respondent's (the company) antagonism to Ethel Greenglass undoubtedly arose by virtue of the fact that she was active in organizing the Union, was a member of the first and second committees, and had urged fellow employees who were working after Goldblatt's (a fellow union organizer) dismissal to cease working and protest against it.[212]

While waiting to perform at a benefit for the International Seamen's Union in 1936, she met Julius Rosenberg, an engineering student at City College and a dues-paying Red. The couple bonded over politics, raising funds and collecting signatures to petition the U.S. government to support the democratically elected Spanish Republic that was under siege from *Generalissimo* Franco's fascist rebels. They wed in June 1939, moved into a three-room flat on the Lower East Side, and started a family; Michael was born in 1943 and Robert four years later. Julius—or Julie, as Ethel called him for the rest of their lives—remained active in the Communist Party, but Ethel put everything on the back burner—her job, her music, and political organizing—to raise her two boys.

Despite federal agents' insistence that Julius was the key actor in the plot to pass nuclear technology developed at the Los Alamos lab to the Soviet Union, it was always Ethel, and those eyes that seemed to return your gaze with the searing intensity of a laser beam, who was the more compelling figure. Standing 4-feet-11-inches tall, she towered over America's internecine class struggle, polarizing rich and poor in the U.S. every bit as much as Argentina's populist First Lady, Eva Peron, who died of cancer the year before Ethel. Her stoicism on the witness stand so unsettled the powerful that President Dwight D. Eisenhower would later write that "in this instance it is the woman who is the strong and recalcitrant character, the man who is the weak one. She has obviously been the leader in everything they did in the spy ring."

Had she indeed been the ringleader of an atomic spy ring, then she was like none other. She cried herself to sleep almost every night that she was in prison, read *Parents* magazine voraciously, and was visiting her psychotherapist four times a week by the time of her arrest, according to her biographer Ilene Phillipson. And yet, she was fierce, calling J. Edgar Hoover's bluff and preferring to go to the gallows rather than betray either her husband or the people. On June 19th, 1953, prison guards at New York's Sing Sing prison strapped the couple into the electric chair. Julius died after the first jolt, but Ethel fought until the last; after administering three jolts of electricity, attendants removed the straps and were astonished to detect a heartbeat. Authorities applied two more shocks, after which witnesses reported seeing plumes of smoke waft from her head.[213]

Letters of support for the Rosenbergs poured in from both Marxists—the writers Nelson Algren, Dashiel Hammett and Bertolt Brecht, artists Frida Kahlo and Diego Rivera—and moderates such as Albert Einstein and the filmmaker Fritz Lang. Brooklyn's all-Black International Longshoremen's Association Local 968 walked off the job for a day to protest the Rosenbergs' scheduled execution, Pope Pius XII appealed to Eisenhower to spare the couple, the Spanish painter Pablo Picasso urged the world to stop "this crime against humanity," and French existentialist philosopher Jean-Paul Sartre denounced the execution as:

> . . . a legal lynching which smears with blood a whole nation. By killing the Rosenbergs, you have quite simply tried to halt the progress of science by human sacrifice. Magic, witch-hunts, autos-da-fé, sacrifices—we are here getting to the point: your country is sick with fear . . . you are afraid of the shadow of your own bomb.

Referring to Ethel as a "Saint on Earth," the *Daily Worker* wrote that she "lifted the hearts and steeled the spirits of countless simple men and women like [herself] in every corner of the earth."

The verdict rendered by history makes clear that at worst, Ethel typed the notes that Julius passed along to his Soviet handlers and that this classified information was either redundant or altogether useless, shaving no more than a year from the time it took the Soviets to develop their own nuclear warheads. Similar to HUAC's attack on Detroit's radicals a year earlier, the Rosenbergs' execution took dead aim at the interracial unity that had emerged as the leadership of the proletarian revolution. It was lost on absolutely no one that the most radical whites tended to be Jews whose historical memories of suffering at the hands of European mobs formed the basis of their support for African Americans. The Rosenbergs' two sons were adopted by the Jewish songwriter Abel Meeropol—who composed the anti-lynching dirge *Strange Fruit*, popularized by Billie Holliday—and his wife, Anne. Before turning to a career in music, Meeropol was a high school English teacher in New York City and among his students was a young James Baldwin.

Less well known is the role that an African American New York City social worker named Evelyn Williams played in the Meeropols' adoption of the Rosenberg boys. Following the Rosenbergs' execution, the state wanted to institutionalize the couple's sons to prevent their radicalization by an adopted Jewish family sympathetic to the Rosenbergs, which the Meeropols most certainly were. As the lead investigator assigned to the boys' case, Williams found herself pressured by her supervisor to uncover, or manufacture, the signs of neglect that would provide child welfare authorities with the pretext to remand the boys to an orphanage. In her autobiography, she wrote:

> Before my investigation was complete Panken called me into his chambers and threatened to fire me if I did not follow

> that recommendation. I made a choice: to base my decision concerning my future recommendations for the children solely on my own investigative findings and the hell with the job.

Williams would go on to earn a law degree and later defend the Black Liberation Army, which included her niece, Joanne Chesimard, who the world would come to know as Assata Shakur.

Other lives touched by the Rosenbergs' martyrdom included a young, interracial couple, Robert Nemiroff and Lorraine Hansberry, who spent the day before the wedding picketing the Rosenbergs' execution outside the federal courthouse in Chicago.

Hansberry, who would go on to write the agonizing play, *A Raisin in the Sun*, recalled:

> We had come to a wedding. We had come to Chicago to lose ourselves in the Bridal Song. And then there were those moments when the news came. And we spoke of it quietly to one another—our voices soft under the discussion of where the cake would be placed and when the photographers would arrive. [. . .] Our voices above the champagne glasses, our eyes questioning one another between the fresh fragrant flowers in their gleaming pots on the coffee tables of the wedding house, festive flowers. The Chicago heat in the vast living room suddenly overpowering the senses, some grim terrible fire within suddenly making it more awful, more stifling—the desire to fling the glass into the flowers, to thrust one's arms into the air and run out of the house screaming at (one's) countrymen to come down out of the apartments, down from the houses, to get up from the television sets, from the dinner tables. [. . .] The bride sits a moment in a corner alone to herself— she thinks: And what shall I say to my children? And how shall I explain such a thing to them?[214]

In her solitude, Hansberry paradoxically symbolized a nation of strangers beginning to tear down the Tower of Babel that had been erected to divide them. The ensuing call and response awakened in the people a great yearning for *liberté, égalité,* and *fraternité,* and combined with the lynchings of the Rosenbergs and Emmett Till, the Korean War, the Montgomery bus boycott, and the Supreme Court's 1954 decision in *Brown versus Board of Education of Topeka, Kansas* to create new vistas from which the nation could start to see both itself and others. From the hilltops to the hollows to the housing projects, fugitive wage slaves began sending up flares to alert others to their exact location or assure them that the coast was clear. This dialogue, in turn, opened new lines of intellectual inquiry and informed the ways in which Americans engaged the world and moved through it.

Three years after the Rosenbergs' execution, a 34-year-old Jewish history professor who had used the GI Bill to finish his doctoral thesis at Columbia University trundled his wife, two kids and all their earthly possessions into a 10-year-old Chevy and drove south, to Atlanta, arriving on a hot and rainy August night. The war veteran was not, as he would write later, looking to do good necessarily, but merely for a job, and the best offer he had was for $4,000 annually to chair the social sciences department at Spelman, the historically Black college for women. Of his arrival, he wrote:[215]

> There were no white students at Spelman. My students, in a rich variety of colors, had wonderful names like Geneva, Herschelle, Marnesba, Aramintha. They were from all over the country, but most were from the South and had never had a white teacher. They were curious and shy, but the shyness disappeared after we came to know one another. Some were the daughters of the black middle class of teachers, ministers, social workers, small businesspeople, skilled workers. Others were the daughters of maids, porters, laborers, tenant farmers. A college education for these young women was a matter of life and death. One of my students told me one day, 'My mother says I've got to do well,

because I've already got two strikes against me. I'm black and I'm a woman. One more strike and I'm out' . . .

I soon learned that beneath my students' politeness and decorum there was a lifetime of suppressed indignation. Once I asked them to write down their first memory of race prejudice, and the feelings tumbled out. One told how as a teenager she sat down in the front of a bus next to a white woman. 'This woman immediately stormed out of her seat, trampling over my legs and feet, and cursing under her breath. Other white passengers began to curse under their breaths. Never had I seen people staring at me as if they hated me. Never had I really experienced being directly rejected as though I were some poisonous, venomous creature.' A student from Forsyth, Georgia, wrote: 'I guess if you are from a small Georgia town, as I am, you can say that your first encounter with prejudice was the day you were born. . . . My parents never got to see their infant twins alive because the only incubator in the hospital was on the 'white side.' . . .

I had been at Spelman six months when, in January of 1957, my students and I had a small encounter with the Georgia state legislature. We had decided to visit one of its sessions. Our intent was simply to watch the legislature go about its business. But when we arrived we saw, and should have expected, that the gallery had a small B section on the side marked "colored." The students conferred and quickly decided to ignore the signs and sit in the main section, which was quite empty. Listening to the legislators drone on, even for a few minutes, about a bill on fishing rights in Georgia rivers, we could understand why the gallery was empty. As our group of about 30 filed into the seats, panic broke out. The fishing bill was forgotten. The Speaker of the House seemed to be having an apoplectic fit. He rushed to the microphone and shouted. 'You nigras get over to where you belong! We got segregation in the state of Georgia.' The

> members of the legislature were now standing in their seats and shouting up at us, the sounds echoing strangely in the huge domed chamber. The regular business was forgotten. Police appeared quickly and moved threateningly toward our group. We conferred again while the tension in the chamber thickened. Students were not yet ready, in those years before the South rose up en masse, to be arrested. We decided to move out into the hall and then come back into the "colored" section, me included. What followed was one of those strange scenes that the paradoxes of the racist, courteous South often produced. A guard came up to me, staring very closely, apparently not able to decide if I was "white" or "colored," then asked where this group of visitors was from. I told him. A moment later, the Speaker of the House went up to the microphone, again interrupting a legislator, and intoned, 'The members of the Georgia state legislature would like to extend a warm welcome to the visiting delegation from Spelman College.'

In 1959, the professor, acting as faculty advisor, proposed that the Spelman Social Science Club move beyond the theoretical. He wrote:

> Someone said, 'Why don't we try to do something about the segregation of the public libraries?' And so, two years before the sit-ins swept the South and "the Movement" excited the nation, a few young women at Spelman College decided to launch an attack on the racial policy of the main library in Atlanta. It was a nonviolent assault. Black students would enter the Carnegie Library, to the stares of everyone around, and ask for John Locke's *An Essay Concerning Human Understanding*, or John Stuart Mill's *On Liberty*, or Tom Paine's *Common Sense*. Turned away with evasive answers ('We'll send a copy to your Negro branch'), they kept coming back, asking for the Declaration of Independence, the Constitution of the United States, and other choices designed to make sensitive librarians uneasy. In the midst of our campaign, I was sitting in the office of Whitney Young,

> dean of the School of Social Work of Atlanta University, who was working with us. We were talking about what our next moves should be when the phone rang. It was a member of the library board.
>
> Whitney listened, said, 'Thank you,' and hung up. He smiled. The board had decided to end the policy of segregation in the Atlanta library system.

The Spelman professor in question was Howard Zinn, who went on to author *A People's History of the United States,* which has sold more than two million copies since it was published in 1980. Among his students were the novelist Alice Walker and the child welfare advocate Marian Wright Edelman, who wrote of her relationship with the "tall, lanky" professor with a warmth that is mindful of the agent Leila Steinberg's description of hers with Tupac Shakur:

> We called him Howie and felt him to be a confidant and friend as well as a teacher, contrary to the more formal and hierarchical traditions of many black colleges. He stressed analysis and not memorization; questioning, discussions, and essays rather than multiple choices and pet answers; and he conveyed and affirmed my Daddy's belief and message that I could do and be anything and that life was about far more than bagging a Morehouse man for a husband.[216]

Initially, the civil rights movement was fixated on the white gaze and integration, with buttoned-down young men and women politely asking to check out books from their local library, or patiently waiting to order the smothered chicken at the Woolworth's lunch counter or registering voters. Said one student of the passive-aggressive resistance strategy:

> We didn't feel we had a choice; the implication was plain that we were being let into the university on the condition that we become white men with dark skins.[217]

The Black-Jewish dialectic as epitomized by the alliance between Zinn and Edelman, however, began to challenge liberalism's understanding of African Americans as merely frustrated whites. In her unpublished memoir, a Jewish writer, Arlene Eisen—who would go on to join the radical Weather Underground, author a book on revolutionary Vietnamese women, and produce a seminal 2013 report on police violence against African Americans—recalled having a typical breakfast of coffee and a cigarette during her freshman year at Cornell University in 1961:

> As I sipped and exhaled, I stared at the headline on the front page of *the Cornell Daily Sun*. 'Patrice Lumumba is dead. Assassination suspected.' . . . The article said Lumumba was a popular leader who had been elected President of the Congo after they kicked the Belgians out. While I was still in high school I had found the autobiography by Kwame Nkrumah in a Greenwich Village bookstore. As I read Nkrumah's writing about the brutality of colonialism, I wept. I hardly knew anything about the Congo, except that my friends said that Lumumba was like Nkrumah—an idealistic man who fought for his peoples' independence. . . .
>
> That January day, as I emerged from the Strait intending to go to my next class, I was relieved to see 15 or 20 Black men—all African and Caribbean students dressed in suits and ties, along with Lucho, Pedro, Paco, Nicole and a few other white students [—] walking in a circle in front of the Student Union. They held signs. "Long Live Lumumba," "Belgium, CIA, Hands off the Congo," "Mobutu is a Traitor." Nicole motioned for me to join them. An extra sign rested against the bench. I picked it up and entered the circle. 'To hell with my class,' I decided.
>
> We walked around and around in a tiny circle. We did not chant. No one had the money to reproduce leaflets that might explain to bystanders why we were there. We tried to ignore the growing crowd of students who surrounded us. They were jeering and snickering at us.

'Commies, niggers, go back to Africa.'

'If you don't like it here, leave.'

'Lumumba got what was coming to him.'

There were more of them than us. Many more. I felt more contempt for them than fear. They reminded me of the people I left behind in Merrick. Finally, the Campus Police came and ordered everyone to leave. We did. I felt exhilarated from the chance to take a public stand for what I believed and, again, proud to be part of a select group of people who understood what was happening in the world. Yet, our embattled status also disturbed me. It was obvious we needed to teach a lot more people about the anticolonial movement in Africa. I decided to join Forum, a campus organization that sponsored educational lectures on world events.

At the first Forum meeting I attended, I felt like I was sitting on the sidelines of a verbal boxing match. In one corner were people who wanted to invite Roy Wilkins, the leader of the NAACP, to speak at Forum's next big public lecture. In the other corner were the advocates for inviting Leroi Jones, a radical Black New York poet who had recently returned from a trip to Cuba. I didn't know the rules of the match and all the debaters were men. It never occurred to me to open my mouth. I was certain I had nothing to contribute.

Yet, I paid close attention.

Wilkins' supporters claimed he was a national leader of the most important civil rights organization in the country. But others said that he may have been important in the 1940s and fifties, but now the NAACP was tired and old and irrelevant. Other organizations like SNCC and CORE had just started leading sit-ins and freedom rides to integrate the South. We should invite someone from one of those groups if we wanted to focus on civil rights. A man from the Leroi

Jones' side interrupted.

'I'm all for SNCC and CORE, but it will take time to contact them. I know someone from the Committee for Fair Play for Cuba in New York who can put us in touch with Leroi right away.'

'But that's a Commie organization,' someone from the other side yelled.

That cinched it for me. When we marched for Lumumba, the hecklers accused us of being Commies. I trusted my friends—Pedro and Nicole—not the hecklers. I had already rejected the side that hated communists.

Then, the only Black person in the room raised her hand to speak. I smiled in her direction. I had already met Angel at one of the foreign students' parties. The others ignored her. She was a tall, lean, dark-skinned woman whose confidence and grace fascinated me—especially because her right arm had been cut off above the elbow. One night, soon after that foreign students' party, she had knocked on my dorm room door. She was wearing baby doll, sleeveless pajamas, had a shoulder bag hanging from the same side as her stump and was carrying a razor. Her total comfort with her body amazed me.

'Arlene, I'm glad you're still awake. I need some help.'

'Sure,' I began to ask, 'what' . . .

Angel lifted the stump of her right arm and sort of waved it in the direction of her left armpit, still holding the razor in her good left hand. 'There's no way I can shave on my left side. Will you do it for me?'

'Sure, yes, of course. Lemme get some shaving cream,' eager to accommodate her. I hoped her request meant she wanted to be my friend.

'No need. I have some here.' And she reached into her

shoulder bag, handed me the can and smiled modestly. 'You know, I was born like this. I've had plenty of time to learn how to prepare for anything.'

Now the men at the Forum meeting continued yelling at each other and ignored Angel's raised hand. Finally, she got the nod to speak. I waved to her as she stood up, but felt vaguely disappointed that she didn't see me.

'You know I'm from New York City and I was in Harlem when Fidel Castro stayed at the Hotel Theresa and met publicly with Malcolm X. . . . '

A lot of the men started talking at once when Angel mentioned the name Malcolm X. Although there was a reverence in her voice when she pronounced his name, some people were asking who he was and others were saying he was some kind of racist crackpot who thought all white people were the devil. Angel raised her voice slightly and persisted.

'I'll tell you who Malcolm X is. He's a very popular and important leader in Harlem. You may not agree with everything he says, but thousands of Negroes follow him because he is showing us how to respect ourselves.

Anyway, I was trying to make a point about Cuba and Leroi Jones, not Malcolm.'

She paused, expecting the others to quiet down and finally they did.

'Leroi Jones represents a new generation of Black people who, like Malcolm, understand that our struggle for freedom is not for civil rights. It's for human rights. We can't be begging the Dixiecrats for the right to vote or to sit at their lunch counters. We need to change the system altogether. Cuba changed its system.'

A white man who favored Roy Wilkins, rose from the front row, waved his hands in the air and turned to face the rest.

Angel paused as he yelled.

'You commie. Shut up. We don't listen to commies. You're gonna get us in trouble.'

Angel gave him a bemused smile and continued as if she hadn't been interrupted. I wanted to clap for her, but was afraid of drawing attention to myself.

'Cuba inspired Leroi Jones and he's not the only one. The purpose of Forum is to encourage a debate on campus that teaches us something we don't already know. We already know Roy Wilkins' story.' Then she sat down.

The vote was close. But those of us for Leroi Jones won.

Towering over Eisen's political education were two intellectuals, one Jewish, one Black: Karl Marx and Malcolm X. Marx remains acutely relevant if for no other reason than that his critique of capitalism remains the standard-bearer, and all other views on the matter, whether in support or denunciation, are in response to his. Burnishing his legacy worldwide are his many disciples who emerged in the early Cold War period, including high-profile figures such as Paul Robeson, Fidel Castro, and Che Guevara, and lesser-known but still important intellectuals such as the British sociologist E.P. Thompson, whose 1963 book, *The Makings of the English Working Class,* described in painstaking detail the autonomy and agency of the British proletariat in the formative years of industrial society and urged scholars to *study the people*, rather than their rulers.

Malcolm X's metamorphosis from pimp to prophet embodied this understanding of the most oppressed as the engine for modernity. Upon his 1952 release from the Massachusetts state correctional facility in Norfolk, Malcolm joined the Nation of Islam, changed his surname from "Little" to "X"—reflecting the unknowable African name that was stolen from him by slavery—and threw himself into organizing for the religious sect, first from the Detroit Temple, and later from his post atop the Harlem mosque.

Estimated at only 400 members nationwide when Malcolm was paroled, membership skyrocketed to 40,000 within seven years, owing in no small part to Malcolm's uncommon skill as an orator.

It wasn't simply a matter of style, however; substantively speaking, the self-taught Malcolm was a revelation, particularly for the young. And while there is no record that he ever joined the party, Malcolm's understanding of Marx was profound. He once told an audience:

> It's impossible for a white person to believe in capitalism and not believe in racism. You can't have capitalism without racism. And if you find one and you happen to get that person into a conversation and they have a philosophy that make [sic] you sure they don't have this racism in their outlook, usually they're socialists or their political philosophy is socialism."

Mike Wallace's 1959 documentary, *The Hate That Hate Produced*, raised Malcolm's profile, and as his speaking engagements on college campuses spiked, so too did the cross-fertilization of Marxism and Pan-Africanism, and questions about the ineffectiveness of sit-ins, rent strikes, and integration, following the failure of the Mississippi Freedom Democratic Party to gain admittance to the 1964 Democratic Convention in Atlantic City.

Harkening back to the freedpeople who wanted to put as much distance as they practically could between themselves and the white community, Malcolm called for African Americans to control their own communities just as whites controlled theirs.

This resonated with Black students. Over a two-year period beginning in 1968, there were protests on nearly two hundred college campuses, the majority of which combined opposition to the Vietnam War with demands for Black studies, or the renaming of buildings, dormitories and libraries after Malcolm X. In her fantastic book, *The Black Revolution on Campus*, the scholar Martha Biondi wrote:

> With remarkable organization and skill, this generation of Black students challenged fundamental tenets of university life. They insisted that public universities should reflect and serve the people of their communities; that private universities should rethink the mission of elite education; and that historically Black colleges should survive the era of integration and shift their mission to community-based Black empowerment. Most crucially, Black students demanded a role in the definition and production of scholarly knowledge. These students constituted the first critical mass of African Americans to attend historically white universities. Deeply inspired by *The Autobiography of Malcolm X* and the charismatic leadership of Stokely Carmichael, yet shaken by the murder of Martin Luther King Jr., they were engaged in a redefinition of the civil rights struggle at a time when cities were in flames, hundreds of thousands of young Americans were at war in Southeast Asia, and political assassination was commonplace. These were 'Malcolm's children,' and they were inspired by the slain leader's denunciation of American hypocrisy and his call for Black Control over Black Institutions.

Of all Malcolm's children, none was more extraordinary than Fred Hampton, who was 16 when Malcolm was assassinated. Growing up in the Chicago suburb of Maywood, Hampton led student protests at his high school demanding more African American faculty, and joined the local NAACP, advocating for increased recreational and educational opportunities for youths. After high school, he enrolled in a pre-law curriculum at nearby Triton Junior College, and eventually rose to the rank of chairman of the Illinois chapter of the Black Panthers. Under his leadership, the Panthers negotiated a nonaggression pact between Chicago's street gangs, and they expanded the arrangement in the summer of 1969 with the formal launch of the Rainbow Coalition, incorporating the

Students for a Democratic Society, the American Indian Movement, the Puerto Rican Young Lords, and the Young Patriots, a group of poor whites from Appalachia who had settled mostly in Chicago's Uptown neighborhood. At a Black Panther conference in Oakland that year, a Young Patriots leader, William "Preacherman" Fesperman, spoke to the need for a class-conscious movement:

> We come from a monster. And the jaws of the monster in Chicago are grinding up the flesh and spitting out the blood of the poor and oppressed people, the blacks in the South Side, the West Side; the browns in the North Side; and the reds and the yellows; and yes, the whites—white oppressed people.[218]

The class struggle collided with the Black liberation movement in 1968, however, when Black and Puerto Rican parents in Brooklyn's Ocean Hill and Brownsville neighborhoods proposed that they assume the responsibility for managing their children's public schools. Influenced by Malcolm's pedagogy of self-reliance, the takeover plan merely acknowledged the failure of white administrators and educators to imbue Black and brown students with either the knowledge or the confidence they would need to succeed. More than a decade after the Supreme Court's desegregation order, New York City's schools were more segregated than ever, test scores were abysmal, dropout rates high, and classrooms overcrowded. And so it seemed only fair to parents in the Ocean Hill-Brownsville school district that if the largely white schools' bureaucracy couldn't meet the needs of their children, they should do it themselves. With support from Mayor John Lindsay and the Ford Foundation, organizers pitched the idea to New York City's Board of Education, which signed off on the pilot project in July 1967.

Nearly a year later on May 9th, 1968, a 38-year-old science teacher at Junior High School 271 in the Ocean Hill-Brownsville district, Fred Nauman, was a few minutes into his first class when he was summoned to the principal's office, where he was handed an envelope. It read:

> Dear Sir:
>
> The Governing Board of the Ocean Hill—Brownsville Demonstration School District has voted to end your employment in the schools of this District. This action was taken on the recommendation of the Personnel Committee. This termination of employment is to take effect immediately. In the event you wish to question this action, the Governing Board will receive you on Friday, May 10, 1968, at 6:00 P.M., at Intermediate School 55, 2021 Bergen Street, Brooklyn, New York.
>
> You will report Friday morning to Personnel, 110 Livingston Street, Brooklyn, for reassignment.
>
> Sincerely,
>
> Rev. C. Herbert Oliver, Chairman Ocean Hill—Brownsville Governing Board
>
> Rhody A. McCoy Unit Administrator[219]

A German Jew who arrived in New York with his parents on the eve of World War II, Nauman was one of 19 teachers and administrators who had received the reassignment notice. He was also a chairman for the United Federation of Teachers, or UFT, representing 55,000 public school teachers, a good many of them Jewish. Signing its first union contract in 1961, the UFT was the successor to the more radical Teachers' Union, which had been destroyed in the 1950s by Taft-Hartley's communist witch hunts. The UFT eschewed the Congress of Industrial Organization's model of civil rights unionism for a conservative approach that was more in sync with the American Federation of Labor's myopic praxis in the interwar years.

This echoed the conversation in the broader Jewish community at the time.

Although a number of leftist organizations protested the Rosenbergs' conviction, others—most notably the American Jewish Committee—endorsed the verdict. With the horror of the Holocaust still in everyone's rearview mirror, elites in the U.S. began to extend the racial contract to Jews, offering them the opportunity to enjoy the same privileges and protections as whites if only they would agree to unambiguously switch sides in the class war and participate in the white settlers' subjugation of the Negro. Not all Jews agreed to this deal; indeed Zinn was a keeper of the radical faith until the day he died of a heart attack in 2010, as were the attorney William Kunstler and many others like Eisen and the Rosenberg's two sons. But it is no accident that the neoconservative movement that flourished in the 1980s was led by Jewish intellectuals such as Nathan Glazer, Milton Himmelfarb, Irving Kristol, Eliot Cohen, Hannah Arendt, Daniel Bell, and perhaps most importantly, the libertarian economist Milton Friedman, who first came to prominence for rushing to the aid of white parents traumatized by the U.S. Supreme Court's 1954 desegregation ruling in *Brown v. Board of Education*. By proposing a voucher system that remains the template for school privatization, Friedman's ultimate goal was to offload the cost of public education to working-class parents, *à la* Virginia's postbellum Funders, and chillingly, discourage the poor from having children as part of a eugenics plot, as the scholar Nancy MacLean explained in a 2021 paper entitled "How Milton Friedman Exploited White Supremacy to Privatize Education."[220]

Narrowly interpreting community control as a challenge to their rights won by negotiating a collective bargaining agreement with the city, Jewish union leaders such as Nauman and United Federation of Teachers' President Albert Shanker followed Friedman's lead in objecting to the governing board's choices for principals in the Ocean Hill—Brownsville schools, opposing changes in the curriculum to reflect the students' African heritage, and insisting that the community did not have the right to reassign uninspired, underperforming teachers. According to Jerald Podair's marvelous account, *The Strike That Changed New York: Blacks, Whites and the Ocean Hill-Brownsville Crisis,* the project's African American superintendent, Rhody McCoy

> . . . had begged union leaders to be more flexible. They wouldn't listen. He had told Nauman and his colleagues that this was an experiment in community control, and if this did not mean control over personnel, finances, and curriculum, what did it mean? They didn't understand. The union seemed to go out of its way to throw bureaucratic impediments at him. He was trying to be reasonable, but the white teachers wouldn't meet him halfway. It was as if they didn't respect him. Perhaps that was it. He didn't have "proper credentials." Most of the sixteen members of the local board were women; many were on welfare. Nauman and the union didn't think they were "professional" enough. Or maybe they just weren't white enough, perhaps that was the problem. In any case, a few days before, McCoy and the local board had decided to do something about it. They had met and made a list of the educators in the district who were the most hostile to community control. Nauman was one of them . . .

When the teachers tried to return to their classrooms, they were blocked by hundreds of community residents. On May 15, 300 police officers escorted the teachers back to schools, breaking the blockade until the schools reopened in the fall of 1968. The UFT led a series of citywide strikes, shutting down New York's public schools for 36 days. The strike ended in November 1968 when the New York state education commissioner took control of the Ocean Hill-Brownsville district and reinstated the dismissed teachers. The damage, however, was lasting. With Jews charging anti-Semitism and Blacks countering with charges of racism, the vanguard of the workers movement that had begun to dig the nation out of a deep hole almost 40 years earlier was irrevocably split. And perhaps just as devastating, the Ford Foundation's cynical support of community control combined with Milton Friedman's school voucher plans to plant the seeds for the privatization of public education that emerged in the Clinton administration.

Under the leadership of McGeorge Bundy, the national security advisor in both the Kennedy and Johnson administrations, the Ford Foundation hoped to domesticate the radical Black polity that posed an existential threat to the white settler capitalist project. McBundy and his liberal aides did not want self-determination for African Americans so much as assimilation, and envisioned community control of schools as a means of appeasement. By the time the State Board of Education had assumed control of the Ocean Hill-Brownsville district, the Ford Foundation was already backing away from the experiment, and qualifying its support for the movement's leaders who saw community control as a means to express an African identity that was clearly at odds with racial capitalism.[221]

The foundation's attempts to manage a social movement from the top down, however, was the opposite of the Communist Party's strategy in defending the Scottsboro Boys and a precursor for Mark Zuckerberg's failed $100 million investment in Newark's public schools, the Gates Foundation's $200 million investment in standardized testing for teachers, and a philanthropic-industrial complex that neutered the Movement for Black Lives Matter.

The tragedy is that the Brooklyn schools' crisis represented a squandered opportunity to patch the fissures that had developed in the biracial working-class coalition that modernized the nation. In response to violence against and mass jailings of civil rights protesters in Birmingham, Alabama, in the spring of 1963, the attorney general at the time, Robert F. Kennedy, requested a private meeting with James Baldwin and several other Blacks at Kennedy's Central Park apartment. In attendance were RFK and his aide, Burke Marshall; Baldwin and his brother David; Harry Belafonte; the Black psychologist Kenneth Clark; Lena Horne; Edwin Berry of the Chicago Urban League; Clarence Jones, an advisor to Martin Luther King Jr.; the actor Rip Torn; the NAACP's June Shagaloff; Lorraine Hansberry; and Jerome Smith, who had founded the New Orleans chapter of the Congress of Racial Equality and was in New York for treatment on a jaw that had been broken in a scuffle with Southern cops. The meeting began politely enough but heated up as Jerome Smith began to openly question the federal government's sincerity in protecting Blacks from white terrorism. Exasperated, Kennedy turned from Smith as if to say (Baldwin would later write), "I'll talk to all of you, who are civilized. But who is he?"

At this point, Hansberry, who had grieved the Rosenbergs' execution on her wedding day, spoke up. "You have a great many very accomplished people in this room, Mr. Attorney General, but the only man you should be listening to is that man [Smith] over there. That is the voice of 22 million people."

Hansberry then dropped the mic.

"We would like from you a moral commitment."

Robert Kennedy reportedly called the meeting a waste of time. But less than a month later, his brother, President John F. Kennedy, introduced what would become the Civil Rights Act of 1964, characterizing it as not just a legal issue but a moral one, borrowing Hansberry's exact language. Later, when Robert Kennedy was running for president, he told the British journalist David Frost:

> I think there has to be a new kind of coalition to keep the Democratic Party going, and to keep the country together. We have to write off the unions and the South now, and replace them with Negroes, blue collar whites and the kids. We have to convince the Negroes and the poor whites that

> they have common interests. If we can reconcile those hostile groups, and then add the kids, you can really turn this country around.[222]

11.

Embedded

If you're not careful, the newspapers will have you hating the people who are oppressed and loving the people who are doing the oppressing.

–Malcolm X

Anytime you catch folks lying, they're scared of something.

–Zora Neale Hurston

On Thursday, December 4th, 1969, at about 4:30 a.m., three unmarked Chicago police cars and a panel truck left the 26th Street office of the Cook County State's Attorney and headed west. The lakefront air was bitterly cold, and the vehicles moved deliberately past the empty lots, gutted warehouses, and walk-ups that dotted the city's west side like rows of rotting teeth. Ten minutes later they'd arrived at their destination: an old yellow brick two-flat at 2337 West Monroe. Parking 50 yards up the street, 14 officers tumbled out, clad in leather jackets and fur hats. Their armaments included one .357-caliber pistol, 19 .38-caliber pistols, one carbine, five shotguns, and one Thompson submachine gun with 110 rounds of ammunition.

They had no tear-gas canisters, no sound equipment, and no spotlights; none were necessary for this mission.

They split up into three groups. Five officers ambled up the six stone stairs at the front of the two-flat and entered through the narrow outer hallway, while six moved through the passageway alongside the building and climbed the back stairs. The remaining three waited outside on the sidewalk. Sergeant Daniel Groth pounded on the front door. "Who's there?" barked a voice from inside the first-floor apartment. Groth demanded that the occupants open the door, and heard more voices and shuffling inside, followed by a pause.

Officer James "Gloves" Davis kicked in the front door commando-style and he, Groth, and the other three officers in his unit burst into the living room, lighting up the bluish darkness with a flash of carbine, pistol and shotgun fire. Simultaneously, the six on the back porch sprang into action. Officer Edward Carmody kicked open the rear door and entered through the kitchen, firing three shots from his revolver. Two of his men followed on his heels, crouching to fire shotgun blasts.

Then the submachine gun rang out; later, the officers would describe what followed as a macabre dance, their fusillade lighting up the room like flickering neon, casting the writhing bodies in sharp relief as they fell to the floor. Finally, after a few minutes, another pause, followed by two more shots in quick succession from a bedroom, and it was over.

"The premises are under control," a patrolman who had just arrived on the scene reported over his squad-car radio. Within minutes ambulances and more patrol cars arrived, hustling two men and a pregnant woman out of the building in handcuffs. Four others were carted out on stretchers, wounded but alive, followed by two corpses: 22-year-old Mark Clark, shot once in the heart, and the chairman of the Illinois Chapter of the Black Panther Party, Fred Hampton, who had been struck once in the chest, once in the shoulder, and twice in the forehead at close range.

He was 21.

As their bodies were loaded into ambulances for transport to the Cook County morgue, the news of their passing was relayed over the police two-way radio, and later, the downtown dispatcher reported hearing cheers from police cars scattered over the city. Said one officer: "That's when to get them; when they're in their beds!"[223]

Six months later, *New York* magazine published a startling story written by Tom Wolfe entitled *Radical Chic: That Party at Lenny's*, illustrated with a cover photograph of three glamorous white women in evening gowns raising their gloved fists in a Black power salute à la Tommie Smith and John Carlos at the 1968 Olympics. Wolfe's account of a lavish fundraiser for 21 jailed Black Panthers held at the composer Leonard Bernstein's tony Upper East Side townhouse was simply unlike anything ever seen before in the annals of American journalism. For starters, there was Wolfe's novelistic treatment of the event, which made no pretense of objectivity and deployed an Oscar Wilde-like sensibility in its rendering of what unfurled inside Bernstein's home. Its poetry notwithstanding, however, *Radical Chic* was a hissing broadside that took aim at Black radicalism and the white limousine liberals who would support it, representing a sharp departure for journalists who had reported in a mostly matter-of-fact tone on the Black Panthers since the organization's inception in 1966, if they bothered to mention the organization at all. For example, when dozens of pistol-packing Panthers marched on the California State Assembly to protest gun-control laws, the incident earned but a single sentence in *Newsweek* and no mention in *Time*. Wolfe, however, abandoned the standard "who, what, when, how" journalistic framework to vilify the left-leaning sympathies articulated by

Bernstein and his guests, mocking the Panthers for everything from their afros to the manner in which they spoke to their apocryphal shakedowns of Jewish merchants. He referenced one Panther as "huge," ridiculed the Bernsteins' hiring of white servants rather than Black or brown ones, repeatedly reminded his readers of the Bernsteins' Jewishness ("stein not *steen*") and the couple's ostentatious wealth, dropped hints about the musician's then-closeted homosexuality, and lamented the tendency of the rich to romanticize the more "primitive" elements of society, invoking the French phrase *nostalgie de la boue,* or "nostalgia for the mud."

> God, what a flood of taboo thoughts runs through one's head at these Radical Chic events. . . . But it's delicious. It is as if one's nerve-endings were on red alert to the most intimate nuances of status. Deny it if you want to! Nevertheless, it runs through every soul here. It is the matter of the marvelous contradictions on all sides. It is like the delicious shudder you get when you try to force the prongs of two horseshoe magnets together . . . them and us . . .

Yet, if Wolfe's reportage trafficked glibly in shopworn tribal tropes and sexual innuendo suggesting ulterior motives for the pairing of Black revolutionaries and white socialites, then Gail Sheehy's two-part series that appeared in *New York* magazine five months later landed like a direct blow from a blunt instrument in an apparent attempt to serialize *The Birth of a Nation.* Centered on the trial of 12 Black Panthers for murdering one of their own in New Haven, Connecticut, Sheehy's article, *The Agony of Panthermania,* was published in the November 16th, 1970, edition of *New York* magazine, and purported to interrogate the relationship between New Haven's middle-class, or "good" Blacks, against the "bad niggers" who joined the local Panthers chapter. What it was, in effect, was "a compendium of every ugly cliche about Blacks one could imagine," according to Michael E. Staub, an English professor at the City University of New York.[224]

According to Sheehy, militant Blacks were often addicted to heroin "chipping a little . . . under the skin of [the] knee" . . . they were overly sexual, had low IQs, and were overly concerned with cool headgear and fancy cars. Sheehy even mobilized the motif of the emasculated Black man "desperate to claim his manhood" fixated entirely on "ego and sex."

Much as the Fusionists' rainbow coalition had unnerved North Carolina's aristocracy 70 years earlier, the Black Panthers' growing appeal to a wide swath of liberals triggered what Staub described as a "moral panic" among the nation's plutocrats and their vassals in the media who were frantic to quarantine an outbreak of class-consciousness. Four days after the assassinations of Hampton and Clark, 350 Los Angeles police officers conducted another early morning raid, this time on the Panthers' headquarters at 41st Street and Central Avenue, bringing to a merciful close Richard M. Nixon's first year in the White House, which had begun with the killings of two Black Panthers, Alprentice "Bunchy" Carter and John Huggins, in a shootout with a rival group just three days before Nixon was even sworn in. These escalating attacks on the Panthers bore the hallmarks of a covert operation coordinated by the FBI, harkening back to the Palmer Raids roundup of leftist dissidents, and foreshadowing the 2007 Pentagon offensive known euphemistically as the "surge," which targeted Iraqi militants for assassination during the United States' occupation of that country.

With the assassinations of Malcolm X and Martin Luther King Jr., the charismatic Hampton was as likely as anyone to inherit the mantle of the messianic figure that the FBI's Hoover warned of in his infamous 1967 memo creating a counter-intelligence program known by its uninspired acronym, COINTELPRO, to "expose, disrupt, misdirect, discredit or otherwise neutralize the activities of Black-nationalist, hate-type organizations . . . "

Reprising Jennett's role from the Wilmington coup 71 years earlier,

Wolfe and Sheehy's New Journalism headed up the counterrevolution's editorial strategy.

To be sure, the savage inequalities visited upon the U.S. represent a failure of all of America's liberal institutions—from the criminal justice system to labor unions to the academy—but none more so than the news media. In updating its authoritarian motherboard, New Journalism, like the old, foments racial terror, isolates progressive ideas, and promotes solidarity among whites regardless of whether they have anything in common other than European ancestry. The prose of Wolfe and Sheehy gave *Orientalism* a fresh coat of paint, eschewing reportorial inquiry for an author's narration, substituting impressions—and even fantasies—for facts, and putting a bull's-eye on the backs of the noisiest change agents.

Much as the freedpeople spearheaded the democratizing political, social, and labor movements of the late 19th century, their grandchildren and great-grandchildren were again leading the charge for a more perfect union in the 1960s, inspiring, among others, gay, Puerto Rican, and even Zionist activists as well as the eruption of more than 300 urban rebellions between the 1964 disturbance in Harlem and the nationwide riots that followed King's 1968 assassination. And to the chagrin of the ruling class, none of the prophetic voices in the Black liberation movement trumpeted a "kill whitey" rhetorical line. Rather, in keeping with a tradition of scholarship passed down from both autodidacts and credentialed intellectuals such as Robeson, Du Bois, and Malcolm X, all of the important Black militants from the era promoted violence only as a means of self-defense. "We don't hate white people," the Black Panther leadership was fond of saying to the media, "we hate the oppressor." Said Hampton:

> We've got to face the fact that some people say you fight fire best with fire but we say you put fire out best with water. We say you don't fight racism with racism, we're going to fight racism with solidarity. We say you don't fight

> capitalism with black capitalism; you fight capitalism with socialism. . . . We're going to fight . . . with all of us people getting together and having an international proletarian revolution.[225]

The Black prophetic fire that Hampton embodied set the country ablaze, spreading across the prairie to the coasts and south, to the sea. A *Fortune* magazine poll in the fall of 1968 found that 368,000 university students considered themselves revolutionaries; three years later, a poll by *Playboy* magazine showed that number had swollen to 1.7 million. A survey in September 1969 showed that 57 percent of Americans opposed the war, up 12 percentage points from June. Another survey of college students by Gallup in 1970 found that 44 percent of respondents felt violence on behalf of social change was justified, and more than a third described themselves as "Left" or "far Left." A few months after the U.S. invaded Cambodia, *The New York Times* reported that four of ten college students, or three million people, believed that revolution was necessary to right America's wrongs. In May 1970, *The Wall Street Journal* reported that at least 500 GIs deserted every day of that month and many Black soldiers returned home to join radical organizations, while remaining soldiers began to "frag" their commanding officers by lobbing grenades into their tents while they slept to voice their opposition to the war in Vietnam. After the National Guard fatally shot four demonstrators at an antiwar protest at Kent State University in the spring of 1970, a Harris poll reported demonstrations on 80 percent of college campuses. Student strikes and sabotage of campus buildings exploded across the country and by May 1970, the National Strike Information Center at Brandeis University announced that 448 campuses were either striking or shut down. An offshoot of the Students for a Democratic Society on New York's Lower East Side dubbed themselves the Motherfuckers and set fire to uncollected trash during the 1968 garbage workers' strike.

"Revolution," the political prisoner and Black Panther Mumia Abu Jamal said of the era, "seemed as inevitable as tomorrow's newspaper."[226]

Initially at least, COINTELPRO's assault on the Panthers did not seem to slow the radicalization of white activists but accelerated it. The New Left, which had sprung from the college antiwar movement, responded to Hampton's murder by organizing working class whites in Chicago (Rising Up Angry), Philadelphia (the October 4th Organization), and the Bronx (White Lightning), using the Panthers' community service model of free breakfast programs and free health and legal clinics as organizing tools.[227] In late 1970, a white, mild-mannered physics professor at Haverford College, William Davidon, asked his friends: "What do you think of burglarizing an FBI office?" A few months later in March 1971, while much of the country was transfixed by the first of the three heavyweight fights between Joe Frazier and Muhammad Ali, eight white antiwar activists, ranging in age from 20 to 44, did exactly that, burgling an FBI office in suburban Philadelphia and stealing every file in sight. Calling themselves the Citizens Commission to Investigate the FBI, they mailed the most damning files to newspaper reporters, revealing the existence of COINTELPRO's massive domestic spying, "particularly of its Black citizens," as *Washington Post* reporter William Greider wrote a year after the break-in.[228]

Of all the white leftists in the Panthers' orbit, however, none were more radicalized by Hampton's murder than the 11 activists who'd splintered from the Students for a Democratic Society in June 1969 to form the Weather Underground. At the ninth annual SDS conference in Chicago, the organization's radical cell, the Revolutionary Youth Movement, issued a 16,000-word manifesto named for a Bob Dylan song, "You Don't Need A Weatherman to Know Which Way the Wind Blows." The document identified African Americans as colonized subjects and proposed that the SDS raise their revolutionary metabolism to "bring the war home," and seed a classless society. In arguing that SDS should commit to guerilla warfare, one of the Revolutionary Youth Movement's leaders, a 27-year-old graduate of the University of Chicago's Law School, Bernardine Dohrn said:

> The best thing that we can be doing for ourselves, as well as for the Panthers and the revolutionary black liberation struggle, is to build a fucking white revolutionary movement.[229]

Dohrn and Bill Ayers, who would later become her husband, were especially close to Hampton, who disapproved of the Weathermen's plans to jump-start the revolution with three days of violent demonstrations in Chicago in October 1969. Regardless of the rift, nearly 300 activists attended the Weathermen's emergency War Council in Flint, Michigan, three weeks after Hampton's assassination. Held at a dance hall in a Black neighborhood where walls were bloodstained from an earlier confrontation between police and dissidents, organizers met for three days, culminating with a decision by the Weathermen to go underground to elude the FBI's widening dragnet, and to turn up the heat with guerilla attacks targeting the state. In May 1970, four months after the Bernsteins' fundraiser, the Weathermen released this communique to the press:

> Hello. This is Bernardine Dohrn. I'm going to read a DECLARATION OF A STATE OF WAR . . . Ever since SDS became revolutionary, we've been trying to show how it is possible to overcome the frustration and impotence that comes from trying to reform this system. Kids know the lines are drawn; revolution is touching all of our lives. Tens of thousands have learned that protest and marches don't do it. Revolutionary violence is the only way. . . . Within the next fourteen days we will attack a symbol or institution of Amerikán injustice. This is the way we celebrate the example of Eldridge Cleaver and H. Rap Brown and all black revolutionaries who first inspired us by their fight behind enemy lines for the liberation of their people. Never again

> will they fight alone.[230]

If the Weathermen wanted war, the 37th president of the United States was only too happy to accommodate. Possessed of remarkable pettiness and venality even by American political standards, Richard Milhous Nixon was also a masterful political strategist whose genius, an aide once said, was "understanding who hates who." His obsession during his five-and-a-half years in the Oval Office was smashing the New Deal consensus that had by 1970 governed the country for nearly 40 years. Aping efforts by his hero, Woodrow Wilson, Nixon sought to revive a laconic race war through a wide range of domestic policies intended to pit white workers against Black and leave the Democrats' out-of-touch, "effete" East Coast liberal leadership holding the bag.

In his 2008 biography, *Nixonland*, the author Rick Perlstein describes Nixon's first inauguration in a fashion that evokes the climactic scene in *The Godfather* in which Michael Corleone attends his nephew's christening while his henchmen dispose of his enemies. After he was sworn in, Nixon spoke of a stirring peace for a troubled nation:

> The greatest honor history can bestow is the title of peacemaker. This honor now beckons America — the chance to help lead the world at last out of the valley of turmoil, and onto that high ground of peace that man has dreamed of since the dawn of civilization.

As he spoke, thousands of antiwar protesters huddled in the freezing January rain for a counter-inaugural demonstration.

> The second third of this century has been a time of proud achievement. We have made enormous strides in science and industry and agriculture. We have shared our wealth more broadly than ever. We have learned at last to manage a modern economy to assure its continued growth. We have given freedom new reach, and we have begun to make its promise real for black as well as for white. We see the hope

of tomorrow in the youth of today.

After he had finished, protesters threw a jug of wine at the marine commandant's convertible, screamed "Romney eats shit" at HUD Secretary George Romney, and set fire to miniature flags along the parade route. A phalanx of Secret Servicemen, Perlstein wrote, swatted down rocks, beer cans and bottles hurled at the president and first lady as they passed by in a retrofitted limousine. Perlstein continued:

> Afterward, the Justice Department's Warren Christopher met with new White House counsel John Ehrlichman. Christopher handed over a packet of documents and instructed the president to keep them on hand at all times; proclamations to declare martial law with blanks to fill in the date and the name of the city.

From the start, the Washington press corps made it known they had no intention of refereeing this fight, describing Nixon and his cabinet as "cool," "efficient," "confident," and "mellow" and the inaugural protesters as "disgruntled remnants out to ruin the new atmosphere of peace and conciliation."[231]

That Nixon himself frowned upon peace and conciliation became clear in April 1970 when he announced plans to extend the Vietnam War into neighboring Cambodia. Five months to the day after Hampton's murder, on May 4th, 1970, Ohio National Guardsmen fired into a crowd of demonstrators at Kent State University, killing four students and injuring nine, triggering a wave of student strikes across the country, and forcing hundreds of universities to close. About a week after the Kent State shootings, police killed six and wounded 20 Black protesters in Augusta, Georgia; a few days later, state and local police killed two and wounded 12 Black students in protests at Jackson State College (now University).

Around the same time, police bayoneted 11 students at the University of New Mexico, wounded seven people with shotgun fire at Ohio State

University, and wounded another 12 with birdshot in Buffalo. And in a scene that was a harbinger of the Trump era, 200 white construction workers surged past a barricade of indifferent New York City police officers to attack anti-war protesters. When the melee was over, nearly 70 people were injured, and the mob of construction workers marched triumphantly through the narrow streets of Lower Manhattan towards City Hall, where they sang the Star-Spangled Banner and demanded that Mayor Lindsay raise the flags that he had lowered to half-mast to honor the Kent State victims. Lindsay complied.

The fatal shootings of four white students at Kent State, however, marked an inflection point reminiscent of the four labor organizers hanged for the 1886 Haymarket bombing in Chicago. Whether intended to send a message or not, Kent State, like Haymarket, was essentially a shot across the bow, discouraging whites from participating in leftist movements in which there was a reasonable chance that their blood might be spilled in the streets just like Blacks who made trouble for the ruling class. Nixon understood that unspooling the Democrats' already tenuous rainbow coalition would usher in a new Republican majority. A Gallup Poll taken days after the shootings suggests that Kent State did indeed have a chilling effect on public attitudes that was similar to the anti-union repression that followed the Haymarket affair: 58 percent of respondents blamed the students for the violence, and only 11 percent held the National Guard culpable.

Lending credence to suspicions that Nixon ordered the attacks on Kent State to lift whites' longstanding immunity from state violence, the president of Black United Students, Charles Eberhardt, spotted the National Guardsmen milling around the campus on the morning of the rally, and deducing that Black students would be targeted as was typically the case, he got word out that African American students should stay inside their dorm room for the duration of the afternoon rally. They did. Said Eberhardt in a 2020 interview:

> I couldn't believe they were shooting, with live ammunition, on a college campus. I couldn't believe they would do that against white students.[232]

Following the Kent State massacre, whites began to abandon their alliance with Black activists, similar to their forefathers' abandonment of the labor movement as the robber barons escalated their attacks on the Knights of Labor. Wrote David Barber in his book, *A Hard Rain Fell: SDS and Why It Failed*:

> The New Left failed because it ultimately came to reflect the dominant white culture's understanding of race, gender, class, and nation. While all these elements are inextricably intertwined, race is the key element in understanding the trajectory of the New Left. Pushed by the black movement, white New Leftists struggled to come to grips with their own white upbringing. But the young white activists of the 1960s never succeeded in decisively breaking with the traditional American notions of race. The New Left 's failure fully to come to terms with its own whiteness finally doomed its efforts.

The FBI actively sowed seeds of racial division to turn white and Black activists against each other. According to a May 1, 1969, FBI memo obtained by *Jacobin* magazine:

> The concept of white students studying in universities while Black Panthers are going to jail or being killed in the ghetto would be encouraged.

Anticipating the relationship between the government and the "embedded" journalists who covered the 2003 U.S. invasion of Iraq, the mainstream news media and the Nixon White House were more or less joined at the hip in the endeavor to drive a wedge between leftist militants. This relationship was a blueprint for reportage such as *The Washington Post's* 2003 article on the daring military rescue of a 19-year-old Army private,

Jessica Lynch, who was described as a blonde Rambo valiantly fending off the Iraqi brutes before succumbing to their superior firepower and, it was suggested, their sexual predation. The truth, as it was later revealed, was much more prosaic: Lynch was unable to fire a single shot when she and her squadron were ambushed by Iraqi forces, and she was, in fact, rescued by friendly Iraqi hospital staffers who nursed Lynch back to health and called the U.S. military to come retrieve her when she was healthy enough to be moved.

Much like the manufactured Black rapists terrorizing Wilmington's white women a century earlier, or Tom Wolfe's insinuation that interracial solidarity was somehow debauched, the *Orientalism* at the heart of Lynch's story is in stark contrast to the deep reportage of the communist organs that emerged during the Great Depression, the *Southern Worker* and the *Waterfront Worker,* or Mike Quin's account of the 1934 San Francisco general strike. Also firmly within the *Orientalist* tradition was a 1980 *Washington Post* profile of an eight-year-old African American heroin addict written by an ambitious young Black city desk reporter, Janet Cooke. Entitled "Jimmy's World," the front-page story was reprinted around the country—about as viral as you could get in the 1980s—and won Cooke and the newspaper a Pulitzer Prize the following year. *The Post* retracted the story and returned the Pulitzer when it was found to be a hoax, an embarrassment that could have been avoided if only top editors such as Ben Bradlee and Bob Woodward and Cooke's assignment editor, David Maraniss—the son of Elliot Maraniss, whose commitment to racial justice had gotten him blacklisted by the House Un-American Activities Committee—had listened to several African American *Post* reporters and editors who had warned in the weeks leading up to publication that it reeked of fabulism. Still, Cooke's exposure as a fraud who invented her Black heroin addict, much as the editor Josephus Daniels had manufactured his Black rapist for his *Raleigh News and Observer* 82 years earlier, raises a question: Why did she manufacture *that* story?

Nixon's domestic policy advisor John Ehrlichman provided us with a key piece of the puzzle in 1994 when he told journalist Dan Baum:

> The Nixon campaign in 1968, and the Nixon White House after that, had two enemies: the antiwar left and Black people. You understand what I'm saying? We knew we couldn't make it illegal to be either against the war or Blacks, but by getting the public to associate the hippies with marijuana and Blacks with heroin, and then criminalizing both heavily, we could disrupt those communities. We could arrest their leaders, raid their homes, break up their meetings, and vilify them night after night in the evening news.

The experience of another African American female *Post* reporter 19 years after the Cooke scandal also helps explain. A feature writer in the newspaper's *Style* section, Esther Iverem, had turned in a profile she'd written on the artist and civil rights icon, Paul Robeson. Fittingly, Iverem's article shined a light on the public life of a global icon of the anti-imperialist struggle, whose politics and artistry influenced freedom fighters worldwide, from Nelson Mandela's African National Congress to Irish mineworkers. But according to Iverem, *Style's* Assistant Managing Editor, David Von Drehle, who is white, refused to run the Robeson profile on the grounds that Robeson "was on the wrong side of history."

To borrow from Fred Hampton, a news media that hitches its wagon to counterrevolution leaves us "with answers that don't answer, explanations that don't explain and conclusions that don't conclude." Robeson is on the wrong side of history only if history is constantly being rewritten, and an eight-year-old Black boy plied with heroin each school day on his way out the door only exists on the wish list of a ruling class that fears its time is up.

In a 2020 article, the writer and former dean of Columbia's journalism school, Nicholas Lemann, criticized as overheated a scholar's claims that white supremacy is the lifeblood of American capitalism.[233] Such assertions, Lemann argued absurdly, overstate the importance of cotton to the U.S. economy in the 19th century, and downplays both the Civil War and the Crown's abolition of slavery in her territories. And in an interview that same month with the internet news program, *Rising*, the writer Zaid Jilani took issue with reportage suggesting that the coronavirus pandemic had disproportionately affected African Americans because 18 states had at that time failed to sort data by race, which, he argued, had become a lazy journalistic shorthand for more probing inquiries.

"Race," Jilani said, "is just skin color at the end of the day."

Anyone who has read the Caribbean psychiatrist and philosopher Frantz Fanon would recognize in Lemann's and Jilani's emphatic denials of racism the phenomenon known as cognitive dissonance, in which someone is so wed to an ideal—in this instance the earned privilege of non-Black peoples—that they ignore even the most incontrovertible science if it disproves their worldview. Yet if New Journalism's promotion of a culture of make-believe has helped convince whites to stay in their lane, it forced Black journalists to cross the double yellow line and swerve into oncoming traffic. Iverem quit *The Washington Post* after her encounter with Von Drehle over the Robeson profile, beginning an exodus of African Americans from newsrooms across the country as the 21st century began. By 2021, African Americans accounted for 6 percent of editorial staffs nationwide,[234] a figure that is roughly half of the overall Black population and slightly smaller, on a per capita basis, than it was in 1890, when the Census counted 300 Black journalists out of a population of 62 million. The biggest problem, however, might not be the Blacks who have left the newsroom but those who remain.

By pitting "good" moderate Negroes against the angry, radical activists in New Haven, Sheehy's *Panthermania* essay, especially, helped set in motion the rise of a quisling Black middle class that parrots white supremacy and the *laissez-faire* capitalism that the Panthers so adamantly opposed, redolent of Jews who repudiated Ethel and Julius Rosenberg in the hopes of assimilating. And with all due respect to Adam Clayton Powell, the case can be made that New Journalism, and not Harvard, "has ruined more Negroes than cheap whiskey." What connects most of the Black recipients of American journalism's top prize, the Pulitzer, in the 40 years since *Jimmy's World* is a willingness to ape Wolfe and Sheehy's expressionistic technique to depict African Americans as generally unfit to participate in public life. Consider Leon Dash's eight-part *Washington Post* profile of an illiterate, drug-addled, HIV-infected, larcenous sex worker named Rosa Lee Cunningham, which won a Pulitzer for Explanatory Journalism in 1995. Dash, who is Black, "explained" how Rosa Lee represented an isolated urban underclass. She was, in fact, quite the opposite: a white supremacist's chimera, a sociological aberration, and an outlier in her impoverished, mostly Black community who was no more representative of a Black underclass than Ted Bundy typified the white, suburban middle-class.

The following year, the *San Jose Mercury News* published a 20,000-word series, *Dark Alliance: The Story Behind the Crack Explosion*, exposing drug trafficking by the CIA-backed Contra rebels to fund their counterinsurgency against Nicaragua's Sandinista government. The mainstream news media largely ignored the article, written by white investigative journalist Gary Webb, until Los Angeles activists began to demand a congressional probe. The historian Donna Murch elaborates in her book, *Crack in Los Angeles: Crisis, Militarization, and Black Response to the Late Twentieth-Century War on Drugs:*

> To contextualize the backlash against Webb, one has to understand the importance of Los Angeles for the national War on Drugs. In the 1980s, the city contained the world's largest urban prison population. It had been the target of the most brutal campaigns against crack use and distribution.

And it had been the venue of some of the Reagan/Bush Era's most provocative War-on-Drugs spectacles, including Daryl Gates co-piloting a tank armed with a fifteen-foot-long battering ram to tear down the side of an alleged "crack house" in Pacoima (only to find a mother and her children eating ice cream). In 1988, the LAPD's implementation of "Operation Hammer" utilized similar shock-and-awe displays of police power through mass sweeps of black and brown youth. In a single day, law enforcement jailed over 1,400 people, the largest total since the Watts Rebellion in 1965. Very few of the arrests stuck, but the scale of internment was so great that the LAPD set up mobile booking units in the parking lot of the Los Angeles Coliseum.

The "Southland's" War on Drugs extended from saturation policing to the creation of a parallel legal structure criminalizing poor urban populations of color. Law enforcement databases listed over half of young African American men in L.A County as gang members, and it was not uncommon for convicted teenage offenders to receive over a century of hard time. By attacking precisely the types of youth that joined militant political organizations like the Southern California Black Panther Party two decades earlier, law enforcement's overlapping wars on drugs and gangs struck at the heart of postwar black radicalism in the city.

In this context, Webb's revelations raced through South L.A. in the late 1990s like wildfire and helped to revitalize dormant anti-statist activism. Radical Angelinos used the *Mercury News* story to mobilize residents against U.S. covert action abroad and the drug war at home, bringing together disparate left-wing community groups together, including historical Black Power organizers and Central American activists. The umbrella group, "Crack the CIA Coalition," united former Panthers, Sandinista supporters, black Communist Party members, the West Coast branch of

> Kwame Ture's (formerly Stokely Carmichael) All-African People's Revolutionary Party, and even a few sympathetic dissidents from the NAACP. They sponsored regular protests and rallies in front of the *L.A. Times* accusing the paper of colluding with the CIA. In one demonstration, protestors dressed in hats and mittens carried an artificial snow blower with signs reading, "L.A. Times Snow Blind to the Truth," "Contra Cocaine Story: Twelve Year White Wash," and "Avalanche of Disinformation." In an amusing piece of agit prop theatre, two rotund snowmen, "Frosty" and "Flakey" marched hand in hand holding a sign, "CIA and L.A. Times Working Together to Keep you Snowed."

Leading *The Washington Post's* denunciation of Black conspiracy theorists were two Black journalists. The columnist Donna Britt wrote:

> What feels true to blacks has fueled numerous conspiracy theories. Some, such as the infamous Tuskegee Experiment in which syphilitic black men weren't treated by doctors who knew their condition, are true. Others are not.[235]

Another Black journalist at *the Post,* Michael Fletcher, echoed Britt's harangue.

> The history of victimization of black people allows myths—and, at times, outright paranoia—to flourish. . . . Even if a major investigation is done it is unlikely to quell the certainty among many African Americans that the government played a role in bringing the crack epidemic to black communities.[236]

The late Manning Marable's 2011 biography, *Malcolm X: A Life of Reinvention*, recalls *Panthermania's* Chatty Patty reportorial technique. Jurors saw fit to award the posthumously published book a Pulitzer despite its thinly-sourced (only 25 interviews) narrative and the use of gossip and innuendo to repeat rumors that one of the 20th century's greatest intellectuals had a homosexual encounter, multiple extramarital affairs, and was, the reader is led to believe, lousy in bed.

So disappointing was the Marable biography that Black writers and academics openly wondered whether Marable actually wrote it. One Malcolm X biographer, Karl Evanzz, called the book a "fraud" and a "failure."

Similar to the policy of meritorious manumission in which slaves were freed for snitching on other slaves who were plotting a plantation revolt, Black journalists are richly rewarded for blaming Blacks for their own oppression. Channeling Sheehy's vitriol towards African American men, Black sports journalist Jemele Hill tweeted in 2017 that "Straight Black Men Are the White People of Black People," articulating a brand of bourgeois feminism associated with the former CIA asset Gloria Steinem, or Steven Spielberg's one-dimensional rendition of *The Color Purple*. It should be noted that Hill's view of African American heterosexual men was not widely shared by the older generation of African American women who were active in the movement, including Hampton's fiancé, Deborah Johnson, who was eight months pregnant when the police raided the Panthers' flat. Unable to wake a drugged Hampton, she dove on top of him as the bullets whizzed by. Said former Black Panther Kathleen Cleaver in a 2016 interview:

> When our Black Panther movement began in the mid-60s . . . the women's liberation movement in the white community began and they were assuming that our pattern was their pattern . . . that they had domination by powerful men and that women have to be liberated in this little context . . . we didn't have that context. What we needed to be liberated from was racism.[237]

The mixed-race son of a suburban New Jersey family, Thomas Chatterton Williams has scored jobs from *the New Yorker* and *Harper's* magazines since the publication of his 2010 memoir *Losing My Cool: How a Father's Love and 15,000 Books Beat Hip-Hop Culture* which, like Sheehy's

Panthermania, is "a compendium of every ugly cliche about Blacks one could imagine." In a review entitled *"Irrational Man: Thomas Chatterton Williams's confused argument for a post-racial society,"* Tobi Haslett wrote[238]:

> It's instantly clear that Williams is of a different species from the people he pals around with; he may be the only black kid in Jersey who fully occupies three dimensions. And the prose in which Williams renders his "hip-hop" milieu wobbles between awkward and appalling. Foiled attempts at vividness quickly curdle into cliché, as when black high school students are described as 'psyching themselves up like child soldiers drunk off blood in some war-ravaged African province.' This language is not merely frank; nor is it unfamiliar. The book is stuffed with ciphers that slot into racist tropes.

In 2016, ESPN hired *the Washington Post's* African American managing editor, Kevin Merida (Donna Britt's husband and Michael Fletcher's college roommate), as the top editor for its niche publication, *The Undefeated.* With a mostly Black staff, *The Undefeated,* under Merida's editorship, was the literary heir to Wolfe and Sheehy's New Journalism, a paean to Black respectability politics, and a declassified dossier of tribal dysfunction, constantly trafficking in narratives in which history is inert, racism exists only inasmuch as it vexes Barack Obama or his wife, Michelle, and no injustice is so grave that it cannot be resolved by Black folks merely pulling up their pants. When George H.W. Bush died in 2018, Merida penned a fawning elegy that fondly recalled their jogs together with the Secret Service detail in tow yet made no mention of the 41st president's illegal 1989 invasion of Panama that resulted in the deaths of 1,000 civilians, most of them Afro-Caribbeans. Similarly, a 2016 *Undefeated* article written by the celebrity intellectual Michael Eric Dyson takes darker-skinned Blacks to task for their begrudging refusal to exalt in the accomplishments of lighter-skinned Blacks such as the National Basketball Association's two-time Most

Valuable Player, Steph Curry:

> The resentment by darker blacks of the perceived and quite real advantages accorded to lighter blacks has sometimes led to a wholesale repudiation of all fairer-skinned blacks. There is, however, a big difference between asking for racial transparency in light privilege, and the unvarying treatment of fairer-skinned blacks as automatically guilty of exploiting their status.[239]

As a work of either reportage or critical inquiry, Dyson's 2,000-word essay is an abysmal failure. Didactic, artless and populated with misshapen strawmen, it fails to identify a single African American who articulates anything resembling envy or disdain for Curry, let alone anyone whose resentment is grounded in his fair complexion. Nor does Dyson at any point in his polemic mention the word "rape," for doing so would be tantamount to handing up an indictment for a 500-year-old crime spree that is unlike anything the world has ever seen. Virtually from the moment they alighted in the Americas, European expatriates set upon indigenous and African women, creating, from whole cloth, a language of sexual defilement—mulattoes, octoroons, quadroons and Latinos—and giving birth, quite literally to the New World, and the Steph Currys who populate it.

Why would African American journalists traffic in such seditious caricatures and moonlight as apologists for white supremacy?

The answer can be found in the role that a Black informant, William O'Neal, played in providing FBI agents with a layout of the Panthers' West Side Chicago headquarters, and slipping a sedative into Hampton's meal the evening of the raid. In a clear admission of culpability, the Chicago Police Department would pay $1.85 million to settle a civil suit filed by Hampton's family, and while no one was held criminally liable, it is clear that Hampton's assassination was political, as evidenced by law enforcement's failure to seal off the apartment, as is customary in forensic investigations. That allowed hundreds of Chicagoans to tour the ransacked, pockmarked, blood-stained apartment, including a Black state lawmaker named Harold Washington. For all intents and purposes, racial capitalism deputized O'Neal—much as it has deputized a generation of Black journalists—in its conspiracy to assassinate the reputation, or the body, of the Black militants who are the tip of the proletarian spear in America. O'Neal had gone on a joy ride in a stolen car and agreed to spy for the FBI to avoid doing hard time.

> We tried to develop negative information to discredit him. . . . I tried to come up with signs of him doing drugs or something and never could; he was clean, he was dedicated.[240]

And so the FBI resorted to Plan B. For O'Neal's "uniquely valuable services which he rendered over the past several months," the FBI paid him a $200 bonus.

12.

U A(in't) W(hite)

My friends, it is solidarity of labor we want. We do not want to find fault with each other, but to solidify our forces and say to each other: We must be together; our masters are joined together and we must do the same thing.

–Mother Jones

At a double-nickel past four in the afternoon on July 15th, 1970, a 25-year-old Black autoworker named James Johnson walked into Chrysler's Eldon Avenue Gear and Axle plant on Detroit's west side, pulled a semi-automatic M-1 rifle from the pant leg of his overalls, and opened fire.

Foreman Gary Hinz was the first to fall; after shooting him twice, Johnson shouted above the factory's preoccupied din "Where's Jones?"[241] Finding Hugh Jones moments later, Johnson squeezed off two rounds, then stood over his fallen supervisor and pumped four more shots into him at point-blank range. The next co-worker Johnson came across was Melvin Cooper. Johnson pointed his gun at Cooper but did not fire; his beef was with plant managers who had suspended him just hours earlier, and Cooper was wearing a blue shirt, not a white one. Moving on, Johnson encountered

Joseph Kowalski, who tried to dissuade him from continuing his shooting spree; failing that, he turned to run and was shot in the back. When all was said and done, three supervisors—one Black, two white—lay dead. Johnson surrendered to plant security and prosecutors quickly charged him with first-degree murder.

Occurring nearly three years to the day after what was at the time the bloodiest riot in U.S. history, the reconfiguration of the Eldon Avenue shop floor into an abattoir took the temperature of a fever that had yet to break. Sparked by a police raid on a Detroit speakeasy—known colloquially as a "blind pig"—the 1967 Detroit intifada had, in fact, prompted two very different responses. Titans of industry and finance such as Old Man Ford's libertine grandson and namesake, Henry Ford II, Marathon Oil Chairman Max Fisher, Chrysler Chairman Lynn Townsend, and head of the United Auto Workers, Walter Reuther, appointed themselves and each other to the blue-ribbon panel known as Detroit Renaissance, which immediately raised $50 million for a gleaming riverfront redevelopment project and arranged another $200 million in loans as part of a renovation project that, had it gone according to plan, would've simply papered over structural deficits by gentrifying the corridor between Detroit's central business district and Wayne State University to its south.

Unenthused about New Detroit's white elephant project was a coterie of young, Black Marxists who'd met at Wayne State University in Midtown Detroit. What the city really needed, in their view, was less capitalism, not more. In the first issue of a new monthly newspaper, the *Inner City Voice*, which began publishing three months after the riot, the headline of its lead editorial read "Michigan Slavery." It began:

> In the July Rebellion we administered a beating to the behind of the white power structure, but apparently our message didn't get over. . . . We are still working, still working too hard, getting paid too little, living in bad

> housing, sending our kids to substandard schools, paying too much for groceries, and treated like dogs by the police. We still don't own anything and don't control anything. . . . In other words, we are still being systematically exploited by the system and still have the responsibility to break the back of that system. Only a people who are strong, unified, armed, and know the enemy can carry on the struggles which lay ahead of us. Think about it brother, things ain't hardly getting better. The Revolution must continue.

Billing itself "The Voice of Revolution," the *Inner City Voice* found its métier four weeks after Martin Luther King Junior's assassination when a group of mostly Polish women at Detroit's Dodge Main plant decided to walk off the job after their lunch break to protest the speed-ups on the assembly lines. They were joined by several of their African American co-workers including one especially outspoken employee named General Gordon Baker, the son of a Georgia sharecropper who had studied political theory at Wayne State University, formed a campus organization named *Uhuru*—the Swahili word for "freedom"—and traveled to Cuba on a fact-finding mission. Plant managers at Dodge mistakenly identified Baker as a strike organizer and promptly fired him; by month's end, Baker had joined with the *Inner City Voice's* top editor, John Watson, and another Black activist named Mike Hamlin to form the Dodge Revolutionary Union Movement, or DRUM.

Unlike the Black Panthers who centered their work on college campuses and among the lumpenproletariat, DRUM focused on the point of production, demanding, among other things, an end to racism in the labor unions, a retooling of the employee grievance process, a rollback of plant speed-ups and constantly expanding quotas, and, rather innovatively, the reinvestment of autoworkers' union dues in the ghetto. Nearly 4,000 employees walked off the job two months later, and ensuing wildcat strikes at Dodge excited Black workers in ways that Detroit Renaissance's limousine liberals could not, inseminating a proliferation of alphabet-soup mutinies nationwide, beginning with the organization of the city's General Motors Cadillac plant, or CADRUM; the Ford assembly line, or FRUM; a UPS chapter, or UPRUM; the Eldon Avenue plant, or ELRUM. Eventually, the shop floor rebellions crisscrossed the continental 48, springing up at auto plants in California, New Jersey, and Georgia, public transit systems in New York, Chicago, and San Francisco, the American Federation of Teachers, the U.S. Steelworkers Union, and the Building Service Employees International Union. In 1969, Hamlin, Watson, Baker, the Black attorney Ken Cockrel, and a handful of other Black nationalists formed an umbrella group, the League of Revolutionary Black Workers, to keep track of all the bees in the hive.

James Johnson did not associate with the ELRUM militants. Co-workers typically described him as saturnine and humorless, a Bible-thumper whose lone conceit was the small house he was buying for himself and his sister. Still, many co-workers viewed his rampage as an act of resistance against plant managers who mistreated workers as chattel—Black employees referred to the shopfloors as *plant-tations*—routinely overworking employees to the point of exhaustion, injury and even death. In a two-week span in 1970, one male and one female employee were killed in on-the-job accidents at the Eldon Avenue shop, reminiscent of the back-breaking conditions at R.J. Reynolds in Winston-Salem a generation earlier. The inside joke among Black autoworkers throughout the Midwest was that it wasn't *automation* that enabled the Big Three to produce staggering year-over-year increases in the number of vehicles manufactured, but *"nigger-mation."*

Defending Johnson would be Cockrel who, at the age of 34, was already as celebrated as any attorney in Detroit, known for his work on the seven-man Executive Committee of the League of Revolutionary Black Workers, and more broadly for his spirited defense of four Black men accused of killing two police officers during a raid at the New Bethel Baptist Church on March 29th, 1969. At a bail hearing the following month for one of Cockrel's clients, a 38-year-old factory worker named Al Hibbitt, Recorder's Court Judge Joseph E. Maher sided with the prosecution in setting bail at $50,000, far higher than Cockrel felt fair. Outside on the courthouse steps, reporters overheard Cockrel mumblingly refer to Judge Maher as a "racist monkey, a honky dog, a racist pirate and a bandit,"[242] and when the word got back to Maher, the judge charged the young defense attorney with contempt of court.

Cockrel missed nary a beat, and immediately went to work calling linguists, etymologists, and civil liberties experts to "prove beyond a reasonable doubt that Judge Joseph Maher is a criminal, a racist, a bandit and a thief."[243] To support his contention that the contempt charge was an abridgment of counsel's First Amendment rights and an act of intimidation, Cockrel, and one of his law partners, Harry Philo, compiled hundreds of pages of documents on the topics of racism, free speech, and English usage, and rounded up support from a wide range of public figures, including Congressman John Conyers, the Wolverine Bar Association, and even celebrity defense attorney F. Lee Bailey. After two days of testimony in which Cockrel managed to put Wayne County's legal establishment on trial, it was clear that the attempt to censure the maverick attorney had backfired. Judge Joseph A. Sullivan dismissed the case.

Once the trial on the shootings resumed, Cockrel and his white law partner, Justin Ravitz, managed to convince a jury of six whites and six Blacks that their clients were the victims of a racist law-enforcement system. (It did not help that one police officer admitted on the stand that he "couldn't swear to the fact that this was the individual that I seen in front of the church doing the shooting.")

The young defense attorneys were unable to seat as many Blacks in the second New Bethel trial, however, leaving them to wonder why the jury pools in Detroit Recorder's Court were often so overwhelmingly white in a city with a population that was about 45 percent Black at the time. Cockrel and Ravitz decided to comb through the jury commissioner's questionnaires and were stunned to find handwritten notes atop the sheets denoting "community activist" or "long hair," or "ADC," a reference to Aid to Families with Dependent Children, or the dole.

The second New Bethel trial was put on hold for a month while the judge heard testimony from the jury commissioner and Cockrel and Ravitz, who identified 824 instances when jurors had been improperly dismissed for reasons as capricious as "having a beard, wearing miniskirts, being on welfare or chewing gum."[244] The judge agreed with Cockrel and Ravitz that the Jury Commission's process was "illegal, unconstitutional and racist" and ordered an overhaul of the city's jury selection process. Rather than request a mistrial, however, Cockrel and Ravitz asked to recall jurors who had been improperly dismissed, and "(f)or the first time ever in Detroit . . . a majority Black jury" sat in the box at Recorder's Court, Ravitz told the historian Heather Ann Thompson. After deliberating for 28 hours, a merged jury of 12 African Americans and two whites acquitted Clarence Fuller and Rafael Viera of the shootings.

As masterfully as Cockrel and Ravitz handled the New Bethel trials, it was readily apparent that Johnson's case was going to be far tougher. The defense conceded that Johnson ambled into the plant on the afternoon in question and hunted down his prey as coolly as Ernest Hemingway on safari but questioned whether he could be held criminally responsible for the triple homicide. Riding the momentum from the New Bethel case, the defense managed to seat a panel of 14 of Johnson's peers: nine were Black, five were white, ten of whom were either hourly employees or married to autoworkers.

In his opening statement, Cockrel told jurors that Johnson's childhood and that of his siblings as the children of sharecroppers in Starkville, Mississippi, was "not so terribly different from the conditions of life of their forefathers and their foremothers who were slaves." A cousin, Maggie Taylor, testified that at the age of nine, Johnson was "forever changed" after witnessing a lynching, an account corroborated by Johnson's mother, Edna Hudson, who testified that her son was haunted by bewitching spells that visited him in the dark of night. He would awake screaming, she said (describing her child in terms similar to Jean Toomer's description of *Cane's* doomed protagonist Kabnis), chased by nightmares of contorted, ghastly faces and an unnatural fear of death that was surely exacerbated by poverty so grinding that Johnson had neither the leisure nor the toys to play with as a boy because the family needed his help in the cotton field, and every spare nickel just to survive. This squared perfectly with the testimony from a Black psychologist, Clemens H. Fitzgerald, who told jurors that Johnson exhibited signs of mental illness and chronic depression.[245]

After a stint in the Army, Johnson caught on with Chrysler in May 1968, feeding six brake shoes per minute into a 380-degree oven for \$3.10 an hour. By the mid-1960s, the auto manufacturer was running three shifts around the clock and needed all the unskilled labor it could find—my father found work at the Indianapolis Chrysler foundry only two months after my birth in January 1965—but typically reserved the most loathed job assignments for African Americans. Case in point were the conveyor loaders at Eldon Avenue Gear and Axle, all of whom were, like Johnson, Black. The intense heat from the raging ovens led Johnson to complain of nausea and chest pains, and eight months after he started, he was reassigned to the cement room, bumping up his pay by 30 cents an hour. It was immediately clear to Johnson that the move represented a promotion because all six of his co-workers in the cement room were white.

According to Thompson in her book, *Whose Detroit: Politics, Labor and Race in a Modern American City*, his white foreman, Bernard Owiesny, routinely referred to Johnson as "nigger" and "boy." Compounding the matter were injuries to Johnson's head and neck sustained in a car accident in May 1970. The injuries were severe enough that a physician insisted that Johnson convalesce at home, but after recuperating only a few days, he received a telegram from his supervisors threatening him with termination if he didn't return to work. Defying his physician, he complied, only to discover that Chrysler had denied him benefits to pay the medical bills that accrued from his accident. Later that month he took a few days off from work but returned to find that he had been marked AWOL; supervisors said they neither received nor approved his time off request. He eventually had both the decisions on his medical benefits and vacation rescinded but was dealt another blow a month later when a job-setter recommended that Johnson fill in for him for two months while he took time off. Johnson was ecstatic; the job-setter position was akin to an assistant foreman, plus it paid $5 an hour. But Owiesny appointed a white employee and friend to fill the temporary position.

The final straw came on July 15th when Johnson arrived for work in the cement room at his usual time, 2:30 p.m. Forty-five minutes later one of the plant's few Black foremen, Hugh Jones, reassigned Johnson to work the number 2 oven. By all accounts, Johnson complied, reaching the ovens only to find that there were no asbestos-lined gloves available for him to wear. Nonetheless, plant managers suspended Johnson for insubordination, sending him home at 3:15. Co-workers would later say Johnson left without making a scene, returning roughly 90 minutes later to exact his revenge.

Climactically, jurors toured the crime scene and despite Chrysler's cleanup effort, were horrified by the deplorable work conditions. Moreover, several Black employees raised a fist in salute, shouting encouragingly, "Hey Brother Johnson," as the group passed. Ignoring prosecutors' contention that the defense had put too much emphasis on 200 years of slavery, jurors found Johnson not criminally responsible by reason of insanity.

On November 2nd, 1972, voters elected Cockrel's partner, Ravitz, to a ten-year term as a Recorder's Court judge, reflecting popular support for his work as Cockrel's second chair. And on May 12th, 1973, came the *mic drop*: represented by another of Cockrel's white law partners, Ron Glotta, Johnson was awarded workmen's compensation at a rate of $75 a week for the emotional injuries he sustained at Chrysler, retroactive to the day of the slayings.

Glotta told me in an interview:

> At our law firm, the idea was to use the law as a tool for social transformation. I was never a careerist; I just wanted to present the case. These auto factories were oppressive. They were hot in summer and cold in winter and they had people working their asses off. Labor law holds that an employer can be held liable for injuries suffered by its employees on the job. Let's put that to a jury and let them decide. Detroit was a major power source for the country at that time and Black nationalism was really driving that.

Each battle was a grind, and no victory was assured, but there could be no doubt that as the U.S. approached its 200th birthday, workers, at long last, were winning the class war.

For starters, paychecks were fatter than ever. Employees in 1973 earned a larger share of national income—about 51 percent of GDP—than at practically any time in recorded history.[246] Correspondingly, fewer Americans were living in poverty by 1973—about 1-in-10—than ever before.[247] Conversely, the wealthiest 1 percent of Americans that same year took home their *smallest* share of national income, roughly 4 percent, than at any year in the history of the Republic.[248] Couples married more and divorced less,[249] and spent less of their income on housing,[250] a kilowatt of electricity,[251] or college tuition.[252]

Secondly, between 1970 and 1974, the number of African Americans enrolled in college increased by 56 percent, and 15 percent for white students.[253] Two months after Johnson gunned down his bosses, the City

University of New York's vast network of postsecondary schools opened its doors to all of New York City's high school graduates, just a year after Black and Puerto Rican students at City College demanded that university admissions reflect the racial makeup of the city's high schools, which was at the time, half non-white. The administration expressed sympathy but moved at a snail's pace in addressing the concerns until nearly 1,000 mostly white students protested in support of their minority classmates. After weeks of demonstrations and sporadic clashes with police, the Board of Education relented in July 1969, announcing that enrollment in the municipal network of postsecondary schools would be open to all of New York City's high school graduates beginning in the fall semester of 1970. Between 1969 and 1972, the percentage of minority students in the freshman class tripled, but in absolute numbers, it was Italian Americans who benefited most from the open enrollment policy, doubling from 4,989 in 1969 to 9,803 in 1971, according to the historian Joshua Freeman.[254]

In January 1970, St. Louis Cardinals' center fielder Curt Flood sued Major League Baseball Commissioner Bowie Kuhn for violating federal antitrust laws. At issue was the league's reserve clause prohibiting players from filing for free agency once their contractual obligation to a team had expired. Flood, who had been traded to the Philadelphia Phillies in 1969, likened the clause to slavery, and attributed his decision to challenge baseball's owners to the militancy in the streets, telling the players' union's executive board:

> I think the change in Black consciousness in recent years has made me more sensitive to injustice in every area of my life.

Despite support from retired players including Jackie Robinson and baseball's first Jewish superstar, Hank Greenberg, Flood lost the lawsuit that was ultimately heard by the U.S. Supreme Court. But the international reserve clause was abolished in 1976. Salaries for all professional athletes skyrocketed.

In August 1970, tens of thousands of protesters poured into the streets across America for the Women's Strike for Equality in the largest women's rights demonstration since the suffragists. The following month, two African American employees at Polaroid in suburban Boston, Caroline Hunter, a chemist, and Ken Williams, a photographer, were on their way to lunch when they noticed a bulletin board mock-up of an identification card. The caption read: "Department of the Mines, Republic of South Africa." The couple did some digging and discovered the ID cards were used by South Africa's white minority to enforce the police state known as apartheid. When Hunter and Williams raised their objection to Polaroid executives, they were initially ignored, and ultimately fired, yet the couple went on to birth the international divestment movement that led to South Africa's first all-races election in 1994.

Even the arch-villain Richard Nixon got in on the act, creating the Environmental Protection Agency in 1970, and introducing plans to provide a guaranteed minimum income to all Americans. Lawmakers did not pass the legislation, but it was the basis of the Earned Income Tax Credit that continues to this day to supplement the paychecks of millions of low-wage employees. Four years later, Congress approved the Section 8 rental subsidy program that provides roughly five million low-income families with housing vouchers. Meanwhile, voters in 1973 elected eight Black, big-city mayors including Tom Bradley in Los Angeles, Maynard Jackson in Atlanta, and Reuther's nemesis, Coleman Young in Detroit. Before the decade was over, at least six other cities would elect Black mayors, including Ernest "Dutch" Morial in New Orleans, Richard Arrington in Birmingham, and Marion Barry in the nation's capital. In 1974, a group of Black lesbian feminists, including the writer Audre Lorde, formed the Combahee River Collective to map a route to self-determination for themselves that steered clear of mainstream feminism—dominated by white, suburban women—or the Black power movement, dominated by Black men.

The art that characterized John Glubb's Age of the Intellect continued to flourish.

Melvin Van Peebles released the movie *Watermelon Man* in 1970 followed by *Sweet Sweetback's Baadasssss Song* the following year. *The Spook Who Sat By the Door* hit the big screen in 1973, *Claudine* in 1974, and *Cooley High* the following year. At the 1973 Academy Awards, Marlon Brando sent Native American actress and activist Sacheen Littlefeather to refuse the Oscar he'd won for *The Godfather,* as a protest against ugly Hollywood stereotypes of Native Americans, and in support of the American Indian Movement. Later, in an interview with Dick Cavett, he credited African Americans for inspiring him to act:

> The Blacks have brought about changes because they were just damn angry about it and they thumped the tub and threatened and made some noise about it but if they had just been silent and thought 'well gradually wisdom will come to those who are in the business of the movies and they will do right by us' the day would never have come. We have a lot to be grateful for that the Blacks were as insistent as they were . . . but it's a block-by-block fight.

In 1971, television audiences were introduced to the sympathetic, blue-collar bigot from Queens, Archie Bunker, and a rumpled homicide detective, Columbo, who regularly managed to outwit the super-rich. And in 1973, television viewers were treated to what *New Yorker* critic Hilton Als would dub "the most profound meditation on race and class that I have ever seen on network television. "Juke and Opal" was a ten-minute comedy sketch written by Lily Tomlin's partner specifically to showcase Richard Pryor's unique talents. By turns poignant and hilarious, the skit revolves around the intimacy between Pryor's character, an unemployed heroin addict, Juke, and Tomlin's Opal, the proprietor of a greasy spoon. The charming couple chase away two well-meaning but out-of-touch white liberals and the skit concludes on the most gorgeous of grace notes when Juke promises to stay clean and returns the $10 he has hustled from Opal to cop a fix.

Pryor and Tomlin's display of tenderness belied the nationwide mutiny that was afoot. Nearly 2.5 million employees walked off the job in 381 labor strikes in 1970, according to the Bureau of Labor Statistics; there were another 298 work stoppages in 1971, 250 in 1972, 317 in 1973 and 424 labor strikes in 1974, the third-highest total ever.

Nearly as telling as the aggregate numbers was the merger of "Soul Power" and "Union Power" —a formulation coined by striking New York City hospital workers—and the impression that this alliance left on the consciousness of white co-workers who were becoming increasingly disillusioned with the wages of whiteness. In their 1973 book, *Detroit, I Do Mind Dying: A Study in Urban Revolution,* authors Dan Georgakas and Marvin Surkin wrote:[255]

> The capitalist work ethic has been discredited. Men and women no longer wish to spend forty to fifty years performing dull, monotonous, and uncreative work. They see that the productive system which deforms their lives for a profit of which they have less and less of a share is also one that destroys the air they breathe, wastes the natural resources of the planet, and literally injures or disables one out of ten workers each year.

In 1973, 25-year-old Eddie "Oilcan" Sadlowski launched a grassroots campaign for the directorship of the United Steelworkers District 31, representing mills on Chicago's South Side and across the state line in Gary, Indiana. Sadlowski's bid for the union position was a rebuke of the collective bargaining agreement negotiated by the USW leadership, in which the rank and file forfeited their right to strike in exchange for regular pay raises. Under the banner, "It's Time to Fight Back," the burly and gregarious Sadlowski garnered wide support from his Black, Latino, and white co-workers, quoted

John Steinbeck, idolized Eugene Debs, and had an understanding of the class question that mirrored Fred Hampton's.

> You can't be a union man and be a redneck. I just can't handle that kind of shit. A guy will come up to me and say 'nigger this' and 'nigger that' and I'll just unload on him. . . . There's no way you can be a union man and a racist.

In another interview he said:

> The biggest thing management has had going over the years is this game of divide and conquer—especially between whites and blacks. Like my pa used to tell me about the sharecroppers down South. The black sharecropper would get a house that was just a little bit better than the white guy . . . but the white guy would get a dime more on a bale of cotton than the black. And so they'd always be jealous of each other about something and always fighting each other instead of the boss.[256]

Sadlowski's takeover attempt failed but was representative of the yawning chasm between rank-and-file employees and their stodgy union leaders. And the proliferation of wildcat strikes indicated that employees were not merely willing to go to war with the bosses but with their own leadership as well. Flouting a law prohibiting federal employees from striking, New York letter carriers on March 17th, 1970, voted 1,555 to 1055 to walk off the job in protest of a 5.4 percent pay raise that was less than the inflation rate and far less than the pay hike of 41 percent that congressional lawmakers awarded themselves that year. Within days, 152,000 postal workers in 671 locations across the country had followed suit, walking off the job in the biggest wildcat strike in U.S. history. Nixon called in 24,000 military personnel to deliver the mail but they weren't up to the task. Negotiators ultimately agreed to a wage increase of 14 percent.

Defying the UAW's leadership, 7,500 employees walked off the job two years later at the General Motors plant in Lordstown, Ohio. Executives sited the plant on an 80-acre cornfield about 60 miles southeast of Cleveland to escape the nettlesome Black workers in the big city only to find that white laborers could be every bit as irksome with their demands. Similar to their peers in Detroit, organizers of the three-week Lordstown strike targeted speed-ups and the soul-killing monotony of assembling an unheard of 101 cars per minute.

"You clip on the color hose, bleed out the old color, and squirt," a 22-year-old paint shop worker told writer Barbara Garson. "Clip, bleed, squirt, scratch your nose. Only now (the bosses) have taken away the time to scratch your nose."

Workers often couldn't finish their tasks in the 36 seconds that GM demanded. Car quality suffered, and the more than 1,000 "disciplinary layoffs" collided with the workers' dreams of a better life. Many of Lordstown's employees were Vietnam veterans whose attitude was, "I was just getting shot at in the jungle, and this guy with a shirt and tie isn't going to tell me what to do," said Tim O'Hara, a former vice president of UAW Local 1112. He added:

> It was a workforce that decided they weren't going to be treated like robots, but like human beings.[257]

Echoing O'Hara and the West Coast dockworkers from four decades earlier, a 27-year-old welder at a Cleveland steel plant, Patrick Stanton, told *the New York Times*[258]:

> It's the petty day-to-day stuff that guys are sick of. You say a job is unsafe and the foreman tells you to go home. And the union says they'll look into it but nothing ever happens. It's a frightening thing to do something that may get you killed but to do it anyway. There are cranes going over your head with hot iron ingots corning out of the soaking pit, and with stuff dropping on your head. People are so intimidated they won't even say anything. And the union bosses won't back

> you up. All the union bosses talk about productivity and partnership. The company gets the profits and we get the layoffs and the injuries, so where is the partnership?

Increasingly, the coupling was between union leaders and C-suite executives who cuckolded the rank and file. The purge of militants from the shop floor by Taft-Hartley's strictures indebted labor leaders to executives who were traumatized by the postwar strike wave. Detroit's Big Three of GM, Ford, and Chrysler realized that the days when Henry Ford forbade his employees from even speaking to one another during their lunch break were gone but recognized the opportunity to make a deal with the UAW to squeeze every penny from their workforce in exchange for steadily rising wages and benefits, within limits. In return, contracts between the UAW and the industry prohibited work stoppages of any kind; unauthorized strikes could be sanctioned by the courts as a breach of contract.

The union acquiesced to company demands such as compulsory overtime—which was far cheaper than hiring additional workers but routinely required employees to work 12 hours a day for six or even seven days a week in noisy, unsafe factories—and for their part, the Big Three agreed to collect union dues directly from employees' paychecks, insulating the UAW from workers who were so dissatisfied with their labor representatives that they chose to withhold their dues payments.

Coupled with his endorsement of Jim Crow practices on the shop floor, Reuther's no-strike pledge left the grievance process as autoworkers' only recourse. Tellingly, James Johnson did not file such a complaint with his union rep because he knew it would go nowhere. By 1970, there were 250,000 written grievances at GM alone, or one for every two workers employed in production. Wrote Georgakas and Surkin[259]:

> Conditions in the auto factories of the sixties were as bad as they had been in the days before the union.

In their 2001 book, *Three Strikes: Miners, Musicians, Salesgirls and the*

Fighting Spirit of Labor's Last Century, Howard Zinn, Dana Frank, and Robin D.G. Kelley described the most effective labor leaders:

> They reach out to the very communities where working people live, dream, and die, and in the process the union movement has been reinfused with the fighting spirit that working-class neighborhoods have nurtured for so long. The most visionary labor organizers are attempting to build a movement without borders, recognizing that any significant challenge to global capital depends on international solidarity.

Conversely, labor leaders such as Reuther put distance between themselves and the communities that produce their rank-and-file membership. As one example, I was nearly four months into my stint at the California Nurses Association in 2015 when I found myself in a half-lit, mildewed, second-floor conference room in the union's downtown Oakland office, seated among a clutch of maybe seven or eight communications staffers, only two of us—an Asian woman and myself—who are non-white.

The task this late April afternoon was to identify "nurses' values," which I had assumed meant that I would help pore over the results of a nurses' questionnaire to produce a coherent ad campaign.

Instead, the communications manager, Sarah Cecile, stood astride an easel that leaned like a sprinter at the finish line, her magic marker poised to add to the wan list of adjectives that glared accusingly at me.

"Wait," I said, "we're *telling* the nurses what their values should be? Shouldn't we be *asking* the nurses what their values are, you know, like in a survey, or a poll?"

"That's a bad word for us," said a graphic artist who'd worked for the nurses' union for several years. "Polling is frowned upon here."

"Maybe they know something I don't," I said sarcastically, "but if we're telling the rank and file what to do, doesn't that make the union just another boss that the nurses have to answer to? Should communications organize a coup of sorts?" I asked provocatively.

I was fired a week later.

Compare the nurses' union's DeMoro to the dockworkers' union leader, Harry Bridges. One of Bridges' vice-presidents, Tommy Trask, recalled a company executive once questioning one of his demands during contract negotiations:

"What do you need this for?"

"How the hell do I know?" Bridges snapped. "The workers tell me they want it."

In the documentary *Finally Got the News,* one white autoworker said of labor executives' coziness with the bosses:

> Management and the union have gotten to the point where they are almost the same. You hear the same rhetoric from both of them.

Implicit in that allegation was the labor leadership's mimicry of the bosses' racism, which served to weaken worker solidarity. Later in the documentary, the same white worker who complained of collusion between union leadership and corporate management said:

> I took three tests, now one of the math tests I took I didn't do too well on. The fella who was running the tests said 'well I tell you what you go home and study up on this a little bit and come back and see me in a week.' I know Goddamn well he wasn't going to tell that to any colored boy.

So disgruntled were African American autoworkers that they would chant at wildcat strikes that UAW stood for "U Ain't White," or openly mock Reuther with chants of "Put a Halter on Walter." Neither the League of Revolutionary Black Workers nor DRUM organized white workers, but Black activists encouraged whites to organize their own. Said one white autoworker:

> White people should respect the black struggle in the factory

> because blacks struggling in the factory will benefit both people. The thing is the League and DRUM organizing the factories that they're working in coordination hoping that a white struggle in the factories will come about. It's real important for white people to start organizing white people and respect the black people's struggle.

In another telling statement, a United Auto Worker official told *the Detroit News*:

> The black militants in Detroit's auto factories pose a greater peril to the UAW than the communist infiltration did in the 1930s.[260]

It was around this time that my father was denied a promotion at Indianapolis Chrysler although he scored the highest on a qualifying examination. As he told the story, a white foreman responded to his inquiries by explaining that "if I gave that job to a nigger, we'd both get fired." My father would go on to become the first Black skilled tradesman at the plant, but he loathed the inhumane speed-ups, discrimination on the shop floor and in the union, which reserved the best jobs for the whitest worker rather than the best. My earliest memory of the class war was my father's uproarious laughter whenever the name Earl Butz was mentioned on the radio or television. I would learn later that when the singer Pat Boone asked Butz, Gerald R. Ford's agriculture secretary, what the GOP could do to attract more Black voters, Butz echoed the Tin Pan Alley songs intended to belittle Black self-determination a half-century earlier, replying:

> The only thing the coloreds are looking for in life are tight pussy, loose shoes, and a warm place to shit.

Butz's buffoonery aside, the oligarchs were beginning to reload in preparation for the class war's version of the Tet Offensive. David Rockefeller, a Chase Manhattan Bank board member, wrote in 1971: "It's clear to me that the entire structure of our society is being challenged."[261]

In August of that same year, prior to accepting the Nixon administration's nomination to the highest court in the land, a courtly Southern corporate lawyer named Lewis Powell delivered a "Confidential Memorandum" to the U.S. Chamber of Commerce. Polemically entitled the *Attack on the American Free Enterprise System,* the seven-page communiqué that became known as the "Powell Memo" made only a single explicit reference to the issue of race, but it recommended that Big Business regain its footing by isolating criticism of its operations to "minority" communities, thereby short-circuiting its disquieting spread to "perfectly respectable elements of society" such as college campuses, the pulpit, the media, literary journals, the arts and sciences, or in short, *white* America. In measured language, Powell proposed nothing less than the corporate takeover of America's dominant institutions, a reshaping of democratic discourse through "constant surveillance" of textbook, newspaper and television messaging, the aggressive promotion of conservative academic voices and, where possible, a purge from public life of the most radical leftist elements.

The Nixon administration, of course, had already gotten a head start on implementing the conclusions of the Powell Memo, seeking, at every turn, to manipulate parochial frustrations such as those exhibited by the hardhats who turned on the antiwar protesters in New York City. For their part, the super-rich began almost immediately putting Powell's plans into action. One hundred and twenty-five of the nation's largest industrial, commercial, and financial corporations formed the Business Roundtable in 1972 to lobby the federal government for corporate tax cuts, deregulation of the transportation and financial industries, and labor law "reform." The Roundtable was followed in short order by the founding of the conservative Heritage Foundation in 1973, the libertarian Cato Institute in 1977, and a series of ad hoc business-based coalitions that helped defeat legislative efforts to create a Consumer Protection Agency.

Full panic set in following the October 1973 decision by the Arab oil cartel known by the acronym OPEC to sharply increase the price of crude oil, largely in retaliation for the Nixon administration's sale of arms to Israel during the infamous Yom Kippur War against Egypt and Syria. The spike in fuel costs triggered the 1974 recession that plunged the global economy into what was, at the time, its deepest downturn since the Great Depression. Economic growth in the world's 24 richest countries plummeted from 9 percent in 1973 to *negative* 9 percent in 1974, and corporate profits in the U.S. fell by 8.6 percent over that same period.

Whites unable to find work on the shop floor began to volunteer for the military or apply for the police and fire academies, which hired few Blacks. One Chicago police detective, Jon Burge, applied torture techniques he had learned during a tour of duty in Vietnam to more than 118 people between 1972 and 1981 to coerce false confessions. "Whether internal divisions will thwart the development of united class action," Georgakas and Surkin wrote presciently in 1973, "is a question that remains to be answered."

The tensions that materialized in the late 1960s reached their boiling point in late 2022 when union executives representing 115,000 railroad workers led the rank and file into an ambush, agreeing with the Biden administration to hold off on a work stoppage until after the midterm elections. Unsurprisingly, after organized labor had helped Democrats maintain control of the U.S. Senate, Biden essentially used the authority vested in him by the 1947 Taft-Hartley Act to intervene on behalf of management, reject rail employees' demands for paid sick leave, and larger, safer, work crews, as well as pass legislation to block freight handlers from walking off the job, even while their employers rake in record profits.

What's more, the government's *laissez faire* approach to regulating big business has put both workers and communities at risk. According to the Federal Railroad Administration, there were at least 1,164 train derailments in the U.S. in 2022, an average of three per day, resulting in one fatality and

16 injuries. In February 2023, a Norfolk Southern train was traveling towards the Ohio town of East Palestine when outdated sensors failed to detect an overheated bearing in time, causing 38 of the train's 150 cars to derail, including 11 that carried hazardous chemicals, and another six carrying oil and fuel additives.

The runoff polluted the water in the stream that ran through East Palestine, killing thousands of fish, and even pets. For days after the derailment, a mushroom cloud hovered over the town of 4,700 near the Pennsylvania border. In the aftermath of the environmental catastrophe, it was revealed that Norfolk Southern had declined to invest any of its windfall profits in upgrading equipment, which would likely have averted the crash. The nation's rail carriers are, in fact, so loosely regulated that they often don't even bother to move train cars from major intersections in midsized cities such as Hammond, Indiana. Wrote the investigative news organization, *Pro Publica* in April 2023:

> Every day across America, their trains park in the middle of neighborhoods and major intersections, waiting to enter congested rail yards or for one crew to switch with another. They block crossings, sometimes for hours or days, disrupting life and endangering lives.
>
> News accounts chronicle horror stories: Ambulances can't reach patients before they die or get them to the hospital in time. Fire trucks can't get through and house fires blaze out of control. Pedestrians trying to cut through trains have been disfigured, dismembered and killed; when one train abruptly began moving, an Iowa woman was dragged underneath until it stripped almost all of the skin from the back of her body; a Pennsylvania teenager lost her leg hopping between rail cars as she rushed home to get ready for prom.

America's dystopian nightmare is all the more frustrating considering the hopefulness of so many workers heading into the country's bicentennial, as exemplified by the conclusion of Lily Tomlin's 1973 comedy sketch. After Pryor's character, Juke, returns the money he'd planned to use to cop a fix, he shares a kiss with Tomlin's Opal—defying the CBS network executives who expressly forbid the interracial peck—and as he heads out into the swirling winter cold, bids adieu:

> I'll think about you. Be glad when it's spring, flower.

Part IV

Return to the Battle of the Crater

13.

The Fog of War

Hell is a place where by design nobody gets their needs met.

–Jean Paul Sartre

Speaking metaphorically, the February 22nd, 1976, episode of *McCloud* resembled a leaflet drop in the run-up to a ground war, agitprop plummeting gently to earth like sheets of Technicolor rain, signaling to the civilian population a sharp escalation of hostilities. With Golden Age prosperity beginning to fade from the nation's rear-view mirror, the popular NBC series reflected the zeitgeist of the super-rich that saw in the Big Apple's thickening fiscal crisis its first viable opportunity to unspool the thread that stitched together liberalism's loose strands into one cozy, colorful quilt.

Part of the network's Sunday evening lineup, *McCloud* was a postmodern parable, its eponymous protagonist—first name Sam—an unassuming, white cop from New Mexico's hinterlands, improbably on loan to the New York City Police Department. Entitled "*The Day that New York Turned Blue*" the penultimate episode of *McCloud's* sixth season assigns the folksy, Stetson-wearing marshal—played by Dennis Weaver, a regular in stock, 1960s Hollywood Westerns—the Sisyphean tasks of protecting a mob-accountant-turned-state's-witness, tracking down a courtesan with a fetish for spraying her Johns in a gaudy, lethal, blue acrylic paint, all while bracing for an epic snowstorm, a walkout by the rank-and-file police officers in a labor dispute, and the arrival of federal regulators to audit the department's books.

Early in the 90-minute telecast, after negotiations between the city and the police union reach an impasse, the rank-and-file agrees to go out on strike at midnight. McCloud pleads with Officer Delaney, the head of the police union, to delay his plans long enough to see the department through the perfect storm that is bearing down on Gotham. Cast in the role of Delaney was the African American actor Carl Weathers, who that same year would make his first appearance in the *Rocky* franchise as the brash, loud-talking Apollo Creed, a character clearly modeled on Cassius Clay, which is to say, a caricature of the loud, brash, Black boxer before he was conscientized by Malcolm X and the Nation of Islam. Nonplussed by McCloud's appeal to his sense of duty, Officer Delaney makes clear that he intends to stay the course, forcing McCloud to persuade another officer, a white patrolman named "Rizzo," that it was his patriotic duty to abandon the union and stay behind. Together the two defend both the witness and the police precinct from an Alamo-like assault by the Mafia, track down the rogue prostitute before she can kill (or paint) again, and withstand both the blizzard and the piercing scrutiny of the federal auditors.

We can plainly see in McCloud the archetypal traits of Jennett's honest white man from 77 years earlier just as we can intuit from Officer Delaney's pouty narcissism a threat to the civic project that is every bit as menacing as Zip Coon's bottomless libido. Less clear but still visible was the association of the murderous prostitute with a stereotypically shrill, man-hating feminism bordering on lunacy. Representative of an emerging genre that included the *Dirty Harry*, *Death Wish,* and *Rocky* franchises, *McCloud*'s televised morality play redeployed these pat narratives for the same reasons that Daniels, Aycock and Simmons dreamt up a lusty, dusky incubus in a North Carolina hotel room: a surging working-class movement of both Blacks and whites was increasingly challenging the plutocrats' authority and cutting into their profit margins. Nowhere was this truer than in the city so nice they named it twice.

If the proletariat began its uprising in an obscure hamlet tucked away in the Alabama hills, it made perfect sense that the empire would launch its counteroffensive here on this serpentine island at the nation's edge, and the center of the known world. New York City was no one's idea of utopia and yet, by the mid-1970s the municipal government, at the behest of its diverse working class, played a bigger role in housing, educating, employing, healing, feeding, transporting, protecting, and even entertaining its citizens than any city in the country, if not North America. Beginning in earnest in the New Deal years, and shifting into high gear in the 1960s, the Big Apple's Jewish, African American, Puerto Rican, Irish, and Italian neighborhoods formed the motor of what historian Joshua Freeman describes as a "social democratic polity." While no other U.S. city ever had more than three public hospitals, New York City funded a network of 24 at its pinnacle in the 1950s and dozens of primary care, pediatric and drug treatment clinics.[262] The city also financed the country's most expansive municipal postsecondary educational system; mandated civil rights and labor protections that far exceeded virtually any other American city; maintained rent control long after it was abolished elsewhere; created playgrounds, recreation and day care centers for low-income mothers; and made public housing subsidies so widely available that pro basketball Hall of Famer Kareem Abdul Jabbar would later fondly recall the uptown tenement where he grew up as a "little multinational enclave" but "without the bunker mentality."

The price tag for such a prodigious welfare state is not insubstantial, however, and by October 16th, 1975, a crisis reminiscent of Virginia's budget shortfall nearly a century earlier was bearing down on the Big Apple.

At 4 p.m. the next day, come hell or high water, $453 million in loans would mature, but the city had only $34 million in its treasury. If New York couldn't pay those debts, the city would officially be bankrupt. *The New Yorker* magazine would describe the dramatic moment[263]:

> At the Waldorf-Astoria, in Midtown, seventeen hundred guests were gathering for the Alfred E. Smith Memorial Foundation benefit dinner, a white-tie fund-raiser for the Catholic charities named in honor of Al Smith, a former governor and the first Catholic candidate on a major-party Presidential ticket. As day turned to night, the bad news continued to come in. Banks were refusing to market the city's debt, which left New York unable to borrow. Federal help was repeatedly refused by President Gerald Ford and his advisers. The only hope left was pension funds. And the only one that had committed to buying the city's bonds—the Teachers' Retirement System—was now pulling back.

The city had first run out of money six months earlier, and as the budget woes deepened, New York's diminutive Democratic Mayor Abraham Beame, despite two stints as the city's comptroller, seemed to shrink with each passing month. *The New Yorker's* retrospective continues:

> Governor Hugh Carey had advanced state funds to allow the city to pay its bills under the condition that the city turn over its financial management to the state. This led to the creation of the Municipal Assistance Corporation [MAC], which was authorized to sell bonds to meet the city's borrowing needs. (Its detractors referred to it as "Big Mac," because of its authority to overrule city spending decisions.)
>
> The MAC, which was chaired by the financier Felix Rohatyn, insisted on significant reforms, including a wage freeze, a subway fare hike, the closing of several public hospitals, charging tuition at the previously free City University, and tens of thousands of layoffs.

Under immense pressure from Wall Street, Beame proposed cancelling a scheduled 6 percent pay hike for city employees or, alternatively, reducing the workweek to four days. When their unions rejected his proposal, the mayor called for huge cuts at the City University of New York, or CUNY, the closure of libraries and clinics, and the elimination of 38,000 jobs from the city's payroll.

Beame's deference to an unelected board triggered tidal waves of protests across the city in the summer of 1975, foreshadowing the days of rage that unfurled in Greece in 2011 when bankers for the European Union and International Monetary Fund exacted from that country's workers their pound of flesh. Hundreds of City Island residents protested cuts to their fire department. When the layoffs went into effect on July 1st, irate New Yorkers poured into the streets. Ten thousand sanitation workers walked off the job to protest the firing of nearly 3,000 of their co-workers, while five hundred laid-off policemen rallied at City Hall, blocking the Brooklyn Bridge, arguing with motorists, and even hurling beer cans and bottles at their uniformed former co-workers who were assigned to the demonstration. The next day a wildcat strike by highway workers snarled rush-hour traffic on the Henry Hudson Parkway. After a week, police stopped bothering to remove the sawhorses that they had positioned in front of City Hall for crowd control. On July 24th, the Manhattan entrance to the Brooklyn Bridge was again blocked, this time by 4,000 doctors, nurses, hospital workers, and even some patients.

The layoffs of 13,500 municipal employees were met with opposition from a broad swath of New Yorkers, from mostly white police and firefighters to the Black and Latino membership of the American Federation of State, County and Municipal Employees District Council 37, with many in the trade unions calling for a general strike in defiance of Taft-Hartley. After the Al Smith gala, Mayor Beame returned to Gracie Mansion where he had convened a team of speechwriters and lawyers to prepare legal briefs and a press statement in the event that the city failed to meet the deadline.

The New Yorker again:

> By ten o'clock, Rohatyn and others had learned that the Teachers' Retirement System wouldn't invest in more mac bonds. The Teachers' trustee, Reuben Mitchell, said, 'We must watch that investments are properly diversified, that all our eggs aren't put in one basket.' Governor Carey left the dinner and phoned state and federal leaders with a simple message: Default was imminent.
>
> The governor placed another call that night, summoning to his office a developer named Richard Ravitch, who had been serving as a minister without portfolio for the governor. When Ravitch arrived at the governor's office, Carey was still in white tie. He told Ravitch to find Al Shanker, the powerful head of the teachers' union, and convince him to buy the bonds that would save the city.

Ravitch, however, failed to reach an agreement with Shanker, and New Yorkers awoke to apocalyptic headlines on the morning of October 17th. *"Balk by UFT pushing city to default,"* blared the *Staten Island Advance; "Teachers Reject 150-Million Loan City Needs Today,"* read *The New York Times.* City officials ordered the sanitation department to stop issuing payroll checks. A scant two hours before the deadline, Shanker, the villain of the Brownsville-Ocean Hill teachers' strike seven years earlier, announced that the teachers' union would make up the city's shortfall. Still, the statement prepared by Beame's team but never released, is notable for echoing the Readjusters' conundrum in Virginia a century earlier:

> I have been advised by the Comptroller that the City of New York has insufficient cash on hand to meet debt obligations due today.
>
> The financing which was to be made available by the Municipal Assistance Corporation will not be forthcoming

> because the Teachers' Retirement Fund failed to approve its participation in the State Financing Plan.
>
> This constitutes the default we have struggled to avoid.[264]

Continuing, Beame said that he had petitioned a state court for bankruptcy protection from the city's creditors.

> Were I to take no legal action at this moment, I have been advised that such funds as the City . . . would first be used to pay debt service rather than life support and other essential services. These priorities to financial institutions, under State Law, would be binding . . . unless legal steps are taken to forestall it.

With the crisis momentarily averted, Beame continued to press President Ford for help plugging New York City's $5 billion budget deficit. It was a tough sell. What the country needed to get back on its feet—both TV's *McCloud* and the Beltway Bourbons suggested—was a return to the exalted individualism, pioneering resolve, and entrepreneurial ethos that animated the white settlers who tamed this sprawling patch of feral land. Delaware Senator Joseph Biden explained to a reporter: "Cities are viewed as the seed of corruption and duplicity. There is a general negative feeling toward New York City."[265]

New York Times reporter Fred Ferretti wrote that "the resistance in Washington to helping the city was grounded largely in the view that the city was a haven for 'welfare cheats' (read that 'lazy niggers'), people with an overabundance of *chutzpah* (read that Jews), for minorities who want a free ride (read that Puerto Ricans and other Hispanics), for arrogant smart-asses who don't give a damn about the rest of the country."

Perhaps no one in Washington was less sympathetic to the Big Apple's budget shortfall than Treasury Secretary William Simon, a senior partner at the Salomon Brothers investment house before arriving in Washington in 1972. Simon's belief in an unregulated marketplace bordered on Darwinian, characterizing the salaries of municipal workers as "absurd" and their pensions as "appalling." These provisions, combined with City University subsidies, rent control, and other housing aid, were in Simon's view, like malignant tumors that not only ate a huge chunk of New York's revenues, but had metastasized throughout the American body politic, shaping a profligate national "philosophy of government." Bailing the city out, Simon advised Ford, would reward elected officials who lacked the will to stanch the inevitable hemorrhaging inflicted by bankrupt liberalism. On the other hand, making an object lesson out of New York could work as a curative for overly generous social programs. In language mirroring Nixon's instructions to Henry Kissinger to make Chile's economy "scream" ahead of the 1973 coup that toppled that country's socialist President, Salvador Allende, Simon told lawmakers in October 1975 that any bailout should be on terms "so punitive, the overall experience made so painful, that no city, no political subdivision would ever be tempted to go down the same road."

Twelve days after the city won a reprieve, on October 29, 1975, President Ford stepped to the podium at the National Press Club, and in an effort to stave off an anticipated primary challenge from California's rabidly conservative governor, Ronald Reagan, took New York City to the woodshed in an address that might well have made Virginia's Bourbons blush.

> The record shows that New York City's wages and salaries are the highest in the United States. A sanitation worker with three years' experience now receives a base salary of nearly $15,000-a-year. Fringe benefits and retirement costs average more than 50 percent of base pay. There are four-week paid vacations and unlimited sick leave after only one year on the job. The record shows that in most cities, municipal employees have to pay 50 percent or more of the cost of their pensions. New York City is the only major city in the country that picks up the entire burden. The record

> shows that when New York's municipal employees retire they often retire much earlier than in most cities and at pensions considerably higher than sound retirement plans permit. The record shows New York City has 18 municipal hospitals; yet, on an average day, 25 percent of the hospital beds are empty. Meanwhile, the city spends millions more to pay the hospital expenses of those who use private hospitals. The record shows New York City operates one of the largest universities in the world, free of tuition for any high school graduate, rich or poor, who wants to attend. As for New York's much-discussed welfare burden, the record shows more than one current welfare recipient in ten may be legally ineligible for welfare assistance.[266]

Later in the speech, he added:

> I can tell you, and tell you now, that I am prepared to veto any bill that has as its purpose a federal bailout of New York City to prevent a default.

The following day, the *Daily News* published its infamous front-page headline in 144-point type:

FORD TO CITY: DROP DEAD.

Earlier that same month, in the wee hours of the morning of October 1st, 1975, 227 miles due south of New York City along Interstate 95, 200 *Washington Post* pressmen walked off the job. In her 1998 memoir *Personal History*, the newspaper's iconic publisher, Katharine Graham, wrote that she was awakened by a phone call from one of her negotiators at 4:45 a.m.:

> There was no time to think. I dressed hastily, jumped in the car without waking my driver who lived nearby and drove myself down quiet and dark Massachusetts Avenue to 15th

Street.[267]

Graham went on to describe being blindsided by the pressmen's union, Local 6, which disabled all nine presses before their walkout and "brutally" beat a pressroom foreman who'd tried to inspect the damage. Central to Graham's defense was the union's damage to the presses, which *the Post*, at one point implied, approached $15 million, or nearly $82 million at 2023 prices. *Post* executives later agreed to a sum of about $270,000, and there is evidence the damage was far less than that figure even. An enterprising *Chicago Tribune* reporter called the company that was hired to manage the repairs and was quoted a figure of $12,900.

The awful truth is that *the Post* had been preparing "for a strike for two years," wrote the newspaper's former national editor, Ben Bagdikian—who supervised coverage of *the Post's* publication of the Pentagon Papers and was later the dean of the University of California at Berkeley's journalism school—"sending 125 management people to a training center to take over union duties, and setting up alternative composing equipment in a secret project on the paper's executive floors."

The reason was simple: money. Those same shareholders who failed to convince Graham to bury the Pentagon Papers when *the Washington Post Company* first went public in 1971, ruled the roost by 1975. The newspaper's overall financial health was sound, with revenues soaring to $122 million in 1974, up from $84 million three years earlier. Profits stood at $10.9 million, or a robust 9.1 percent, but investors prodded Graham to restore profit margins to their 1969 level of 15.1 percent.

"The first order of business at *the Washington Post* is to maximize the profits from our existing operations," Graham told market analysts in January 1972. "Some costs resist more stubbornly than others. The most frustrating kind are those imposed by archaic union practices. . . . This," she concluded, "is a problem we are determined to solve."

The pressmen overwhelmingly rejected *the Post's* final offer. Said Local

6 leader Jimmy Duggan: "To have accepted that final offer would have meant there was no union. There was no doubt in my mind *the Post* wants to bust its unions."

Graham acknowledged as much in a conversation with a family friend, the conservative president of the AFL-CIO, George Meany, who asked her in the strike's final days what she would do if the pressmen accepted her final offer. "I guess I'd slit my throat from ear to ear," was her response.

To understand how integral the pressmen's strike was in reshaping labor relations, it's important to contextualize the period in which it occurred. As *the Post's* publisher, Graham succeeded her late husband, Phil, and her father, both of whom had decent relations with the newspaper's craft unions.

And, of course, race played a vital role in Graham's dissembling ploy, though not in the typical fashion. It would have been pointless to scapegoat Blacks in dealing with an overwhelmingly white union, so Graham cynically adjusted the divide-and-conquer playbook to isolate Local 6 by portraying the union as a kind of racial bubble in a city that was, at the time, two-thirds African American.

"The pressmen were all-white," Craig Herndon, a Black former *Post* photographer who started at the newspaper in 1968 and refused to cross the picket line told me. Continuing he said:

> A lot of those guys lived in West Virginia and they would drive into town for the week, and then go back home on the weekends, and that cost them a lot of support in Chocolate City. There just wasn't a lot of support for them either in the newsroom or at City Hall.

By December, Graham had crushed Local 6 of the Newspaper and Graphic Communications Union, replacing the fired pressmen with non-union scabs, inspiring her friend Ronald Reagan to do the same to 11,345 striking federal air traffic controllers six years later, and introducing a new era of labor docility. Graham cynically boasted that the first scab hired was a Black man, though *the Post* was never viewed as an ally of the District's Black community, and at the relationship's nadir in 1980 the paper published its fabricated profile of an eight-year-old Black heroin addict. Moreover, Bagdikian wrote in the January 1976 issue of *the Washington Monthly,* a month after the strike concluded, *the Post's* redoubled emphasis on the bottom line exemplified "a crucial change in American newspapering" and reflected the "transformation of the daily newspaper in the United States from a family enterprise to a corporation with an obligation, first and foremost, to its stockholders to 'maximize' profits."

The 1975 pressmen's strike represented not only the twilight of the American working class but of journalism as well, cementing the newsroom's unholy alliance with the boardroom. In her zeal to maximize profits for *the Washington Post Company's* new shareholders, Graham is as responsible as any media mogul for reshaping news coverage to meet investors' narrow and elitist tastes, leading to the "fake news" environment today that eschews on-the-ground reportage in exchange for access to the rich and powerful. Graham herself seemed cognizant of her true legacy, devoting 50 pages of her memoir to the pressmen's strike, or nearly double the number of pages exploring her decision to publish the Pentagon Papers.

Sixteen years after *the Washington Post's* pressmen's strike, I was a young City Hall reporter for the *Minneapolis Star Tribune* that was entering into contract negotiations with its guild union representing the editorial staff. The union was a closed shop, and the publisher was a man named Roger Parkinson, an ex-Green Beret in Vietnam and former *Post* executive who had helped break the strike by arranging for helicopters to land atop the newspaper's downtown headquarters and whisk the page plates past picketers to nearby printing plants while *the Post's* own presses were being repaired. One morning, Minneapolis' mayor, an unassuming, wonkish liberal named Donald Fraser, summoned me into his office, which was unusual since he was hardly a headline-chaser; he was interested in the finer points of public policy.

He told me that he had recently met with Parkinson, who had asked him if there was any way the newspaper could skirt the city ordinance forbidding helicopters to land on downtown buildings for any reason other than an emergency. I was 26 at the time, and dumber than the day was long, and there was a pregnant pause while I tried to grasp Mayor Fraser's point. When I finally did, I blurted out a long "ohhhh," and Mayor Fraser delivered the punchline:

> I told him there was not.

While Graham and Parkinson plotted their offensive in the nation's capital, a junta of top financiers—including Felix Rohatyn of Lazard Frères, Frank Smeal at Morgan, Metlife CEO Richard Shinn, and First National's Walter Wriston—carried out the other phase of the operation further north in New York City. Staffed almost wholly by bankers and corporate executives, the MAC was authorized by the state to sell up to $3 billion in city bonds, using the proceeds to retire existing municipal debt, or in other words, repay their own loans, the exact same scheme that the European Union, International Monetary Fund, and other international lenders pursued in collecting from Greece 36 years later. The caveat was that the MAC was statutorily authorized to deny the city loans if it was not convinced that City Hall was doing enough to reel in public spending.

It was a case of the proverbial fox guarding the henhouse.

Something other than payroll was driving the budget imbalance, however. While New York City's labor costs increased by 46.7 percent between 1961 and 1975, that figure was only about half of the growth rate for municipal workforces across the country, and the 313.6 percent rise in the total costs of wages, benefits, and pensions was significantly slower than the 392.7 percent growth for all city operating costs, William K. Tabb wrote in his book, *The Long Default: New York City and the Urban Fiscal Crisis*.

Neither was the dole to blame. Enrollment in the now-defunct Aid to Families with Dependent Children program, or AFDC, had nearly quadrupled since 1961, but that was consistent with the growing number of caseloads in other big cities, and welfare as a proportion of New York's budget had actually dropped by 6.2 percent between 1969 and 1975. Similarly, Medicare and Medicaid financed the bulk of the city's hospital operations, and city taxpayers' share of public health expenses grew by less than half the rate of all city expenses. Employment at CUNY had tripled since 1961 but at $537.3 million in 1975, it accounted for only 4.6 percent of all city spending.[268]

What *had* begun to gobble up a larger portion of taxpayer funds were two budget items that are seldom scrutinized publicly: contracts, supplies, and equipment that are the playpen of pork barrel politics and crony capitalism; and debt service paid to lenders. New York City shelled out 29.4 percent more in taxpayer funds to contractors between 1966 and 1971. And the costs of supplies, materials, and equipment mushroomed by almost 19 percent between 1971 and 1975.

But it was debt service that was fast becoming the mother of all municipal expenditures, growing by 68 percent between 1961 and 1970, and 188 percent in the first five years of the decade.

The reason was simple. New York was borrowing more and more money at higher and higher interest rates. Awash in more cash than they knew what to do with after wooing Saudi Arabia and other OPEC countries to stash more and more of their petrodollars in U.S. banks, Wall Street began scouring the globe for new investment opportunities, urging state and local governments stateside to borrow more. Municipal paper paid relatively high interest rates, entailed low risk, and was exempt from federal income taxes, and state and local taxes as well in New York.

This lending was facilitated by a change in public financing laws in the 1960s, enabling cities to raise bond revenues for private development projects with even a vague public benefit. In a harbinger of the exotic financial products and bundles of junk mortgages that led to the historic 2008 collapse of the real estate market, New York was one of several cities to form something called Real Estate Investment Trusts with the sole purpose of using bond revenues to funnel taxpayer money to private developers. By 1974, REIT assets had mushroomed to more than $420 billion nationwide. When the economy began to tank in late 1973, the asset bubble burst. Office occupancy rates plunged, and by 1975 real estate investment trusts had lost 80 percent of their value. Chase lost $169 million—nearly a billion dollars in 2024 dollars—and First National had to write off 10 percent of its real estate portfolio.

Overextended in emerging markets such as Chile as well, bankers decided to lessen their exposure in the municipal markets and recoup 100 percent of their investment, which as of early 1975, amounted to well over $1 billion in loans to New York City alone.

The timing couldn't have been worse. With rising unemployment and falling tax revenues bleeding the city's coffers of cash, New York City needed the then-staggering sum of nearly $5 billion to stay afloat. Smelling blood in the water, investment managers and CEOs seized the opportunity to humble a working class that was calling the shots at City Hall.

When Beame fired only 1,700 city employees rather than the 30,000 pink slips demanded by lenders, the banks refused to underwrite a half-billion-dollar bond sale in February 1975, forcing the city to negotiate an extraordinarily high interest rate with a syndicate of smaller banks and brokers. Soon thereafter, the banks made it clear that they could no longer find buyers for the city's bonds, effectively shutting off New York City's line of credit. Unable to raise the cash it needed to make a scheduled payment on money it had already borrowed, the city stood on the precipice of default in 1975.

In mid-July, the Municipal Assistance Corporation urged Beame to adopt a policy of "overkill" to "shock" organized labor and compel its leadership to agree to wage freezes, additional layoffs, four-week unpaid furloughs, a transit fare hike, tuition at CUNY, and a reduction in welfare benefits.

Just as McCloud would later win over Rizzo, and the Confederate soldiers at the Battle of the Crater persuaded the captured white Union infantrymen to turn on the colored troops, Wall Street bankers persuaded two of the city's most powerful union leaders, both white, to turn on the rank and file, especially the African American and Puerto Rican vanguard.

Given his role and rhetoric in the Brooklyn schools strike, Shanker's defection was no surprise. When a reporter asked his stance on the possibility of a general strike to protest the mayor's austerity budget, he sounded the polarizing call to arms that had been used by management at the R.J. Reynolds plant to weaken workers' solidarity decades earlier:

> A general strike is a political weapon associated with the communist unions of Europe. For us to use it would be irresponsible.

The president of District Council 37, Victor Gotbaum, was another matter however. Gotbaum had led the efforts in 1968 to coax Shanker into calling off the Brooklyn teachers' strike; his top deputy in the local was a Black woman he had personally recruited for the job, and even though DC 37 adhered to the top-down management style that had become commonplace in organized labor after Taft-Hartley, his administration was seen as more responsive to the rank and file than many other locals. But Gotbaum's subordinates, labor journalists and activists, say that Rohatyn and Wriston made a concerted effort to woo Gotbaum, meeting with him regularly in their office suites during the summer of 1975 to discuss the finer points of finance over contraband Cuban cigars and top shelf cognac.

Other labor activists say that Gotbaum defected because he was misled by the Svengali-like Jack Bigel, a top officer in the left-leaning United Public Workers that was destroyed by red-baiting and loyalty oaths in the '50s. Bigel left the shop floor to become a millionaire consultant, and it was his counsel that ultimately convinced Gotbaum to switch horses midstream. After some back and forth, Gotbaum and Shanker ultimately agreed to Wall Street's cost-cutting concessions and sank nearly $2.5 billion of employee pension funds into the city's bonds, paradoxically incentivizing trade unions to champion cost-cutting measures that reduced the city's chance of default. By 1978, New York's six major banks had offloaded virtually all of their investments in city paper, reducing their exposure to one percent of their banks' total assets, while the employees' pension fund had invested 38 percent of its assets in municipal debt. With this stake, New York's workers, through their unions, traded places with investors as the underwriter of city paper and muddied industrial relations with endemic conflicts of interest.

For years after the 1975 fiscal crisis, the joke among DC 37 's rank-and-file was that Rohatyn and Wriston had given Gotbaum his "white man's wakeup call," or that if the bankers planned to seduce the leadership of the municipal unions into betraying the rank and file, they'd certainly chosen the "*white* man for the job." Others suggested printing T-shirts that read: *Vic and Al Got Blow Jobs; Now We Got NO Jobs.* Shortly before his death in 2002, Bigel acknowledged that he and other union leaders had no idea what they were doing and were motivated by fear more than facts. "We shot craps with the assets of 350,000 pension fund members," he said.

Bill Clinton's Health and Human Services secretary, Donna Shalala, a Columbia political science professor in 1975 and the only non-businessperson on the MAC board, echoed Bigel's assessment, recalling as perfunctory the meeting at which the panel signed off on the city's final austerity package. There were no staff papers or background work or any data of any kind that demonstrated how the spending cuts would plug the budget deficit. "We had," she would say later, "no hard facts."

That is supported by the fact that even after the workers' concessions, a $32 million cut in CUNY's budget, and hikes in the city's transit fares and other fees, the budget crisis was only resolved after President Ford reversed his unpopular decision and awarded New York with a $2.3 billion bridge loan.

In his book, *Working-Class New York*, the historian Joshua B. Freeman wrote that Gotbaum and his partner, Joe Bigel,

> . . . preferred to make concessions and invest their members' pension money in city debt in return for a place at or near the table, where discussions about the city's future were being made by financiers, businessmen, and state and federal officials. Gotbaum became so entranced by the power elite . . . that within a few years he and (investment banker Felix) Rohatyn were calling each other best friends, even holding a joint birthday party in Southampton.[269]

In his betrayal of his members (and Blacks and Latinos especially), Gotbaum bridged the misleadership of Walter Reuther's generation and the California Nurses Association's Rose-Ann DeMoro. Similar to the Nixon administration's overthrow of Allende's socialist government in Chile two years earlier, and the 1898 Wilmington massacre, New York City's reorganization was akin to a coup, ushering in a new neoliberal order in which the state no longer played the role of arbitrator in the relationship between labor and management, but rather served as the *guarantor* of corporate profits.

The MAC, in fact, became the model for the International Monetary Fund's debt collection efforts across the developing world, in which the organization represented international creditors in much the same fashion that bagmen represent the mob; rather than threatening to break legs, however, the IMF threatened to withdraw financial support unless the indebted country abandoned free health care or educational policies, food assistance for the poor, or agricultural subsidies. And perhaps most importantly, it reinforced in the minds of investors—such as those who urged Katharine Graham to fleece her workers—their absolute entitlement to profits that are no more owed to them than winnings at the blackjack table in a Las Vegas casino. This mindset would shape the government's response when another speculative scheme—the bundling of subprime mortgages into bonds—went belly up 33 years later.

In his 1984 book, *The New Politics of Inequality*, the journalist Thomas Edsall wrote: "During the 1970s, business refined its ability to act as a class, submerging competitive instincts in favor of joint, cooperative action in the legislative arena . . .."

The proof is in the pudding, or perhaps the lack thereof. New York shed 63,000 jobs—a quarter of its workforce—between 1975 and 1980. Trash pickups were cut. Subways cost more, came less frequently, and broke down more often. Crime against passengers rose sharply, driving many riders to their cars, clogging up city streets, and slowing the average speed on some Manhattan side streets to 4.4 miles per hour. The cost of tuition at CUNY reduced enrollment by 62,000 students in only four years. The ratio of teachers to pupils shot up sharply.

The banks, on the other hand, have never been richer than in the years since the 1975 coup.

In contrast, the budget axe fell heaviest on Black and Latino neighborhoods. Layoffs reduced the percentage of African Americans and Spanish-surnamed teachers from 11 to 3 percent wiping out the progress in integrating city classrooms post-*Brown v. Board of Education.* At CUNY, Black and Latino freshmen enrollment that had risen steadily every year after the implementation of open enrollment declined by half between 1976 and

1980. Unemployment accelerated the abandonment of mostly African American and Puerto Rican neighborhoods in the South Bronx, Brownsville, East New York, Harlem, East Harlem, and the Lower East Side, as families with steady incomes moved to better neighborhoods and landlords walked away from their buildings rather than pay outstanding mortgages, taxes and utilities. In the months following the fiscal crisis, New York was in flames—literally—as bored youths and landlords set fire to buildings to collect insurance or drive out the few renters who remained. Shortly before Union Carbide's widely publicized 1977 decision to relocate its New York headquarters, a company official described its dilemma thusly:

> It's an image we have to contend with. And it isn't just crime and high living costs. It's the city's changing ethnic mix which makes some people uncomfortable, and the graffiti on the subways, the dirt on the streets, and a lot of other things.[270]

In 1976, New York City's housing and development administrator, Roger Starr, suggested that the city should ape private capital and walk away almost entirely from neighborhoods like Brownsville and the South Bronx, reducing police and fire service, shuttering schools, hospitals and subway stations to allow swaths of the city to "lie fallow until a change in economic and demographic assumptions makes the land useful once again." The idea, he said, was to induce Blacks and Puerto Ricans to relocate, not only to other parts of the metropolitan area but even other parts of the country. "Our urban system," he said, "is based on the theory of taking the peasant and turning him into an industrial worker. Now there are no industrial jobs. Why not keep him a peasant?"

Astrophysicists say that there are solar systems so distant that even the most powerful telescope cannot locate their suns. Yet they can discern its existence from the movement of planets and other celestial bodies. From what transpired in the generation that followed New York's meltdown, we can be reasonably sure that Starr's vision clearly reshaped the American metropolis writ large into what the sociologist Saskia Sassen calls "extraction zones," at precisely the moment that Blacks and Latinos were poised to succeed Irish, Italian, and German emigres as the custodians of urban political power. Wall Street's takeover of both the nation's financial capital and its news media was tantamount to a European power's bid to maintain control of its colonial possession even while transferring the reins of governance. Think Belgium's assassination of Patrice Lumumba in the early days of Congo's independence. But now bonds, not bullets, are the rulers' weapon of choice.

In a 1975 congressional hearing, Detroit Mayor Coleman Young addressed the spiraling debt crisis that had forced his administration to seek state approval to raise the ceiling on interest rates paid on the city's paper.

> I believe that all mayors here look upon New York's problem as symptomatic of a national crisis in American cities. . . . The impact of New York's crisis obviously spreads far beyond the borders of that city . . . I can cite my own city as an example. . . . It does not matter to the bond market whether cities have taken steps in order to correct their situation or whether they have not. In Detroit for instance, we have within the last 18 months reduced the number of our public employees from 25,000 to 20,000. That's a 20 percent cut in services to our people. We've taken every measure that we can and yet as we have approached the bond market over the last year we've found that the eminence of the crisis in New York City has affected our ability to sell our bonds . . . never prior to 1974 did Detroit pay in excess of 6 percent on a general obligation bond. . . . Again approached the bond market on a 30 million dollar issue where we paid 9.8 . . . which we feel to be extortion. I gather that is the going rate. . . . We need to meet what is a national urban crisis and we need to meet it on the same basis that the federal government recognized in the '30s that the

national crisis on our farms threatened the existence of our nation. We need to mobilize . . . the full resources of our federal government because if our cities go down, our nation will go down. . . . We stand on the brink of a national and international catastrophe.[271]

14.

Asymmetrical Warfare

I came to you to tell you this: If you do not purge yourself of white-skinned privilege and fight the state that tries to enshrine it, it will destroy you as a human being. . . . And to black people here I say to you that if you do not understand the necessity for you to make a commitment to the liberation of your people you will be destroyed by that same power. . . . So you see we have a common interest; you must save your humanity and we must save our very lives.

–Dhoruba bin Wahad

On the evening of September 18th, 1977, Richard Pryor took the stage at the Hollywood Bowl for a gay rights fundraiser and delivered what was perhaps the most incendiary monologue of a career that was both famously—and literally—combustible.

What the audience of 17,000 mostly gay white men expected was to be regaled by the virtuoso in his prime. What they in fact got was a *conflagration*, as Pryor lit into the LGBT community for what he characterized as their indifference to African Americans' struggles.

Amazingly enough, it didn't begin that way. As Scott Saul wrote in his

2014 book, *Becoming Richard Pryor*, the headliner ambled onto center stage, and after prowling the platform briefly like a caged big cat, he finally spoke:

> I came here for human rights and I found out what it was really about was not getting caught with a dick in your mouth.

The crowd roared with laughter. Pryor continued:

> You don't want the police to kick your ass if you're sucking the dick, and that's fair. You've got the right to suck anything you want! I sucked one dick. Back in 1952. Sucked Wilbur Harp's dick. It was beautiful, but I couldn't deal with it. Had to leave it alone. It was beautiful because Wilbur has the best booty in the world. Now I'm saying booty to be nice. I'm talking about asshole. Wilbur had some good asshole. And Wilbur would give it up so good and put his thighs against your waist. That would make you come quick.

The crowd erupted again, half in delight, half in disbelief.

> I was the only motherfucker that took Wilbur roses. Everybody else was bullshitting. I took Wilbur [the roses] and said, 'Here, dear.'

At this point, as Saul described the scene, Pryor paused, and the monologue took a sharp detour into some dark recess of the comedian's mind. While waiting backstage to go on, Pryor had noticed how the white stagehands ignored an all-Black dance troupe known as the Lockers when the dancers asked for help adjusting the stage lights. And when they returned after what Pryor thought was a spectacular performance—one dancer jumped over six chairs—the comedian watched incredulously as the show's promoters did nothing to defend the Lockers who were dressed down by a fire marshal for detonating a small explosive as a special effect.

And then an hour later, just before Pryor was scheduled to go on, the stagehands who earlier couldn't be bothered by the Lockers' appeal for help, suddenly leapt into action when two white ballet dancers asked for help with the very same light fixture.

By the time he reached the stage, Pryor—who it's safe to assume had snorted, smoked or imbibed something of a chemical nature before going on that night—was fuming. As the crowd laughed at his recollections of Wilbur Harp, Pryor mumbled softly into the microphone, surveying the sea of white faces, as though in a catatonic trance.

> "How can faggots be racists?" he asked. "How can faggots be racists?"

And then, he *exploded.*

> "I hope the police catch you motherfuckers and shoot your ass accidentally, because you motherfuckers ain't helpin' niggers at all." The audience howled, but was clearly puzzled, Saul wrote. "When the niggers were burning down Watts, you motherfuckers were doing what you wanted on Hollywood Boulevard, didn't give a shit about it." By this point, some clarity had begun to wash over the audience and the laughter was beginning to turn to hissing and boos.

Pryor continued, addressing a feminist movement defined largely by the concerns of white, suburban women. "Motherfuck women's rights. The bitches don't need no rights. What they need to do is pay the people on welfare." Again, the crowd roared its disapproval. Pryor shot back with his own rage.

> "Yeah, get mad. 'Cause you're going to be madder than that when [Los Angeles Police Chief] Ed Davis catches you motherfuckers coming out of here in the lot." By this point, all confusion on the part of the crowd had dissipated, with hecklers not just taunting Pryor but openly threatening to do him bodily harm. Undaunted, Pryor pivoted on his heels,

> exhorted the enemy combatants to "kiss my happy, rich, black ass," and walked off the stage.

In the days that followed, the *Los Angeles Times*, *Vanity Fair* magazine, and the Hollywood media mostly excoriated the comedian as rude, deranged, and even homophobic. The first allegation was most certainly true, the second arguable, but the last, given his stunning public admission of his own same-sex experience, was way wide of the mark.

However crude, Pryor's reproach of Southern California's gay community signaled the transition from John Glubb's Age of Intellect to the Age of Decadence and Decline, and the splintering of the rainbow coalition that had engineered the most prosperous working class in the history of the world. Incentivized by the white backlash that followed the National Guard's attack on white students at Kent State, a news and entertainment media that increasingly portrayed Blacks as sexual degenerates and loutish drug addicts, and a renewed competition for jobs and educational opportunities, white workers were deserting the class struggle in bunches, repudiating any affiliation with African Americans and retreating to the impermeable silos of racial identity and privilege. Similar to their response to the Haymarket aftermath, and the dawn of the Jim Crow era, Irish, Italians, Germans, Poles, Scandinavians, Russians, Hungarians, Jews, Anglos and the LGBT community began to demobilize and turn, with increasing vitriol and frequency, against their former allies, and rally around ethno-nationalist narratives advanced by everyone from Dirty Harry to Rocky Balboa, and soon the Redeemer-in-Chief, Ronald Wilson Reagan.

Fueling this new attitude was a tectonic shift in Americans' material realities as the Golden Age of Industrialism came to a close and the Age of Austerity ratcheted up. By the time of Pryor's scathing monologue, the supply of decent-paying manufacturing jobs that galvanized a critical mass of Black and white workers a generation earlier was beginning to dry up. Nearly a third of all workers were employed in the industrial sector in 1953;

by 1977, that number had dipped to a quarter and would plummet to less than 11 percent by 2018. The ax, however, did not fall on everyone equally: Between 1975 and 1980, the number of unemployed white workers fell by 562,000 while the numbers of jobless Blacks *increased* by 200,000 over the same period.[272]

Nowhere was the rising tide of racial resentment more evident than in the culture wars beginning to take shape as the nation's 200th birthday approached. If artists as diverse as Humphrey Bogart and the Beat Poets mirrored a nation's ache for community in the 1940s, the prevailing ambition 30 years later seemed merely to be left alone. White aggrievement in this era resembled the temper tantrum thrown by white Southerners during radical Reconstruction, figuring prominently in movies like *Rocky*, *Saturday Night Fever* and *Death Wish*. And the old, standby narratives of the Honest White Man and Zip Coon began to reappear with greater frequency and emphasis as the decade wound down.

In the 1979 sci-fi classic *Alien*, for example, the only thing more menacing to Sigourney Weaver's crew than the extraterrestrial monster that boarded their spaceship was the selfishness and greed of the lone Black crew member, played by Yaphet Kotto, the son of a Cameroonian immigrant. And Hollywood's Oscar-winning 1979 dramatization of the efforts by Black and white employees to organize a North Carolina textile mill, *Norma Rae*, while well-done, focused on the protagonist's love life more than it did on the real-life collaboration between Black and white mill employees that resulted in a unionized shop floor.

It was music, however, that became a cultural shibboleth for bourgeois art and epitomized the New Deal's metamorphosis into a cheap knock-off of the Weimar Republic's hedonism. For all its saccharine qualities, disco formed a bridge, however flimsy, "between what George Clinton famously called the chocolate cities and the vanilla suburbs, encouraging women, gays, Blacks, Latinos, and ethnic whites to enjoy a polyrhythmic point of integration . . ."[273] But as jobs dried up and meat prices soared, white brittleness intensified, emasculating young white men who rejected the integration of musical traditions that produced the Beatles, Rolling Stones, and early iterations of groups like the band Chicago. As the decade wound down, an anti-disco movement picked up considerable steam, causing one critic to comment at the time that "white rock was sounding whiter and Black music was sounding Blacker."

So intense was the musical backlash that a Chicago disc jockey, Steve Dahl, invited White Sox fans to turn up at Comiskey Park on July 12, 1979, with a disco record to gain admittance to the game for 98 cents. Dahl planned to fill a Dumpster with the records between the scheduled doubleheader and blow them up as a publicity stunt.

In a 2019 retrospective for *the Guardian* newspaper entitled "Disco Demolition: The night they tried to crush Black music," Alexis Petridis wrote of one African American usher, Vince Lawrence, who

> . . . realized something wasn't right: people weren't just turning up with disco records, but anything made by a black artist. 'I said to my boss: Hey, a lot of these records they're bringing in aren't disco—they're R&B, they're funk. Should I make them go home and get a real disco record?' He said 'no: if they brought a record, take it, they get a ticket.' He laughs. 'I want to say maybe the person bringing the record just made a mistake. But given the amount of mistakes I witnessed, why weren't there any Air Supply or Cheap Trick records in the bins? No Carpenters records—they weren't rock'n'roll, right? It was just disco records and black records in the dumpster.'
>
> Things turned uglier after Dahl's demolition took place and the crowd—estimated at 50,000—rushed the field. Unable to cope with the surge of people the ushers were told to go home and that the police would have to deal with what was degenerating into a riot. 'Someone walked up to me said:

> "Hey you—disco sucks!" and snapped a 12 (inch) in half in my face,' Lawrence says. 'That's when I started feeling like: OK, they're just targeting me because I'm black. I've got a Loop T-shirt on—what's the difference between me and the next usher trying to get back to his locker? I was one of the few African American people in the stadium. Steve Dahl said it wasn't discriminatory, he was an equal opportunities offender or whatever, but Steve didn't invite no brothers to Comiskey Park.'

This segregation of sound partitioned New York City as well: Uptown, Blacks and Puerto Ricans blended funk, disco, and the Black Arts movement to create an explicitly political genre that came to be known as rap, or hip-hop, the first authentically American art form since jazz; while downtown at hotspots like CBGB, disaffected white youths consciously shunned all Black musical influences—the creative opposite of the Beat Poets or John Cassavetes a generation earlier—to create a sound known as punk rock. Of the latter, the Ramones were by far the most well-known group in the U.S. Wrote Jefferson Cowie in his splendid historiography, *Stayin' Alive: The 1970s and the Last Days of the Working Class*:

> The Ramones returned rock 'n' roll to its proper garage setting, promising a do-it-yourself kit for those interested in emancipation from the chains of mainstream seventies music that (rock critic) Greil Marcus could dismiss as little more than 'a habit, a structure, an invisible oppression.' They were the United States' most important contribution to, and much of the catalyst for, the Anglo-American punk movement, but what was curious about the band, especially as opposed to their British cousins, was their distinct lack of class politics—and when they had them, their often conservative bend. Rather than being class conscious or even political, they tended to embrace simply being "dumbbell pillhead teenagers" stripped of any sentimentality and who could whipsaw angst into contempt and farce. It is not that

> the Ramones were not often witty or even brilliant, but simply, in contrast to much of the punk movement across the Atlantic, they were part of the breakdown of class as a category of analysis rather than a re-imagining of it.[274]

It's hardly a coincidence that the biggest white musical acts of the 1980s—the Clash, U2, the Police, Madonna, and Bruce Springsteen—all consciously embraced the blues, reggae or Motown and even Black dance styles, beguiling white audiences who knew something was missing from their mixtapes even if they couldn't quite put their finger on it.

Cowie continues:

> The most important thing that a band like the Clash had that almost all American music of the late seventies lacked was a conscious infusion of black musical traditions. As rock critic Lester Bangs put it, 'Somewhere in their assimilation of reggae is the closest thing yet to the lost chord, the missing link between black and white noise, rock capable of making a bow to black forms without smearing on the blackface.'

Born in 1940 at the exact moment when the white working class was beginning to reconsider its allegiances, Pryor was known for his collaborations and close friendships with Gene Wilder, Lily Tomlin and Robin Williams, and he proposed marriage to his white girlfriend only days after the Hollywood Bowl debacle. Before leaving the stage on that evening in 1977, with his face contorted into a mask of sorrow and rage, he challenged the crowd in an almost Biblical tone:

> I wanted to test you to your motherfuckin' soul.

Two years after Pryor's wrathful monologue, on July 3rd, 1979, amid dwindling gas supplies and soaring inflation, the 39th president of the United States, Jimmy Carter, boarded a helicopter for Camp David and vanished from public view, resurfacing 12 days later to deliver what is possibly the most prophetic presidential address in the nation's history.

Our most vexing problem, a subdued Carter told the television audience, was not the serpentine lines unfurling at gas stations across the nation, but a crisis in confidence that had cast a dark spell from sea to shining sea. Somewhere between the last World War, and Watergate, Carter scolded, America had lost its way. He said:

> In a nation that was proud of hard work, strong families, close-knit communities, and our faith in God, too many of us now tend to worship self-indulgence and consumption. Human identity is no longer defined by what one does, but by what one owns. But we've discovered that owning things and consuming things does not satisfy our longing for meaning. We've learned that piling up material goods cannot fill the emptiness of lives which have no confidence or purpose.

Continuing, he said:

> What you see too often in Washington and elsewhere around the country is a system of government that seems incapable of action. You see a Congress twisted and pulled in every direction by hundreds of well-financed and powerful special interests.

And then:

> We are at a turning point in our history. There are two paths to choose. One is a path I've warned about tonight, the path that leads to fragmentation and self-interest. Down that road lies a mistaken idea of freedom, the right to grasp for ourselves some advantage over others. That path would be one of constant conflict between narrow interests ending in chaos and immobility. It is a certain route to failure.

Though he never uttered the word, Carter's address was famously dubbed the "Malaise Speech" by the press, and it presaged the "death of industrial pluralism, and the New Deal system."[275] *The Washington Post* and other mainstream media outlets panned the speech but voters loved it; polls showed a double-digit bump in Carter's approval ratings in the immediate aftermath. For all its divination, however, Carter's address belied his reticence to resuscitate postwar liberalism, and replenish the cupboard for the party's blue-collar constituency. In plain proletarian English, he talked it better than he walked it. Unlike Bobby Kennedy who'd planned to patch up FDR's comfy, cozy electoral quilt that was beginning to fray at the edges, Carter threw it out with the trash, becoming the first president to govern in a post-New Deal framework.

Perhaps Carter's biggest squandered opportunity was his tepid support for legislation that would've created a single nationwide labor market, thereby reducing regional and racial competition for jobs. Sponsored by Lyndon Baines Johnson's vice president, Minnesota's U.S. Senator Hubert Humphrey, and California Congressman Augustus Hawkins, one of the founders of the Congressional Black Caucus, the Humphrey-Hawkins bill proposed a federal guarantee of full employment—defined as a jobless rate of no more than three percent—and would've buoyed efforts by unions to organize both in the South—which was fast becoming the destination for industries fleeing the heavily unionized Midwest and Northeast—and the growing low-wage service sector. An expansion in collective bargaining rights, wrote *the Nation* magazine at the time,

> . . . represents nothing less than the economic consolidation and extension of the limited legal and political gains won by the civil rights movement in the 1960s. By alleviating the poverty of both blacks and poor whites, unions can allay the economic enmity which lies at the root of so much of the South's racial tension. The labor movement's self-interest lies in aggressively promoting integration in the region.

Noted Pittsburgh's famous labor priest, Monsignor George Higgins:

> The struggle to achieve a more humane economic order will

> not be fought along racial lines but will be defined by broader class interests.[276]

Modeled on the Full Employment Act of 1946, the Humphrey-Hawkins Act had broad support from the labor and civil rights communities, including such iconic figures as Martin Luther King Jr.'s widow, Coretta Scott King. Concerned, rightly, that full employment would strengthen unions and raise labor costs for Big Business, conservative lawmakers on both sides of the aisle gutted the Roosevelt administration's bill requiring the executive branch to prepare annual projections for industrial output and budget estimates of the labor force necessary to fulfill those benchmarks. However many jobs private industry could not—or would not—provide would be absorbed by the public sector at the prevailing wage.

Despite the original bill's failure, full employment remained the holy grail of liberal reformers. But in his Machiavellian plans to undermine the New Deal coalition by pitting whites and Blacks against one another, Nixon preferred hiring quotas for minorities in federal contracts. Most civil rights leaders certainly understood Nixon's cynical ploy as a poison pill, and as they had in the Reconstruction and New Deal eras, articulated a universal vision for lifting all boats, including those already underwater. Their faith in ample jobs to go around had not waned in the Black Power era and if anything, had grown stronger. One of the founders of the Coalition of Black Trade Unionists, Cleveland Robinson, explained the need for a federal jobs guarantee to complement affirmative action:

> Consequently you will have a situation where the white worker who is hungry cannot see any reason why he shouldn't have the job, just because the black worker has traditionally been left out. It's actually asking too much to say to that white unemployed, 'You should understand (how important it is for a black person to have this job).' So together with the struggle for affirmative action, we have to struggle for full employment.[277]

Robinson's ambivalence to affirmative action underscores African Americans' profound understanding of the phenomenon of white backlash, and helps explain their historic preference for universal programs that benefit all workers rather than race-specific reforms. Blacks' endorsement in the 1970s of the full-employment mandate, a basic income grant for all U.S. households, and a single-payer health care system modeled on Medicare, underscores the sophistry at play in white liberals' growing criticism of identity politics and race-based solutions to problems that affect the entirety of the laboring class. Broad support in the Black community for reparations is a notable exception, but that issue only re-entered the national conversation following the 2008 implosion of the housing bubble that resulted in the greatest loss of wealth for African Americans since the Freedman's Bank closed in 1874.[278]

By 1976, when Senator Humphrey and Representative Hawkins—who represented Watts and was a protege of A. Phillip Randolph—introduced the bill, New Dealers, trade unionists, and the civil rights community were acutely aware of white workers' defection from a movement that had lifted their standard of living but was now beginning to bus Black children into their neighborhoods to attend school with their own sons and daughters. In open defiance of Molly Ivins' dictum—"you got to dance with them what brung you" —the white proletariat had begun to turn the page on the very movement that had boosted their incomes in a sophomoric attempt to reclaim the full rights and privileges afforded their racial classification.

The Democrats hoped to at least delay white flight from their big tent by passing full employment legislation, forcing President Ford to veto the bill in an election year, and subsequently deliver the White House to a Democrat who would, presumably, sign the legislation on its second pass. After rigorous negotiations with top labor leaders such as the AFL-CIO's dour President George Meany and the Congressional Black Caucus, Humphrey-Hawkins threw down the gauntlet by proposing to recognize full employment as the law of the land, and calling for job banks, increased federal aid to the states, and greater coordination with the Federal Reserve. House Majority Leader Tip O'Neill touted the measure as "the centerpiece of our party's 1976 platform."

Alan Greenspan, the chair of Ford's Council of Economic Advisors—who would later trigger the housing market crash with his investor-friendly monetary policies as Federal Reserve chairman—testified against the bill in congressional hearings. Treasury Secretary William Simon, who had insisted that families of modest means shoulder the burden of closing New York City's budget gap, ridiculed the naivete of legislation promising "an instant panacea to all our economic woes," the scaffolding of which was "the economic illiteracy of the American people." The libertarian University of Chicago economist Milton Friedman, who pioneered the school voucher movement and authored the instruction manual for Chile's fascist overhaul under General Augusto Pinochet, described Humphrey-Hawkins as "close to fraud," and an economist in the Nixon administration, Herbert Stein, complained that the bill "was so smothered in sentimentality that anyone who speaks out against it runs the risk of being considered brutal."[279]

Such critiques from conservatives were hardly unexpected. What wasn't anticipated were similar criticisms leveled by Keynesians such as the economist John Kenneth Galbraith, who pleaded against Humphrey-Hawkins:

> Let us not imagine that God is a liberal gentleman who will work miracles for liberals merely because He loves his own.[280]

Carter would ultimately sign Humphrey-Hawkins into law in 1978 but it had been watered down to the point of merely suggesting full employment. What united both liberal and conservative economists in their condemnation of the bill's first draught was a neoclassical view of wage inflation as larceny, robbing capital of its divine right as kings to enrich themselves off the labor of others. At issue was the inverse relationship between inflation and employment as illustrated by the Phillips Curve, which correlates a steep drop in unemployment with a spike in consumer prices, or alternately, a rise in unemployment with a decline in prices.

Inflation is no picnic for working stiffs either, but for obvious reasons—without a job you can't afford that loaf of bread at *any* price—it's vastly preferable to unemployment, because it's offset by fatter paychecks and shrinking debts. If, for instance, you borrow $1,000 this year and the annual rate of inflation is 10 percent, the principal you owe will effectively be shaved to $900 next year.

For this reason, wage inflation triggers the same murderous obsession in speculators as Moby Dick inspired in Captain Ahab. Critics of full employment in the 1970s were the intellectual heirs of the Bourbons who steadfastly refused entreaties from the Greenbackers, Populists and Grangers to restore the scrip minted during the Civil War or the coinage of free silver for use as legal tender. Either of these measures would have likely resulted in rising inflation, tipping the balance of power, if only marginally, from employer to employee, and lender to borrower. That's a nonstarter for capital and the elected officeholders, intellectuals, and lobbyists who carry their water.

To the chagrin of Humphrey-Hawkins' supporters, consumer prices had begun to increase dramatically in 1974. Simultaneously, economic output began to slow, introducing a new term into America's political lexicon, "stagflation," combining the words "stagnation" and "inflation." Heterodox economists argued, however, that inflation was rising because of a deficit of cash and not its surfeit, as exemplified by the fact that unemployment was *rising* in the mid-1970s, not falling.

This was largely because the labor market was struggling to absorb both the Baby Boomers and women who were beginning to flood the labor force in unprecedented numbers. Coupled with soaring oil prices, inflation was ticking up, these economists argued, not because there were too many consumers chasing a limited supply of goods and services, but too few, causing demand to fall and prices to rise. Humphrey-Hawkins, they said, would actually lower inflation by increasing consumer purchasing power, and therefore, the demand for goods and services.

To this day there's no consensus on what causes inflation, and indeed there are myriad global examples of skyrocketing inflation in a low-wage or high unemployment environment. The Marxist economist Richard Wolff attributes inflation to price gouging by corporate executives to capitalize on what they perceive as even the tiniest increase in consumer purchasing power.

What everyone agrees on, however, is that if you kill jobs and gut wages, prices will surely drop because no one can afford to buy anything. Herein lies the seed of our national discontent in the neoliberal era: Since at least the Carter administration, the federal government has doggedly pursued austerity policies, or what Reagan termed "supply-side" economics, which are, in essence, the direct opposite of Keynesianism in that they do not invest in jobs and raise wages but *divest* in jobs and *gut* wages. The ensuing victory for investors is a pyrrhic one: They cut their labor costs but in doing so they also slice into their customers' buying power.

Neoliberalism's illogic was very much on display in 2023 as the Federal Reserve had, over the course of a year, raised interest rates by nearly five percentage points, explicitly to kill jobs and lower wages. And yet both wages and the employment rate—the percentage of able-bodied adults who are attached to the labor market—are near historic lows and couldn't possibly be the source of the post-pandemic bout of inflation. The most obvious culprit is the Fed's decade-long policy of money-printing since the Great Recession began in 2008 to help investors recoup their losses that accrued to their over-speculation in the real estate market.

Just as William Mahone's political equivocations helped diminish his constituents' enthusiasm for the Readjusters nearly a century earlier, and widespread discontent with Barack Obama's centrist leadership paved the way for Trump, Carter's rudderless presidency primed the pump for Ronald Reagan's ascension in 1980, renewing the marriage vows between capitalism and racism.

A peanut farmer and former Georgia governor, Carter had no real affinity for organized labor, and his relationships with African Americans were largely paternalistic. Once elected, he quickly backed away from pledges made during the 1976 campaign to support universal health care, and his policies of deregulation and disinvestment widened the gap between the party and its electoral base.

In 1979 a journalist asked William "Wimpy" Winpisinger, the president of the International Association of Machinists and Aerospace Workers, "Is there any way the president can redeem himself in your eyes?"

"Yes, there's one way he can do it," replied the blunt-spoken labor leader.

"What's that?" asked the reporter.

"Die."

Calling Carter the "best Republican president since Herbert Hoover," Winpisinger would go on to support Ted Kennedy's primary challenge in the 1980 campaign, and when that fell short, led a walkout of the Democratic Convention when Carter was renominated.

That same year, Federal Reserve Chairman Paul Volcker, a Carter appointee, applied a novel form of shock therapy to combat inflation that was rising at a pace of about 1 percent per month. Instead of setting the interest rates, or the *price* of money, the Fed would curb the *supply* of money by setting strict quotas on money printing, allowing the market to set the price. Wall Street responded by doubling the interest rate at which the central bank loaned money to commercial banks—known as the Federal Funds rate—to a historic high of 21.5 percent, triggering what was at the time the worst economic downturn since the Great Depression.

In Volcker's obituary, *the New York Times* wrote in 2019:

> As consumers stopped buying homes and cars, millions of workers lost their jobs. Angry homebuilders mailed chunks of two-by-fours to the Fed's marble headquarters in Washington. But Mr. Volcker managed to wring most inflation from the economy.

In doing so, he strangled the goose that laid the golden egg—a robust manufacturing economy—and reset the global economy. Consider that in the years since 1980, the poverty rate has soared to historic highs, the number of employees belonging to a union has dropped, falling from almost 4-in-10 to 1-in-10, and the number of work stoppages in 2022 was 23, or roughly one-half of one percent of the total number of work stoppages from 40 years earlier. Conversely, the Federal Funds rate hovered at about a quarter of one percent until the Fed began its attack on rising prices, and inflation that once ran at a clip of 1 percent per month inched along at roughly 1 percent *per year* until the pandemic.

All of these statistics are part of the bankers' power play intended to prop up asset prices while gutting wages, strengthening creditors' position in the marketplace while weakening the position of employees left increasingly dependent on high-interest debt to get by. Volcker's monetary policy was akin to chemotherapy that kills both the cancerous tumor and the patient.

At base, capitalism is a pyramid scheme, and the contradictions between speculators and labor are simply unsustainable over the long term. But, as evidenced by the New Deal's trajectory, the marketplace can keep a lid on things for a while if labor and capital are engaged in constant negotiation over the distribution of wages, which circumscribes the chaos and allows for a certain equilibrium to be struck between unemployment and inflation. The farcical idea at the heart of Reagan's trickle-down economics is that investors can wrest more money from borrowers than employees.

The term "neoliberalism" refers to the classical economic notion to free, or liberate, the marketplace from artificial encumbrances, and yet Adam Smith never dreamt of the scenario that confronted the U.S. economy in the aftermath of the Great Recession; fresh out of paying customers, the central bank was reduced essentially to printing the profits for Big Business for more than a decade.

In the same vein that the Funders' austerity budgets a century earlier maximized bondholders' returns while reducing Virginians' buying power, one president after another—Carter, Reagan, Bush, Clinton, Dubya, Obama, Trump, and Biden—has sliced into the jugular vein that is workers' disposable income, leaving capital with few options short of fraud or strongarm robbery. The fulcrum of an economy that makes nothing of value is what the French call rent-seeking, and it is populated not by industrialists but *rentiers*, or parasites.

Absent consumer demand, the Federal Reserve, for nearly a decade, credited the accounts of the biggest banks and corporations to offset Americans' inability to spend. How else to explain the contradiction between soaring stock prices and earnings that are either flat or falling? Rather than guarantee every American worker a job, the federal government today guarantees the biggest banks and corporations a profit. So much for free enterprise.

Consider that in a single month, June 2020, the Treasury Department printed more banknotes than it had for the first 200 years of the Republic, most of which was deposited in the bank accounts of the super-rich, who need only so many Aspen vacation homes. The velocity of money in the U.S. in the fourth quarter of 2019—before the Covid pandemic—was 1.427, which means that a single dollar was used less than one-and-a-half times, the lowest level since at least 1960, according to the Federal Reserve. In other words, money that workers could use to buy goods and services is instead being hoarded by people who don't need it.

You needn't possess a Ph.D. in history or economics (in fact given the state of the economics profession, it's probably better if you don't) to understand that weaponizing monetary policy against employees raises critical questions, chief among them: How can capital *extract* wealth without *producing* wealth?

Between 2008 and 2020, the Fed's balance sheets increased from $900 billion to nearly $9 trillion as a result of buying non-performing assets, or bad loans, often *above* par, from the very same too-big-to-fail banks that oversold predatory mortgages known as subprime. This government bailout, named quantitative easing, or QE, is tantamount to socialism for the speculators who fleeced millions of homeowners out of their life savings. Over that same period, banks evicted nearly 10 million families from their homes. "This is money laundering, essentially," said Max Keiser, former host of the Keiser Report on the Russian-owned network, RT.

Think of two neighboring villages, miles apart, one housing the employers and the other their employees. When the workers are finally able to afford both meat and potatoes, the ruling class burns every potato farm in sight. But when the affluent are forced to cut back on their daily champagne consumption from two bottles to one—similar to Kay Graham's diminishing but still robust returns at *the Washington Post* in 1975—the central bank airdrops aid packages of cash, in large denominations, over their village.

Such a heist requires a criminal mastermind, and Ronald Reagan was the kingpin sent, almost literally, by central casting. The Gipper cut his teeth in Hollywood bickering with communists such as John Howard Lawson and was California's governor when the Black Panthers stormed the state capitol.

He was only half as smart as Richard Nixon, if that, but had twice the charisma, and as a child of the Radio Age he could deliver his lines with gusto. Announcing his campaign for the White House in the same Mississippi county where the Klan had murdered three civil rights workers just 16 years earlier served as a subliminal message posed once again to Europe's sons and daughters:

Are you a worker or are you white?

Carter had already loosened the cap; Reagan merely allowed the genie to escape from the bottle. The same year that he invited whites to return to the fold in Mississippi, an all-white North Carolina jury acquitted six white nationalists for opening fire on a peaceful, multi-racial "Death to the Klan" rally in Greensboro, killing five and injuring ten. Organized by the local Communist Party, the march on November 3rd, 1979, was held at a local public housing project and was attended by a number of Black mill workers. Anticipating the 2017 terrorist attack on protesters in Charlottesville, Virginia, and mindful of the violence that followed the withdrawal of federal troops from the conquered Confederacy, and the Haymarket affair, a caravan of armed Klansmen and neo-Nazis attacked the demonstrators, a few of whom were armed and returned fire. Despite an informant who warned police of the white nationalists' plans, patrol officers were nowhere to be found when the 88-second clash began. As was the case with Fred Hampton, no one was ever convicted for the slayings.

In his tome, *Black Reconstruction in America*, W.E.B. Du Bois wrote that the Confederacy's flight and fight response to emancipation reflects the landowning aristocracy's failure of imagination. Had they freed the slaves, and paid them a nominal amount for their labor, they would have expanded consumer buying power exponentially and consolidated their monopolistic control of the economy. Similarly, a study published in 2020 by Carter C.

Price and Kathryn Edwards of the RAND Corporation asserts that if the U.S. had maintained its income distribution from the postwar period between 1945 and 1974, the aggregate annual income of Americans earning below the 90th percentile would have been $2.5 trillion higher in the year 2018 alone. That is an amount equal to nearly 12 percent of the nation's entire economic output, and enough to more than double median income by putting $1,144 per month in the pocket of every single worker in the bottom nine deciles.[281]

Another study published in 2020, by Citigroup, estimates that racial discrimination has cost the U.S. roughly $16 trillion in lost output, or nearly an entire year's GDP.

America is a failed state because its reflexive answer to every crisis is to steal more money from workers, beginning with African Americans. Either unable or unwilling to generate new ideas, President Carter merely did as he was told, parroting the pablum vomited up by his rivals and donors. This set in motion a pattern that continues to this day with Joe Biden, another uninspiring Democrat in the White House. Wrote Louis Proyect of the Democratic Party's 2020 presidential nominee:

> He proposed banking at the post office and that the Federal Reserve guarantee all Americans a bank account. Such 'socialist' measures perturbed Wall Street bankers to the point that his campaign had to phone them up and tell them to relax.

The response from Biden's campaign, said one investment banker on the condition of anonymity, referenced progressives who supported U.S. Senator Elizabeth Warren of Massachusetts:

> They basically said, 'Listen, this is just an exercise to keep the Warren people happy, and don't read too much into it.'

The bipartisan devotion to austerity helps explain the federal government's militarist expansion abroad over the last quarter century.

Unwilling to invest in jobs at home, politicians have few options to turn a profit for their donors other than by looting, as in Libya, or supporting foreign officeholders who are more amenable to borrowing money from Wall Street at usurious interest rates, such as Ukraine in 2014 or Argentina in 2015.

In their book, *The Smartest Guys in the Room: The Amazing Rise and Scandalous Fall of Enron,* the authors Bethany McLean and Peter Elkind describe a 2001 story McLean wrote in *Fortune Magazine* that asked a simple question: "How does Enron make its money?

The question marked the energy trader's downfall. If only someone had asked that question of the ruling class in 1980.

What has happened to the American body politic since is eerily similar to what happens to a human body when it's been infected with the virus that causes AIDS, which entered the public consciousness at roughly the same moment that Volcker's monetarist policy was beginning to weaken the nation's economic immune system. The medical professionals who treat and study HIV say that most people will, upon infection, come down with an awful flu bug, lasting for a period of two weeks. The term for this is seroconversion, meaning that the good blood coursing through your veins is turning bad, and the body becomes weak, sick, and feverish during this interregnum.

In all probability, our national seroconversion began in the Carter administration; the disease settled in under Reagan, and by Trump's inauguration, the U.S. body politic had developed full blown AIDS. It's only a matter of time before a fatal infection, possibly in the form of a public health crisis or a proxy war abroad, finishes us off. To carry the HIV metaphor to its logical conclusion, friends of the late Rudolf Nureyev say the celebrated Russian dancer lived in denial after he was diagnosed with the virus, carrying on with business as usual. It is said he suffered a particularly wrenching death.

In 2021, more than 40 years after Pryor's acerbic monologue at the Hollywood Bowl, another astute African American comedian, Dave Chappelle, appeared in a comedy special, *The Closer*, broadcast on Netflix. Like Pryor, Chappelle's monologue was widely denounced by celebrities, journalists, podcasters and social media influencers as hateful, homophobic, and transphobic for "punching down" on a marginalized group. That seems spurious; much as Pryor fondly acknowledged his same-sex relationship with Wilbur Harp, Chappelle spoke at length of his friendship with a transgender comedian, Daphne Dorman, who committed suicide in 2019.

What's missing from these appraisals, however, is a class analysis; when contextualized through a historical lens, both Pryor and Chappelle's standup routines addressing the LGBTQ community are reminiscent of Karl Marx's reproach of the British proletariat who the Irish largely viewed as patsies. Writ large, the LGBTQ community is by no means unique in its abandonment of the class struggle. Indeed, the oligarchy has managed to subdue racial democracy by thinning out the ranks of the proletariat and creating a buffer—of Italians, Irish, Germans, white women, Jews, gays and even the Black elite as we shall discuss in the next chapter—to isolate the vanguard of the revolution: the African American working class.

Chappelle even says at one point in his monologue that his problem is not with trans people but white people for whom the only suffering that matters is their own.

And James Baldwin, who was openly gay, had a similar critique of the LBGTQ community as allies in the class struggle:

> Their reaction seems to me in direct proportion to their sense of feeling cheated of the advantages which accrue to white people in a white society. There's an element, it has always seemed to me, of bewilderment and complaint. Now that may sound very harsh, but the gay world as such is no more prepared to accept Black people than anywhere else in society."

15.

‘A Man Who Got Down With His Country in the Wrong Way’

We are not remotely interested in the all-insulting concept of the exceptional Negro, we are not remotely interested in any tea at the White House. . . . What we are interested in is making perfectly clear that between the Negro intelligentsia, the Negro middle class, and the Negro this and that, we are one people and as far as we are concerned, we are represented by the Negroes of the streets of Birmingham.

Lorraine Hansberry

. . . and before you know it, we’ll have Negro imperialism.

Fred Hampton

Intimately familiar with winter’s tempestuousness, Chicagoans were nonetheless caught unprepared for the avalanche that blanketed the city with nearly two feet of snow over an early January weekend in 1979, pelting the prairie with flakes bigger and wetter than reality, shutting down O'Hare International Airport for only the second time ever, and producing snowdrifts that resembled a lumpen Sahara of marshmallow-white sand, swallowing cars, collapsing roofs, and disabling "L" trains. Transportation came to a standstill as commuters crammed into the remaining transit cars, squabbled over parking spaces, or laid claim to them with so many pieces of repurposed furniture that second-hand merchants began scouring the streets for sofas, recliners and loveseats.

Frustrated Chicagoans blamed the late pharaoh-like Mayor Richard J. Daley's handpicked successor Michael Bilandic for their impassable streets, and Blacks were particularly incensed by the L trains that skipped stops in their neighborhoods and whizzed off to the lily-white northwestern suburbs, leaving them stranded while temporarily reducing public transportation, for all intents and purposes, into a taxpayer-funded private shuttle service. Exacerbating the problem was the revelation that Bilandic's administration had paid a crony $90,000 for a snow removal plan that was never finished.

By 1979, Chicago's Black electorate had little to show for its loyalty to the most powerful big-city machine in U.S. history, dating back to the days when Al Capone and Mayor "Big" Bill Thompson were thick as thieves. Through a byzantine network of aldermen and Democratic precinct captains, City Hall doled out a few crumbs—a job on the city payroll here, an endorsement there, a pint of cheap whiskey, a canned ham, maybe a bed in a nursing home—to destitute voters, their pastors, and docile African American politicians like William Dawson in exchange for their vote. When carrots didn't work, the machine wasn't shy about brandishing the stick, threatening to evict a tenant from public housing, or withholding a welfare check from anyone who dared to vote against the machine.

Daley actually lost the white vote in 1963, but overwhelming support from African American voters re-elected him.[282] Complaints about this attenuated quid pro quo became increasingly animated, however, as the stocks of affordable housing shrank, police terror against communities of color escalated, and Daley—known both affectionately and derisively as "Boss"—continued to maintain segregated schools, separate and unequal, for years after the Supreme Court's 1954 decision in *Brown v. Board of Education.* Moreover, despite their numbers and rock-ribbed allegiance to the machine, Blacks were denied all but the most menial patronage jobs, accounting for scarcely one in every 30 managers in the City of Big Shoulders. When a 24-year-old Jesse Jackson met with Daley about job prospects in 1965, Daley offered him a job as a toll booth operator, despite his college degree and a letter of recommendation from North Carolina's governor, a fellow Democrat.

Finally, African Americans issued the machine a no-confidence vote in 1972 when they cast their ballots for the Republican candidate for Cook County State's Attorney, ousting the incumbent, Edward Hanrahan, who was responsible for supervising the raid that ended in Fred Hampton's assassination. This effectively derailed the machine's succession plan when Daley died unexpectedly five days before Christmas in 1976, though his contempt for his Black constituents survived him when his subordinates and Democratic ward bosses physically blocked his logical successor, the African American president pro tem of the city council, from taking office in the interim.

For months after the January blizzard, the snow continued to fall in the winter of 1979, dumping 87 inches on Chicago, more than double the average, signaling perhaps a change in the political season for a Black community under siege, turning out for the April primary in then-record numbers to replace Bilandic with a lakefront liberal who campaigned as a reformer, Jane Byrne.

If anything, she was worse. Despite overwhelming support from African American voters, Byrne seemed to have it in for them in a cynical and unimaginative bid to get a jump on her re-election campaign by wooing white ethnic voters, who were increasingly anxious in a city that was divided roughly into thirds between whites, Blacks and Latinos. After campaigning to rid City Hall of an "evil cabal" of white men, Byrne's first few months in the mayor's office seemed to augur a new day in Chicago. She quickly named five Blacks and three Latinos to the 11-member school board, shifting the balance of power on the panel that represented a system-wide enrollment that was 80 percent non-white yet had, to that point, always seated a majority of whites. She chose a Black man to head the Chicago Transit Authority (CTA) and a Black interim police chief, both Chicago firsts. But by her administration's midterm, she'd turned on a dime, as if possessed, easing out the Black interim chief to give the permanent job to a white officer. She fired the head of the CTA and hired a white successor, removed two of the five African Americans on the 11-member school board and replaced them with white women who'd cut their teeth in the racially charged anti-busing movement, passed over an accomplished Black educator for a white superintendent, and replaced two Black board members on the Chicago Housing Authority with whites.[283] Her move into an apartment in the notoriously violent Cabrini Green housing projects in 1981 was widely dismissed as a publicity stunt to defuse growing backlash from Black voters, and a feeble one at that after she aborted the experiment 25 days in. And to add insult to injury, it did not go unnoticed that Byrne was one of the few big-city mayors unwilling to publicly criticize Reagan's enervating austerity budgets.

The "Snow Queen's" contempt for the very voters who'd catapulted her into office was unmistakable proof that if Black Chicagoans continued to merely show up at their precinct every four years to cast a ballot for a candidate they had no say in choosing, they might well be buried alive by the avalanche of racial animus emanating from City Hall, their petrified corpses dug up centuries later like the ancient ruins of Pompeii, frozen in time as a monument to some Homeric battlefield. If they were to thrive—or even just survive—they would need to come up with a new strategy.

Beginning in 1980, a group of about 20 Black activists began meeting periodically in the basement of a muckraking journalist's home to discuss Byrne, voter registration, the maldistribution of municipal services that left Black neighborhoods inundated with snowed in winter and uncollected trash in summer, and Daley's oldest son, Richard M., who was sure to be a candidate in 1983. But before long, the meetings began to center on a single question, reminiscent of the shipyard cooperative created a century earlier by Baltimore's African American stevedores after the white hate strike had cost them their jobs: What if the Black community fielded its own mayoral candidate?

Leading these brainstorming sessions was the blunt-spoken Lutrelle Palmer—known as "Lu"—who was not exactly known as a consensus-builder. But if there was one thing that both his friends and foes could agree on, it was that the veteran journalist and political gadfly was a race man of the first order. Born in Newport News, Virginia, in 1922, the son of a prominent educator, Palmer came within a thesis of earning his Ph.D. from the University of Iowa, and was known to regularly and publicly scold peers who self-identified as "journalists" first, and "Black" second, which had become increasingly commonplace in the post-*Radical Chic* era. As a columnist at the *Chicago Daily News*, Palmer convinced a *capo* in the notorious street gang, the Blackstone Rangers, to surrender to him at the newspaper's downtown office on charges that he had shot a cop. A white editor working at the paper wrote that the gang leader had surrendered to the newspaper; Palmer objected on the grounds that no Black gang leader would surrender to a white news organization; he had surrendered to a Black reporter working *for* said white news organization. The distinction spoke to journalistic credibility. When the editor refused to recast the article, Palmer summoned the street gang's infamous leader, Jeff Fort, to the newspaper's downtown office, to convince the editor that it would be in his best interest to comply with Palmer's suggestion. He did.

Palmer characterized that particular episode as a rare victory in his losing battle against racism in the newsroom, and when he inevitably quit after the editors had published a point-by-point refutation of one of his articles, he worried that the newspaper's executives might try to stop him from removing the volumes of notebooks he'd accumulated over the years. So he called an old friend, Bobby Rush, who had succeeded Hampton as the chairman of the Illinois chapter of the Black Panther Party, and asked him to send over a few men to conspicuously retrieve the boxes of files from the *Daily News* office.

His association with the Panthers was integral to his political identity. Palmer was one of the first journalists to assert publicly that Hampton's death was, in fact, a state-sponsored assassination, earning him the *nom de guerre*, "Panther with a pen."

With Byrne rather than Old Man Daley now running roughshod over the Black community, the principal problem identified by Palmer and the others was that the Cook County Democratic machine's monopolization of the political process was profoundly anti-democratic. Its clique of aldermen, precinct captains, ward heelers and central committeemen infantilized the electorate by requiring voters to do nothing more than cast their ballot and go home. Under this arrangement, the best Black Chicagoans could ever hope for was choosing the lesser of two evils, or maybe lodging a protest vote, which in the case of Byrne had gotten them nowhere. The group led by Palmer proposed they flip the script, recruit the candidate who best represented the Black community's interests, and then do whatever it took to elect him or her.

To be sure, this represented a seismic shift in Palmer's thinking. Listeners of his radio show had grown accustomed to hearing Palmer explain that Blacks would fare better by reconnecting with the African cultural identity that had been wiped from their hard drive by centuries of subjugation. By this time, however, there were Black mayors in Los Angeles, Detroit, Atlanta, Washington, D.C., and even Birmingham, and Palmer had begun to cotton to the idea that electing one of their own to the mayor's office might be restorative to the wounded Black soul.

Palmer's ad hoc committee never truly considered anyone other than Harold Washington. Born three years after the 1919 Chicago riot, Washington grew up within shouting distance from the stockyards that inspired Carl Sandburg to write the line "hog butcher to the world" in his iconic poem. He was the fourth child of Bertha and Roy, who worked as a precinct captain for Mayor Anton Cermak, widely considered the father of the city's Democratic machine at a time when most African Americans still voted Republican. With his Motown baritone, the soaring cadence of a Baptist preacher, and a striking resemblance to the actor Ossie Davis, Washington had Palmer and his cohort at "hello." Both a bookworm and star athlete at DuSable High School, Washington went to night school, like his father, to earn his law degree, and was a state senator and a part of the Daley machine when the word went out to shun Martin Luther King Jr. 's 1966 visit to Chicago. Washington defied the order, making it a point to march alongside the iconic cleric, but that experience coupled with Hampton's murder and Daley's bid to topple Washington's mentor—a Black congressman who'd dared challenge the mayor on the issue of police brutality—had caused Washington to go rogue. He tossed his hat into the ring for the special election following Daley's sudden death, and though he lost badly, he continued to march to the beat of his own drum. His record was by no means unblemished; he'd been rather bizarrely sentenced to 40 days in the Cook County jail for failing to *file* his taxes (he'd paid them), and so profligate was his womanizing that one friend reportedly said that if "every woman Harold had slept with stood at one end of City Hall the building would sink five inches into LaSalle Avenue."[284]

Still, his attributes far outweighed his negatives in the minds of Lu Palmer's cadre, and when the members approached Washington about running for mayor in the 1983 election, he played it coy, agreeing to the mayoral bid only if the group registered at least 50,000 new voters and raised $200,000 by the fall of 1982. While Washington was intrigued by the possibilities, mounting a mayoral bid struck him as a tad quixotic. Moreover, he already had a good job, representing Illinois' 1st District in the U.S. House of Representatives. He had hoped to dissuade supporters by setting the bar high.

No one so much as flinched, least of all Palmer and his wife, Jorja, who began teaching political education classes—modeled on the Panthers' efforts under Hampton—at the nonprofit organization the couple had founded, Chicago Black United Communities, or CBUC, on the city's South Side. In a 1992 interview, Palmer recalled:

> After every four-week period we would have a graduation, and every graduation speaker was Harold Washington. He'd come by, make a nice little speech, give out the citations. The first graduation we had was on the coldest day in Chicago history when the wind chill factor went down to 80 something below zero. We were so poor we had no heat in the building and so the people kept their scarves on, and I mean you could see the breath coming out of their mouths.
>
> But nobody left. I turned to Jorja and said 'these brothas and sistas are ready' because you know how our people are about the cold. [285]

By the fall of 1982, Chicago's Black radio station, WVON, crackled with Palmer's clever taunt, "We shall see in '83." Chicago Black United Communities had unleashed 2,000 trained organizers on the streets of Chicago, and with their zeal and expertise, they exceeded Washington's initial demands, working with the Urban League, NAACP, and Jesse Jackson's Operation Push to register 237,000 new voters—including

180,000 Blacks—eclipsing all citywide voter registration efforts combined over the previous decade. And to that army of voters Palmers' soldiers added a war chest of nearly half-a-million dollars to be spent on Washington's campaign.[286] It was going to be a dogfight, but Washington's campaign aides theorized that with Daley and Byrne neutralizing the white vote, Washington could leverage the 80/80 rule—80 percent Black turnout and an 80 percent share of the African American vote—and a plurality of Latino ballots to win the primary, practically guaranteeing victory in the general election.

Washington did not neglect the white, lakefront liberals or the southside Hyde Park community that is home to the ivy-canopied University of Chicago, but he honed in on Black public employees like Fraser Robinson—whose daughter, Michelle, would go on to be the First Lady of the United States—and the poor who lived in notorious housing projects like Cabrini Green, State Street, and Ida B. Wells. A key player in Washington's campaign was Charles Hayes, an African American and international vice president of the United Food and Commercial Workers Union, who led a faction of white, Black and Asian meatpackers who challenged and ultimately replaced the conservative, virtually all-white union leadership in the 1940s. The union went on to support the 1955 Montgomery bus boycott, raised funds for the Southern Christian Leadership Conference's voter registration drives in the Deep South, and did much of the heavy lifting for Washington's campaign, raising money, organizing phone banks and mobilizing voter registration drives.

In one notable stump speech delivered at a South side church, Washington's soaring, nationalist rhetoric could easily have been confused with an African liberation hero such as Patrice Lumumba or Kwame Nkrumah:

> We've been pushed around, shoved around, beat, murdered, emasculated, destroyed. There's been an unfair distribution

> of all the goodies. No system works for us. We influence no institutions in this country except our own. We have no power. We have no land. . . . We've been giving white candidates our votes for years and years unstintingly hoping that they would include us in the process. Now it's come to the point where we say it's our turn. It's our turn.[287]

In *Fire on the Prairie: Chicago's Harold Washington and the Politics of Race*, the journalist Gary Rivlin wrote:

> Washington anticipated the criticism that would rain down on him for using 'our turn.' So he offered a quick history of ethnic politics in Chicago. The Irish were treated like white trash at the turn of the century. "Paddy Wagons" were so named because crime and the Irish were closely linked in people's minds back then, much the same way today crime has a black face. But the Irish took power and then offered no apologies when they attained representation well beyond their share of the population. Now it was the black community's turn, Washington said. Two-fifths of the city were shortchanged in the distribution of education dollars, basic city services, and jobs; even shortchanged was their share of federal antipoverty dollars slated for low and moderate income communities. The weight of these abuses, Washington said, was so overwhelming as to brook (no) debate. He urged those listening to 'make it unfashionable and uncomfortable' for any black not to vote for him. It was a suggestion that this particular audience would not have to hear a second time.

Polls consistently showed that Washington scared white voters, so his aides resorted to voiceover for radio ads aired on stations popular with whites and reverted to Washington's voice for ads broadcast on Black-formatted radio stations. The astute Washington often tailored his message by belting out "the battle cry is reform!"[288] with white audiences yet shifting gears with African Americans. Speaking to a largely Black audience of the late Daley:

> He was a racist to the core, head to toe, hip to hip, there's no ding or doubt about it. He eschewed and fought and oppressed black people to the point that some thought that was the way they were supposed to live, just like some slaves on the plantation thought that that was the way they were supposed to live. I give no hosannas for a racist, nor did I appreciate or respect his son. If his name were anything other than Daley, his campaign would be a joke.[289]

Rivlin wrote that at this point in his speech Washington chuckled at his abrasiveness, and softened his tone in speaking of the redemptive spirit that has historically guided African Americans in their relationship with their white countrymen.

"That redemption is not going to come out in hatred. It's going to come out in positive action towards our fellow man," he said. Blacks had a responsibility to lead "even if we have to beat 'em across the head and knock 'em down and make 'em take it."

Even as polls began showing Washington with the lead in the weeks before the primary, Chicago's mainstream media dismissed his campaign as "racially polarizing."[290] Anticipating contemporary nonblack journalists like Matt Taibbi in the aftermath of the George Floyd killing and the protests that followed, John McDermott, editor and publisher of the liberal newspaper, the *Chicago Reporter*, lamented in an op-ed that "race is not a legitimate issue."

Washington garnered 36 percent of the ballots to Byrne's 34 percent and Daley's 30 percent in the primary; his margin of victory was 33,000 votes out of 1.2 million cast. Striking a conciliatory tone ahead of the general election, he tried to reassure white ethnic voters that his agenda would enable "all Chicago to move forward." The sectarian slogan for Washington's Republican opponent, Bernard Epton, on the other hand, was "Epton for Mayor: Before It's Too Late" and he came within 50,000 votes of beating the Democratic nominee in a city that had been blue for half a century at that point, polling 200,000 more votes than the previous three Republican nominees for mayor combined.[291] Washington won only 5 percent of the white vote in the general election, but nine of ten ballots cast by African Americans, and two-thirds of all Latino votes.

For Black Chicago, said Robert Starks, a political science professor at Northeastern University and a key political strategist for Washington, the campaign "took on almost a religious or gospel character. . . . It became almost a civic religion."[292]

Describing his election as a "pilgrimage" and promising a coalition of "more people and more kinds of people than any government in the history of Chicago,"[293] Washington began to deliver the spoils almost immediately, working assiduously to cut everyone in on a sweet deal that had previously been reserved for a privileged few. Despite stiff opposition from white aldermen and state lawmakers, his administration represented nothing less than an outbreak of good governance and pluralism.

Washington expanded media access to municipal government by rewriting the guidelines for Freedom of Information Act requests, rescinded a municipal ordinance prohibiting street musicians from panhandling and strengthened renters' rights. He made Chicago the first sanctuary city in the Midwest, issuing an executive order forbidding municipal employees from enforcing immigration laws; computerized city departments; and extended collective bargaining rights for public trade unions whose rank-and-file members were often kept in the dark about the wink-and-a-nod labor contracts struck between their corrupt leadership and the Daley machine.

He awarded a record number of city contracts to minority-owned vendors, increased the number of women and Blacks at City Hall, distributed city services more evenly across all neighborhoods, capped campaign contributions for contractors doing business with the city at $1,500, and professionalized the city's workforce by banning patronage jobs, all of which would've been unthinkable under the old machine. He even mothballed the city's limousine for an Oldsmobile 98.

When a West Side toy factory announced plans to close five years after procuring a $1 million city grant to subsidize job creation, Washington forced the company to delay the closing to help its employees find new jobs. And his administration responded to homeless advocates protesting the demolition of single-room occupancy hotels by requiring the developers of the luxury Presidential Towers in the West Loop to donate $5 million to what would become the new Low Income Housing Trust Fund; it continues to subsidize the rent of more than 20,000 Chicagoans to this day. When condominiums and apartments began encroaching on a Northside industrial corridor, Washington protected jobs by creating designated manufacturing districts.

By the time an overworked and overweight Washington keeled over dead from a heart attack while working at his office desk on Thanksgiving Eve of 1987, Chicago's white political establishment was already plotting a strategy for reclaiming lost ground. The next year, a Harvard-educated Black Rhodes scholar named Mel Reynolds challenged Washington's ally, Gus Savage, for the Illinois 2nd Congressional District, which included a swath of Chicago's South Side lakefront. It would take Reynolds three tries to finally unseat Savage, but as Frederick Harris wrote in his 2012 book, *The Price of the Ticket: Barack Obama and the Rise and Decline of Black Politics,* the city's two major daily newspapers, the *Chicago Tribune* and *Sun-Times* endorsed Reynolds, as did conservative *Washington Post* columnist George Will. The main business daily, *Crain's*, did not endorse him, but went out of its way to praise him for his tendency to "downplay race as a factor in politics."

Feted by foundations and the media, and bankrolled by wealthy campaign contributors, Reynolds' meteoric rise led one Black state lawmaker to wonder aloud how he managed to amass such campaign cash.

> White politicians have bought and paid for a novice who wasn't even a block captain, or community leader, or even a member of a recognized church. There's something wrong. His whole staff comes from City Hall, which tells you they're being supplied to get rid of Gus Savage.[294]

Reynolds' career would ultimately be derailed by a sex scandal involving a teenage girl, but in his three years on Capitol Hill he amassed a voting record that was solidly neoliberal, voting for the Clinton Administration's North American Free Trade Agreement and the omnibus crime bill, both of which were catastrophic for workers.

The same year that Reynolds won his congressional seat, a young, 31-year-old community organizer named Barack Obama approached Lu Palmer asking for his support for a voter registration effort. As Palmer told the story, he thought the Harvard-trained lawyer both arrogant and unoriginal, and sent him on his way. But three years later, he would encounter Obama again. An old ally in the Washington campaign, Alice Palmer (no relation) had finished third in the special election to succeed the now-disgraced Reynolds, and she wanted to return to Springfield. Palmer asked Obama to withdraw his name out of respect for the widely respected Alice Palmer, but Obama refused. Palmer couldn't recall Obama's exact words but something about the way he spoke sounded oddly familiar. That's when it clicked.

"Man, you sound like Mel Reynolds," Palmer told Obama.[295]

Absent an understanding of Chicago's first Black mayor you cannot begin to make sense of the Republic's first Black president. Obama owed his electoral triumphs to a top-down political movement that was antithetical to the grassroots organizing that produced Washington, and each man governed accordingly. As such, the pro-business policies of Black politicians such as Obama, Kamala Harris, New York City Mayor Eric Adams, New Jersey's U.S. Senator Cory Booker, former Chicago Mayor Lori Lightfoot, D.C. Mayor Muriel Bowser, and countless others can only be explained as a response to an insurrection, and the radical Black polity that was its engine. Or to put it another way, Obama was the figurehead for a *counterrevolution* that takes dead aim at its foes in the American working class.

Substantively and stylistically, Washington was everything that Obama was not. Washington reversed public policies steeped in white supremacy, Obama deepened them. Washington weakened the influence of money in politics, Obama strengthened it. Washington accommodated immigrants and helped transform Chicago into a sanctuary, while Obama deported more migrants than any president in history, and outrageously, stopped and frisked the presidential airplane of Bolivia's first indigenous president, Evo Morales, in search of the whistleblower, Edward Snowden. Washington rewarded organized labor for its support, Obama gave unions the cold shoulder when he wasn't trying to bust them altogether. Washington opened space for workers in the informal sector who were trying to make a living any way they could in a shrinking economy; by failing to prosecute so much as a single white vigilante or police officer for violating an African American's civil rights, Obama encouraged the kind of wanton disregard for Black life that resulted in the lynching of an unemployed Black man merely for selling loose cigarettes on a Staten Island street corner.

Washington invoked Fanon, exalted the messianic quality of the African's experience in the Americas, and exhorted people of color to never give up the fight against injustice and oppression; Obama invoked Reagan, trafficked in folklore, and scolded Black men for feeding their children cold Popeye's chicken for breakfast. Washington's prophetic Blackness embodied Bessie Smith's blues, Obama's performative Blackness the mediocre, Black capitalist hip-hop of Jay-Z.

None of this was by chance. If Washington's election is viewed in its most irreducible form—namely, the pinnacle of what the ex-president of the NAACP's North Carolina chapter, Rev. William Barber, characterizes as the nation's second Reconstruction—then Obama can only be contextualized as the plutocrats' man in the White House, installed for the singular purpose of preventing a third.

The proof is in the bitter pudding. Never have African Americans lost more wealth than they did during Obama's eight years in office, suggesting rather strongly that Obama was chosen by bankers for the same reason that their forefathers selected Frederick Douglass as the Freedman's Bank was collapsing in 1874: to restore faith in a system that was robbing them blind.

In early 2008 as the primary season was getting underway, the writer Pam Martens found that seven of Obama's top 14 donors were connected to the biggest actors in the subprime mortgage heist.[296] A month before the 2008 election, a Citigroup executive submitted to the Obama campaign a list of its preferred candidates for cabinet positions, corresponding almost exactly to the White House cabinet in Obama's first term.[297]

Speaking to South Carolina voters in January 2008, Obama said:

> Washington lobbyists haven't funded my campaign, they won't run my White House, and they will not drown out the voices of working Americans when I am president.

Yet that's exactly what they did as evidenced by his trip to Michigan in April 2016 to reassure Flint residents that the contaminated water was safe to drink. Appearing alongside Republican Governor Rick Snyder, Obama asked for a glass of filtered tap water that had been drawn from corroded pipes; raising the glass to his lips and appearing to take a sip, he proclaimed the water safe to drink.

One Black woman in attendance later told reporters that the audience responded to Obama's ploy with an audible gasp, signaling widespread disgust.

That Michigan's political class poisoned Flint's water to satisfy the Bourbons is hardly a new story. What is new, however, is the complicity of such a vast segment of the Black elite in the Bourbons' kleptocratic schemes.

There is no national precedent for this moment. The closest comparison is Napoleon Bonaparte's decision in 1802 to reclaim Haiti for France and re-enslave its African population following the island's triumphant slave revolt 13 years earlier, which was supported by mulatto planters who were, under the colonial arrangement, free, but relative to whites, second-class citizens. Arguing that they were more French than Black, Napoleon convinced the mulatto planters to switch sides. This is essentially what the plutocrats have done with a large swath of the Black Talented Tenth since Harold Washington's 1983 bid.

Three years after he rebuffed Palmer's overtures, Obama challenged Bobby Rush for his congressional seat.

"A dozen years after the death of Harold Washington, there is a generational shift in the leadership of the Black community," wrote *Chicago Sun-Times* columnist Steve Neal in 1999.

Chicago's Black community was less impressed, however, at least initially.

"Barack is viewed in part to be the white man in blackface in our community," said Donne Trotter, an Illinois state legislator who was also challenging Rush for the 1st Congressional District.

> Who pushed him to get where he is so fast? It's these individuals in Hyde Park who don't always have the best interests of our community in mind.

While Washington auditioned for his job in a freezing South Side Chicago community center, Obama's close-up moment was at a 2003 fundraiser at the Washington home of Democratic fixer and Bill Clinton's Black BFF, Vernon Jordan, getting facetime with such Democratic establishment fixtures as former White House Counsel Greg Craig, Mike Williams, a lobbyist for the Bondholders' Association, and K Street law partners Tom Quinn and Robert Harmala.

In a 2006 article for *Harper's Magazine*, Ken Silverstein noted that Craig "liked the fact that Obama was not a racial polarizer on the model of Jesse Jackson or Al Sharpton," and Williams was "soothed by Obama's reassurances that he was not anti-business."

"There's a reasonableness about him," Harmala told Silverstein, "I don't see him being on the liberal fringe."

The African American political scientist Adolph Reed wrote after meeting Obama in the late '90s:

> In Chicago, for instance, we've gotten a foretaste of the new breed of foundation-hatched black communitarian voices; one of them, a smooth Harvard lawyer with impeccable do-good credentials and vacuous-to-repressive neoliberal politics, has won a state senate seat on a base mainly in the liberal foundation and development worlds. His fundamentally bootstrap line was softened by a patina of the rhetoric of authentic community, talk about meeting in kitchens, small-scale solutions to social problems, and the predictable elevation of process over program—the point where identity politics converges with old-fashioned middle-class reform in favoring form over substance. I suspect that his ilk is the wave of the future in U.S. black politics . . ..

Obama was hardly the first African American politician enthralled with neoliberalism. In 1977, just nine years after Martin Luther King was assassinated while protesting with striking Black garbage workers, Atlanta's first African American Mayor Maynard Jackson fired striking Black sanitation workers. And five years earlier, the March on Washington's principal organizer, Bayard Rustin, told disgruntled Black workers at the International Association of Machinists convention to "stop griping always that nobody has problems but you Black people" and that the privileges and positions of power white workers held in the union were not on account of race. The historian Robin Kelley noted that the international had barred non-whites for 60 of its 80 years in existence at that juncture.

Still, it's clear that Democratic Party power brokers have unleashed a veritable army of turncoat Black lawmakers, mayors, school superintendents, prosecutors, judges, journalists, academics and police to thwart the rise of progressives like Washington, Jesse Jackson, or Vermont's socialist Senator Bernie Sanders by tightening its control of the purse strings and through gimmicks such as superdelegates. Conservative party leaders launched the Democratic Leadership Council in 1985 to chart a more moderate political path, and four years later a young California congressman named Tony Coelho resigned his seat to avoid an ethics investigation and went on to reinvent party fundraising by strengthening ties to Wall Street donors while relying less on the Democrats' traditional base of organized labor. When two Dixiecrats, Bill Clinton and Al Gore, won the party's 1992 nomination with a "Third Way" platform that was effectively a response to Reagan's efforts to drive a wedge through the New Deal consensus, the die was cast, and the "butter biscuit brigade" of Black politicos was born.

As one example, consider the careers of two African American mayors—Marion Barry in Washington, D.C., and ex-NBA star Kevin Johnson in Sacramento. First elected in 1979, Barry may have been the most transformative mayor in the second half of the 20th century, enacting policies and legislation that created the wealthiest Black-majority jurisdiction in the country across the District's border in Maryland's Prince George's County. Here is what *Washington Post* columnist Courtland Milloy wrote upon Barry's death in 2014:

> When Barry was elected to his first term as mayor in 1979, less than 5 percent of the District's $100 million government contracting and procurement business went to black businesses.
>
> By 1989, hundreds of minority-owned businesses were receiving 40 percent, or roughly $233 million in city contracts.

For expanding the Greater Washington area's consumer base, Barry was hounded out of office by an exhaustive FBI investigation that famously videotaped him consorting in a D.C. hotel room with a government informant who was not his wife and taking a drag from a crack pipe. Convicted on a single count of drug possession, he served six months in federal prison.

Johnson's biggest achievement, on the other hand, was brokering a deal to spend $258 million in taxpayer money to construct a new arena for Sacramento's NBA franchise. Like Barry, Johnson has also been the subject of a federal probe, but unlike Barry he has never seen the inside of a jail cell. According to a 2009 report released jointly by the Senate Finance Committee and the House Committee on Oversight and Government Reform, investigators for Gerald Walpin, the inspector general for the Corporation for National Community Service, found that between 2004 and 2007, Johnson misspent nearly a million dollars intended for St. HOPE Academy, the charter school organization he had founded in his hometown of Sacramento. The report alleged, for instance, that Johnson paid people to "wash his car . . . and run personal errands" with federal funds that were earmarked for the hiring of tutors.

Walpin concluded that Johnson's financial malfeasance alone warranted criminal charges, but his investigation uncovered more evidence of misconduct. In 2007, a teenager told a St. HOPE administrator, Jaqueline

Wong-Hernandez, that Johnson had "inappropriately touched" her. Women and teenage girls have repeatedly made similar allegations against Johnson, including one 16-year-old Arizona girl who Johnson paid $236,000 on the condition that she not speak of the allegations to anyone other than "a priest, a therapist or a lawyer."

School reformer and ex-Washington, D.C., Schools Superintendent Michelle Rhee—who Johnson would later marry—would squash the St. HOPE allegations. Obama fired Walpin in 2010 then reinstated Johnson's eligibility for federal educational grants after Johnson agreed to repay the government a portion of the $845,018.75 in funds that Walpin had alleged were misused by Johnson.

What is, in fact, most remarkable about today's Bourbons are their African American accomplices. As California's Attorney General, Kamala Harris declined to prosecute One West's CEO Steve Mnuchin for thousands of illegal foreclosures despite recommendations by her own staff that she do so. New Jersey Senator Cory Booker blocked legislation to lower drug prices. The son of Howard Zinn's protégé, Marian Wright Edelman, Josh Edelman, was a key player in Chicago Mayor Rahm Emmanuel's closure of 50 public schools in 2013, and in 2018, Washington, D.C.'s African American Mayor, Muriel Bowser, signed legislation that overturned a ballot measure in which 6 of 10 voters in the city approved a wage hike for hospitality workers.

And so it goes in post-racial America. Not only does the modern Talented Tenth defend white supremacy, but each other as well. Black pundits like Angela Rye, Bakari Sellers and Andrew Gillum urge African Americans to vote for the Democratic ticket of Joe Biden and Kamala Harris despite their extensive records of racist law enforcement policies and praxis. In his hagiography of Obama, *We Were Eight Years in Power*, the celebrated Black writer Ta-Nehisi Coates wrote ridiculously:

> The central thread of this book is eight articles written

> during the eight years of the first black presidency—a period of Good Negro Government. Obama was elected amid widespread panic and, in his eight years, emerged as a caretaker and measured architect. He established the framework of a national healthcare system from a conservative model. He prevented an economic collapse and neglected to prosecute those largely responsible for that collapse. He ended state-sanctioned torture but continued the generational war in the Middle East. His family—the charming and beautiful wife, the lovely daughters, the dogs—seemed pulled from the Brooks Brothers catalog. He was not a revolutionary. He steered clear of major scandal, corruption, and bribery. He was deliberate to a fault, saw himself as the keeper of his country's sacred legacy, and if he was bothered by his country's sins, he ultimately believed it to be a force for good in the world. In short, Obama, his family, and his administration were a walking advertisement for the ease with which black people could be fully integrated into the unthreatening mainstream of American culture, politics, and life.

The irony is that liberal media pundits complain constantly about sellout Black politicians yet fail to acknowledge that this brand of identity politics was, in fact, created by a white ruling class to help them defend their bounty from radical Black actors like Harold Washington, Marion Barry, and Coleman Young, all of whom steadfastly championed *universal* policies in education, the workplace, health care, and finance designed to lift all boats.

In a 1992 interview, 12 years before his death at the age of 82, Palmer spoke wistfully of Washington's triumph.

"We had built Chicago to a peak of Black solidarity by the time it came to elect Harold," Palmer said. "You'd better not even *think* about not voting for Harold Washington. I mean it better not even come in your mind, or somebody would go upside your head."[298]

"I'm actually depressed now because everything we fought for between 1981 and 1989 has been wiped away, destroyed, stepped on, stomped on," Palmer added. He sighed heavily, and said almost prophetically:

> "I don't know what' its going to take to bring our people back together."

Ronald Glotta, the white Detroit lawyer who won workmen's comp benefits for the Black autoworker James Johnson after he'd been acquitted of murder charges, told me in an interview:

> Where I think we dropped the ball is in failing to realize that there is always a counterrevolution. In retrospect, it's plain to see that the ruling class decided to use the Black middle class to neutralize the Black power movement that they had no answers for. They changed their tactics and now it's incumbent on us to do the same.

Obama actually compares favorably to Washington, but Booker T., not Harold. A Black Alabama tenant farmer named Ned Cobb foretold the counterrevolutionary dangers posed by race managers like Walter White, Obama, Kamala Harris, and others in 1909:

> Booker T. Washington was an important man but he didn't feel for and didn't respect his race of people to go rock bottom for them. He never did get to the root of our troubles. The veil was over our people's eyes and Booker T. Washington didn't try to pull the veil away like he should have done. He should've walked out full faced with all the courage in the world and realized 'I was born to die. What's the use of me to hold everything under the cover if I know it? How come I won't tell it in favor of my people?' Wrong-spirited Booker T. Washington was. He was a man got down with his country in the wrong way.[299]

16.

Cancel Culture

I have a foreboding of an America in my children's or grandchildren's time—when the United States is a service and information economy; when nearly all the key manufacturing industries have slipped away to other countries; when awesome technological powers are in the hands of a very few, and no one representing the public interest can even grasp the issues; when the people have lost the ability to set their own agendas or knowledgeably question those in authority; when, clutching our crystals and nervously consulting our horoscopes, our critical faculties in decline, unable to distinguish between what feels good and what's true, we slide, almost without noticing, back into superstition and darkness.

–Carl Sagan

Shortly before midnight on Thanksgiving Eve in 1915, a white Methodist preacher named William Joseph Simmons led an entourage of about 15 men up Stone Mountain just outside of Atlanta. Reaching its peak, they built an altar of 16 boulders, upon which they laid an American flag, a copy of the Holy Bible, and an unsheathed sword. Then, standing in the moonlight, they raised a behemoth wooden cross, set it afire, swore an oath of allegiance to the "Invisible Empire" and announced the resurrection of the Ku Klux Klan. In anointing himself Imperial Wizard, Simmons haughtily proclaimed:

> The angels that have anxiously watched the reformation from its beginnings must have hovered about Stone Mountain and shouted hosannas to the highest heavens.[300]

Simmons' ritual was inspired by D.W. Griffith's classic film, *The Birth of a Nation*, which was released earlier that year, and was itself a riposte to the upheaval in the labor market caused by industrialization and the Great Migration of Blacks from the Deep South. Similar to the Tin Pan Alley tunes at that time warning "darkies" to stay in their lane, Simmons hoped a revitalized "Second Klan" and its ethos of racial terror would discipline African Americans' demands for a fairer share of the spoils.

In the years that followed, Stone Mountain became a mecca for settler jihadists who raised funds for what would ultimately become the world's largest bas-relief sculpture. Soaring 400-feet-high and occupying an acre and a half, the mountain carving depicts Jefferson Davis, Stonewall Jackson, and Robert E. Lee astride their majestic steeds.

With its surrounding streets named for Davis, Jackson, and Lee, Stone Mountain Park was the site of the Klan's annual Labor Day cross-burning jubilee and a popular summertime laser show concluded with the unfurling of an enormous Confederate flag and a recording of Elvis singing "Dixie." The late Georgia Congressman John Lewis said that when he first moved to the Atlanta area from Alabama, "we didn't dare go to Stone Mountain because that's where the Klan had rallies."[301]

Wrote the author Nathan Robinson:

> The rallies persisted until 1991. A speaker at the 1985 event called for a new wave of 'white vigilantes' across the country. 'Death to the race mixers,' he said, forecasting that 'when the hour of retribution strikes, there will be ten million dead ones in America.' . . .

> There was a reason, then, that in Dr. Martin Luther King's 'I Have a Dream' speech, he made sure to single out a specific plea: 'let freedom ring from Stone Mountain of Georgia.' A dream that freedom could ring from Stone Mountain was ambitious indeed; perhaps no other location in the country has remained so closely associated with white supremacy for so long.[302]

All of which is to say that there's not the slightest chance on God's green earth that a politician as astute as William Jefferson Clinton was unaware of the message he was sending when he appeared just before the 1992 Super Tuesday primaries at the Stone Mountain Correctional Institution alongside Georgia Governor Zell Miller, U.S. Senator Sam Nunn, and Congressman Ben Jones—who played "Cooter" on the *Dukes of Hazzard*—for "a press conference of little apparent purpose except to show them standing in front of a phalanx of dour, jump-suited inmates, all but a sprinkling of whom were Black," wrote Robinson.

Responding to the newspaper photographs of the event, Clinton's rivals for the Democratic Party's nomination were quick to denounce the Arkansas governor. California Governor Jerry Brown compared Clinton and his mates to "colonial masters" soothing white settler fears of a rumored slave revolt or an attack by a Native American tribe. "Don't worry, we'll keep them in their place. . . . Two white men and forty Black prisoners, what's he saying? He's saying we got 'em under control, folks."

Publicly, Clinton decried his critics' racial politicking. His intent, he protested, was merely to help rehabilitate youths who'd lost their way. Privately, however, Slick Willy must've been over the moon that his rivals were helping him make his case to white voters. By 1992, the Democrats hadn't won the White House in 16 years and two dueling ideologies were vying for the soul of the party. Advancing from the left was Jesse Jackson, whose 1984 and 1988 presidential campaigns consciously parroted Harold Washington's mayoral bids and had some success in wooing Black and white workers with progressive platforms that included a single-payer health care system that continues to elude the U.S. nearly 40 years later.

Advancing from the right were the Republicans who were reinvigorated by the Reagan Revolution's exhumation of Jim Crow politics.

Often described by newspaper columnists as a man of both great intellect and rapacious appetites, the Ivy League-educated Clinton's real genius was reheating old ideas and repackaging them as his own. His Stone Mountain photo op almost certainly was intended to ape Reagan's campaign debut 12 years earlier in Mississippi's Neshoba County, where three civil rights workers were slain by the Klan in 1964.

All the more revealing was that Clinton's electoral strategy did not reach out to disaffected African American voters as Jackson's had, but instead focused on white suburban Democrats who were attracted to Reagan's sectarianism. No jurisdiction in the country represented that electoral bloc known as "Reagan Democrats" better than the Detroit suburb of Macomb County. According to a 1992 *Washington Post* profile written by Thomas Edsall:

> Macomb. . . is a working-class county that in 1960 won attention as the suburban area casting the nation's highest margin of votes for Democrat John F. Kennedy. Since then, the overwhelmingly white electorate has moved steadily toward the GOP, with much of the momentum driven by racial issues: the Detroit riots of 1967, a 1974 federal court order for intercounty busing with Detroit that was overruled by the Supreme Court, constant battles over tax dollars with predominantly black Detroit.
>
> In combination with the accelerating decline of the auto industry during the Democratic administration of Jimmy Carter, these forces produced a rebellion against the Democratic Party and 2-1 ratios for Republican presidential candidates. In the mid-1980s, this insurgency briefly threatened Democratic control of local offices, and desperate

party leaders brought in pollster Stanley Greenberg, who in 1985 did not have good news. In a study of defectors, he found:

> 'These white Democratic defectors express a profound distaste for blacks, a sentiment that pervades almost everything they think about government and politics. . . . Blacks constitute the explanation for their vulnerability and for almost everything else that has gone wrong in their lives; not being black is what constitutes being middle class; not living with blacks is what makes a place a decent place to live.'

Quoting 64-year-old Richard Powers, a retired gas company worker and union member, *The Post* continued:

> 'I used to be a Democrat,' said Powers. 'When did I change? Reagan. Democrats, well, they always want to give too much away. . . . They want me to pay for someone who doesn't want to work, and I don't like that.'

Greenberg concluded that Democrats had become "too identified with minorities and special interests to speak for average Americans." Their only chance to compete in statewide and national elections, he said, was to "keep demands for racial and gender justice meager."

Wrote Louis Proyect in summing up research by the labor historian David Roediger:

> Eventually, Greenberg's study became part of the core philosophy of the Democratic Leadership Council (DLC) that served as the premier think tank for politicians like Bill Clinton, Joe Lieberman, Bruce Babbitt, and Dick Gephardt. It was also home to campaign managers like James Carville, who eventually founded a consulting company with Stanley Greenberg that groomed politicians in the centrist politics that has dominated the Democratic Party to this day. They have also lined up clients with little to do with the DLC's

> pro-working-class orientation ... (that) include(s) Monsanto, BP, and Boeing.[303]

Clinton's contention that he was "a different kind of Democrat" belied his inauguration of the Third Klan. The only difference was that while Simmons' mountaintop trek occurred in the context of deepening industrialization, Clinton's Stone Mountain stunt heralded the beginning of the *post-industrial* era. Indeed, the man from Hope, Arkansas, was merely a more polished version of demagogues like South Carolina's Ben "Pitchfork" Tillman a century earlier, and his vision, like Trump's a generation later, uncomfortably similar to Charles Manson's plan to start a race war by murdering everyone in Roman Polanski's Hollywood Hills home and blaming it on Black militants.

Calculating and cynical, Clinton was determined that he would not be typecast as a carpetbagging liberal as was the party's 1988 nominee, Massachusetts Governor Michael Dukakis, whose bid for the White House was undone by GOP ads showing a menacing Black inmate named Willie Horton who had raped a white woman while free on a furlough scheme that Dukakis endorsed while he was governor. At one point during the 1992 campaign, Clinton made a point of returning to Arkansas for the execution of an African American man convicted of murder, Ricky Ray Rector, who had an IQ of 70 and cognitive impairments so severe that he asked correctional officers to save his last meal for him to finish later. "I can be nicked on a lot," Clinton said at the time, "but no one can say I'm soft on crime."

Clinton's attempts to placate the fears of "the people who used to vote for us" meant legitimizing imaginary white grievances and gaslighting real Black ones. In their 1992 campaign book, *Putting People First*, Clinton and Al Gore mentioned race only once and that was to rebuke racial quotas, according to Robinson. A chapter on civil rights centered almost exclusively on the disabled. Wrote the political scientist Corey Robin: Clinton intended to "win over white voters by declaring to the American electorate: We are not the Party of Jesse Jackson, we are not the Rainbow Coalition."

In antagonizing the Democrats' most loyal constituents, Clinton gambled that Blacks would not abandon the party for the GOP led by Newt Gingrich, Jesse Helms, and Strom Thurmond. In her 2016 presidential campaign, Hillary Clinton made the exact same bet and lost. The super couple had gone to the well once too often; so fed up were African Americans by that time with the Clintons' backstabbing that many simply stayed home rather than cast a ballot for either Hillary or Trump. Black voter turnout declined by 7 percentage points in 2016 accounting for Donald Trump's victory in swing states such as Wisconsin, Michigan and Florida.[304]

During his two terms in the White House, Clinton nailed shut the New Deal's coffin while belting out an off-key duet with the GOP covering the tune, "Anything You Can Do I Can Do Better." Reagan loosened Wall Street regulations, Clinton razed them. When Reagan left the White House, the number of conglomerates controlling the bulk of U.S. media outlets had been whittled from 50 to 29; by the time Clinton left office, the number was six. And while Reagan talked a good game about lifting trade barriers, the U.S. tariff regime was largely intact when he left office; the North American Free Trade Agreement signed into law by Clinton opened the floodgates for employers to ship the nation's manufacturing sector offshore.

It was, however, Clinton's 1994 crime bill that was the focus of intense scrutiny in the 2020 U.S presidential season, and rightly so. The Reagan and Bush administrations nearly doubled the nation's federal prison population yet Clinton jailed more inmates in eight years than the Reagan and Bush administrations did in 12. What's seldom broached in most critiques of Clinton's crime bill, however, is that it also served as a jobs program, career ladder and source of cheap labor for attorneys, police officers, prison guards, criminologists, sociologists, bail bondsmen and CEOs, all of whom benefitted materially from the swollen prison population.

In fact, virtually everything that Clinton did in his eight years in office can best be understood as an effort to create opportunities for financiers to extract more money from the surplus labor supply *after* they had sent the country's industrial sector overseas. Clinton's 1996 repeal of the New Deal's 61-year-old public relief program is a case in point. Occurring amid a tight labor market, the welfare overhaul kicked millions of single mothers off the rolls and into the workforce, helping employers lower their labor costs.

In a 1997 *Washington Post* article, I wrote:

> Ada Thompson's entry into the labor force comes as something of a bargain for the hotel where she works—and a bit of a threat to her coworkers. During her 90-day probation, Thompson will wipe, dust and vacuum on eight-hour shifts, five days a week, the same as any other housekeeper. In return, she will get $410 a month in welfare benefits from the state and a $30 weekly stipend from the Omni Inner Harbor Hotel.
>
> After probation, the hotel's managers will decide whether to hire Thompson permanently for $6.10 an hour. But the company is not legally obligated to do that for her or any of the 13 temporary, taxpayer-subsidized housekeepers drawn from the city's public assistance rolls. The city's efforts to move Thompson off the dole and into the workplace have pushed her smack-dab into the middle of a long and acrimonious labor dispute between Baltimore's largest hotel and its 300 bellmen, housekeepers, doormen and kitchen workers.
>
> 'The situation at the Omni should be a warning for all working people that welfare reform was never intended to lift poor people out of poverty,' said the Rev. Douglas Miles, former co-chairman of Baltimoreans United in Leadership Development. 'It was intended to provide greater subsidies to corporations, and this brand of welfare repeal has merely shifted taxpayers' subsidies from the neediest to the

greediest.'

Continuing I wrote:

> Six weeks into the program, [Sue] Fitzsimmons, [a spokeswoman for Baltimore's Department of Social Services] said, 'Omni executives have agreed to hire two of the 13 housekeeping trainees.' Peter A. Bheda, the hotel's general manager, said the company's only interest in collaborating with the city is 'helping people to get a second chance in their lives. There is no profit for us with this program.'
>
> But Bheda would not discuss the year-long labor dispute between the Omni, Baltimore's largest hotel, and Local 7 of the Hotel Employees and Restaurant Employees Union. The Omni's union contract expired in September 1995 after the workers voted not to accept a new contract with wage concessions and a reduction in benefits, said Paul Richards, the local's executive secretary. . . .
>
> 'They're bringing in cheap help. That's what they're doing,' said Ella Mae Walker, 60, who is paid $7.25 an hour and has prepared salads in the hotel's kitchen for almost 24 years. 'They're just trying to break up our union, is all.'

Similarly, Clinton's repeal of key provisions of the Glass-Steagall Act—a 1933 law prohibiting commercial banks from investing in risky securities—spoon-fed real estate speculators' irrational exuberance, culminating in the worst economic downturn since the Great Depression. Worse even than the subprime mortgages that targeted African Americans and Latinos was the government's handling of the bubble *after* it burst. Policymakers have historically responded to debt crises by forcing big creditors to accept a reduction or "haircut" on their loan portfolios to reduce borrowers' monthly installments and free up consumer cash for new spending.

Secondly, government regulators traditionally indict, prosecute and ultimately jail lenders for fraud to discourage repeated wrongdoing, or "moral hazard." During the savings and loan crisis, for example, the Department of Justice, under Reagan and George H.W. Bush, jailed hundreds of bank executives, including Charles Keating, whose Lincoln Savings and Loan scandal cost taxpayers $3.4 billion.

Lehman Brothers' 2008 collapse cost taxpayers nearly 10 times that amount, and yet the Obama administration did not prosecute a single Wall Street executive for malfeasance. Nor did Obama give Wall Street's grifters a haircut. In fact, he did quite the opposite, bailing out everyone except the disproportionately Black borrowers who were swindled out of their homes and life savings, by purchasing bad debts from unscrupulous lenders for 100 cents on the dollar, repaying the investors who purchased the liars' loans, and showering the big banks and corporations with trillions in cheap money in a bid to re-inflate the speculative bubble and send the stock market soaring again.

The pandemic lockdowns further depleted consumer buying power, forcing the Treasury Department to ratchet up its money-printing another notch and turn over those newly minted bank notes to what the French call *rentiers*, who produce nothing of real value but manipulate public policy for personal gain. This practice, known as rent-seeking, explains why bankers who should've gone belly up after the 2008 crash are instead the beneficiaries of government largesse much as the shipping magnates were following the enactment of the Jones-White boondoggle in 1928.

Consider, for instance, the 2005 bankruptcy reform law written by Delaware's senior U.S. Senator Joe Biden, enabling creditors to squeeze borrowers of even more cash; the Obama administration's 2011 smash-and-grab of Libya's oil and gold reserves, or its 2012 fire sale of foreclosed homes owned by the government-backed lender Fannie Mae. Wrote *the Atlantic* magazine:

> Between 2011 and 2017, some of the world's largest private-

> equity groups and hedge funds, as well as other large investors, spent a combined $36 billion on more than 200,000 homes in ailing markets across the country. In one Atlanta zip code, they bought almost 90 percent of the 7,500 homes sold between January 2011 and June 2012; today, institutional investors own at least one in five single-family rentals in some parts of the metro area, according to Dan Immergluck, a professor at the Urban Studies Institute at Georgia State University.[305]

Hence, the key to riches today is not innovation or hard work but cronyism that is enabled by white workers' inability to identify the highwaymen who are robbing them blind. Think of the nation's income as a pizza pie consisting of 10 giant slices. In the golden industrial era that began after World War II and lasted until the early 1970s, investors and their employees split national income roughly in half. In the neoliberal age, however, investors gobble up six slices, leaving workers to fight it out between themselves for the remaining four slices. Much like the Russian tsars pitting tribes against each other to deflect scrutiny of their pilfering of state resources, Bill Clinton's modus operandi was to isolate the African American worker and incentivize whites to nickel-and-dime as much money from their Black co-workers—through discrimination in the labor and housing markets, privatization of education, insurance fraud, banking, and the jobs, fees and civil forfeiture generated by the criminal justice system—as they can lay their hands on.

Referred to as "racialized lending" by other countries, the subprime mortgage scandal is again the perfect example. From hedge fund managers to mid-level mortgage brokers to young college grads mortgaging their parents' homes to buy and flip properties, everyone seemed to profit from the swindle targeting Black and brown borrowers. This explains why the Obama administration made virtually no effort to shave off a portion of the swindled borrowers' debts as has mostly been the case in the aftermath of previous asset bubbles.

Another example is a close friend, Sunni Khalid, an experienced and accomplished African American journalist who was forced to drive a cab after news executives blackballed him for championing more balanced coverage of Israel's illegal occupation of Palestine. In 2019, he earned $91,000 for Uber and Lyft driving six days a week and often ten hours per day in northern California's Bay Area. But Uber and Lyft skimmed a little more than half—53 percent—off the top, despite producing nothing of value, and a business model that relies on government deregulation and parasitic technology designed to pick the pocket of their drivers, who are disproportionately people of color.

Uber was valued at nearly $60 billion in the spring of 2020, yet failed to record a profit in 2016, 2017, 2018, or 2019, racking up nearly $19 billion in losses over that four-year span.[306]

Similarly, by extracting wealth rather than producing it, Wall Street's *rentiers* have further sickened an already wheezing health care system by transforming medical professionals into the equivalent of Uber drivers or Amazon warehouse workers, said Armen Henderson, an African American internist in South Florida. While physicians in the past could build lucrative private practices over time, doctors today are typically employees of health care providers such as Tennessee-based Hospital Corporation of America, or HCA, which operates 186 hospitals and more than 2,000 clinics across the country. Consequently, physicians are not paid for how many patients they heal but by how many they *see* and are incentivized to perform costly—but often unnecessary—medical procedures, similar to auto mechanics.

"We make more, obviously but it's the same way that an Amazon worker says 'oh, they only let me take two bathroom breaks a day,'" Henderson told me. "If you are a proceduralist you make money based on the number of procedures you perform. The problem with that is that sometimes people might not need that heart catheterization or colonoscopy but they still get them. There is a lot of waste . . . from [health care corporations] defrauding the system."

Moreover, Henderson said, "incentive-based pay packages exert tremendous pressure on doctors, and it's becoming increasingly common for hospitals and clinics to delegate more and more of doctors' workloads to nurse practitioners—who make a lot less money than doctors—thereby allowing physicians to see even more patients and generate more revenue. This severs or weakens the doctor-patient relationship."

Unsurprisingly, that has a far greater impact on African Americans, whose health outcomes—including amputations, mortality rates for infants and mothers, and even pain, because doctors often *under-prescribe* opioids to Black patients they suspect are drug addicts—are exponentially worse than whites.

For all intents and purposes, the U.S. has, over a generation, become a laboratory for fascist schemes that typically rely on a marginalized, super-exploited class of workers to grease the wheels. Ask yourself: How did Elon Musk become the wealthiest man in world history? Certainly, the streets are not teeming with Tesla sedans. With banks essentially handing out no-interest loans to rich people following the collapse of the real estate market in 2008, Musk has simply borrowed hundreds of millions of dollars to buy his company's stock, inflating its value.

Also expanding Musk's wealth—estimated at nearly $300 billion at its apex in early 2022 before he purchased Twitter—are the carbon credits that carmakers are legally required to purchase from Tesla to comply with federal environmental regulations. This is the definition of rent-seeking: Wouldn't the money paid to Tesla benefit more people if it was collected by the government and used to invest in renewable energy sources?

Furthermore, it is hardly a coincidence that Musk—whose father was an investor in a South African mine during apartheid—has been accused of racism. In 2021, a federal jury in San Francisco awarded $137 million in damages to an African American elevator operator who accused Tesla executives of ignoring a barrage of racial slurs hurled at him while working at the automaker's plant in Fremont, California. A judge would later reduce the award to $15 million but affirmed the jury's verdict. (The elevator operator refused that offer, and a later jury trial produced a $3 million award.) And a study found that the number of anti-Black slurs on Twitter more than tripled after Musk purchased the social media platform.

As the country spins out of control, the growing consensus among both white liberals and conservatives is that identity politics, "wokeness" or "cancel culture" is to blame. Much like the cowardly white Union soldiers who betrayed their fellow Black infantrymen at a critical moment, a broad swath of whites today seeks to avoid any accountability by blaming America's decline on the *acknowledgment* of Black suffering, rather than their class treachery.

What I set out to prove in writing this book is that Blacks are not America's problem;

We are its salvation!

This gnashing of white's teeth, the efforts to censor Black books and African American studies, and to immunize white motorists who plow into Blacks protesting the latest police killing of an unarmed Black man reflects a white settler Republic at the end of its rope, reminiscent of the Nazis burning records of the Holocaust as the allies closed in.

And yet this inverse meritocracy is remarkably inefficient. Studies show that a lack of diversity enervates newsrooms, boardrooms, and executive suites, curbs innovation, and encourages groupthink. Moreover, the constant dissembling required to sustain a political and economic system centered on pathologizing a Black identity diminishes critical thought, debases the language, and ultimately eats away at whites' confidence, reminiscent of Sylvester Stallone's Rocky character when he discovered that his trainer was protecting him by only allowing him to fight "tomato cans."

Americans have been lying to each other for so long that the vast majority can no longer discern fact from fantasy. Faced with almost any crisis, the default position of the white working class especially is to ape their ancestors at the Battle of the Crater and betray their most ardent allies.

The result, a quarter of the way into the 21st century, is that the wealthiest 1 percent is beating the living daylights out of the 99 percent.

If the workers have any chance of mounting a comeback, they would be wise to follow the advice of the Russian novelist Fyodor Dostoevsky, who wrote in his classic novel *The Brothers Karamazov:*

> Above all, don't lie to yourself. The man who lies to himself and listens to his own lie comes to a point that he cannot distinguish the truth within him, or around him, and so loses all respect for himself and for others.

Epilogue: A Prayer for George Jackson

The people made their recollections fit in with their suffering.

Thucydides

Those who do not have power over the story that dominates their lives, the power to retell it, re-think it, deconstruct it, joke about it and change it as times change—truly are powerless because they cannot think new thoughts.

Salman Rushdie

No sooner had the guns fallen silent at Appomattox than the rumors of war began anew.

Word spread west from the Carolinas across the vanquished Confederacy, accumulating more detail with each retelling, and stoking fears among white Southerners of a vast conspiracy cooked up by emancipated slaves:

Was murder afoot?

Historian Dan T. Carter wrote of a moral panic that gripped the postbellum South in 1865:

> Everywhere there were vivid, secondhand accounts of armed blacks drilling in nightly conclaves, waiting only for the signal which would trigger a coordinated massacre sometime during the Christmas holidays.[307]

A Boston minister, Reverend Mansfield French, was one of the first to document the growing anxiety below the Mason-Dixon line during a six-week-tour of Georgia for the Freedmen's Bureau in July, scarcely three months after the Civil War had ended. He wrote that he had observed in many whites a "fearful apprehension that the freedmen have a deep-laid plot for an insurrection and slaughter."[308]

In North Carolina, a nurse at a Wilmington army hospital sounded the alarm, alleging that one of the coup-plotters had tipped him off to a scheme to "murder the white race [and] the old slave owners to get their land and houses."[309]

Assigned the task of rebuilding the devastated Southland, agents for the Freedmen's Bureau and commissioned U.S. Army officers had no choice but to investigate the allegations, regardless of how far-fetched they were. Major Samuel Oliver of the Second Massachusetts Artillery spent two weeks in August 1865 questioning African Americans in the Wilmington area and found nothing to substantiate the gossip. Yet his report did little to assuage the fears of Wilmington's white denizens who continued to insist that "armed" Negroes were conducting military drills at night, and assailing whites by day with "insolence and insubordination."[310] They pleaded with the state's provisional governor to arm them with rifles and revolvers so that they could form a *posse comitatus*. Similarly, Reverend French's attempts at dissuasion in Georgia were to no avail, and as winter approached, white women and children were evacuated from counties with large Black populations, leaving the menfolk to batten down the hatches and prepare for battle.

Whites in the eastern South Carolina town of Kingstree found suspicious the arrival of two Black schoolteachers from up North, and in late autumn, demanded federal protection from the "imminent rising." Before a government investigator could make the trip from Charleston, however, a "citizens' council" decided to take matters into its own hands, chasing down and whipping 16 African American agitators and expelling the two carpetbagging educators.

By November, rumors of a holiday putsch stretched across the Black Belt in the form of a crescent, surfacing in more than 200 counties and a dozen parishes from the Atlantic coastline to the Gulf of Mexico. One white Alabama farmer swore that he spotted freedmen conducting military drills in the woods, although after robust questioning from a Bureau agent, he acknowledged that it was "possible" that he only saw a prayer meeting. Another white farmer reported seeing Blacks steal hundreds of rifles from a nearby armory, only to discover that no such depot existed and there had been no cache of weapons reported missing anywhere in the state. Notwithstanding the evidence to the contrary, white delegates attending the state convention in September 1865 petitioned Alabama's provisional governor to organize militias for protection.

And when a Mississippi plantation owner, William B. Wilkinson, went missing on November 1 after selling his cotton harvest for a cool $1,000—worth nearly $19,297 at 2024 prices—his neighbors surmised that his former slaves had murdered him and buried his body in a secret grave on his farm, as payback for selling "their" cotton before they could annex the property. A group of white vigilantes went to Wilkinson's plantation, according to the historian Carter, and finding a shovel that had been recently used and a knife with specks of dried blood, "beat and tortured three freedmen in an attempt to coerce a confession." The Black farmworkers denied both killing Wilkinson and engaging in any subversive activity; mercifully, their lives were spared by the serendipitous arrival of federal troops.

Wilkinson was found, very much alive, the following day, celebrating his windfall profits in a nearby brothel.

One-hundred-and-fifty years later, on June 17th, 2015, 21-year-old Dylann Roof sat outside the Emanuel African Methodist Episcopal Church in Charleston, South Carolina, finishing off a bottle of Smirnoff's Ice before pulling a Glock handgun from his waistband, walking into the church and opening fire, killing a pastor and eight of his parishioners, all of them Black. Redolent of Furnifold Simmons, Josephus Daniels and Charles Brantley Aycock in 19th century North Carolina, Roof's objective, he wrote in his manifesto, was to start a race war by sounding the alarm and alerting his fellow whites to the African Americans who "are raping our women and taking over the country."

So constant is whites' fear of the Fire Next Time, and so quotidian is the violence against Blacks that it is almost impossible to discern its ebb from its flow. But Roof's blasphemy inside a House of God only a mile west of where the first shots of the Civil War rang out was a call to arms to disgruntled young white men. Seven years after Roof's rampage, another young man fearful of "white genocide," 18-year-old Payton Gendron, walked into a Buffalo supermarket with a semi-automatic rifle, and opened fire, killing 10, all of them African American. In his manifesto, he cited Roof, and the Great Replacement Theory, as his inspiration.

Scantly a year later, a white, 24-year-old ex-Marine, Daniel Penny, strangled to death an aggressive African American panhandler, Jordan Neely, aboard a New York subway, while FBI agents accused another young, disillusioned white man, 21-year-old National Guard member, Jack

Teixeira, of leaking a trove of classified military intelligence. Prosecutors allege that the Massachusetts man was preparing for a race war. In a video published by *the Washington Post,* Teixeira is dressed in camouflage fatigues with his finger wrapped around the trigger of a semi-automatic rifle. Facing the camera, he says:

"Jews scam, niggers rape, and I mag dump."

Whether it is increased competition for jobs from millions of freed slaves or Blacks fleeing Southern farms for factories in the North, or the transition to a speculative, post-industrial economy a century later, white workers typically respond to financial uncertainty by abandoning the class struggle to instead punch down on African Americans, who they invariably see as a threat to their racial identity and the privileges afforded to it.

Hence, the question at the heart of this book:

Are you a worker or are you white?

With employees fighting each other, the bosses are making out like bandits. The wealthiest 1 percent's share of all assets in the U.S. has ballooned from less than 3 percent in 1989 to nearly 26 percent in 2022, according to the Federal Reserve. Robbed of their intellectual and emotional resources by the ruling class, far too many whites are governed almost wholly by their id and its primitive, psychosexual impulses; consequently, they are hard-pressed to identify—let alone address—the broader political forces that circumscribe their economic mobility. If it is indeed true that to a hammer every problem resembles a nail, then to angry, infantilized whites like Gendron, Roof, Penny, and Teixeira, any crisis can be resolved simply by re-asserting your right to murder every African American in sight, just as your forefathers did at the Battle of the Crater.

The Anti-Defamation League attributed 25 homicides to right-wing extremists in 2022, of which 21 were at the hands of white supremacists like Gendron, whose shooting spree accounted for ten of the slayings.[311] Similarly, law enforcement killed at least 1,096 people in 2022—more than three people per day on average—representing the deadliest year on record for police violence since *the Washington Post* began tracking the slayings nationwide in 2015.[312] *The Post* database also found that while nearly half of all of those slain by police were white, African Americans are 2.5 times more likely to be killed by on-duty police than are whites.

And the Gun Violence Archive identified 647 mass shootings in 2022 and 690 in 2021. Both figures are more than double the number of mass shootings, 282, in 2014 when the Archive first began tracking such assaults and are commensurate with an FBI analysis of 2019 data that found that the number of hate crimes had risen by 42 percent over a five-year-span, representing the highest nationwide total since the onset of the Great Recession in 2008. The increase is predicated mostly on a spike in hate crimes targeting African Americans. Analyzing data submitted by more than 15,000 state and local law enforcement agencies, the FBI identified 7,759 hate crimes, 2,755 of which identified Black victims, representing a 40 percent increase from the previous year. Anti-Asian assaults increased by 70 percent over the same period, but the aggregate numbers were relatively minuscule, from 158 to 274, while anti-white violence rose by 16 percent to 773. (Attacks targeting Muslims and Jews fell by 42 and 30 percent respectively over the same span.)

Following a similar trend, the number of reported hate crimes in Los Angeles County rose by 23 percent in 2021, to 786, representing the highest total in nearly 20 years, according to LA County's Commission on Human Relations.[313] African Americans account for only 9 percent of the population in the county, but nearly half, or 46 percent of the total number of victims. Dominique DiPrima, the African American host of an AM radio show in southern California, told the *Los Angeles Times*:

> Anti-Blackness is the tip of the sphere. It's almost like we've normalized hate against Black people. It's the default.[314]

Capri Maddox, executive director of Los Angeles' Civil Rights Department, told the *Times* that the city's numbers are a microcosm of the country as a whole:

> The FBI has been tracking hate crimes for 30 years and the consistent number one population of victims are African Americans.[315]

And just as Ethre Jennett's cartoons animated the murderous white mob in 1898, so too does social media continue to stir up racial violence today. The director of the Center for the Study of Hate and Extremism at California State University at San Bernardino, Professor Brian Levin told the *Los Angeles Times*:

> What we have seen is when invective goes up online, we see it go up on the streets in the form of violence time and time again.[316]

It is within this context of anti-Blackness that we can best understand white leftists who have joined with white conservatives such as Tucker Carlson and Florida Governor Ron DeSantis in decrying "cancel culture," "identity politics," and "wokeness," as a key factor—if not the source—of America's malaise. Ironically, it is this kind of treachery by the white left that inspired Blacks to coin the phrase "stay woke" as a warning to remain vigilant, or metaphorically, not fall asleep at the wheel. More substantively, these attacks from white progressives would seem to suggest that white men losing their jobs for careless remarks is of graver concern than are Black men losing their lives while praying, grocery shopping or panhandling on the F train on Manhattan's Lower East Side.

And perhaps most egregiously, their critique conflates legitimate demands for racial justice with the same, feckless liberalism that is responsible for Vichy Black politicians such as Obama, Vice-President Kamala Harris, and Willard Townsend, who was sent by the Congress of Industrial Organizations to undermine the tobacco workers' Local 22 in postwar Winston-Salem.

De-emphasizing the role that racism plays in pitting worker against worker is a tacit acknowledgment that even the white intelligentsia is heavily invested in a system in which jobs go to the whitest rather than the best and have no truck with a system of social redress that stipulates that everyone's blues are *not* the same. The essence of racial capitalism is that it creates both an exploited and a super-exploited class of labor, and modernity requires a *triage* system in which those who are bleeding from the head are moved to the front of the line ahead of those with a bruised knee.

This was the basis of Lenin's belief that liberating the working class required the Bolshevik Revolution to fully recognize the history of oppression visited upon Russia's ethnic and religious minorities by the tsars, as evinced by Harry Haywood's experience on the Moscow streetcar. But for the most part, the white working class in the U.S. has difficulty envisioning the American economy as anything other than a zero-sum game in which it is always the winner.

What good would it be to be white in a country where everyone's needs are met?

Two months before the Los Angeles County Commission on Human Relations published its data on the rise in hate crimes, the *Los Angeles Times* published excerpts from an audiotaped conversation between Los Angeles City Council President Nury Martinez, two of her Latino colleagues on the city council, and the Latino president of the Los Angeles County Federation of Labor. During the private meeting to discuss gerrymandering, Martinez seemed to channel her inner Tom Wolfe or Gail Sheehy, taking aim, seemingly, at every ethnic group in the city. Of Koreatown, she said: "I see a lot of little, short dark people there." Later, punctuating her dislike of indigenous Oaxacans, she is heard to say "tan feos," which means "[they're] so ugly" in Spanish.

Jews and Armenians also take on incoming fire, but the Latino politicos reserve their bitterest vitriol for the city's shrinking African American population. Of the district attorney, Martinez said, "Fuck that guy . . . He's with the Blacks." And after referring to the adopted African American son of her white city council colleague, Mike Bonin, as a "changuito" or "monkey" in Spanish, she said:

> They're raising him like a little white kid . . . . I was like, 'This kid needs a beatdown. Let me take him around the corner, I'll bring him right back.'

The boy was 2 years old at the time.

For anyone who has studied class relations, it is obvious that the remarks made by Martinez and her conspirators represented a petition to be white, or at least white-adjacent, and to put distance between themselves and Los Angeles' poorest and most oppressed demographic, the Blacks, reminiscent of the Irish immigrants who did not warm to the mostly Italian workers who struck the Connecticut textiles factory in 1912 because they had already become white.

In that sense, Martinez' belligerence is no different than Victoria Price's mendacious claims that she and Ruby Bates had been raped by nine Black teenagers aboard a train in Alabama, or Milton Friedman's plans to privatize public education in the aftermath of the 1954 *Brown* Supreme Court decision, or Victor Gotbaum's betrayal 21 years later of AFSCME District Council 37's African American and Puerto Rican workers so that he could hang out with the cool kids on Wall Street.

The Cameroonian scholar Achille Mbembe refers to this feature of the settler colonial project as *necropolitics.* While Frank Wilderson's theory of *Afropessimism* posits that all racial and ethnic groups are invested in the death of the African slave, Mbembe goes a step further in explaining that necropolitics is the understanding that for one group to live, another group must die, if not physically then at least socially. Much as it did a century ago at the beginning of the industrial era, the so-called American melting pot is again choosing up sides, as the post-industrial era dawns.

And yet, any discussion of class struggle is conspicuously absent from our news and entertainment media, as though it is not, like Mary Turner's lynching, a story to pass on. This culture of "not knowing" puts me in mind of Plato's Allegory of the Cave, in which the Greek philosopher imagined inmates imprisoned in a grotto since childhood, their legs and necks shackled so that they are unable to either escape or see anything other than the shadows cast on the wall directly in front of them by puppeteers using a fire pit as a projector. One prisoner escapes, and discovering a world of sun and sea and mountains and presumably, humanity, returns to the cave and shares what he has learned with the others, who denounce him as a madman; they are comfortable with this shadowy, walled-off un-reality.

Plato intended his allegory as a meditation on education, yet it dovetails nicely with the Italian intellectual Antonio Gramsci's theory that neither violence nor its threat is sufficient to sustain the hegemons' control of a population; culture, and the ability to shape the narrative and ultimately manufacture new, anesthetizing realities such as the images that appeared on the wall of Plato's cave is critical to the bosses' rout of America's working class.

In plain proletarian English, our stories fail us when we need them most.

Any thorough reading of history strongly suggests that the U.S. is on the precipice of an economic and political catastrophe, and as the nation's 250th birthday approaches, we are living through what Gramsci called the "interregnum," which is characterized by a litany of "morbid symptoms." "The old is dying," Gramsci wrote, "and the new cannot be born." Yet history is also unambiguous in anticipating a third Reconstruction to follow the conflagration to come. America is not one thing or another but all things and the other. Inasmuch as Roof, Gendron, and Teixeira are harbingers of things to come, there are also signs of a racial reckoning and perhaps an ensuing American Spring.

Consider an account in the African American newspaper, the *Los Angeles Sentinel.* In the aftermath of the leaked audiotape scandal, Black Lives Matter protesters showed up outside the home of one L.A. city councilmember, Kevin de León, who participated in the redistricting hearing.

The *Sentinel* wrote:

> A large group of Latino De León supporters showed up in the afternoon but, after a conversation with BLMLA leaders, switched sides and joined in the calls for De León to resign.

Again, my own experience shines a light on the class war's complicated, Jekyll-and-Hyde-quality. Sometime during Barack Obama's second term, I befriended on Facebook a white woman who we'll call Mabel, who was at the time a political science professor at the University of Pittsburgh's feeder campus in Titusville. We became fast friends, bonding over our progressive ideals. In 2017, she arranged for me to speak at her university, in exchange for a $2,000 honorarium, and during my time in Titusville, she was extraordinarily kind to me, treating me like family.

So I didn't think twice about asking her to loan me $330 in March 2020 when I had just been hired to teach English in Vietnam. The school would not pay my airfare upfront but would reimburse me upon arrival. I assured Mabel that I would repay her in a couple of months once I had been reimbursed. Just weeks later, however, the COVID-19 pandemic triggered a lockdown in the U.S. and Vietnam, putting my plans on hold. Thinking that the pandemic would quickly run its course, I reassured Mabel that I would travel to Vietnam in a few months' time and repay her then.

By the time it became clear that the coronavirus had much more staying power than initially believed, Mabel had begun to sing a different political tune, parroting white nationalists' insistence that the pandemic was a hoax intended to enslave Americans, and defending her friends who wrote on Facebook that the white Minneapolis police officer who had murdered George Floyd was in fact, innocent. I responded that they were a coven of "Karens," setting off a heated exchange between Mabel and me.

Unable to resolve our differences, Mabel and I decided in 2021 to part ways, at least on social media. I acknowledged my debt and thinking (naively as it turns out) that a refund from Expedia was imminent, reassured her that I would repay her once I had collected. Expedia, of course, gave me the run-around, and admittedly, distracted by the writing of this book, looking for work and several other projects, I dropped the ball in pursuing my collection efforts, although at no point did I receive an email from Mabel nudging me for payment. So I was surprised to hear that late in 2021 Mabel had written a plea on Facebook for anyone who was friends with me to demand repayment on her behalf because, as she told it, I had repeatedly rebuffed her efforts to collect the money she had loaned me.

Using a burner account to read through the scores of responses to Mabel's post, however, I was stunned; it was the social media equivalent of a Klan rally, with some threatening me with bodily harm and others joking that I considered her loan a form of reparations for slavery. The *piece-de-resistance*, however, was from Mabel, who at one point wrote this about me:

> And have you noticed how he craved the attention of white women?

I was reminded of Rebecca Felton exhorting Wilmington's white men in 1898 to "lynch a thousand Negroes a week" to avenge the series of phantom rapes. And yet what happened next was even more stunning: Dozens of Facebook friends—Black and brown and yes, many whites—were outraged by Mabel's gracelessness, and offered to repay her on my behalf. Several proposed starting a GoFundMe page, and several more still went on Mabel's Facebook page to tell her in no uncertain terms what they thought of her.

My father was the first class warrior I ever met, and while it's true that I spent the first ten years of my life thinking that "stupid peckerwood" was someone's name, what inspired his wrath was that element within the 99 percent that sided with the wealthiest 1 percent. And while he would not have used such language, his disdain for anyone who he viewed as a class traitor was visceral, imbuing any time spent in the company of strangers with the threat of spontaneous combustion similar to his confrontation with the gas station attendant in 1976.

And yet in the dozens of Thanksgivings, Christmases and holiday events spent in the company of my younger brother and his father-in-law, a beefy, charismatic German-descended *bon vivant* named Dave Heldman, I never detected a moment of discomfort between my father and Dave, and none of my three siblings could recall hearing my father speak ill of Dave. Their respect for one another was confirmed for me at my father's repast on a snowy January day in 2011. As I was unlocking my car and preparing to leave, Dave ambled up to me, clasped my hand in a hammerlock, looked me straight in my eye, and said with almost startling sincerity: "Jon, I am so sorry for your loss; your father was a *great* man, he truly was."

It was at that moment that I got it: Although they worked for different plants, Dave and my father were both autoworkers and they recognized in each other an ally in their fight against the bosses.

My birth at the height of American industrialism to a millwright who was the grandson of a slave, and my good fortune to have been a journalist in the final days of one millennium and the beginning of the next has led me to describe myself alternately as one of the fugitives from Plato's cave, and a kind of dusky Forrest Gump who has been present for every major battle of the global class war's neoliberal phase.

But I'm no fool: the denizens of an apartheid state constructed atop a foundation of enmity and murder are not going to suddenly reverse centuries of scission and come together to sing Kumbaya as in some Coke commercial. But as demonstrated by my father, and Dave Heldman, those Latinos who were persuaded to support the Black Lives Matter protesters, the dozens of whites and Blacks who rushed in to support me in my acrimonious dispute with Mabel, and the eruption of pro-Palestinian rallies on college campuses nationwide as this book goes to press, there exists in this wretched country a great yearning for *community*. Consequently, our national situation is dire, not hopeless, and I continue to believe it's possible that the U.S. might yet achieve Fred Hampton's vision of a confederacy of equals, in which Black workers exercise power over their community just as white workers govern theirs, and Latinos and Asians and Native Americans are vested with self-determination as well. All of us deserve some peace, and none of us needs a boss. If that is communism then play it as it lays, I say.

My research for this book has left my soul scarred, like the back of a runaway slave. Still, my heart is full to the point of bursting with all that I have learned and seen.

I need to testify:

Shoehorned between the state line and the Allegheny River in Pennsylvania's northwest corner, the city of Titusville is as red as America gets, a place where virtually every one of its 5,601 residents identified his or her race as "white" on the 2010 U.S. Census, and a few storefront windows, rather bewilderingly, displayed Confederate flags and "Trump: Make

America Great Again" campaign banners more than a year after the 2016 presidential election.

If they've heard of it at all, African Americans tend to view the bucolic enclave and its environs with some trepidation, peppering their goodbyes with so many warnings to "be careful" and "be safe" that Black students enrolled at the University of Pittsburgh's feeder campus in Titusville often joked that their parents mistook Crawford County for a combat zone in Kabul or Fallujah.

In all fairness, though, African Americans seldom experience Titusville's racial antagonisms as bodily violence, but rather as the gaping spiritual wound left by a battery of invectives, bullying, and profiling that locals often characterize as "drive-bys." Still, it did not go unnoticed when both the frequency and intensity of these microaggressions began to escalate sharply in the days and weeks leading up to Election Day in 2016.

One Black student complained that he was just minding his business at an off-campus hangout, the Sheetz convenience store, when he was accosted by a white customer exhorting him to "go back to Africa." In the same vein, a department store cashier demanded that a Black student produce proof that he had the means to pay before ringing up the merchandise, and yet another insisted on rummaging through an African American student's backpack.

And in an incident during the 2016 homecoming weekend, the vice-president of the Black Student Union, Tyra Hollinger, was buying snacks at Sheetz when she and her friends were confronted by the driver of a pickup truck who proudly displayed a Confederate flag in his rear window. Revving his engine, and "whooping and hollering," as Tyra recalled later, the young man glared menacingly and conspicuously at the women while they pumped gas, as though he were auditioning to play the role of a skinhead in an *American History X* sequel.

Funny thing about that one though: Tyra and her friends were on their way to the Friday night bonfire at The Well on East Point, a popular coffee shop in town, when they encountered the angry young white man at Sheetz. Arriving at their destination moments later, they told the cafe's owner, Sarah Muir, about the incident, half out of bemusement, half out of annoyance.

That did not sit well with Muir, who is white and grew up in neighboring Pleasantville. The next day, she repeated the story to her husband and childhood sweetheart, Brent, a tattoo artist who was even more steamed than she was. He immediately sprang into action, phoning Tyra for a description of the truck; he made a few inquiries and five minutes later texted Tyra a photograph of a blue pickup with a wooden bed.

"Is this the one?" he asked.

Tyra verified that it was, and Brent promptly put in a call to Titusville Police Chief Harold Minch, who immediately recognized the truck as belonging to the son of one of Titusville's most esteemed families and summoned the young man to his office for an early Monday morning meeting to read him the riot act.

"We want our college students to feel comfortable and to enjoy their college years," said Minch, who describes himself as a lifelong Republican, albeit one experiencing a crisis of faith in the Trump era. "I sure as heck enjoyed mine and a lot of us are committed to letting our African American students know that we've got their back."

Brent Muir puts it more bluntly:

> I was just fed up with the way some of our kids are treated in town. There's always been this attitude about people coming into town from the outside but there's been a kind of surge over the last year, and a lot of us have taken it upon ourselves to address the problem. We're not going to stand idly by and just let this happen.

Tyra knew that the Muirs would not gaslight her but "I really just wanted to vent," she said. "I never expected the Muirs and the police to do what they did."

Trump's election caused this rustic enclave on Lake Erie to take a long, hard look at itself. Suffice it to say, many of them did not like what they saw.

And so it came to pass that wide swaths of Titusville—from university administrators and faculty to the YWCA to the Chamber of Commerce; from the police to faith leaders, parishioners, bloggers, and mom-and-pop shop owners such as the Muirs—decided to do something about it, launching an urban renewal project aimed at refurbishing hearts and minds more so than bricks and mortar.

On Friday nights, the town drunk and his drinking buddies taught young, dreadlocked Black men from Philadelphia and Cleveland to roast marshmallows and hot dogs over a campfire while telling tall tales. Young Black women babysat the Muir's adopted Puerto Rican daughter almost every weekend, braiding her hair and eating so much free food that university administrators called to inquire if they'd lost their meal cards. When a customer photographed a "Nigger Job Application" posted on the bulletin board of the only hardware store in town, the university stopped doing business with the store.

A second-year pre-med student from Baltimore, 20-year-old Briana Davis, was running errands in the winter of 2017 with three of her girlfriends, all Black, when one of Minch's patrol officers stopped her for running a yellow light. Briana dutifully complied with the officer's request for her driver's license and car's registration, then sat motionless, her hands affixed at 10 and 2 on the steering wheel, as the officer somberly inspected her documents.

Suddenly, he smiled.

"Oh, is your mom's name Charlotte?" he asked. "That's my mother's name too," he said, flashing a broad grin and sending the young women on their way with only a warning.

"He was very professional," Briana said. "This whole community has really made an effort to make African Americans feel comfortable."

No one in Titusville adheres to any illusions. Barring something biblical, racism will outlive everyone in the state.

And yet, there is this:

"I just know that as a woman of color, I feel welcomed and free here," said Briana.

And this:

"I think we've made significant progress," said Tammy Carr, who is white and the university's vice-president for marketing and assistant to the president. "The name-callers always thought they had free rein because they're never called on it. A lot of us have just decided . . . that we're just not going to put up with it anymore."

State budget cuts closed the university in 2020, but the formal name for Titusville's anti-racism campaign was Stand Up Together and, like most things these days, the seed was planted online, as frustrated locals turned to social media networks to articulate their fears in the days after Trump's victory. "A lot of us were basically licking our wounds," said Ashleigh English, who is white, and the executive director of the Titusville YWCA. "We knew we wanted to educate and advocate but not push people away."

From those digital dialogues a mission statement emerged:

> As part of a global society, Titusville is committed to creating an inclusive, respectful and safe community that will actively confront and challenge all forms of harassment and discrimination. By embracing and celebrating the ideals of diversity and equality, we will create a culture of empowerment, goodwill, innovation [and] economic empowerment.

The group's inaugural was the first-ever citywide Martin Luther King

Day celebration just days before Trump's inauguration. English said she would've been thrilled if 20 people had shown up; but, by her estimate, roughly 125 people attended, standing in a semi-circle in the YWCA courtyard holding aloft votive candles while listening solemnly to the "I Have a Dream" address. From there, they moved across the street to the St. James Episcopal Church to sip hot chocolate, eat muffins and cookies, and, most importantly, talk.

Stand Up Together's motto was seemingly the same as New York City's antiterrorism campaign: "If you see something, say something." When the campus police chief complained to Dean David Fitz that some Black male students were protesting the nationwide spate of police shootings of unarmed African Americans by throwing up their hands and mockingly declaring "hands up, don't shoot," whenever campus police officers walked by, Fitz suggested that he resolve the situation by explaining to the students that their protests unfairly painted law-enforcement with too broad a brush. The chief did just that; the protests stopped.

Carr, the university's marketing director, invited Blacks to speak to the Black Student Union, and Mary Ann Caton, an assistant professor of history and political science, invited African Americans to speak to her classes or deliver town-and-gown lectures, while the YWCA's English coordinated discussions between Black college students and white high-schoolers.

Chief Minch appealed to merchants to help ease racial tensions by removing their Confederate flags and, although all three declined, Minch and others involved with Stand Up Together say the most vital step is merely initiating the conversation.

Said Minch: "We knew going in that we had to make some changes and, specifically, white people had to make some changes. Black people get it already."

A logger and 23-year-old church volunteer from Pleasantville, Tyler Brown was enthralled with the idea of a community coming together and finding a place where "someone like me can brush shoulders with people who are different."

And so, about eight months into the Stand Up Together project, he began organizing the weekend bonfires at The Well. The first in early September of last year got off to a slow start, with Tyler posted at the edge of the road recruiting pedestrians to stop by for free coffee, a hot dog or a s'more.

One of the first to walk by—well stumble actually—was John, a white man then in his 70s who was widely considered the town drunk. "I have *never* seen him sober," says Tyler. John sat on a metal chair with foam padding and was chatting with Tyler when he spotted a friend walking into a nearby bar and promptly yelled: "Ben, get your ass over here and get a cup of coffee."

Ben did as he was told and, before long, began telling John and Tyler and a few others gathered around the fire that he had recently been diagnosed with cancer, and it didn't look good. He was in the midst of confessing that his biggest concern, in fact, was finding someone to care for his dog, when Tyler spotted a group of six Pitt students walking towards them and invited them over. Of the three who stayed, two were young Black men from Philadelphia, and the third from Baltimore.

The Indian summer night wore on, the flames heaved and fell as the crowd expanded to as many as 20 people, their frames cast in sharp relief by the nearly full moon. Tyler counted at least a half-dozen conversations happening simultaneously by the time John left for home sometime past midnight, only to be replaced by a forty-ish white man named Mark whom Tyler describes as "the most committed redneck I know."

Hitting it off particularly well were Ben and the three Pitt students. As Tyler recalled:

> I remember that Ben was amazed when all three of the students said they had never been to a campfire, and so he's

> there, showing them how to roast a marshmallow. And then later, he had them in stitches telling the story of how he once chased a baby black bear with a broomstick.

The three Black Pitt-Titusville students would admit later that they had been on the hunt for some weed when they ambled past the bonfire but settled for s'mores and small talk instead.

As 2 a.m. approached and the bars let out, a thirty-ish white woman ran past the bonfire in hot pursuit of a speeding car. She was alternately cursing and crying and "just an emotional wreck" as Tyler recalled. Minutes later, an older woman came running after her. When she finally caught up, the older woman attempted to comfort her friend in her moment of despair. Tyler fetched them both coffee and they sat, with the younger woman explaining that she'd had an argument with the man in the fleeing car who'd resorted to calling her a "cunt." And, to make matters worse, she said, her night out was intended to help her numb the pain of her sister's recent death.

The older woman—who gave her name as Mama D—was as sober as her friend was drunk, though not for a lack of trying; she'd had every intention of tying one on when she headed out earlier in the evening. Like Ben, she'd also been diagnosed with cancer recently and wanted to drown her sorrow in bottled spirits, but just couldn't seem to get there.

The crowd began to dissipate slowly after 3 a.m., as Tyler recalled. The drunken young woman had sobered up some but, as she left, she hugged each of the dozen or so people gathered around the fire, embracing a few so tightly that she left them gasping for air. "I'm so sorry," she said, apologizing for her behavior earlier, "but I'm so glad you guys were all here tonight. I feel like what I really needed was just someone to be nice to me and here you all were, just waiting, to give me exactly what I needed."

The "redneck," Mark, offered the three Black Pitt students a ride back to campus, which they accepted.

"There was not even a whiff of any racial tension," he said. "There was a lot of laughing like we were all just best friends, and like we all belonged."

Central to Titusville's spirit of solidarity are the Muirs, who reported Tyra's encounter with the belligerent pickup truck driver to Chief Minch.

When the youngest of the couple's three biological teenage children started high school, they decided to become foster parents, taking in nearly 20 children over a three-year span, including three Black Puerto Rican siblings from Erie, aged 4, 7, and 8. With their parents unable to shake their demons, the Muirs formally adopted the three, and last autumn began the process of adding their newborn baby brother.

The kids adjusted well to the normalcy of their new family life, but one day, as they drove through town, their four-year-old daughter said innocently to Sarah: "Mom, I like Titusville, but there's no one here who looks like me."

And so it came to pass that Sarah was on a mission at Stand Up Together's MLK Day event, her eyes scouring the room for someone who resembled her daughter until she spotted the clot of Black women sitting at a table. She walked up to Tyra and introduced herself.

> I wanted to contact some of the girls at Pitt to teach me how to do my daughter's hair but more importantly, I wanted to create some real, authentic relationships.

In the year after they met, Sarah, Tyra and a few other Black women at Pitt became thick as thieves. "I love me some Sarah," Tyra said enthusiastically.

Said Sarah: "I'm very thankful for the girls. . . . With them, I really feel like my [adopted kids] are being raised by an entire community."

Two years earlier, Sarah and Brent had driven to Erie, Pennsylvania, in a blinding snowstorm to pick up four Black children whose grandmother had been arrested for stealing diapers. As the children climbed into the back seat, the three youngest were just "bawling," Sarah recalled, their cries so loud and guttural that they pierced the bitterly cold air. The oldest, a 15-

year-old boy named Shakur Franklin, was a "rock," consoling his sisters and brother, reassuring them for the duration of the 45-minute drive to Crawford County. "It's okay," he repeated, hugging his sisters, tugging at them. "We're all together. We're going to be alright."

The three months that followed were a joy for Sarah and Brent. "Singing, dancing, laughing, yelling, fighting, and making up again," the Muirs' foster kids were like a solar system unto themselves, Sarah said, of which Shakur was clearly the sun around which his siblings orbited. Tall and angular with a smile so bright and honest that it seemed to warm the entire house, he helped Sarah bake Christmas cookies and sang Bruno Mars.

Once, she took the kids to her church in Titusville and Shakur's younger brother asked her "Why are there so many white people here, Sarah?" Then he started to count: "one, two, three, four . . . ". He stopped at 20. "I had no good answer for him. Why are only white people showing up at our church?"

Shakur and his siblings were reunited with their mother. A year passed, and the Muirs took the kids they would later adopt on a ten-day Disney World vacation. They'd only been home a few hours when Sarah got the news: Shakur had been fatally shot in a drive-by targeting another youth.

Attending his wake, Sarah couldn't help but notice the irony: "Why are there so many Black people here? One, two, three, four. I got to twenty and then stopped counting.

Why are only Black people showing up for a young man killed by gun violence?"

In a Facebook post months later, she wrote:

> I know virtually nothing about race issues, gun violence or injustice, but I am listening. My life until now has been blissfully ignorant, consumed in rural whiteness. These issues were removed, were other, were not my life. They didn't matter to me in a real way until a child who sang in

> my shower, ate spaghetti at my table and danced with my children was MURDERED. He is not my child, but he is all of our children . . .
>
> The only thing that I know how to do is to show up. I will show up in the city to visit his family. I will show up at the cemetery to remember his life. I will continue to offer my futile condolences, to send messages saying 'I'm thinking of you' and 'What can I do to help?' I will talk to my children about injustice. I will teach them the best that I know how . . .
>
> Rest in peace sweet boy. I will forever hear your voice singing 'Today I don't feel like doing anything, I just want to lay in bed.' I will hear you complaining about my cats keeping you awake at night. I will see you putting together my Christmas tree with my other children.
>
> I will see you hugging your siblings. . . . I will remember your energy. I will keep your smile forever in my heart. . . . You made a difference. You changed my world. You give me the motivation to be a world changer.

The night is dark and cold when a middle-aged white woman boards the uptown C train bound for Brooklyn. Looking distraught, she asks for directions to a church; someone has died and she is going to a memorial service or wake. She asks an attractive young Black couple, and they give her directions. She thanks them, breathes a sigh of relief and begins to tell the couple about who she has lost. I cannot hear everything above the din of the train, but the Black couple listens patiently, and when the middle-aged woman begins to cry, they huddle around her, comforting her.

This goes on for a few minutes, with the Black woman whispering in the white woman's ear to console her; finally, her husband grabs the woman's hand and his wife's, and they pray. And he is loud and clear as though he has a microphone tucked into his lapel, asking God to bless the grieving woman and to welcome her friend to heaven for he has most surely earned a place there.

Half the train marveled at this gesture and when the older woman arrived at her stop, she stood and hugged the couple, sobbing and grateful, and lingering so long that she almost missed her stop. The Black woman made a joke that I could not hear, all three laughed and she was gone, a richer person than she had been when she boarded the train, 15 minutes earlier.

Early on the morning of September 14th, 2020, Doris Smith—who described herself as an "86-year-old woman of English-Irish-Scotch-German-Czech descent, born in a midwestern rural community of 1,500 white people"—had a dream so lucid, and resplendent, that she had to share it for fear that her heart might explode.

> In this dream I find a younger me sitting at the end of a long gold-hued wooden pew, half-way back in the middle section of the large, high-ceiling nave of a church. I'm looking in the direction of long stained-glass windows, their beautiful warm light filling the space. It's not really the environment of modern-day megachurches—more like the traditional churches of working-class and middle-class communities of old, but a larger version. There is no ostentation, just comforting beauty that makes you feel that in the midst of your suffering, all's well in the world and for a time you can rest from the struggle, life is bountiful, and you are protected in a cocoon of love.
>
> It is the regular Sunday morning service in this congregation of African American parishioners. I am the only white person visible to me in that room of a couple hundred people, and even though I had come there alone, I felt very

> comfortable being there. It was my place; I wasn't a visitor.
>
> The sermon is going along when it is interrupted for an announcement: George Jackson has been pardoned and will be released from prison!
>
> A moment of stunned silence, then wild clapping and cheering, but soon tears are flowing everywhere and we sit, silently weeping. The depth of our weeping—my weeping—brings me out of my dream, and I am still weeping as I wake up.

And so what is to be done now as the country disintegrates into political chaos and those of us who are fully awake wait anxiously for the rest of the nation to join us in reclaiming this land from the bloodsucking capitalists who have robbed us blind? Perhaps the best advice, for all of us who ache to live in that Beloved Community, was written by Ethel Rosenberg in her poignant final letter to her sons just hours before she was executed:

> . . . [M]y most precious children . . . Your lives must teach you, too, that good cannot flourish in the midst of evil; that freedom and all the things that go to make up a truly satisfying and worthwhile life, must sometime be purchased very dearly. Be comforted then that we were serene and understood with the deepest kind of understanding, that civilization had not as yet progressed to the point where life did not have to be lost for the sake of life; and that we were comforted in the sure knowledge that others would carry on after us. . . . Always remember that we were innocent and could not wrong our conscience. We press you close and kiss you with all our strength.

Notes

1 Richard Slotkin, "The Battle of the Crater," *The New York Times*, July 29, 2014,
https://archive.nytimes.com/opinionator.blogs.nytimes.com/2014/07/29/the-battle-of-the-crater/

2 Brendan Wolfe, *Crater, Battle of the*, in Encyclopedia Virginia, 2009, https://encyclopediavirginia.org/entries/crater-battleof-the/

3 Nelson Morehouse Blake, *William Mahone of Virginia: Soldier and Political Insurgent*, (Garrett & Massie Publishers, 1935), 56.

4 Richard Slotkin, *No Quarter: The Battle of the Crater, 1864:* (Random House, 2009), 368

5 Slotkin, *No Quarter: The Battle of the Crater*, 1864, 368

6 Drew Desilver, Pew Research Center, *For most U.S. workers, real wages have barely budged for decades*. August 7, 2018

7 Faith E. Pinho, "Black woman describes terrifying attack by Trump mob in L.A.: 'I'm thinking I'm dead,'" *Los Angeles Times*, January 8, 2021

8 George Jackson, *Blood in My Eye*, (Random House, 1971), xii.

9 Donna Britt, A white mother went to Alabama to fight for civil rights. The Klan killed her for it. *The Washington Post*, April 17, 2017

10 Blake, *William Mahone of Virginia, Soldier and Political Insurgent*, 72.

11 Blake, *William Mahone of Virginia, Soldier and Political Insurgent*, 72

12 Jon Jeter, D.C. Less Black More Green, *The Root*, September 15th, 2010

13 Charles Lane, *The Day Freedom Died: The Colfax Massacre, The Supreme Court and the Betrayal of Reconstruction*, (Macmillan, 2009), 6

14 John Hope Franklin, *Reconstruction After the Civil War*, (University of Chicago Press, 1962), 17

15 Blake, *William Mahone: Soldier and Political Insurgent*, 6

16 Blake, *William Mahone: Soldier and Political Insurgent*, 62

17 Franklin, *Reconstruction After the Civil War*, 115

18 Peter Rachleff, *Black Labor in Richmond, 1865-1890*, (University of Illinois Press, 1989) 71

19 Rachleff, *Black Labor in Richmond, 1865-1890*,

20 James T. Moore, Black Militancy in Readjuster Virginia, 1879-1883, *Journal of Southern History*, Vol. 41, No. 2 (May, 1975), 167-186

21 Moore, Black Militancy in Readjuster Virginia, 1879-1883

22 Blake, *William Mahone of Virginia, Soldier and Political Insurgent*, 163

23 Jane Dailey, *Before Jim Crow: The Politics of Race in Post Emancipation Virginia*, (The University of North Carolina Press, 2000), 45

24 Brent Tarter, *A Saga of the New South: Race, Law, and Public Debt in Virginia*, (University of North Carolina Press, 2016) 33

25 Blake, *William Mahone of Virginia: Soldier and Political Insurgent*, 157

26 Blake, *William Mahone of Virginia: Soldier and Political Insurgent*, 158-159

27 Daniel Barclay Williams, *A Sketch of the Life and Times of Capt. RA Paul*, (Library of Congress,1885), 14

28 Blake, *William Mahone of Virginia: Soldier and Political Insurgent*, 165

29 Carl N. Degler, Black and White Together, Bi-racial Politics in the South, *The Virginia Quarterly Review*, Volume 47, Number 3 (Summer 1971) 421-444

30 Blake, *William Mahone: Soldier and Political Insurgent*, 150

31 Moore, *Black Militancy in Readjuster Virginia*, 1879-1883, 171

32 Blake, *William Mahone of Virginia: Soldier and Political Insurgent*, 176

33 Moore, *Black Militancy in Readjuster Virginia*, 1879-1883, 178

34 Charles Chilton Pearson, *The Readjusters Movement in Virginia*, (Oxford University Press) 1917, 149

35 Rothstein, Richard, *The Color of Law: A Forgotten History of How Our Government Segregated America*, (Liveright, 2017), 46

36 Ben Joravsky, "Rahm's Latest Plan: Close the Schools, Build an Arena," *Chicago Reader*, May 23, 2013

37 Wright, Chris, "Neoliberalism on Trial: A History of Tax Increment Financing in Chicago," 2012

38 Weber, Rachel, Farmer, Stephanie, Donoghue, Mary, Why These Schools? Explaining School Closures in Chicago, 2000-2013, *Great Cities Institute*, University of Illinois at Chicago, November, 2016

39 Royden Harrison, British Labor and American Slavery, *Science and Society*, Volume 25, Number 4 (December 1961) 291-319

40 Karl Marx and Friedrich Engels, *Collected Works*, Vol. 19 (International Publishers, 2009), 297

41 Philip Foner, *Organized Labor and the Black Worker, 1619 to 1981*, (Haymarket) 1982, 16

42 Philip Foner, A Labor Voice for black Equality: The Boston Daily Evening Voice 1864 to 1867, *Science and Society* (1974) Volume 38, Niumber 3, 304-325

43 Foner, *Organized Labor and the Black Worker*, 18

44 Foner, *Organized Labor and the Black Worker*, 18

45 Foner, *Organized Labor and the Black Worker*, 19

46 Foner, *Organized Labor and the Black Worker*, 28

47 C. Vann Woodward, *Origins of the New South 1877-1913* (1951; reprint Baton Rouge: Louisiana State University Press, 1971), 229

48 Foner, *Organized Labor and the Black Worker*, 27

49 David Roediger, *The Wages of Whiteness: Race and the Making of the American Working Class*, (Verso, 2007), 133

50 Roediger, *Wages* 133

51 Roediger, *Wages*, 134

52 Marx to Meyer and Vogt, 9 April 1870, in David Fernbach (ed), The First International And After: Political Writings. Vol. 3, (London, 1974), 167-171.

53 Herbert Hill, The Problem of Race in American Labor History, *Reviews in American History*, June 1996, Volume 24, No. 2 pp 189-208

54 Hill, The Problem of Race in American Labor History, 194

55 Monica Hunt, "Organized Labor along Savannah's Waterfront: Mutual Cooperation among Black and White Longshoremen, 1865-1894." *The Georgia Historical Quarterly* 92, no. 2 (2008): 177—99. http://www.jstor.org/stable/40585054.

56 Monica Hunt, "Organized Labor along Savannah's Waterfront: Mutual Cooperation among Black and White Longshoremen, 1865-1894." *The Georgia Historical Quarterly* 92, no. 2 (2008): 177—99. http://www.jstor.org/stable/40585054.

57 John W. Blassingame, Before the Ghetto: The Making or the Black Community in Savannah, Georgia, 1865-1889," *Journal of Social History 6* (Summer 1973): 481

58 Eric Arneson, *Waterfront Workers of New Orleans: Race, Class, Politics, 1863-1923*, (University of Illinois Press, 1994), 92

59 Gerald N. Grob, The Knights of Labor and the Trade Unions, 1878-1886, *The Journal of Economic History*, Jun., 1958, Vol. 18, No. 2 (Jun., 1958), 176-192

60 Foner, *Organized Labor and the Black Worker*, 48

61 Foner, *Organized Labor and the Black Worker*, 48

62 Michael Goldfield, Race and the CIO: The Possibilities for Racial Egalitarianism during the 1930s and 40s, *International Labor and Working Class History*, Fall 1993, Volume 44, page 4

63 Matthew Hild, "Organizing Across the Color Line: The Knights of Labor and Black Recruitment Efforts in Small-Town Georgia." *The Georgia Historical Quarterly* 81, no. 2 (1997): 287—310. http://www.jstor.org/stable/40583646.

64 Hild, Organizing Across the Color Line,

65 Foner, *Organized Labor and the Black Worker*, 59

66 Hild, "Organizing Across the Color Line

67Hild, Organizing Across the Color Line

68 Hild, Organizing Across the Color Line, 287-310

69 Foner, *Organized Labor and the Black Worker*, 67

70 Foner, *Organized Labor and the Black Worker*, 68

71 David S. Ceseleski, Timothy S. Tyson, *Democracy Betrayed, The Wilmington Race Riot of 1898 and Its Legacy*, (The University of North Carolina Press, 2000), 73

72 Ceseleski, Timothy S. Tyson, *Democracy Betrayed*, 74

73 Faulkner, Ronnie W. "North Carolina Democrats and Silver Fusion Politics, 1892-1896." *The North Carolina Historical Review* 59, no. 3 (1982): 230—51. http://www.jstor.org/stable/23535100.

74 Doug Henwood, Federal Offenses, *Grand Street*, Vol. 8, No. 1 (Autumn 1988), 209-218

75 William Alexander Mabry, "Negro Suffrage and Fusion Rule in North Carolina." *The North Carolina Historical Review* 12, no. 2 (1935): 79—102. http://www.jstor.org/stable/23515171.

76 Tim Tyson, The Ghosts of 1898: Wilmington Race Riot, *Raleigh News and Observer*, Friday November 17, 2006 Raleigh News and Observer

77 Tyson, Ghosts of 1898:

78 Tyson, Ghosts of 1898,

79 Josh Sanburn, "All the Ways Darren Wilson Described Being Afraid of Michael Brown," *Time*, November 25, 2014

80 Tyson, Ghosts of 1898

81 Jeremy Lybarger, The Price You Pay: On the Life and Times of the Woman Known as the Welfare Queen, *The Nation Magazine*, July 2, 2019, https://www.thenation.com/article/archive/josh-levin-the-queen-book-review/

82 Simon Constable, The Facts about Food Stamp Fraud, *Forbes Magazine*, April 4, 2018, https://www.forbes.com/sites/simonconstable/2018/04/04/the-facts-about-food-stampfraud/#6a1c9b4df880

83Eric Schnurer, Just How Wrong is Conventional Wisdom About Governmental Fraud, *The Atlantic Magazine*, August 15, 2013, https://www.theatlantic.com/politics/archive/2013/08/just-how-wrong-isconventional-wisdom-about-government-fraud/278690/

84Nordell, Jessica, *The End of Bias: A Beginning, The Science and Practice of Overcoming Unconscious Bias*, (Metropolitan Books, 2021), 22

85David Niewert, White Supremacists' Favorite Myths About Black Crime Rates Take Another Hit From BJS Study, *Southern Poverty Law Center*, September 23, 2017, https://www.splcenter.org/hatewatch/2017/10/23/white-supremacists-favorite-myths-about-black-crime-rates-take-another-hit-bjs-study

86Sean Hill, Opinion: Ma'Khia Bryant, George Floyd point to why police should be abolished, *The Columbus Dispatch*, April 25, 2021, https://www.dispatch.com/story/opinion/columns/guest/2021/04/22/sean-hill-makhia-bryant-george-floyd-point-why-police-should-abolished-now/7327463002/

87 Alana Rosenberg, Allison K. Groes, Kim Blankenship, Comparing Black and White Drug Offenders: Implications for Racial Disparities in Criminal Justice and Reentry Policy and Programming, *National Library*

of Medicine, 2016, https://www.ncbi.nlm.nih.gov/pmc/articles/PMC5614457/

88 Earl Ofari Hutchinson, Obama Lay off Black Fathers, *PJ Media*, June 17. 2008, https://pjmedia.com/earl-ofari-hutchinson/2008/06/17/obama-lay-off-black-fathers-n19379

89 Dennis Rome, *Black Demons: The Media's Depiction of the African American Male Criminal Stereotype*, (Prager, 2004), 2

90 Robert Pape, What an analysis of 377 arrested or charged in the Capitol insurrection tells us, *Washington Post*, April 6, 2021,

91 Mary Stanton, *Red, Black and White: The Alabama Communist Party 1930 -1950*,(University of Georgia Press, 2019), 40

92 Ceseleski, Timothy S. Tyson Democracy Betrayed, 74

93 Makaveli Media, Leila Steinberg Breaks Down Her Complex Relationship with Tupac Shakur, 12:10, May 23, 2020, https://www.youtube.com/watch?v=hJinsyJ30X8&list=PLC7C3FE75A5472C84&index=369

94 Julie Buckner Armstrong "The people . . . took exception to her remarks": Meta Warrick Fuller, Angelina Weld Grimké, and the Lynching of Mary Turner, *The Mississippi Quarterly*, Vol. 61, No. 1/2, Special Issue on Lynching and American Culture (Winter-Spring 2008), 113-141

95 Buckner Armstrong "The people . . . took exception to her remarks

96 Julie Buckner Armstrong, Mary Turner's Blues, *African American Review*, Vol. 44, No. 1/2 (Spring/Summer 2011), 207-220

97 Source: St. Louis Federal Reserve, *Compensation of Employees: Wages and Salary Accruals/Gross Domestic Product*, https://fred.stlouisfed.org/graph/?g=2Xa

98 Source: Tuskegee University, *Lynchings: By Year and Race* law2.umkc.edu/faculty/projects/ftrials/shipp/lynchingyear.html

99 Source: Statista, *Rate of fatal police shootings in the United States from 2015 to March 2024, by ethnicity*
www.statista.com/statistics/1123070/police-shootings-rate-ethnicity-us/

100 Richard Wormser, *The Rise and Fall of Jim Crow*, (Macmillan, 2014), 65-67

101 Walter Francis White, *White, A Man Called White*, (University of Georgia Press, 1995)3-27,

102 David F. Krugler 1919, *The Year of Racial Violence: How African Americans Fought Back*, (Cambridge University Press, 2014) page 1,

103 Stanley B. Norvell, William M. Tuttle, Jr., Views of a Negro During "The Red Summer" of 1919, *The Journal of Negro History*, Vol. 51, No. 3 (Jul., 1966), 209-218

104 Abigail Huggins, Red Summer of 1919: How Black WWI Vets Fought Back Against Racist Mobs, *History*, July 26, 2019

105 David Roediger, *Working Toward Whiteness: How America's Immigrants Became White* (Basic Books, 2018) 108

106 Gerald Horn, *Class Struggle in Hollywood*, 1930-1950, (University of Texas Press, 2001) 39

107 Christopher Klein, The Strike that Shook America, *History.com*, September 3, 2012

108 Klein, The Strike

109 Ross Levin, I Like the Way You Lose: Radicals, Rebellion and the Struggle for a Better Life:

Middletown, Connecticut's Wobbly Organized Strike of 1912, 2013

110 Harry Haywood, *Black Bolshevik: Autobiography of an Afro-American Communist*, (University of Minnesota Press 1978), 3

111 Haywood, *Black Bolshevik*, 4

112 Jon Jeter, Left, Undone: As Women March, Blacks Increasingly Question the Quality of Their Allies, *Mintpress News*, January 19, 2018

113 Jeter, Left, Undone

114 Philip Dray, *At the Hands of Persons Unknown: The Lynching of Black America*, (Random House, 2002) iv (preface)

115 Gabriel L. Schwartz, Jacquelyn L. Jahn, Mapping police violence across U.S. metropolitan areas: Overall rates and racial/ethnic inequities 2013-2017, PLOS One, June 24, 2020

116 Megan Leonhart, "Black and Hispanic Americans often have lower credit scores — here's why they're hit harder," CNBC, January 28, 2021

117 Steven Tumulski, "Study: African Americans more likely to have bad credit," *badcredit.org*, October 18, 2016

118 Susan Will, Stephen Handelman, David C. Brotherton, *How they Got Away With It: White Collar Criminals and the Financial Meltdown* (Columbia University Press, 2013), 10

119 Matthew Fleischer, "Opinion: 50 years ago, LAPD raided the Black Panthers. SWAT teams have been targeting Black communities ever since." *Los Angeles Times*, December 8, 2019

120 Jonathan Mummolo, "Militarization fails to enhance police safety or reduce crime but may harm police reputation." *PNAS*, August 18, 2018

121 Cheng Cheng, Mark Hoestrka, Does Strengthening Self-Defense Law Deter Crime or Escalate Violence? Journal of Human Resources July 2013, https://jhr.uwpress.org/content/48/3/821

122 Ellen Feldman, *Scottsboro, A Novel*, (W.W. Norton, 2009) 11

123 Red Black, White: The Alabama Communist Party, 1930-1950, Mary Stanton, page 24

124 Harry Haywood, *Black Bolshevik: A Black Communist in the Freedom Struggle*, (Liberator Press, 1978),167

125 Haywood, *Black Bolshevik*, 166-167

126 Haywood, *Black Bolshevik*, 81

127 Paslovsky, Leo, Moulton, Harold, Russian Debts and Russian Reconstruction, A Study of Russia's Foreign Debts to her Economic Recovery, McGraw Hill, 1924, pg. 21

128 The South Comes North in Detroit's Own Scottsboro Case, An Address Delivered in Detroit by Harry Haywood, General Secretary, League of Struggle for Negro Rights, May 22, 1934

129 J.A. Zumoff, The American Communist Party and the "Negro Question" from the Founding of the Party to the Fourth Congress of the Communist International, 55

130 Eugene Debs, The Negro in the Class Struggle, *International Socialist Review*, Vol. IV, No. 5. November 1903,

131 Kate Richards O'Hare, Nigger Equality, *The National Ripsaw*, March 25th, 1912

132 Timothy Johnson, American Communist History, "Death for Negro Lynching "The Communist Party USA's Position on the Negro Question, *Taylor and Francis Online*, 2008

133 Karen Ferguson, *Black Politics in New Deal Atlanta,* University of North Carolina Press, 2003), 30

134 Robert R. Korstad, *Civil Rights Unionism: Tobacco Workers and the Struggle for Democracy in the Mid-Twentieth Century South*, (University of North Carolina Press, 2003), 99

135 Michael Kazin, American Dreamers: *How the Left Changed a Nation*, (Knopf, Doubleday, 2012), 8

136 James A. Barnes, The Scottsboro Case: An International Cause Celebre, Graduate Student History Conference, Temple University

137 Ada Wright, "My Two Sons Face the Electric Chair," *Labor Defender*, September 1931, 172- 182

138 James A. Miller, Susan D. Pennybacker, and Eve Rosenhaft, Mother Ada Wright and the International Campaign to Free the Scottsboro Boys, 1931-1934, *American Historical Review* 106, no. 2 (2001), 387-430

139 James Goodman, *Stories of Scottsboro*, (Vintage, 2013) 48

140 Goodman, *Stories of Scottsboro*, 7

141 Goodman, *Stories of Scottsboro*, 8

142 Ada Wright, "My Two Sons Face the Electric Chair," *Labor Defender*, September 1931, 172-182

143 Kelley, Robin D,G., "Comrades, Praise Gawd for Lenin and Them!" Ideology and Culture among Black Communists in Alabama, 1930-1935

144 Daniel Anker, Barak Goodman, The Scottsboro Accusers, American Experience, PBS, January 19, 2002

145 Lizabeth Cohen, *Making a New Deal: Industrial Workers in Chicago*, 1919-1939, (Cambridge University Press, 1990) 224

146 Cohen, 225

147 Foner, Organized Labor and the Black Worker, 188

148 Cohen, Making a New Deal, 225

149 Foner, *Organized Labor and the Black Worker*, 191

150 Roy Rosenzweig, 'Socialism In Our Time' The Socialist Party and the Unemployed, 1929—1936,"

151 Foner, *Organized Labor and the Black Worker*, 191

152 Mary Stanton, Red Black and White: The Alabama Communist Party, 1930-1950, page 47

153 California Historical Society Quarterly, June 1959, Volume 38, Issue 2, page 178

154 Mike Quin, The Big Strike, (Olema Publishing, 1949)

155 Victoria Johnson, *How Many Guns Does it Take to Cook One Meal? The Seattle and San Francisco General Strikes*, (University of Washington Press, 2015) 69

156 Foner, *Organized Labor and the Black Worker*, 194

157 Johnson, Victoria, *How Many Machine Guns*, 72

158 Cal Winslow, "Bloody Thursday: The Strike That Shook San Francisco And Rocked The Pacific Coast," *BeyondChron*, July 3, 2014

159 Johnson, *How Many Machine Guns*, 73

160 Johnson, *How Many Machine Guns*, 81

161 Johnson, *How Many Machine Guns*, 77

162 Quin, *The Big Strike*, 41

163 Johnson, *How Many Machines Guns* 85

164 Johnson, *How Mamy Guns Does It Take*, 81

165 Johnson, *How Many Machine Guns Does It Take*, 96

166 Quin, *The Big Strike*, 33

167 Johnson, *How Many Machine Guns*, 99

168 Foner, *Organized Labor and the Black Worker*, 191

169 Johnson, *How Many Machine Guns*, 98

170_Berry Minott, Harry Bridges: A Man and His Union, Create Space Studio, 1993

171 Johnson, *How Many Machine Guns*, 100

172 Peter Cole, St. Francis Square: How a Union Built Integrated, Affordable Housing in San Francisco, *JSTOR Daily*, January 2,2016

173 Eric Arneson, *Waterfront Workers of New Orleans: Race, Class, Politics, 1863-1923*, (University of Illinois Press, 1994), 11

174 Robert Korstad, *Civil Rights Unionism: Tobacco Workers and the Struggle for Democracy in the Mid-twentieth Century South*, (University of North Carolina Press 2003), 16

175 Korstad, *Civil Rights Unionism*, 17

176 Korstad, *Civil Rights Unionism*, 20

177 Korstad, *Civil Rights Unionism*,21

178 Korstad, *Civil Rights Unionism*, 24

179 Foner, *Organized Labor and the Black Worker*, 209

180 Foner, *Organized Labor and the Black Worker*, 211

181 Foner, *Organized Labor and the Black Worker*, 212

182 Foner, *Organized Labor and the Black Worker*, 213

183 Foner, *Organized Labor and the Black Worker*, 214

184 Foner, *Organized Labor and the Black Worker*, 218

185 Foner, *Organized Labor and the Black Worker*, 220

186 Foner, *Organized Labor and the Black Worker*, 219

187 Robert Kornstad, Civil Rights Unionism: *Tobacco Workers and the Struggle for Democracy* (University of North Carolina Press, 2004) 252

188 Rick Hutchins, Myrna Loy: Hero On and Off Screen, *Heroes: What They Do and Why We Need Them*, March 13, 2012, blog.richmond.edu/heroes/2012/03/13/myrna-loy-hero-in-both-fact-and-fiction/

189 Ira Berkow, Two Men Who Did the Right Thing, *New York Times*, November 2, 2005

190Sidney Fine, Sit-Down, the General Motors Strike of 1936-1937, (University of Michigan Press, 1969) 201

191 Lewis Macadams, Birth of the Cool and the American Avant Garde, (Free Press, 2001), 223

192 Alabama News Beacon, "This one is a bit brash for what we usually post . . . "Facebook, January 31, 2024

193 Joe Allen, *People Wasn't Made To Burn: A True Story of Housing, Race, and Murder in Chicago*, (Haymarket, 2011)

194 Foner, *Organized Labor and the Black Worker*, 267

195 Foner, *Organized Labor and the Black Worker*, 267

196 Korstad, *Civil Rights Unionism*, 255

197 Korstad, *Civil Rights Unionism*, 257

198 Glass, Fred, "Golden Lands, Working Hands," Oakland General Strike 1946 (part 1) https://www.youtube.com/watch?v=KfUmIeCTJTA YouTube video, 9:36

199 The Oakland General Strike of 1946, Philip J. Wolman, *Southern California Quarterly*, Vol. 57, No. 2 (Summer 1975) 147-178

200 Glass, "Golden Lands, Working Hands

201 St. Louis Federal Reserve, Compensation of Employees: Wages and Salary Accruals/Gross Domestic Product (1950-2020)

202 Robert Korstad, Nelson Lichtenstein, Opportunities Found and Lost: Labor, Radicals and the Early Civil Rights Movement, *The Journal of American History*, Dec,. 1988, Vol. 75, No. 3, 786-811 https://www.jstor.org/stable/1901530

203 Korstad, Lichtenstein, Opportunities Found and Lost

204 David Maraniss, *A Good American Family: The Red Scare and My Father*, (Simon and Schuster, 2019), 68

205 Foner, *Organized Labor*, 276

206 Foner, *Organized Labor*, 286

207 Foner, *Organized Labor*, 286

208 Foner, Organized Labor, 286

209 Victor G. Devinatz, A Cold War at International Harvester: The Schactmanites and the Farm Equipment Workers Union's Demise, 1946-1955, Science and Society, Vol. 72, No, 2 (Apr., 2008), 182-207

210 Serrin, William, interview with Studs Terkel, The Studs Terkel Program, WFMT-98.7, April 26, 1973

211 Herbert Hill, "The Importance of Race in American Labor History." *International Journal of Politics, Culture, and Society* 9, no. 2 (1995): 317—43. http://www.jstor.org/stable/20007240.

212 NLRB, Volume I, 1936, p. 1016

213 Phillipson, Irene, *Ethel Rosenberg: Beyond the Myths*, 351-352

214 Imani Perry, Looking for Lorraine: The Radiant and Radical Life of Lorraine Hansberry

215 Zinn, Howard, Reflections of a White Professor at Spelman College in the 1950s, *The Journal of Blacks in Higher Education* , Spring, 1995, No. 7 (Spring, 1995), pp. 97-99

216 Edelman, Marian Wright, Spelman College A Safe Haven for a Young, Black Woman, *The Journal of Blacks in Higher Education*, Spring, 2000, No. 27 (Spring, 2000), pp. 118-123

217 Martha Biondi, The Black Revolution on Campus, (University of California Press, 2014), 14

218 Michael Mccane, The Panthers and the Patriots, *Jacobin Magazine*, May, 2017,

219 Jerald E. Podair, *The Strike That Changed New York: Blacks, Whites and the Ocean Hill- Brownsville Crisis*, (Yale University Press, 2002), 2

220 Maclean, Nancy, How Milton Friedman Exploited White Supremacy to Privatize Education, *Institute for New Economic Thinking*, September 1, 2021, Working Paper no. 161

221 Karen Ferguson, *Top Down: The Ford Foundation, Black Power and the Reinvention of Racial Liberalism*, 131-136

222 Jefferson Cowie, *Stayin' Alive: The 1970s and the Last Days of the Working Class*, (The New Press, 2012), 75

223 Robert McClory, "The Neutralization of Fred Hampton," *The Chicago Reader*, November 30, 1989

224 Staub, Michael E., Black Panthers, New Journalism and the Rewriting of the Sixties, Representations, University of California Press, Issue #57, 1997, pp. 52-72

225 Hampton, Fred, "Power Anywhere There's People," Speech delivered at Olivet Church, 1969

226 Staub, Black Panthers

227 Sonnie, Amy, Tracy, James, Hillbilly Nationalists, Urban Race Rebels and Black Power: Community Organizing in Radical Times, Melville House, 2011, 209-221

228 Medsger, Betty, The Burglary: The Discovery of J. Edgar Hoover's Secret FBI, Alfred A. Knopf, 2014, 42

229 Kolbert, Elizabeth, "The Prisoner," *The New Yorker Magazine*, July 16, 2001, 49.

230 Kifner, John, A Radical Declaration Warns of an Attack by Weathermen, *New York Times*, May 25, 1970

231 Rick Perlstein, *Nixonland: The Rise of a President and the Fracturing of America*, (Scribner, 2008), 411-414

232 Sandy Banks, "Haunting photos from Kent State made me wonder: Where were the black students?" *The Los Angeles Times*, May 3, 2020

233 Nicholas Lemann, "Is Capitalism Racist? A scholar depicts white supremacy as the economic engine of American history" *New Yorker magazine*, May 18, 2020

234 "Journalist Demographics and Statistics In The US," *Zippa*, 2022, zippa.com/journalist-jobs/demographics/

235 Donna Britt, "Finding the Truest Truth," *Washington Post*, October 3, 1996

236 Michael Fletcher, "Conspiracy Theories Can Often Ring True: History Feeds Blacks' Mistrust," *Washington Post*, October 3, 1996

237 SYKOPATHeist, Black Panther Woman Speak on Feminism - YouTube

238 Tobi Haslett, Irrational Man: Thomas Chatterton Williams' confused argument for a post-racial society, *Bookforum Magazine*, September 2019

239 Michael Eric Dyson, The Color Line: Steph Curry's prominence resurfaces issues of colorism among blacks, *The Undefeated*, June 1, 2016

240 O'Neal, William, "Eyes on the Prize, Part 5," Film and Media Archive, Washington University in St. Louis, January 1987

241 Heather Thompson, *Whose Detroit?: Politics, Labor and Race in a Modern American City*, (Cornell University Press,2001) 126

242 Thompson, *Whose Detroit?*, 130

243 Thompson, *Whose Detroit?*, 130

244 Thompson, *Whose Detroit?*, 134

245 Thompson, *Whose Detroit?*, 137

246 Sources: Data from "Compensation of Employees: Wages and Salary Accruals/Gross Domestic Product, 1947 to 2021," St. Louis Federal Reserve, fred.stlouisfed.org/graph/?g=2Xa

247 Chaudry, Ajay, Wimer, Christopher, Macartney, Suzanne, Frohlich, Lauren, Campbell, Colin, Swenson, Kendall, Oellerich, Don, Hauan, Susan, "Poverty in the United States: 50-Year Trends and Safety Net Impacts," Office of Human Services Policy Office of the Assistant Secretary for Planning and Evaluation U.S. Department of Health and Human Services, (2017): 21

248 Sources: Data from "The Unequal States of America: Income Inequality in the United States," Economic Policy Institute, epi.org/multimedia/unequal-states-of-america/

249 Cruz, Julissa, Marriage: "More Than a Century of Change," National Center for Family and Marriage Research, http://ncfmr.bgsu.edu/pdf/ familyprofiles/ file131529.pdf (2013)

250Home Price to Median Household Income Ratio, US, Aug. 31, 1952-Aug. 31 2022, Longtermtrends, https://www.longtermtrends.net/home-price-median-annual-income-ratio/

251 Annual Energy Review, "Average Retail Prices of Electricity," 1960-2011, September 27, 2012, U.S. Energy Information Administration - EIA - Independent Statistics and Analysis

252 Sources: Data from "Average undergraduate tuition and fees and room and board rates charged for full-time students in degree-granting postsecondary institutions, by level and control of institution: Selected years, 1963-64 through 2018-19" National Center for Education Statistics:

253 Martha Biondi, *The Black Revolution on Campus*, (University of California Press, 2012) 3

254 Joshua B. Freeman, *Working-Class New York: Life and Labor Since World War II*, (The New Press, 2001), 229

256 Dan Georgakas and Marvin Surkin, *Detroit, I Do Mind Dying: A Study in Urban Revolution*, 6,

257 Jefferson Cowie, *Stayin' Alive" The 1970s And the Last Days of the Working Class*, (The New Press, 2011), 40

257 Steve Wishnia, "The Lordstown Strike of 72: Dreams of Factory Liberation Deferred," *Labor Press*, March 18th, 2019

258 Nick Kotz, Oilcan Eddie takes on the old guard, *New York Times*, December 19, 1976

259 Georgakas and Surkin, *Detroit, I Do Mind Dying*, 33

260 Geschwender, *Class, Race and Worker Insurgency*, 114,

261 Freeman, *Working Class New York*, 256

262 Kim Phillips Fein, *Fear City: New York's Fiscal Crisis and the Rise of Austerity Politics*, (Metropolitan Books, 2017) 16

263 Jeff Nussbaum, "*The Night New York Saved Itself From Bankruptcy*," The New Yorker, October 16, 2015

264 Nussbaum, *The Night New York Saved Itself From Bankruptcy*

265 Freeman, *Working Class New York*, 260

266 Ford, Gerald, Address to the National Press Club, October 29, 1975

267 Katharine Graham, *Personal History: A Memoir*, (Vintage, 1997) 742, 743

268 William K. Tabb, *The Long Default: New York City and the Urban Fiscal Crisis*, (Monthly Review Press, 1982) 37

269 Freeman, *Working Class New York*, 267

270 Freeman, *Working Class New York*, 274

271 Detroit Mayor Coleman A Young, "Before the United States Joint Economic Committee," September 24th 1975, YouTube

272 Barry Bluestone and Bennett Harrison, *The Deindustrialization of America: Plant Closings, Community Abandonment, and the Dismantling of Basic Industry* (Basic Books, 1982), 42,

273 Jefferson Cowie, *Stayin' Alive" The 1970s And the Last Days of the Working Class*, The New Press,210

274 Cowie, *Stayin' Alive* 223-224

275 Melvyn Dubofsky, *The State and Labor in Modern America*, (The University of North Carolina Press, 2000) 226

276 Cowie, *Staying Alive*, 263

277 Cowie, *Stayin' Alive*, 178

278 Angela Hanks, Danyelle Solomon, Systematic Inequality: How America's Structural Racism Helped Create the Black-White Wealth Gap, Christian Weller, *Center for American Progress*, Feb. 21,2018

279 Cowie, *Stayin' Alive*, 274

280 Cowie, *Stayin' Alive*, 274

281 Nick Hanauer, The Top 1% of Americans Have Taken $50 Trillion from the Bottom 90 %--and That's Made the Future Less Secure, *Time Magazine*, September 14, 2020

282 Gary Rivlin, *Fire on the Prairie: Harold Washington, Chicago Politics, and the Roots of the Obama Presidency*, (Temple University Press, 2012) 18

283 Richard A. Keiser, *Subordination or Empowerment? African American Leadership and the Struggle for Urban Political Power*, (Oxford University Press, 1997) 169

284 Rivlin, *Fire on the Prairie,* 27

285 Henry CB, Voices from Yesterday, March 5, 1992, You Tube, 2https://www.youtube.com/watch?v=4e_SlttxTB8

286 Twiley W. Barker, Political Motivation of Black Chicago: Drafting a Candidate, *American Political Science Association*, Volume 16, No. 3, (Summer 1983) pp. 482-485

287 Rivlin, *Fire on the Prairie,* 66

288 Chicago elections: the numbers and the implications, Paul M. Green

289 Rivlin, *Fire on the Prairie,* 79

290 Rivlin, *Fire on the Prairie*, 111

291Rivlin, *Fire on the Prairie*, 119

292 Rivlin, *Fire on the Prairie,* 122

293 Kevin Klose, Washington Winner in Bitter Chicago Election for Mayor, *Washington Post* April 13, 1983

294 Frederick C. Harris, *The Price of the Ticket: Barack Obama and the Rise and Decline of Black Politics,* (Oxford University Press, 2012) 59

295 Harris, *The Price of the Ticket: Barack Obama and the Rise and Decline of Black Politics*, 58

296 Pam Martens, Obama's Money Cartel, ZNet, February 23, 2008

297 David Dayen, The Most Important WikiLeaks Revelation Isn't About Hillary Clinton, *The New Republic*, October 14, 2016,

298 Henry CB, Voices from Yesterday, March 5, 1992, You Tube, 2 https://www.youtube.com/watch?v=4e_SlttxTB8

299 Theodore Rosengarten, *All God's Dangers: The Life of Nate Shaw*, (Vintage, 2013)

300 DeNeen Brown, The preacher who used Christianity to revive the Ku Klux Klan, *the Washington Post*, April 10, 2018

301 Nathan Robinson, Bill Clinton's Stone Mountain Moment, *Jacobin Magazine*, September, 2016

302 Robinson, Bill Clinton's Stone Mountain Moment

303 Louis Proyect, Myths of the White Working Class, *Counterpunch*, September 25, 2020

304 Jens Manuel Krogstad and Mark Hugo Lopez, Black voter turnout fell in 2016, even as a record number of Americans cast ballots, *Pew Research Center*, May 12, 2017

305 Alana Samuels, How Wall Street Bought Up America's Homes, *The Atlantic Magazine*, February 13, 2019

306 Dmytro Spilka, "Profiting on Innovation: Will Uber Ever Start Making Money?" *Business2 Community*, August 22, 2022

307 Carter, Dan T., The Anatomy of Fear: The Christmas Day Insurrection Scare of 1865, *The Journal of Southern History*, Volume 42, No. 3 (August 1976) pp. 245-264

308 Carter, *The Anatomy of Fear*

309 Carter, *The Anatomy of Fear*

310 Carter, *The Anatomy of Fear*

311 Anti- Defamation League, Murder and Extremism in the U.S. in 2022, 2-22-23, https://www.adl.org/resources/report/murder-and-extremism-united-states-2022

312 Source: "*1087 people have been shot and killed by the police in the past 12 months.*" The Washington Post, May 8, 2023

313 Taylor Torregano, "Los Angeles sees record-breaking increase in hate crimes," *Los Angeles Times*, December 14, 2022

314 Torregano, Los Angeles sees record-breaking increase

315 Torregano, Los Angeles sees record-breaking increase

316 Torregano, Los Angeles sees record-breaking increase

www.ingramcontent.com/pod-product-compliance
Lightning Source LLC
LaVergne TN
LVHW021626120125
801077LV00027B/222

* 9 7 8 1 9 6 5 7 5 3 0 0 2 *